Consumer Behaviour in Tourism

This book is, as ever,
dedicated to our son John,
a great travel companion and
a terrific bass guitarist.

Consumer Behaviour in Tourism
Second edition

John Swarbrooke and
Susan Horner

AMSTERDAM • BOSTON • HEIDELBERG • LONDON • NEW YORK • OXFORD
PARIS • SAN DIEGO • SAN FRANCISCO • SINGAPORE • SYDNEY • TOKYO

Butterworth-Heinemann is an imprint of Elsevier

Butterworth-Heinemann is an imprint of Elsevier
The Boulevard, Langford Lane, Kidlington, Oxford, OX5 1GB
30 Corporate Drive, Suite 400, Burlington, MA 01803, USA

First edition 1999
Second edition 2007
Reprinted 2007, 2008

British Library Cataloguing in Publication Data
A catalogue record for this book is available from the British Library

Library of Congress Cataloging-in-Publication Data
A catalog record for this book is available from the Library of Congress

ISBN: 978-0-7506-6735-7

For information on all Butterworth-Heinemann publications
visit our website at www.elsevierdirect.com

Printed and bound in Hungary

08 09 10 10 9 8 7 6 5 4 3

Working together to grow
libraries in developing countries

www.elsevier.com | www.bookaid.org | www.sabre.org

ELSEVIER   BOOK AID International   Sabre Foundation

Contents

Preface   vii

Acknowledgements   ix

Part 1   Context

1   Introduction   3
2   The History of tourist behaviour   12
3   Main concepts in consumer behaviour, including
    models of consumer behaviour adapted for tourism   40

Part 2   The Purchase-Decision Process

4   Motivators   53
5   Determinants   62
6   Models of the purchase decision-making process   69

Part 3   Typologies of Tourist Behaviour

7   Typologies of tourist behaviour and segmentation
    of the tourism market   83

Part 4   Tourism Demand and Markets

8   The global pattern of tourism demand   103
9   National differences: domestic, outbound and inbound   113
10 The nature of demand in different segments
    of the tourism market   128
11 Consumer behaviour and markets in the different
    sectors of tourism   140

Part 5   Consumer Behaviour and Marketing

12   Researching tourist behaviour: marketing research   153
13   The marketing mix and tourist behaviour   161

Part 6   Topical Issues in Consumer Behaviour

14   The green tourist: myth or reality?   177
15   Rise of the global/Euro tourist?   189
16   The emergence of new markets and changes
     in tourist demand   201
17   Quality and tourist satisfaction   211

Part 7   Conclusions and Future

18   Conclusions   225
19   The future of tourist behaviour   229

Part 8   Case Studies

 1   PGL adventure holidays   241
 2   Thomas Cook's Club 18–30   252
 3   The segmentation of the outbound Japanese market   261
 4   Segmenting the leisure shopping market   266
 5   The Savoy Hotel, London   270
 6   First Choice Holidays' all-inclusive package   277
 7   The cruise market: Carnival Cruise Lines   285
 8   Wensleydale Creamery, Hawes, North Yorkshire   300
 9   Société Roquefort, Roquefort, France   306
10   Industrial tourism in France   310
11   British Airways – environmental policy   313
12   TUI, Germany – environmental policy   327
13   Ragdale Hall – health hydro   338
14   The international spa market   345
15   Adventure tourism in New Zealand   351
16   Gay and lesbian tourism in Australia   361
17   easyJet   367
18   Las Vegas, Nevada, USA   375
19   Taiwan: the emergence of a new major outbound
     tourism market   393
20   The inbound market to the Republic of Cyprus   395
21   Susi Madron's Cycling for Softies   402

Glossary of terms   410

Bibliography and further reading   417

Index   425

Preface to the Second Edition

It is now seven years since we wrote the first edition of *Consumer Behaviour in Tourism*. Since then, the world of tourism and tourist behaviour has changed dramatically in ways we could not have even dreamt of in the late 1990s.

The events of 11 September 2001 in the USA in which civilian airliners were used as terrorist weapons put the travel industry at the heart of the growth of terrorism. Tourists have always become the specific targets for terrorist attacks in the years since 11 September with attacks on tourists in countries as diverse as Egypt, Kenya and Indonesia. Hotels here became popular targets for terrorist groups, which has also helped put tourism at the centre of the upsurge in terrorism.

But, at the same time, there have been other threats and scares that have affected the confidence of tourists including SARS, the tsunami in South East Asia, hurricanes in the Caribbean, and – at the time of writing – the spread of Asian flu.

In spite of all these threats and problems, tourism has continued to grow since the late 1990s. Furthermore, the market has been changing in fascinating ways, from the growth of outbound tourism from China and India to the rapid rise of the United Arab Emirates as a major tourist destination. Over the past few years we have also seen an explosive growth in the use of the Internet by tourists as well as the continued rise of budget airlines around the world.

All these changes mean that tourist behaviour itself has experienced over the past ten years a level of change that can truly be called 'revolutionary'. Unfortunately, tourism academics have not been able to keep up with these rapid changes in the tourism market and tourist behaviour. There has been a growing interest in consumer behaviour by tourism researchers but there are still major gaps in our knowledge, which is a challenge for future researchers.

The subject of tourist behaviour and how it is changing is also now more relevant than ever for students, as they will be the future managers and policy-makers who have to grapple with the effects of the changes in behaviour.

When writing this new edition we have tried to retain much of the core text because the main principles, issues and techniques of consumer behaviour in tourism remain constant. We have even kept some of what we wrote in the late 1990s but it now has an almost 'historic' interest. However, we have also thoroughly updated the data in the text and have added new sections on important topics, for example, the Internet and terrorism. We have updated some case studies, revised others and added a number of new ones.

We must always remember that without tourists there can be no tourism, and recognize that if we are to manage tourism effectively, we need to understand tourists and their behaviour. We hope this book will help develop such understanding and that it will stimulate academics and policy-makers to conduct more research in this field which is still underdeveloped.

Happy reading!

John Swarbrooke and Susan Horner

Acknowledgements

We would like to thank the following people for their help in writing this second edition:

- The students who have asked difficult questions, which have helped us clarify our own thinking, and the students from many countries who have provided us with interesting insights into the national and cultural differences in tourist behaviour.
- The many colleagues around the world who gave us positive feedback on the first edition and who convinced us of the importance of a book on this subject for tourism academics.
- Our good friends: Betty Fromer Piazzi and Adriano Piazzi at Aleph in Sao Paolo who worked hard to make this book available to people in Brazil.
- Our friend Judy Mitchell, who has helped make a manuscript out of our illegible scribbling.

PART 1

Context

Part 1 sets the scene for the rest of the book, through three chapters:
1 This introduction includes key definitions and explores the importance of consumer behaviour in tourism as a subject.
2 This chapter provides a history of consumer behaviour in tourism, both in terms of different types of tourism and the various regions of the world.
3 The final chapter in this part discusses the main general concepts in consumer behaviour that were developed from other industries and/or industry as a whole. It also looks at those which authors have sought to adopt for tourism. At the end of the chapter is a brief consideration of the specific characteristics of tourism which make it difficult to apply general consumer behaviour concepts and markets to tourism.

Introduction

The subject of consumer behaviour is key to the underpinning of all marketing activity which is carried out to develop, promote and sell tourism products. Clearly, if we are to optimize the effectiveness and efficiency of marketing activities, we must try to understand how consumers make their decisions to purchase or use tourism products. If we understand their behaviour patterns, then we will know when we need to intervene in the process to obtain the results that we want. We will know who to target at a particular time with a particular tourism product. More importantly, we will know how to persuade them to choose certain products which we will have designed more effectively to meet their particular needs and wants. An understanding of consumer behaviour is therefore crucial to make marketing activity more successful.

The problem with the academic disciplines of consumer behaviour, however, is that while many general models of consumer behaviour have been advanced, there has been little empirical research conducted in order to test these models against actual behaviour patterns. This is especially true in the tourism sector where research on consumer behaviour is very much in the early stages of development. Despite a lack of empirical research, however, there have been several examples of models of consumer behaviour in tourism which have been suggested. It is important that, in this book, we consider these models and consider the stage which the development of the subject has reached. This will allow us to identify further areas of research and will offer the reader some judgements as to how useful the research is to date for the application to practical marketing activities.

Consumer behaviour is a fascinating but difficult subject to research. This statement is particularly relevant in the tourism field, where the decision to purchase by a consumer is of emotional significance. Purchase of a holiday, for example, involves the consumer in a large spend. The holiday that the consumer buys will probably provide the consumer with the major highlight of the year – a chance to escape from work and grey skies and to revitalize the spirit. Consumers are influenced in their decision-making processes by many internal and external motivators and determinants when they choose products. It is very difficult to research how these many motivators and determinants affect the consumer when they are making their choices. They may be affected in different ways, according to the type of product or service that they are purchasing. The experience of purchasing a holiday, for example, will be very different from the experience of purchasing an everyday food item in a supermarket. It is likely to take much more time and involve more careful consideration and selection, particularly as the purchase of a holiday usually involves a high proportion of income.

Before we get into the detail, however, it is necessary for us to define some of the key terms.

We can start with a definition of tourism. Definitions of tourism were explained by Horner and Swarbrooke (1996) as having several components and considerable overlap with hospitality and leisure.

Tourism is defined as a short-term movement of people to places some distance from their normal place of residence to indulge in pleasurable activities. It may also involve travel for business purposes. Horner and Swarbrooke (1996) continue to discuss the reasons for tourism not being a simple concept:

> It does not encompass the lucrative field of business tourism where the main purpose of the trip is for work rather than play. We also have difficulty in deciding how far you have to travel to be a tourist or how many nights you have to stay away from home to be classified as a tourist.

Tourism can be described as an activity which is serviced by a number of other industries such as hospitality and transport. The rise of the mass package tourism business with the development of package holiday companies and retail travel agencies is probably the nearest that tourism comes to being an industrial sector.

Tourism also incorporates the hospitality sector. Collin (1994) defined *hospitality* as 'looking after guests well'. The term 'hospitality' is becoming increasingly used in Europe to replace more traditional terms such as hotel and catering. This is because the word 'well' suggests a qualitative dimension which is a fashionable concept in a time when quality management is growing in importance as a discipline. Hospitality therefore includes all organizations which provide guests with food, drink and leisure facilities. Not all hospitality is concerned with tourism, however. It may just involve people going to a leisure centre or out for a drink.

Horner and Swarbrooke (1996) also suggested that tourism incorporates leisure. According to Collin (1994), *leisure* as a noun means 'free time to do what you want'. He also defines the *leisure industry* as 'companies which provide goods and services used during people's leisure time'. This includes holidays, cinema, theatres, visitor attractions, etc. This shows that like hospitality, not all leisure organizations are concerned with tourism.

The distinctions between tourism, leisure, and hospitality is blurred. A number of examples of this were suggested by Horner and Swarbrooke (1996) and are shown in Figure 1.1. The best example of the blurring of the distinction between tourism, hospitality and leisure is the American import, the resort complex concept.

The tourism market is very diverse and incorporates a range of market segments which each have their own demand characteristics. We will return to this in Chapter 10 when we consider the nature of demand in different segments of the tourism market. It is sufficient here to define the different market segments of tourism, as follows:

- *Business tourism* is a tourist trip that takes place as part of people's business occupational commitment, largely in work time, rather than for pleasure, in people's leisure time (Horner and Swarbrooke, 1996). It incorporates individual business trips, attendance at meetings, training courses and conferences; visiting and organizing trade fairs and exhibitions; undertaking product launches; and incentive travel. There is a blurring of business tourism with leisure tourism, particularly when a business person takes their family with them on business, or extends their business trip to incorporate a relaxing holiday after their work is finished.
- *Hedonistic tourism* involves the tourist in seeking pleasurable activities. The tourism experience is based on physical pleasure and social

---

- The resort complexes such as Club Méditeranée and Center Parcs offer both hospitality services and leisure facilities on the same site, under the ownership of one organization. Furthermore, they offer this mixture to a market which largely consists of tourists, in other words, people who have travelled away from home and are spending at least one night away from their normal place of residence.
- Theme parks are increasingly offering on-site accommodation units to encourage visitors to spend more time, and thus more money, on site. A good example of this is the Futuroscope theme park in Western France which now has several hotels, of different grades, within the boundaries of the park.
- The trend amongst hotels in most European countries is to build in-house leisure facilities for their guests such as gymnasia and swimming pools. This is seen as necessary to attract two very different groups of clients, namely leisure visitors at weekends, and business customers on weekdays.
- Leisure shopping is being developed as a tourist activity. Shopping is now used as a way of motivating trips to destinations as diverse as Liverpool in the UK, with its Albert Dock complex, the craft centres of rural Norway and the gold shops of Dubai.
- Sophisticated catering operations are being developed at visitor attractions to boost income. These can range from fast-food outle ts to themed restaurants. Interestingly many of these current developments in Europe are mirroring earlier ones in North America.

Figure 1.1

Examples of the blurring of tourism, leisure, and hospitality organizations
Source: Horner and Swarbrooke (1996).

life. The hedonistic tourist is often younger and travels in a group with other like-minded people.

- *Educational tourism* involves the tourist travelling for education. This form of tourism is not a new phenomenon, but is still an important segment of the tourism business.
- *Religious tourism* is one of the oldest forms of tourism and involves people travelling often as a sense of duty rather than for pleasure and leisure.

We will expand this analysis of different market segments in tourism further in Chapter 10.

Let us now turn our attention to defining consumer behaviour. Horner and Swarbrooke (1996) have defined *consumer behaviour* in tourism: 'Consumer behaviour is the study of why people buy the product they do, and how they make their decision'.

Before we consider definitions and models which have been adapted for the tourism sector, it is important for us to consider the general definitions developed by researches who were considering consumer behaviour as a general topic.

The process by which a consumer chooses to purchase or use a product or service is defined as the *consumer behaviour process*. Consumer behaviour has been defined by Engel, Blackwell and Miniard (2001) as 'those activities directly involved in obtaining, consuming, and disposing of products and services including the decision processes that precedes and follows these actions'. This definition emphasizes the importance of the psychological process which the consumer goes through during the pre-purchase, and post-purchase stages.

Solomon (1996) incorporated the concept of consumer needs and wants into his definition as follows: 'Consumer behaviour is the process involved when individuals or groups select, purchase, use, or dispose of products, services, ideas or experiences to satisfy needs and wants'. This definition introduces the idea that consumers may make purchase decisions in groups, and not just simply as individuals. The processes which are highlighted in these definitions are very complex and for this reason, it has been more common to illustrate the consumer behaviour process with reference to models rather than definitions. These will be reviewed in the next section.

Before we consider consumer behaviour models in more depth, however, it is important that we consider the role of consumer behaviour in the marketing process. The understanding of consumer behaviour is vital if the marketing activity which is carried out by organizations is to be effective. Marketing is concerned with the relationship between consumer or buyer and seller. Marketing relies on the idea that organizations should have the consumer as the central focus for all their activities.

Organizations often consider their consumer's wants and needs, but also rely on persuading them to buy their products and services. This is often referred to as *consumer persuasion*, rather than putting the consumer at the centre of the organization in a process which is often referred to as *consumer sovereignty*.

The marketing concept does suggest, however, that the overriding inclination of the organization will be to serve the final consumer's wants and needs, as their main priority. This will mean that the organization constantly researches consumer demand and the reasons for this demand. The organization will seek constantly to find out what the consumer wants both today and in the future and work hard to produce the products and services that are requested by the assembly of correctly designed marketing mixes. The provision of these well-designed products and services will require an understanding of consumer behaviour and the ability to predict how this will change in the future. The organization will also have to understand how and why a consumer makes a choice. This will enable them to persuade the consumer to choose their products and services, rather than those offered by the competition. It will also allow the organization to develop products and services which are correctly *positioned* for their target market.

The definitions of *marketing* demonstrates the different approaches which have been taken to the marketing philosophy. Kotler and Armstrong (2004) defined marketing as a 'social and managerial process by which individuals and groups obtain what they need and want through creating and exchanging products and values with others'. Their definition emphasizes the requirement for products and services to reflect consumer wants and needs.

Levitt (1986) emphasized the fact that organizations must provide consumers with added-value appeal in his definition, as follows: 'a truly marketing minded firm tries to create value satisfying goods and services that consumers will want to buy'. Levitt's definition also highlights the importance of consumer needs and wants as being central to the marketing function. The UK-based Chartered Institute of Marketing definition also emphasizes the fact that the marketing philosophy involves putting the consumer or customer as the central focus for the organizational decision-making process: 'Identifying, anticipating, and satisfying customer requirements profitably'.

Piercy (2002) suggested that a market-led approach which considers consumer demand is essential for two reasons:

- Ultimately, all organizations are forced to follow the dictates of the market (i.e. the paying customer) or go out of business.
- The organization can pursue organizational effectiveness by being 'market led' and focusing on the customer's needs, wants and demands.

Piercy (2002) has also explained the reasons for organizations finding it difficult to adopt marketing. He suggested that there are considerable barriers to the introduction of marketing, such as ignorance of customer characteristics, lack of information, inflexible technology and competitive threats. It can be suggested, however, that the most likely reason for organizations not adopting a truly marketing led approach is the fact that they do not really understand consumer behaviour in depth. They have simply learnt how to persuade consumers to purchase by trial and error, rather than having a sophisticated understanding of these complex purchasing processes.

Organizations have, however, become very sophisticated at persuading consumers to purchase, despite an apparent lack of understanding. As far back as 1957, Vance Packard in his book, *The Hidden Persuaders*, portrayed a frightening manipulative view of the marketing function. He showed how organizations, even at that time, could further manipulate consumers, including children, into buying products and services.

This work suggested that the ability to persuade consumers to purchase products may not necessitate a detailed understanding of their behaviour patterns and motives. It may be enough just to have the ability to persuade them to purchase. Despite this view, the authors suggest that a deeper understanding of the consumer behaviour process will help with the marketing of products and services.

Calantone and Mazanec (1991) outlined the value of consumer behaviour for the marketing management process in tourism. An understanding of consumer needs, attitudes and decision processes will allow marketing managers to improve their decision-making process. It will allow marketing managers to forecast behaviour in the future and therefore avoid being overoptimistic or underestimating consumer demand (Calantone, di Benedetto and Bojanic 1987, 1988). An understanding of consumer behaviour is also important for the *product development* of new tourism products and facilities. It will allow the marketing manager to have a clearer view of the types of benefits that consumers are looking for, and enable these to be reflected in the development process.

The development of effective and efficient *advertising campaigns* also requires an understanding of consumer behaviour. Benefit segmentation is often used here so that managers can design the advertising campaign based on the particular benefits sought by the market segment. Calantone, Schewe and Allen (1980), for example, identified five benefit segments of consumers, which could be used to develop effective advertising campaigns. The use of benefit segmentation also allows the marketing manager to understand changes which may occur with time (Calantone and Sawyer, 1978) and from season to season (Calantone and Johar, 1984). This will allow the advertising copy to be amended to reflect the different benefits sought during different periods.

Benefit segmentation also allows the marketing manager to identify very well defined groups of people and target them with well-designed products and services. Several tourist practitioners have recently developed promotions specifically for target groups. Saga, for example, targets the over-fifties market exclusively with well-designed direct-mail brochures. The targeting of the older consumer has been developing for some time. Savini (1986), for example, noted the rise in direct targeting of the lucrative over-fifties market. Similarly, PGL, have a long history of targeting the child and young adult who is looking for an outward-bound type of holiday away from their parents. We will return to the use of benefit segmentation in the marketing process in later chapters.

To finish this section, we consider the marketing planning process and how an understanding of consumer behaviour helps with the marketing planning process in tourism marketing. Marketing planning was developed as a systematic way of incorporating marketing into an organization. The marketing planning process is defined by McDonald and Morris (2000) as a series of steps which incorporates all aspects of the marketing process (Figure 1.2).

We can use this model of the marketing planning to consider the usefulness of an understanding of consumer behaviour in this process. This is explored in more depth in Figure 1.3.

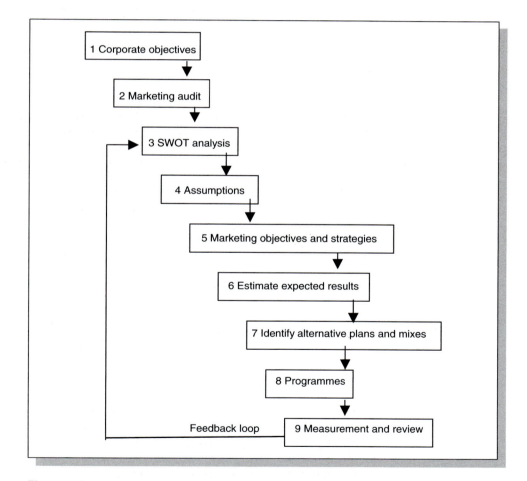

Figure 1.2
A summary of the steps involved in the marketing planning process
Source: adapted from McDonald and Morris (2000).

1. Corporate Objectives	
2. Marketing Audit	*An understanding of current consumers and the benefits they seek from our products/services and the competition.
3. SWOT Analysis	*Consumer perceptions of our products/services and their Unique Selling Propositions (USP's).
4. Assumptions	*Comparisons with competitor views of brand, consumers. *Forecasts of consumer demands will allow opportunities to be defined.
5. Marketing Objectives & Strategies	*Overall objectives and strategies should reflect consumer demands both now and in the future. Segmentation techniques will be important here.
6. Estimate expected results	*Forecasting models for consumer demand essential here.
7. Identify alternative plans and mixes	*Products – should reflect consumer wants and needs
8. Programmes	*Promotion – should target customers with effective and well designed campaigns and understanding of consumer. *Pricing in relation to demand is essential here. *Distribution – an understanding of patterns of consumer purchase essential here.
9. Measurement and Review	*Market Research of consumer responses essential here.

Figure 1.3
The marketing planning process and the usefulness of an understanding of consumer behaviour

It can be seen from Figure 1.3 that an understanding of consumer behaviour will allow a more effective marketing planning process. Some examples of where this understanding helps include:

- understanding why consumers currently choose products and services and the benefits they seek, including their unique selling proposition (USP)

- forecasting consumer demand which will bring efficiencies
- targeting particular market segments
- correct positioning of product
- designing effective marketing mixes and reflection of consumer behaviour in all elements – product, promotion, price and place (distribution)
- reviewing how new products and services have been received and an exploration of this in relation to consumer behaviour.

We can conclude therefore that the marketing planning process will be helped immensely if the marketing manager has a thorough understanding of consumer behaviour. Whether this understanding is developed as a result of thorough and systematic research or as a result of 'gut feel' and past experience is a matter of opinion and circumstances.

There are many examples of individuals who have spotted an opportunity and developed products to exploit them without much detailed research. These organizations are usually headed by entrepreneurs, who, we could argue, have an interest and understanding of consumers and who do not require sophisticated research to confirm their ideas. Even these organizations, however, tend to investigate consumer behaviour in more depth as the organization reaches maturity and more competitive products arrive on the market.

Now that we have considered the role of consumer behaviour in the marketing process, we will move on to the history of tourist behaviour.

Discussion points and essay questions

1 Discuss the reasons for tourism, leisure, and hospitality marketing becoming increasingly blurred.
2 Evaluate the importance of the fact that consumers may make purchase decisions for tourism products in groups, rather than as individuals.
3 'Tourism marketing relies entirely on the fact that consumers can be persuaded to buy by powerful communication techniques' (Horner and Swarbrooke, 1996). Critically evaluate this statement.

Exercise

Conduct a small-scale survey to investigate the importance of the high-spend nature of tourism products on the purchase decision of consumers.

The history of tourist behaviour

Introduction

We do not know the name of the first tourist or the era in which the first holiday was taken. This may be because it is so difficult to define what is meant by the words 'tourist' and 'holiday'. Or does it reflect the fact that chroniclers did not believe that the phenomenon of tourism was significant enough to be worth recording? Perhaps, but we know that for centuries tourism has existed in one form or another and has given us a legacy of travel writing, dating back to Roman times. It has also stimulated some of the world's greatest literature, like Chaucer's Canterbury Tales, for instance. Therefore, while we may talk of mass tourism as a twentieth-century phenomenon, tourism in the broadest sense of the word, has existed for centuries.

In this chapter, the authors will endeavour to address briefly the chronological development of tourist behaviour. It is difficult to understand current tourist behaviour, or predict future behaviour, unless one understands a little about the past.

As we shall see, the history of tourist behaviour is a complex subject. Furthermore, there is relatively little by way of empirical data or artefacts from which we can derive a history or chronology of early tourist behaviour. Most historians of tourism have tended to focus on Europe, from the Greeks and the Romans to the railway and Thomas Cook in the UK. However, it is important to recognize that tourism has existed in other continents for centuries. Furthermore, we need to remember that there are many different types of tourism, including, for example, business tourism, health tourism, religious tourism, educational tourism, and hedonistic tourism. Finally, there is a need to distinguish between domestic and international tourism, together with inbound and outbound tourist flows.

The first tourists

We do not know for certain who the first tourists were or where they lived. It is often thought that the beginnings of tourism date back to ancient Greece and ancient Rome because we have evidence of tourism from these eras, in terms of travel writing, for example.

However, as archaeologists know, it is dangerous to be too dogmatic about history, based on current knowledge and the artefacts we have found up until now. Who is to say that we will not find, in due course, evidence that tourism pre-dates the Greeks and Roman times? This has already happened over the years in other areas of history, leading to historians having to rethink accepted ideas on everything from who discovered the USA to who built the so-called 'Roman roads' in England.

Future research may ultimately show us that tourism pre-dates the Greek era and may indeed have first developed outside Europe. To date, little research appears to have been undertaken on the development of tourism outside Europe. Furthermore, in countries like the USA which were settled by people from the 'Old World', the study of the history of tourism begins with the first holiday-making activities of these colonists. However, some forms of tourism, notably visiting friends and relatives, undoubtedly already existing among Native Americans long before the Europeans arrived.

Unfortunately, in this chapter, by and large, the authors must base their comments on existing knowledge rather than hypothesizing about what we may come to know in the future. Nevertheless, it is important that you read what follows with the last two paragraphs in mind.

Regions of the world

We will now look at the chronological development of tourist behaviour, in two respects:

- the varied type and pace of development in the different regions of the world
- the way different types of tourism have developed, including visiting friends and relatives, business tourism, religious tourism, health tourism, educational tourism and hedonistic tourism.

In the first instance, therefore, we will outline the historical development of tourism in the following regions of the world:

- Europe
- North America
- Central America, the Caribbean and South America
- Africa
- the Middle East
- Asia

- Australasia and the Pacific Rim
- Antarctica.

The emphasis in this section will be on international rather than domestic tourism.

Europe

Today, Europe is the most popular continent as a destination for international tourists, although it is slowly losing its position in the world tourism market to other regions, such as the Pacific Rim. It is appropriate that Europe should continue to hold this pre-eminent position, for most commentators consider it to be the birthplace of modern tourism.

The development of tourism in Europe, as elsewhere, rested on two essential pre-requisites:

- a desire to travel
- the removal of obstacles that prevented people from taking trips.

As we shall see, the desire to travel until relatively recently, was predominantly based on religious devotion, concerns over health or on trade, rather than pleasure. The obstacles that needed to be overcome so that people could become tourists of whatever kind, were largely related to transport, both in terms of the lack of adequate roads and sea transport, and the risk of attack faced by travellers. Tourism could only begin to develop when these problems were removed or ameliorated.

The earliest recorded tourism in Europe dates back to the time of ancient Greece. It tended to be specialist in nature and related to religious practice. People visited religious festivals and consulted oracles. They also visited sporting events such as the Olympic Games which began in 776 BC – but even these had a religious significance.

The oldest recognized travel writing also dates from that millennium. For example, we have the writings of Herodotus, a historian who lived in the fifth century BC, who travelled by sea to Egypt, Persia, Sicily and Babylon. He recorded his experiences in ways which both informed and entertained the reader. Travel writing is thus an activity with a history that stretches back over 2000 years.

It was the Romans who were largely responsible for introducing the idea of tourism for pleasure, rather than for utilitarian purposes such as religious devotion, health or business. They started the hedonistic, sensual tradition in tourism, which has perhaps reached its peak in our age. The Romans were perhaps the first to create purpose-built tourism resorts, both at the coast and inland. These resorts often combined leisure pursuits such as bathing, or the arts, with health in terms of thermal spas. Such resorts were not only found in Italy itself, but also in the Roman provinces. They also gained a reputation as being places where Romans could escape from the moral codes which constrained their everyday lives. This led to 'loud parties, excessive drinking, and nude bathing' (Sharpley, 1994). So we can see that there is little new in the behaviour of today's tourists. However, the Romans also developed tourism based on sightseeing within their empire, utilizing the roads which had been built for the convenience of troops and trade. Romans visited famous buildings while young Romans were sent to Greece to be educated.

Yet, although the Romans pioneered the idea of hedonistic tourism, it was an elitist activity beyond the means of most Romans. It is this fact which distinguishes it from today's mass tourism. The steady march of tourism development in Europe was halted by the Dark Ages. With the end of the Roman Empire came the end of most tourism in Europe, although there was still some business tourism in the form of trade. Historians are rethinking the so-called Dark Ages and are questioning whether they were as dark as we have been led to believe.

However, one form of tourism, that was to become the earliest form of mass tourism, was born in Europe at this time, namely, the pilgrimage. This form of tourism reached its peak during the Middle Ages, and the numbers travelling were large, given the population of Europe at the time. For example, by 1300 some 300 000 people visited Rome in that year alone (Sharpley, 1994).

Other major destinations for European pilgrims included Jerusalem and Santiago de Compostella. There were also shorter pilgrimages such as those taken by the English to Canterbury, for instance. The pilgrimages were supported by a well-developed infrastructure of accommodation, eating places and even guidebooks, and were thus the forerunners of the modern tourism industry.

Towards the end of the Middle Ages there was a growth in what might be termed educational tourism, where people travelled to see great paintings and buildings, meet famous artists, and learn more about language and culture. Italy was the favoured destination for such trips, which were the origin of the 'Grand Tour'. However, in contrast to pilgrimages which were more democratic, such trips were largely the preserve of the wealthy and well educated. Both pilgrimages and the Grand Tour were the origins of the tradition of Northern Europeans travelling to Southern Europe as tourists, which continues to this day.

The Grand Tour reached its zenith in the seventeenth and eighteenth centuries, with the sons of aristocrats spending up to four years travelling around Europe. As many as 20 000 young English people alone could be on the Continent at any one time (Sharpley, 1994). As well as Italy, the tour usually encompassed France, the Netherlands, Germany, Austria and Switzerland. In the latter decades of the eighteenth century the Grand Tour changed in nature, with more people travelling but taking shorter trips. They tended to be older than previously and more middle class than aristocrat, and were more interested in sightseeing and hedonism than learning. The aristocracy began to desert the Grand Tour and look for more exclusive leisure activities elsewhere.

Nature and the scenic beauty of landscapes started to become a major attraction for some tourists, stimulated by the growth of the

Romantic Movement in art. This movement created the perceptions that still determine the way we view rural landscapes and visit the countryside today. At the same time as the rise of the Grand Tour came the rediscovery of the spas which had been so popular with the Romans. The poor sanitary conditions of the burgeoning towns of Europe in the fifteenth and sixteenth centuries stimulated an interest in health among the upper classes. Doctors, such as Turner in 1562, extolled the medicinal virtues of spa waters. Bath in England was a pioneer in the European spa movement but there were many others such as Royal Tunbridge Wells in England, and numerous examples in France, Germany and Italy. Many of these were not new spa resorts but old Roman resorts. In later years, in the nineteenth century, other spas were developed, most notably in Poland, Belgium and the Czech Republic. The spas became major centres of fashion, social activities and gambling. Over time, like the Grand Tour, the spas became less exclusive as middle-class people began to visit them. This process led to the spas' commercialization and to their becoming places to live as well as just visit.

In Britain the early seaside resorts, such as Scarborough, were developed on the premise that people would bathe in the sea to improve their health, rather than for pleasure.

In the nineteenth century we see the real foundations being laid for the development of modern tourism, owing most notably to the introduction of railways. This, and the results of the Industrial Revolution in Britain and some European countries, created the conditions for the growth of larger-scale forms of tourism. The seaside resort was the main beneficiary of this change, particularly in Britain where the Industrial Revolution occurred first. Some of the newly urbanized and industrialized population had some leisure time and disposable income to enable people to travel for pleasure, while the squalor of many towns and cities created a desire to escape for a short time. In Britain this new demand was met by resorts which served largely regional markets. Blackpool catered for Lancashire, Scarborough for Yorkshire, and Margate and Brighton accommodated the needs of London. This pattern of regional catchment areas for many resorts lasted well into the 1950s and 1960s, and has not yet disappeared. However, as rail services improved and journey times reduced, resorts grew up which were further from the major centres of population and industry, such as Torquay. These tended to attract more affluent tourists from all over Britain. The rise of seaside resorts was also seen in continental Europe, where resorts developed to meet the needs of the urban dwellers of France, Belgium, the Netherlands and Germany, from the North Sea to the Atlantic shores of Brittany.

Just as we have seen throughout history, as resorts developed by the upper classes became favoured by the middle classes, the former moved on in search of more exclusive destinations. Thus, wealthier Britons, for example, began to visit resorts in mainland Europe. Sir George Young has estimated that 100 000 Britons were crossing the

English Channel in 1840, while the number had risen to 1 million by the turn of the century (Sharpley, 1994). These Britons began to choose resorts in southern France where the climate was better, as places to spend the winter, away from the cold of Britain. Here we see the fore-runners, albeit a small elite, of today's flow of elderly Britons who travel to Benidorm for several months every winter for exactly the same reason.

It was sun-seeking affluent Britons who in the late nineteenth century stimulated the growth of resorts such as Nice and Biarritz. These resorts were also frequented by royalty from other European countries; they thus became fashionable places. Their image as glamorous risqué playgrounds for the rich was enhanced by the opening of casinos and the growth of gambling.

Another development in the nineteenth century that was to have a profound impact on the growth of tourism was the creation of the modern tour operator, which traditionally is thought to be the excursion business started by Thomas Cook in 1841, in Britain. This company, which has since become a byword for tourism, started by organizing local rail excursions in Leicestershire, but by the end of the nineteenth century it was taking British tourists to Egypt. It also dealt with the travel arrangements of travellers from many other countries. By taking responsibility for organizing trips for tourists, Thomas Cook made travel accessible to those who lacked the language skills or the confidence to travel independently. It thus laid the foundations for modern package tourism.

By the beginning of the twentieth century the seeds of long-haul international leisure tourism were taking root. Sharpley, writing in 1994, estimates that in the years leading up to the First World War, up to 100 000 Americans visited Europe each year. Other future tourism markets were also being pioneered in the early years of the twentieth century including skiing holidays which have reached their zenith in our time. Tourism continued to develop after the First World War. The 1920s were the heyday of the transatlantic cruise market. Sunbathing also developed as a leisure activity in the hedonistic days of the same decade. A suntan became fashionable rather than being associated with lower-class rural dwellers and manual labourers. From the 1930s onwards, the growing availability of the motor car further stimulated tourism. It opened up areas that were beyond the public transport system. During the interwar years the aeroplane began to play a small role in the tourism market as an option for the wealthier classes, particularly in Europe. These improvements in transport coincided in Europe with an increase in leisure time as a result of legislation on the length of the working week, in many European countries. An example of this trend is the Holidays with Pay Act of 1938 in Britain. This era also saw the growth of the holiday camp concept, particularly again in Britain, through the activities of entrepreneurs such as Billy Butlin. These camps reached their peak in the early years after the Second World War and were clearly the forerunners of modern inland complexes such as Center Parcs.

The rapid growth of mass tourism in Europe since the late 1940s, has been well documented. It has been explained by the coincidence of a number of interrelated factors occurring at the same time, including:

- increases in disposable income
- advances in aircraft technology
- the greater availability of motor cars
- further increases in leisure time
- education
- the growth of tour operators and the package holiday.

The first wave of mass tourism in Europe consisted of annual migrations to the Mediterranean, in search of sun, by the residents of Northern Europe. Until recently this was largely a one-way flow, although now there is a rapid growth in outbound tourism from these Mediterranean countries, notably from Italy and Spain. Furthermore, not all Europeans have shown the same desire to visit other countries even though they can afford to, as we can see from the example of the French, who still show a preference for holidaying at home. This may reflect the variety of tourism opportunities that exist within their own country, as well as being the result of government initiatives designed to encourage people to holiday at home for economic reasons. These initiatives include the development of new purpose-built resorts on the Languedoc and Aquitaine coasts and in the French Alps.

These developments illustrate another major recent trend in the European tourism market, namely, the increasing role of governments as both attraction developers and destination marketers. Governments have also often been the catalyst for the growth of a modern form of tourism in Europe, that is, social tourism, where holiday-taking is viewed as a right and may form part of the social security system. While never popular in Britain, it is an important element of the market in France and Germany.

However, it would be wrong to suggest that the past four or five decades have been a period of growth for all forms of tourism. In the 1950s, 1960s and 1970s the opportunities offered by jet travel and new Mediterranean destinations considerably reduced demand for both transatlantic cruises and the seaside resorts of Northern Europe. Interestingly, in recent years, we have seen the renaissance of the European cruise market, but now it is more about mass appeal and budget prices rather than elegance and exclusivity. Nothing typifies better the march of mass tourism and the democratization of travel than this.

It would also be incorrect to imply that the growth of tourism has been a pan-European phenomenon. Until the political change of the late 1980s and early 1990s in Eastern Europe, the countries of the east were locked in their own tourism world. Domestic tourism existed on a large scale and cross-border tourism also existed, although it largely took place wholly within the Eastern bloc. Visits to Western Europe were rare and reserved for the political elite. This process is now changing and new markets are opening up for Mediterranean resorts just as

European tourists are starting to look further afield to the USA, Asia and the Caribbean for their holidays.

The final trend we should note in the historical development of tourism in Europe is the fact that Britain is no longer at the forefront of developments. Germany is the world's largest generator of international trips and the Dutch, Belgians, Swedes and Danes take more holidays per head than the British. Even the most successful tourism developments in the UK are now often imported, such as the Center Parcs concept from the Netherlands or the Waterfront developments that were based on experience in the USA. Perhaps the most significance example of this trend is the fact that Thomas Cook is now German owned.

However, the future of tourism in Europe may in future not be about what happens in different European countries, but rather about events in the rest of the world. Tourism is increasingly a truly global market but it is a market in which Europe is losing its dominant position.

North America

Some histories of tourism in the USA and Canada begin in the nineteenth century, but clearly the first peoples, the Native Americans, had been travelling around the continent of North America for centuries before the colonists arrived. This travel, while not often recorded by historians, must have been motivated by religious devotion, the desire to keep in touch with relatives and the need to look for new hunting grounds. We should also recognize the role played by these Native Americans in helping the early settlers find their way around their newly adopted homeland. However, it is correct to say that the modern tourism industry in the USA only dates back to the mid-eighteenth century. It is not surprising that the earliest growth of tourism in the USA should have occurred in New England, one of the first areas of the country settled by Europeans. In the latter half of the century, coaching inns and taverns began to develop to meet the needs of tourists. An early example is now part of the Old Deerfield Village Museum complex in Massachusetts. City centre hotels began to develop later, with the first recognized such hotel being the Tremont in Boston, which opened in 1829.

However, it was the railway which really first stimulated tourism in the USA, both for pleasure and business. It particularly opened up the 'Wild West' to settlers, commercial travellers and curious tourists. Lundberg notes that in 1830 there were only 23 miles of rail track in the USA, but that by 1880 the figure was 93 267, and that by 1920 it had reached 240 293 (Lundberg, 1990). The railway companies also contributed to the growth of tourism through the building of hotels and resort complexes in New England. They were heavily involved in the development of Florida from the turn of the twentieth century.

The next major phase of tourism growth in the USA was stimulated by the growth of car ownership. In 1914 there were already 2 million private cars on the roads but by the 1930s, at the height of the Depression, there were some 25 million (Lundberg, 1990).

Car ownership stimulated two new developments in US tourism:

- the creation of the roadside motels, offering accommodation that was convenient for motorists. While the motel concept did not extend to Europe until the 1980s, it dates back to the 1920s in the USA
- a growing number of visitors to remote national parks that were beyond the public transport network. This started what has become a major theme of US domestic tourism, namely, visiting wilderness areas in a private car or RV (recreational vehicle).

The development of US tourism was also stimulated by the creation of travel agency chains, beginning with 'Ask Foster' in 1888 and American Express three years later. Since the Second World War, both domestic and outbound tourism have increased in the USA. Indeed, for many Europeans the stereotype of a tourist is normally an American. Yet the truth is that, given the size of the population, Americans are not great world travellers. Relatively few possess a passport and the majority exhibit a preference for domestic holidays. This may well reflect the great size and diversity of their own country, but it may also be related to other issues such as the notably modest level of skill in foreign languages possessed by most Americans.

In recent decades, the USA has pioneered a number of new forms of visitor attractions which have been adopted elsewhere in the world. These include:

- theme parks, beginning with Disneyland in California which opened over forty years ago
- leisure shopping
- open air museums, with live interpretation, such as Old Sturbridge Village, the Plimoth Plantation, and Mystic Seaport in New England
- waterfront redevelopment projects, for example, those of Baltimore, Boston and San Francisco.

Furthermore, they have led the way in the development of some new tourism markets that have spread to Europe. For example, the 'Snowbirds' who travel to Florida and the South West from the North to escape the harsh winter are now being imitated by Britons who winter on the Spanish and Portuguese coasts. The USA also provided the model for the development of destination marketing agencies around the world, based on the principle of public–private sector partnership, through the Visitor and Convention Bureaux, which are found in most US towns and cities.

If we now turn our attention to Canada, much tourism has traditionally been based on the beauty of the natural environment. In the late nineteenth and early twentieth centuries it was the railroad which stimulated the growth of Canadian tourism. Rail companies such as Canadian Pacific developed hotels as well as providing the transport for tourists.

In recent years, however, Canada has started to broaden its tourism appeal in a number of ways, notably by:

- becoming a destination for skiers from Europe
- offering city breaks that explore the different linguistic cultures, such as English-speaking Toronto and French-speaking Montreal.

Central America

Tourism in Central America, (including Mexico) has a relatively long history, but it has experienced rapid growth since the 1960s. In 1960 the region received 749 000 international arrivals, according to the World Tourism Organization, but this figure had risen to 2.9 million in 1970 and more than 7 million by 1989. According to the World Tourism Organization, in 1990 there were major differences in the place of origin of tourists visiting different countries within the region. Mexico, for example, received 92 per cent of all its visitors from the USA and Canada, and only 3 per cent came from other Latin American countries. On the other hand, the equivalent figures for Guatemala were 26 per cent and 56 per cent respectively. Mexico's situation is clearly explained by its proximity to the USA.

However, while Mexico has focused on beach and coach tour holidays, other countries in the region have pioneered new forms of tourism, notably eco-tourism. It is in this field that Belize and Costa Rica have built their fledgling tourist industries in the past decade.

The Caribbean

The Caribbean is a single name that covers hundreds of very different islands. It includes countries with different colonial histories, including Dutch, French, Spanish and British colonies, and countries with distinctly different modern political histories. Cuba is part of the same region as the American-influenced capitalist 'tax havens' of the Virgin Islands and the Bahamas. So it is no surprise to learn that its tourism takes many different forms, but two factors we have already mentioned have determined the tourism history of the area, that is, colonial history and modern politics. The first point is evident in the markets for different Caribbean Islands. Former British colonies such as Jamaica and Barbados attract British visitors, while former French colonies and French 'Outre Mer Départements' like Guadeloupe and Martinique attract mainly French tourists. At the same time a shared history and language draws Spanish tourists to the Dominican Republic. However, this pattern is showing evidence of breaking down with upmarket British tourists being attracted to the French-speaking Caribbean and those in search of value-for-money visiting the all-inclusive resorts of the Dominican Republic.

Cuba illustrates the second point about modern politics perfectly. Seaton recognized that, 'up to the 1958 revolution, Cuba was the most successful Caribbean destination with a thriving tourism industry primarily controlled by US interests and made up of US visitors' (Seaton, 1996). Gambling was perhaps the major motivation for these tourists. After the revolution, the US government introduced a trade blockade of Cuba and the flow of American tourists dried up. To some extent they were replaced by visitors from Europe who were sympathetic to the politics of the new regime of Fidel Castro. The story continues today with Cuba trying to broaden its appeal and attract mass market package tourists to offset its loss of financial support from the old Soviet Union. Interestingly, though, while we have seen that the Caribbean is a very diverse region, its countries have a long tradition of working together in mutually beneficial destination marketing campaigns. This has been achieved largely through the Caribbean Tourism Organization, a governmental agency whose origins date back to 1951, and which has an office in New York.

In recent years, the Caribbean has attracted primarily three types of tourism – cruises, beach holidays, and visits from people who emigrated or whose parents emigrated from the region.

South America

Tourism to South America has a history that dates back decades but it did not really grow dramatically until the 1960s. The World Tourism Organization in 1991 reported that between 1950 and 1960 the number of international arrivals grew only from 410 000 to 426 000. However by 1970 the figure was 2.4 million and by 1989 it was up to around 8 million arrivals. In the early days of tourism in South America, cruises were a major product and air travel developed rapidly in the region between the First and Second World Wars, at a time when cities such as Buenos Aires were seen as sophisticated places to visit. Business tourism has existed in the region for decades based on, for example, the exploitation of crops such as coffee, vital raw materials such as the nitrates required by the fertilizer industry, and the mining of tin.

Recent decades have seen the rise of newer forms of tourism in South America, such as visits to the cultural heritage sites of Peru and trips to the carnival in Rio de Janeiro, Brazil. Political instability has always been an inhibiting factor for the development of tourism in some countries such as Bolivia and Paraguay. However, this very instability has become quite a motivator for a small niche market of adventure travellers. The market for South America has developed considerably in Spain and Portugal in recent years, owing to the common shared language and the growth of foreign holiday-taking by Spanish and Portuguese tourists.

Africa

The continent of Africa is so diverse that making generalizations about it is at best problematic, and at worst, meaningless. But we can say that tourism has existed in Africa for many centuries. We know, for instance, that the Greeks and Romans visited the sights of Egypt. There has also been more outbound tourism from some parts of Africa over the centuries than one might think, particularly in terms of business tourism and religious tourism. For example, Nigerians who are Muslims have, for a very long time, made pilgrimages to the Middle East. However, Africa is undoubtedly largely a receiver rather than a generator of international trips, and has been since the nineteenth century. We should remember that Thomas Cook was offering tours to the historic treasures of Egypt at the end of the nineteenth century. During the first half of the twentieth century, the British played a major role in opening up Africa as a tourist destination, particularly in the countries which were then still part of the British Empire.

In the 1920s and 1930s the two main regions which attracted foreign visitors, apart from Egypt, were:

- Kenya, where the appeal was big game hunting
- Morocco, which was a popular winter sun destination, favoured by, among others, Winston Churchill.

After gaining their independence, many African countries sought to attract tourists to help develop their economies. Between the 1960s and 1980s, a number of African countries began to attract foreign tourists. Tunisia and Morocco became popular summer sun destinations, and wildlife holidays were being offered in Tanzania and Botswana, for example. In the 1960s, Scandinavian tourists discovered Gambia, which in the 1980s was to become a popular winter sun destination for British tourists.

Africa also saw some early experiments in what is now termed sustainable tourism. For instance, there were experiments in small-scale rural tourism in the Casamance region of the former French colony of Senegal. However, the growth of tourism in Africa has been constrained by political instability and poverty in many countries. For instance, in the past three decades tourism has been disrupted by a range of problems, including:

- war in Uganda
- civil war in Nigeria
- a coup d'état in Gambia
- the threat of terrorism in Egypt and Algeria.

The link between politics and tourism is most clearly seen in regions of South Africa. After the country was ostracized by the international community because of its apartheid policies, relatively few international tourists visited South Africa and few residents of the country travelled abroad. Only the white minority could participate actively in the well-developed domestic tourism industry. At the same time, some whites travelled to the so-called 'tribal homelands', for example Bophuthatswana, and resorts such as Sun City where mixed race relationships were tolerated.

With the end of apartheid and the election of a new government, South Africa has begun to attract large numbers of foreign tourists. Indeed, buying property in the country has become popular among Europeans and Americans. There has also been a large growth in business tourism, with the resumption of normal trade relations between South Africa and the rest of the world.

Finally, as some African economies have developed, most notably that of Nigeria, outbound tourism from these countries has grown, both in terms of business and leisure tourism.

The Middle East

The countries of the Middle East have a long history of involvement in the tourism industry, most notably in terms of religious tourism. This region is the most important pilgrimage destination in the world for three major religions:

- Muslims for whom both Mecca and Jerusalem are very sacred places; the tourist flow to Mecca is probably the largest single annual movement of tourists in the world
- the cities of Nazareth, Bethlehem, Jerusalem and Jericho, which are the most important religious cities for Christians
- Jerusalem which is the holiest city for Jews.

However, it is not only religion which has brought tourists to the region. The Middle East has also always been an important crossroads for business travellers. Some silk route caravans used to be routed through Syria and Jordan to the Mediterranean coast, for instance. Until its civil war, the Lebanon, and Beirut specifically, was one of the world's most fashionable and sophisticated tourist destinations. This is clearly illustrated by an advertisement placed by the British airline BOAC in 1962 which described Beirut as an 'international playground'. It offered a return flight for £105 – a fortune in 1962 – and promised passengers, 'exotic night spots', great skiing, and 'fabulous beaches'. The wars between Israel and her neighbours in 1962 and 1973, and the civil war in Lebanon in the 1970s and 1980s, greatly hindered the rise of tourism in the region. However, in recent years the Middle East peace process has helped stimulate a rejuvenation and growth of the industry. It has particularly stimulated the development of cross-border tours of the region's heritage, typically featuring Jordan, Israel, Palestine and Egypt. However, at the time of writing, tension still exists in Israel and the Palestinian territories, which is threatening the future of pilgrimage and cultural tourism in the region. Nevertheless, Israel is still seeing its tourism arrivals growing on its Red Sea coast in resorts such as Eilat, particularly in relation to winter sun packages and water sports holidays.

Finally, some Middle Eastern countries that have never before tried to attract tourists are either attempting to develop tourism or at least are starting to make it easier for tourists to enter them, for example:

- Dubai, with its emphasis on shopping and desert safaris in four-wheel drive vehicles
- Iran, which is increasingly opening its borders to foreign tourists
- Lebanon, which is rebuilding its tourism industry and attempting to re-enter the international tourism market.

Asia

Clearly, Asia is a large continent which encompasses a wide variety of national tourism markets with very different characteristics. In countries like Thailand and the Philippines inbound tourism began with visiting sailors, followed by the arrival of package tourism in the 1980s and 1990s. For example, according to Richter, writing in 1989 (in Hitchcock, King and Parnwell, 1993), Thailand's market grew as follows:

- 1960 – 81 340 arrivals
- 1970 – 628 671 arrivals
- 1980 – 1 858 801 arrivals
- 1986 – 2 818 292 arrivals.

Thailand's resorts are now a cheap, good quality destination for Europeans seeking a sun, sand and sea holiday, but Bangkok has still maintained its reputation for sex tourism, which dates back to its days as a shore trip for sailors.

In India, there is a strong tradition of domestic tourism of two types:

- trips to hill stations during the hot summer months
- visits to religious festivals.

Inbound tourism, on the other hand, has tended to focus on historic cities but coastal resorts such as Goa and Kerala have become major destinations for foreign package tourists looking for winter sun holidays.

While most Asian countries have been trying to attract foreign tourists, Japan, for example, tried to encourage its population to holiday abroad, 'as a way of alleviating trade friction with neighbouring countries' (Mackie, in Harrison, 1992) and in 1986 some 5.5 million Japanese were taking foreign holidays (Inove, 1991). However, the holiday market in recent decades in Japan has been constrained by the continued habit among Japanese people of working long hours and taking fewer holidays than other nationalities. The tastes of Japanese tourists and their tendency to demand familiar food, drink and accommodation can be a controversial issue, as for example on the Gold Coast in Australia. They also show a preference for other Asian countries with cultures similar to their own such as South Korea.

More recently the newly industrialized nations of Asia such as South Korea and Singapore have started to become significant generators of international tourist trips.

In recent years, some countries in Asia have begun to attract foreign tourists in significant numbers, including China and Burma. One of the most spectacular growth rates in international arrivals has been seen in Vietnam. This growth can be seen with reference to figures in the 1990s, quoted in Hitchcock, King and Parnwell (1993), when visitors to Vietnam rose from just 20 000 in 1986 to 187 000 in 1990 and to 500 000 in 1995. This growth has been fuelled by political change in the country, a desire by foreigners to see its cultural and heritage attractions, and a growing trade in visits by American Vietnam War veterans. Across the region, special interest and beach-based tourism are taking over from the 'travellers' of yesterday. Finally, the 'jet-age' has created important 'stopover markets' for certain Asian countries such as Hong Kong and Singapore, on air routes between Europe and Australasia.

Australasia and the Pacific Rim

Australia and New Zealand, though they have relatively small populations, have a long tradition of outbound tourism, particularly among the younger population of both countries. This growth in outbound tourism occurred steadily from the 1960s to the 1990s. Harcourt et al. (1991), offered the following figures on the growth of outbound tourism from Australia:

- 1965 – 161 692 departures
- 1975 – 911 815 departures.

These tourists have traditional taken relatively long trips to Europe and North America, but Asia is now attracting large numbers too. At the same time, the main market for inbound tourism to Australasia has traditionally been people from Europe visiting friends and relatives (VFR) who have emigrated to the region. In the early days, this market was largely English speaking but it increasingly reflects the multicultural nature of Australian society. Many of the VFR tourists are now equally likely to be Greek or Asian. Australia has also attracted considerable numbers of leisure tourists from Japan, who have shown a particular preference for the Gold Coast of Queensland. This has led to the growth of infrastructure that is geared to the tastes of Japanese visitors. Australasia is also attracting growing numbers of tourists from Europe and North America, who are attracted by the natural beauty. For example, there are trips to the Kakadu National Park in Northern Australia and whale watching in New Zealand. The islands of the South Pacific have long held an appeal for Western tourists as they are perceived to offer exotic 'paradise' experiences. They are also attracting Japanese visitors making nostalgic trips to Second World War battle sites on islands such as Guam.

Antarctica

Antarctica is unique in the tourism world in that its lack of a permanent resident population means that the only tourism is inbound, rather than outbound or domestic. The region did not begin to attract tourists until the 1950s. However, while numbers are still small, the growth rate has been dramatic. Statistics quoted by Hall and Johnston (1995), in an edited work on Polar tourism, present the following picture of the growth of arrivals in Antarctica during the period from 1957 to 1993:

- 1957–58 – 194 arrivals
- 1967–68 – 147 arrivals
- 1977–78 – 845 arrivals
- 1987–88 – 2782 arrivals
- 1992–93 – 7037 arrivals.

The same text tells us that more than 90 per cent of visitors to the region arrived by sea, on cruise ships, as they still do today. These cruises originate principally from ports in Australasia, Argentina and Chile. While the cruises may last for an average of 12 to 15 days, most cruise passengers spend only a few hours on land in the Antarctic.

Inter-regional comparisons across the world

There have clearly been considerable differences in the nature and volume of tourism demand between different countries and regions of the world. Some have been generators of international trips while others have generated very few such trips. Certain regions have traditionally been popular tourists destinations while others have until recently attracted relatively few tourists. There are also very different levels and patterns of domestic tourism between different countries, even within the same region of the world. For example, French people take far more domestic holidays that their neighbours in Germany.

The nature of tourism in different countries has been influenced by a myriad of factors including, for example:

- climate
- geographical location
- history
- language
- the development of transport systems
- levels of economic development
- the quality of landscapes and townscapes
- government policies towards tourism
- the degree of economic and political stability.

However, in recent years the picture of world tourism demand has begun to change dramatically. Newly industrialized countries such as

Korea have started to become major generating countries for tourism trips. At the same time, countries renowned for receiving tourists, such as Spain, have also begun to generate tourist trips. Political change has created opportunities for Eastern Europeans to travel outside their own region.

At the same time, there has been a general growth in long-haul travel which has taken tourists to countries where they did not travel before, outside their own continent.

The most significant trend in the period from 1950 to 1990 was the relative decline in the share of tourist arrivals in the Americas and the increase in the share of arrivals in East Asia and the Pacific. However, we must put this in context. According to the World Tourism Organization, while the Americas show a reduction of a third in their share of international tourist arrivals, between 1980 and 1990, their number of visitors actually grew from 7.5 million to 84 million over the same period. In other words, these figures have to be seen in the context of the phenomenal rise in international tourism experienced between 1980 and 1990. Nevertheless, there was a clear trend towards the Pacific Rim, and to a lesser extent Africa, which is evident in the history of international tourism over the past few decades, and particularly during the period from 1970 to 1990.

Different types of tourism

Having looked at the chronological development of tourism from a geographical perspective, it is now time to consider it in terms of different types of tourism. Dividing tourism up into subtypes is always subjective, but the authors believe that the way chosen here allows interesting points to be made about the growth of tourism and the development of tourist behaviour. This section, therefore, covers the following types of tourism:

- visiting friends and relatives
- business tourism
- religious tourism
- health tourism
- social tourism
- educational tourism
- cultural tourism
- scenic tourism
- hedonistic tourism
- activity tourism
- special interest tourism.

Visiting friends and relatives

This phenomenon clearly dates back to the earliest days in pre-history when migration first separated families. Notwithstanding the immense difficulties of travelling in ancient times, it is natural that, from time to time, family members would have wanted to see each other. The same is true of friends who were permanently or temporarily parted by migration and nomadic lifestyles. Weddings and religious festivals provided opportunities for the earliest form of VFR tourism.

In recent centuries this form of tourism has been further stimulated by a range of factors, including:

- increased leisure time
- improved transport systems
- better housing so that people can now accommodate their friends and relatives more comfortably in their own homes.

The VFR market is notoriously difficult to measure, for two main reasons:

- the fact that much of it is domestic and no national boundaries are crossed
- VFR tourists do not usually make use of commercial accommodation establishments, where visitor data could be collected.

However, the growth of economic migration in recent decades, around the world, has given a new impetus to this market. The families or individuals who migrate permanently or temporarily, to improve their economic well-being, create markets for VFR trips. While such trips bring little benefit for accommodation suppliers, they can bring considerable new business for transport operators and travel agents, as the following examples illustrate:

- so-called 'guest workers' in Germany returning home by air and rail to Turkey to visit friends and family
- trips to India, Pakistan and Bangladesh from the UK
- Moroccan and Algerian people, who live in France, using ferries and flights to visit their families in North Africa
- expatriate British workers returning home for brief visits to the UK from Middle East countries such as Saudi Arabia and Kuwait.

Clearly, the demand for visiting families is potentially greater among those communities where the extended family, rather than the nuclear family, is the norm.

Business tourism

We are inclined to think of business tourism as a fundamentally modern phenomenon. In our minds it is purpose-built convention centres, business people jetting around the world, product launches, training seminars and incentive travel packages. Yet, business tourism is one of the oldest forms of tourism; it is just that the type of business tourism has changed over time.

Until this century, business travel was largely related purely to trade, to selling and transporting goods to customers who resided outside the area of production. It thus involved:

- visits to potential customers by 'sales people', the so-called commercial travellers
- the transporting of goods to the customer.

This activity has been going on for longer than we often imagine and each new piece of archaeological research seems to indicate that its history extends even further back into the mists of pre-history. Furthermore, early business tourism is not restricted to any single continent. Evidence of business tourism has been found, in terms of artefacts discovered by archaeologists that could only have been produced elsewhere, all over Africa, the Americas, Asia, the Middle East and Europe. There is evidence of trade taking place in all these countries. There is a tendency to believe that, because of the poor state of transport systems until the modern era, most trade generally only involved short-distance movement. This clearly is not true.

Not only were ships used widely for longer-distance trade, but also well-developed, long-distance overland routes existed many centuries ago. Perhaps the greatest example of this phenomenon is the former 'Silk Route' which brought silk from China to Europe by way of such magically named places as Samarkand and Constantinople. This route, or more accurately set of interconnecting routes, covered thousands of kilometres and was used for hundreds of years.

From its early days, business tourism developed its own infrastructure, reflecting the needs of the business traveller. In the case of the Silk Route this revolved around food, accommodation for the travellers, and the supply of water for their beasts of burden in the arid regions of Central Asia. Many of the buildings that served these travellers, such as the caravanserai where caravans of merchants would stop for rest, remain today as a memorial to early business tourism. Some of these are now being restored as tourist attractions, in Turkey, for example. Indeed, one of the authors recalls a meal taken in a fourteenth-century caravanserai in the Azerbaijani city of Baku, more than a decade ago! The desire of merchants to travel together for safety led to the growth of caravans, and thus the development of a new type of professional, the caravan master. But early trade and business tourism also led to the growth of a range of professions over the years, including sailors, carters and canal boat operators, all with their own unique lifestyles. Alongside individual business trips and the activities of those involved in transporting goods, the third major stream of business tourism has been the trade fair. Here people from a region or a specific industry gather together to sell to each other and exchange professional news. Such trade fairs are not a recent invention, they date back hundreds of years. For example, in the Middle Ages there was a famous annual fair at Beaucaire, on the banks of the Rhône, which was known all over the Western world.

In Europe, at least, the growth of business tourism was greatly stimulated by the Industrial Revolution, and throughout the world it was made easier by the introduction of the railway. However, like leisure tourism, the real boom in business tourism did not occur until after the Second World War. Its rapid growth has been fuelled by a number of factors, including:

- improvements in transport technologies
- the rise of the global economy
- the growth of supra-national trading blocks such as the European Union and the trade agreement between the USA, Canada, and Mexico, the North American Free Trade Agreement (NAFTA), for example
- the effort made by governments to attract high-spending business tourists to their country
- the development of new forms of business tourism such as incentive travel.

Business tourism is no longer just about sales trips and the transport of goods. It now involves conferences where information is exchanged, lavish events to launch new products, survival weekends to motivate or reward staff and intensive training courses. New forms of business tourist have appeared, linked to these developments in business tourism. There is the company troubleshooter, the trainer and the conference circuit traveller. However, certain traditional types of business traveller are declining in numbers, notably the commercial traveller, who has been made increasingly obsolete by developments in communication technologies. Their passing has been the death knell for many small, privately owned commercial hotels in the UK. A whole new industry has arisen to serve these modern types of business tourists, as well as the 'traditional' individual on a business trip. It is an increasingly specialist field with major corporations seeking to achieve competitive advantage in this most lucrative of tourist markets.

It is important to recognize that throughout history, there has been a strong link between leisure tourism and business tourism. Business tourists become leisure tourists when the working day is over and they are often accompanied by partners, who are full-time leisure tourists. Furthermore, as they are often travelling at someone else's expense, business tourists can represent a particularly high-spending segment. The way business tourists have chosen to spend their leisure time has, however, often been controversial. For example, business tourists have often been the stimulus for the growth of red-light districts and prostitution, from Amsterdam to Bangkok.

Religious tourism

We saw earlier in this chapter that, in Europe for example, religion was a major catalyst for early tourism. Religious tourism usually includes visiting places with religious significance such as shrines, or attending religious events such as saint's day festivals. However, it would be a mistake – one often made by tourism historians – to talk about religious tourism mainly in terms of Christian pilgrimages in Europe. Religious tourism undoubtedly existed long before Christianity. Devotion to a religion motivated trips by ancient peoples including the Egyptians, Greeks and Jews. Travel for religious reasons existed in India and Asia, for example, before Christ was born. Many early religions that encouraged pilgrimages in ancient times are now marginal or forgotten, such as the fire-worshippers or Zoroastrians. At a time when Europe was in the Dark Ages the Islamic religion came into existence. We in the West often forget that the Islamic pilgrimage to Mecca is still perhaps the greatest single tourist flow in the world, eclipsing in size modern Christian pilgrimages. Having made this important point, we now return to Christian tourism in Europe.

It is often said that the difference between tourism in the past and modern tourism is that the former was small scale and elitist while the latter is on a mass scale and more democratic. Yet if we look at the European Christian pilgrimages we can see a very different pattern. We can observe that this form of religious tourism peaked in the Middle Ages and has since declined, as religious observance has declined, particularly in Northern Europe. It also reflects the rise of Protestantism in Europe which has never placed the same emphasis on pilgrimages as has Catholicism. Where the latter religion is still practised by the majority of the population, such as in Ireland, the pilgrimage is still popular. For one market segment, there is a strong link between religious and health tourism. These are the people who visit more modern shrines such as Lourdes in the hope that they will be cured of their diseases. Finally, religious tourism in Europe is a good example of how infrastructure developed for one form of tourism can be used in the future for another type of tourism. The great cathedrals that were built as symbols of, and places for, religious devotion and pilgrimages are now merely another sightseeing attraction for the package tourist. Events with great religious significance, such as processions parading the towns' patron saints through the streets, become entertainment for tourists. Pilgrimage routes, such as Santiago de Compostella, became themed tours for ordinary non-religious tourists, while accommodation built to shelter pilgrims become trendy stopovers for tired cyclists. However, this can only happen when the original fundamental purpose has largely become obsolete or of relatively minor significance. This is therefore not happening to Islamic infrastructure, in an era when the Islamic religion is growing and flourishing.

Health tourism

As we saw in the context of Europe, health tourism laid the foundations for the development of much of the modern tourism industry in Europe. While it was pioneered by the Romans, it did not become popular again until the sixteenth and seventeenth centuries. It grew then as a response to the unsanitary conditions in many towns and cities.

At first, health tourism was simply about exploiting natural phenomena for their medicinal benefits, for example mineral springs and sea water. However, as time went on, these resorts also became centres of fashion and social activity. The history of these spas and resorts was described in more detail earlier in the chapter, in the section on Europe; however, it would be wrong to suggest that this development was only confined to Europe. Spa resorts grew up in other continents such as those found in the USA in upstate New York.

It would be also incorrect to give the impression that seaside bathing and spa visiting were the only forms of health tourism. In the seventeenth and eighteenth centuries, many wealthy Europeans paid lengthy visits to reputed doctors at renowned medical schools such as at Montpellier in France. These visits resulted in some of the most famous travel writing of the era, for example Smolletts' account of his visit to Montpellier in 1763. Also, for centuries, climate has played a major part in health tourism. While in Northern Europe, this usually means travelling in search of the sun, it has motivated very different types of tourism flow. Particularly during the age of colonial expansion, European colonists often sought to escape summer heat by moving up to the cooler hills. An excellent example was the practice in India of spending the summer at hill stations such as Simla. However, in doing this, the colonists were only continuing a much earlier tradition established by the Maharajas.

Health tourism, in Europe at least, is an excellent example of fashion cycles in tourist behaviour. Many of the spas which were so popular between the sixteenth and nineteenth centuries in Europe went into decline in the first half of the century. They ceased to be socially fashionable, and improvements in health care standards made them less necessary. In some resorts political instability and the onset of war made them less accessible to their former markets. While this is generally true, there are exceptions, for example Germany, where the involvement of trade unions and social tourism organizations in spa tourism has meant that some have maintained their position. However, in France, although not in the UK, spas have enjoyed a renaissance in recent years with the growing interest of tourists in health. They have again become smart places where health care is combined with leisure facilities and entertainment. The Auvergne region of France, in particular, is exploiting this new interest in spas to develop high-spending forms of health tourism. In recent years the interest in health has even led to a rediscovery of seawater bathing as a health-enhancing activity. Thalassotherapy is very popular in France, for example, where companies such as Accor have invested heavily in the necessary facilities. We have also seen the rise of the health farms in Europe and the USA where many men and women take a short break to lose weight and improve their fitness. The most sophisticated modern form of health tourism is that where people travel abroad for medical treatment, to institutions which are perceived to be world leaders in their field.

Two case studies in Part Eight of the book offer more detail on the international spa market and the health farm market respectively.

Social tourism

In general, the holiday market is a commercial market where consumers are asked to pay a full market price for their vacation. However, in a number of countries, tourism and holiday-taking is also encompassed within the realms of welfare policy. Here, holidays are subsidized in some way, either by government or voluntary sector agencies such as non-profit-making organizations or trade unions. This may be termed social tourism.

This form of tourism is largely absent from the UK where its only manifestation is in the area of subsidized holidays for carers, offered by some charities and local authorities. However, it is much more prevalent in other countries, notably Germany, Spain and France. In the latter country, social tourism is well developed and its 'infrastructure' includes:

- Chéques-Vacances which can be exchanged for tourism services
- social tourism holiday villages and centres, operated by non-profit-making associations.

This provision is subsidized by employers, trade unions and the government. However, pressures on public spending are currently casting a shadow over the future of social tourism in France.

While not strictly speaking social tourism, we have seen, in recent years, attempts being made by the tourism industry to provide a better service for groups in society who have been largely ignored, or even discriminated against, by the industry. These groups include two in particular:

- consumers with disabilities including those with mobility problems, impaired sight or hearing difficulties
- single-parent families who are often unable to take advantage of the usual 'family' offers that stipulate that a family means *two* adults and a number of children. This is clearly discriminatory in a world where an increasing number of families have a single parent.

As yet, however, little effort appears to be being made, overall, by the tourism industry, in Europe at least, to encourage people from ethnic minority communities to participate in the mainstream tourism market. Yet, in many European countries these communities represent markets that run into hundreds of thousands of consumers. Perhaps, however, the situation reflects the feeling that many ethnic communities have their own established patterns of tourism demand, such as visiting friends and relatives in the country from which their parents and grandparents came. This market is often serviced by specialist suppliers, drawn from the communities themselves. However, the USA shows that in due course such communities do develop a demand for mainstream travel services, but these may still be met by specialist operators drawn from these communities. This is true, for instance, of the Black American market.

Educational tourism

Educational tourism, or travelling to learn, has a long history, from the days when wealthy members of the Greek and Roman elites travelled to increase their understanding of the world. Centuries later came one of the greatest manifestations ever of education tourism, in Europe at least, the Grand Tour.

In recent decades, educational tourism has developed in a number of ways, of which two are perhaps particularly worthy of note:

1 *Student exchanges*, where young people travel to other countries to study and learn more about the culture and language of other people. Such exchanges have developed strongly between educational institutions in North America and Europe. For example, many Americans travel to Aix-en-Provence in France to attend special courses put on for them by the local university. Sometimes the relationship goes even deeper, as in the case of the Université Canadienne Française which operates a campus for inbound Canadian students, at Villefranche-sur-Mer on the French Riviera. Exchanges are also well developed between member states of the European Union, thanks to the ERASMUS programme which is now being superseded by the SOCRATES scheme.
2 *Special interest holidays* where people's main motivation for taking a trip is to learn something new. This market has grown rapidly in recent years and now encompasses everything from painting holidays to cookery classes, gardening-themed cruises to language classes. This market is particularly strong among early retired people, the so-called 'empty-nesters'.

Cultural tourism

Cultural tourism is clearly linked to the special interest tourism we have just been discussing, but is broader in scope. The desire to experience other current cultures and view the artefacts of previous cultures has been a motivator in the tourism market since Greek and Roman times. Today, it is extremely popular and is often viewed positively by tourism policy-makers, as a 'good' form of tourism, as 'intelligent tourism'.

Cultural tourism encompasses many elements of the tourism market, including:

• visits to heritage attractions and destinations, and attendance at traditional festivals
• holidays motivated by a desire to sample national, regional or local food and wine
• watching traditional sporting events and taking part in local leisure activities
• visiting workplaces, for example farms, craft centres or factories.

Cultural tourism is the core of the tourism product in many countries and is the main reason why tourists visit these countries. However, concern is often expressed at the impact tourists can have on the cultures they wish to experience, making this a very sensitive sector of the tourism market.

Scenic tourism

The desire to view spectacular natural scenery has stimulated tourists since time immemorial. However, it perhaps really came of age in the nineteenth century, through the influence of the Romantic Movement in the arts. Artists and writers drew inspiration from the natural environment and created popular interest in landscapes. Tourists then began to come to view these same landscapes for themselves, and to follow in the footsteps of the artists.

An example of this phenomenon in the UK is the way in which Wordsworth, through his poetry, stimulated tourism to the Lake District. Today, his houses in the heart of the area, Dove Cottage and Rydal Mount, attract tens of thousands of tourists in their own right. Scenic tourism grew dramatically in the last century in both Europe, particularly in the Alps, and in the USA, where the steady growth of tourism was one of the factors that led to the creation of the world's first national park in 1872. As well as mountains, water-related scenery also became a draw for tourists in the nineteenth century. The Lakes region of Italy and the dramatic coastal scenery of Brittany and Cornwall became popular during this era. We must remember that the original appeal of seaside resorts we now see as urban areas, to their first visitors was often their natural scenery.

Hedonistic tourism

We tend to believe that hedonistic tourism, motivated by a desire for sensual pleasure, is a modern creation, encapsulated in the now classic four Ss of sea, sand, sun and sex. However, hedonistic holiday-making has a much longer history. We saw earlier that the Romans practised this form of tourism in their resorts. In the UK such tourism has given rise to the term, the 'dirty weekend', often associated with the south coast resort of Brighton. Here Londoners in the strict Victorian era took their 'partners', or someone else's partner, off to Brighton where they could behave in ways which were not acceptable in London!

Paris, from the nineteenth century onwards developed as Europe's first capital of hedonistic tourism. Young men from affluent families were sent there to complete their 'education' in the ways of the world. This often involved visiting brothels, going to risqué shows and gambling. However, other cities too based much of their appeal on hedonism and pleasure-seeking. Writing about Vienna, Steward said 'By far the strongest component of the city's place image were its reputation for frivolity [and] the pleasure-loving nature of its inhabitants' (Steward, 1996).

Hedonistic tourism has reached new peaks, though, in the current era with the rise of the 'sea, sun, sand and sex' package holiday, from the 1960s onwards. The promise of hedonistic experiences is now the core offer of some operators such as Club 18–30, in the UK market. We have also seen the rise of distinct hedonistic market segments in recent years, such as the so-called 'Shirley Valentines', that is, Northern European married older women who travel to the Mediterranean resorts in search of romance with local men.

Though often harmless fun, hedonistic tourism is often seen to have a negative impact on both the tourists themselves and the host community; both are at risk from diseases such as AIDS while the latter is often offended by the tourists' behaviour. There is currently considerable international debate about sex tourism, particularly involving Europeans travelling to developing countries, for sex with children. This is clearly far from harmless and represents the morally unacceptable face of hedonistic tourism.

Activity tourism

Activity holidays are a more recent development but are a rapidly growing market. They are based upon the desire for new experiences on the part of the ever more sophisticated tourist, and are also a reflection of growing social concerns such as health and fitness.

Activity tourism is a broad field that encompasses, for example:

- using modes of transport to tour areas which require effort on the part of the tourist, such as walking, cycling and riding
- participating in land-based sports such as golf and tennis
- taking part in water-based activities such as diving and wind-surfing.

Some forms of activity holidays can be criticized in terms of their impact on the physical environment. Golf courses take up valuable greenfield sites, while walking and riding cause erosion. On the other hand, activity tourism is often viewed positively because it is seen as a phenomenon which improves people's health.

Special interest tourism

In recent years we have seen the growth of special interest tourism, where the motivation is a desire to either indulge in an existing interest in a new or familiar location, or develop a new interest in a new or familiar location. Like activity-based tourism, special interest tourism can be either the focus of the whole holiday, or a way of spending one or two days during a holiday.

Special interest tourism is a niche market acting like activity tourism, but it differs in that it involves little or no physical exertion. Nevertheless, the types of interest are diverse, some of the most popular being:

- painting
- gastronomy, both learning to cook and enjoying gourmet meals

- in restaurants
- military history and visiting battlefields
- visiting gardens
- attending music festivals.

Summary

The list of types of tourism we have just examined is clearly subjective but, hopefully, it does show the breadth of the tourism market. It illustrates too that the different types of tourism are linked. For example, religious tourism can also be seen as cultural tourism. At the same time it has been shown that few forms of tourism are new. But what about the future? Perhaps the next major development in tourism will be the rise of techno-tourism, that is, tourism based on new technologies such as virtual reality. This could be a revolutionary change where tourism no longer involves travel, and tourism experiences of a kind can be enjoyed from the comfort of the tourist's own home.

Conclusions

To understand present and future tourist behaviour it is essential that we have an appreciation of the history of consumer behaviour in tourism. For that reason we have focused on discussing the history of tourism demand. However, it is important to recognize that this chapter has still only been an outline, full of generalizations, where whole countries have been reduced to a paragraph or less.

Nevertheless, hopefully, the reader will have identified a number of key points, notably:

1 Tourism is older than we often appreciate.
2 Tourists have existed for centuries in many countries, not just in Europe and the USA.

The emphasis in this chapter has been on international tourist flows, but we must also recognize that domestic tourism has, perhaps, a longer history, and is certainly much greater in volume. However, it is harder to measure and it is the growth of mass international tourism which has been at the forefront of the rise of modern tourism.

Discussion points and essay questions

1 Discuss the ways in which Britain played a major role in the growth of modern tourism.
2 Critically evaluate the contention that, 'tourism history was born in Europe but its future lies in Asia and the Pacific' (Horner and Swarbrooke, 1996).

3 Discuss the ways in which business tourism demand has changed over the past 2000 years in terms of both the types of business tourism and business tourism destinations.

4 Using examples, evaluate the suggestion that 'few, if any, tourism markets are new' (Horner and Swarbrooke, 1996).

Exercise

Choose a country from *each* of the following regions of the world:

- Europe
- the Americas
- Africa
- Asia.

For each country, produce a summary of its history as a destination for inbound foreign tourists, using statistics wherever possible.

Finally, compare and contrast the situation in each country and suggest reasons for the similarities and differences.

Main concepts in consumer behaviour, including models of consumer behaviour adapted for tourism

The purpose of consumer behaviour models is to attempt to give a simplified version of the relationship of the various factors that influence consumer behaviour. Various models have been developed to describe consumer behaviour with the intention of trying to control the behaviour patterns. The models, however, fall short of these objectives and at best give the reader an appreciation of interactive factors that influence behaviour patterns. It is only possible to review some of the general consumer behaviour models here. One of the earliest models of consumer behaviour was proposed by Andreason (1965). This model is shown in Figure 3.1.

The model recognizes the importance of information in the consumer decision-making process. It also emphasizes the importance of consumer attitudes although it fails to consider attitudes in relation to repeat purchase behaviour.

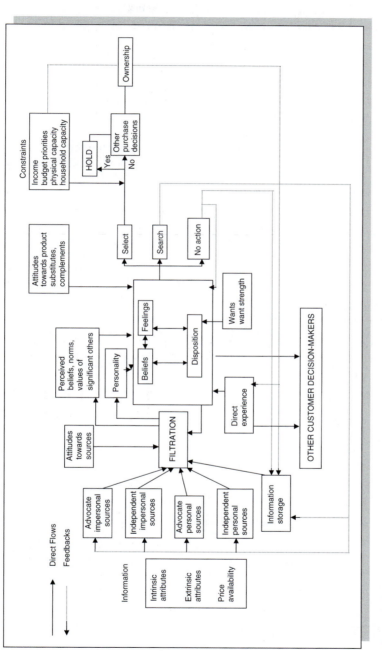

Figure 3.1

Andreason model of consumer behaviour

Source: adapted from Andreason (1965).

A second model, which concentrates on the buying decision for a new product was proposed by Nicosia (1966). This model is shown in Figure 3.2. The model concentrates on the organization's attempts to communicate with the consumer, and the consumers' predisposition to act in a certain way. These two features are referred to as Field One. The second stage involves the consumer in a search evaluation process which is influenced by attitudes. This stage is referred to as Field Two. The actual purchase process is referred to as Field Three, and the post-purchase feedback process is referred to as Field Four. This model was criticized by commentators because it was not empirically tested (Zaltman, Pinson and Angelman, 1973), and because many of the variables were not defined (Lunn, 1974).

The most frequently quoted of all consumer behaviour models is the Howard–Sheth model of buyer behaviour which was developed in 1969. This model is shown in Figure 3.3. This model is important because it highlights the importance of inputs to the consumer buying process and suggests ways in which the consumer orders these inputs before making a final decision.

The Howard–Sheth model does have limitations, and does not explain all buyer behaviour. However, it was a comprehensive theory of

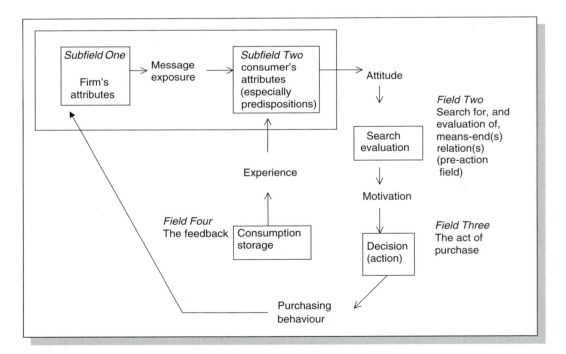

Figure 3.2
A summary description of the Nicosia model
Source: adapted from Nicosia (1966).

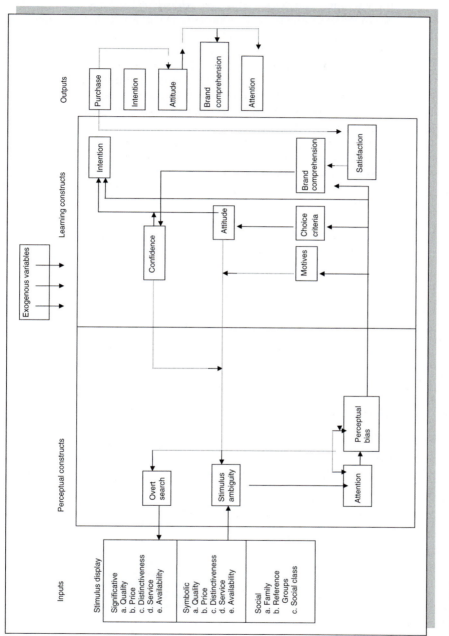

Figure 3.3

The Howard–Sheth Model of buyer behaviour

Source: adapted from Howard and Sheth (1969).

buyer behaviour that was developed as a result of empirical research (Horton, 1984).

More recent research on consumer behaviour has concentrated on the exchange processes and has attempted to look at the marketer's perspective on the process. One example of such an approach is shown in Figure 3.4. This model was developed by Solomon (1996). He also suggested that consumer behaviour involves many different actors. The purchaser and user of a product might not be the same person. People may also act as influences on the buying processes. Organizations can also be involved in the buying process. One example of an organization which may make purchase decisions is the family.

The models considered so far are useful in academic research. Foxall and Goldsmith (1994) suggested that these models mean little in the absence of a general understanding of how consumers act. They suggest that consumer behaviour is a sequence of problem-solving stages, as follows:

- the development and perception of a want or need
- pre-purchase planning and decision-making
- the purchase act itself
- post-purchase behaviour, which may lead to repeat buying, repeat sales and disposition of the product after consumption.

Much of marketing activity, they suggested, concentrates on adapting product offerings to particular circumstances of target segment needs

	CONSUMER'S PERSPECTIVE	MARKETER'S PERSPECTIVE
PRE-PURCHASE ISSUES	How does a consumer decide that he/she needs a product? What are the best sources of information to learn more about alternative choices?	How are consumer attitudes toward products formed and/or changed? What cues do consumers use to infer which products are superior to others?
PURCHASE ISSUES	Is acquiring a product stressful or pleasant experience? What does the purchase say about the consumer?	How do situational factors, such as time pressure or store displays, affect the consumer's purchase decision?
POST-PURCHASE ISSUES	Does the product provide pleasure or perform its intended function? How is the product eventually disposed of, and what are the environmental consequences of this act?	What determines whether a consumer will be satisfied with a product and whether he/she will buy it again? Does this person tell others about his/her experiences with the product and affect their purchase decisions?

Figure 3.4

Some issues that arise during stages in the consumption process
Source: adapted from Solomon (1996).

and wants. It is also common to stimulate an already existing want through advertising and sales promotion, rather than creating wants.

The definitions and models which have been presented so far have been from general marketing theory. Tourism is, by its very nature, a service rather than a product which may have a considerable effect on consumer behaviour. Services have been defined by Kotler and Armstrong (2004) as: 'Any activity or benefit that one party can offer to another that is essentially intangible and does not result in the ownership of anything. Its production may or may not be tied to a physical product'.

The intangible nature of the service offering has a considerable effect on the consumer during the decision-making process involved with purchase. This, coupled with the high-spend aspect of tourism, means that tourism for the consumer is a high-risk decision-making process. Therefore the consumer will be highly interested and involved in the purchase decision. This was recognized by Seaton (1994):

> They involve committing large sums of money to something which cannot be seen or evaluated before purchase. The opportunity cost of a failed holiday is irreversible. If a holiday goes wrong that is it for another year. Most people do not have the additional vacation time or money to make good the holiday that went wrong.

There is a philosophical question as to whether service marketing is substantially different to product marketing (Horner and Swarbrooke, 1996). It is clear, however, that tourism products have many distinctive features which mean that consumer behaviour will be fundamentally different. To cope with these differences, academics have developed definitions and models of consumer behaviour, specifically for tourism. These range from the more general definitions to more detailed models.

Middleton and Clark (2001) presented an adapted model of consumer behaviour for tourism which was termed the stimulus – response model of buyer behaviour. The model is shown in Figure 3.5 and is based on four interactive components, with the central component identified as 'buyer characteristics and decision process'.

The model separates out motivators and determinants in the consumer buying behaviour and also emphasises the important effects that an organization can have on the consumer buying process by the use of communication channels.

Other models which attempt to explain consumer buying behaviour in tourism have been advanced. Wahab, Crampton and Rothfield (1976) suggested a linear model of the decision-making process in tourism. This is shown in Figure 3.6.

Mathieson and Wall (1982) suggested a linear five-stage model of travel buying behaviour, which is shown in Figure 3.7.

Gilbert (1991) suggested a model for consumer decision-making in tourism, which is shown in Figure 3.8. This model suggests that there are two levels of factors which have an effect on the consumer.

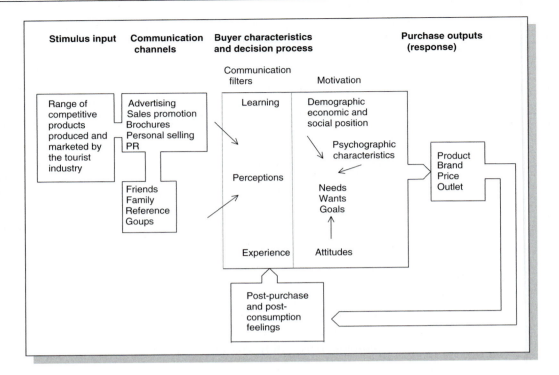

Figure 3.5
A stimulus-response model of buyer behaviour
Source: adapted from Middleton and Clarke (2001).

Initial framework ⟶ Conceptual alternatives ⟶ Fact gathering ⟶ Definition of

assumptions ⟶ Design of stimulus ⟶ Forecast of consequences ⟶ Cost

benefits of alternatives ⟶ Decision ⟶ Outcome

Figure 3.6
A 'linear model of the tourism decision-making process
Source: adapted from Wahab, Crampton and Rothfield (1976).

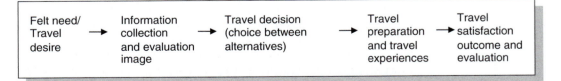

Figure 3.7
Travel-buying behaviour
Source: adapted from Mathieson and Wall (1982).

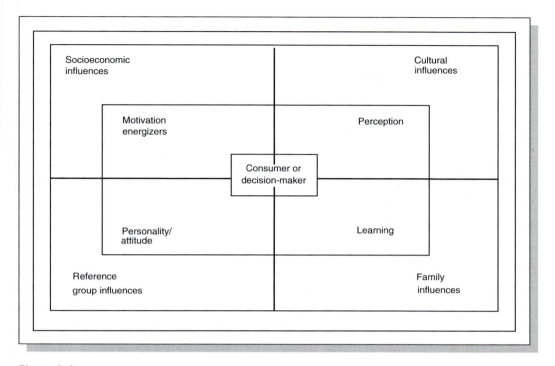

Figure 3.8
Consumer decision-making framework
Source: adapted from Gilbert (1991).

The first level of influences is close to the person and include psychological influences such as perception and learning. The second level of influences includes those which have been developed during the socialization process and include reference groups and family influences.

All these models that have been adapted for tourism offer some insights into the consumer behaviour process involved during the purchase and post-purchase decision stages. The problem with the models is that little empirical research has been conducted to test them against actual consumer behaviour. This is an area which requires further detailed research. We will return to this discussion later in the book, when we consider models of consumer behaviour in tourism in more depth.

Conclusions

Most consumer behaviour models in tourism seem to be linear and rather simplistic when compared to general consumer behaviour models. Yet, as Figure 3.9 illustrates, the diverse characteristics of tourism mean that consumer behaviour in tourism will inevitably be very complex. The inadequacy of models of tourist behaviour is a subject we will return to in Chapter 6.

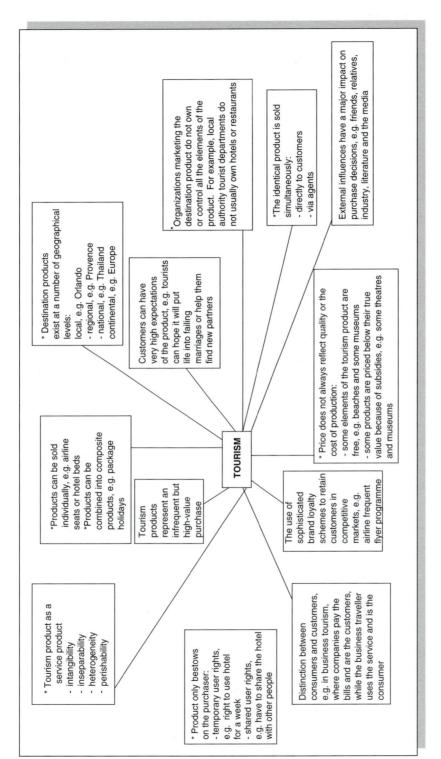

Figure 3.9
Characteristics of tourism

Discussion points and essay questions

1 The purchase of a holiday does not result in the consumer owning any physical product. Discuss the effect of this on consumer behaviour.
2 Evaluate the reasons for a consumer choosing to buy a composite tourism product rather than the individual components.
3 The media can have a major influence on consumer choice in tourism. Evaluate the ways in which a tour operator can use this feature to boost sales.

Exercise

Design a small-scale consumer panel which could be used to evaluate the reasons for consumers choosing a particular tourism product.

PART 2

The Purchase-Decision Process

In this part, we look at the factors which influence the tourist to purchase a particular tourism product. Part 3 will go on to consider the ways in which we can model how these factors are translated into the final purchase decision.

As far as the factors are concerned, we divide these into:

- the *motivators*, those factors which motivate the tourist to wish to purchase a particular product
- the *determinants*, those factors which determine to what extent tourists are able to purchase the product they desire.

However, before we move on to the two chapters that cover these issues, perhaps we should begin with a few words about the tourism product itself.

1 *The product is complex and multilayered* in that:
   (a) it has both tangible elements (hotel beds, food etc.) and intangible elements (service delivery)
   (b) it can range from a simple one night stay in a hotel or a day trip to a theme park to a tailor-made eight-week round-the-world itinerary.

2 *The tourist buys an overall experience rather than a clearly defined product*. The experience has several clear phases:
   (a) the anticipation phase, before the trip commences
   (b) the consumption phase during the trip
   (c) the memory phase after the trip has ended.

3 *The tourist is part of the production process in tourism* which means that their:
   (a) attitudes, mood, and expectations affect their evaluation of their tourist experience rather than just the quality of the product which they are offered by the industry

(b) behaviour directly impacts on the experience of their fellow tourists with whom they share a resort, aircraft or hotel.

4 *The tourist experience is heavily influenced by external factors*, which are beyond the control of the tourist or the company that sells them a product. These external influences include weather, strikes, war, and outbreaks of disease.

In this part of the book, we restrict ourselves to a consideration of one type of tourist product, the package holiday. This is the most complex tourism product and is the one which distinctly separates tourism products from those of other industries such as hospitality and transport.

Out of necessity, we will have to generalize about the subject and about the motivators and determinants that affect tourists. But we must recognize that, as Ryan (1997) says: 'The context, meanings, and experiences of tourism can vary from holiday to holiday, from tourist to tourist. To talk of the "tourist experience" seems to imply a homogeneity which, in reality, is not always present.'

Motivators

Introduction

A wide range of factors motivate consumers to buy tourism products. In this chapter, we examine the motivators which encourage tourists to make particular purchase decisions. We begin by outlining the range of motivators that are thought to influence tourists and then discuss how motivators vary between different types of tourism product and different groups of people.

It is important to recognize that there is still a dearth of detailed reliable research on this subject, across the whole breadth of tourism. Some of the comments in this chapter, therefore, represent subjective observations on the part of the authors. However, in most cases, many other academics and practitioners would concur with these observations.

The number and range of motivators

Motivating factors in tourism can be split into two groups:

- those which motivate a person to take a holiday
- those which motivate a person to take a particular holiday to a specific destination at a particular time.

There are many potential motivators that could relate to either or both of these factors. Furthermore, there are a number of potential 'variations on a theme' for each individual motivator, and myriad ways in which they can be combined.

No widely recognized way exists of categorizing the main motivating factors in tourism. However, some of the major ones are outlined in Figure 4.1.

However, there are other ways of classifying motivators in tourism and the wider field of leisure. We now go on to outline some of these.

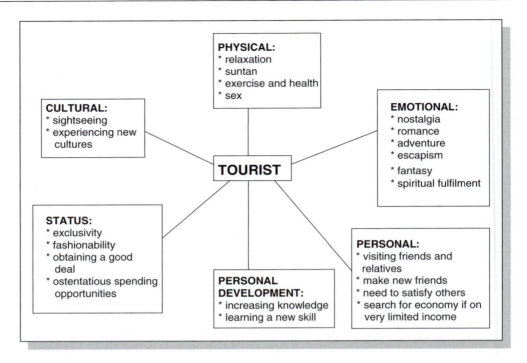

Figure 4.1
A typology of motivators in tourism

The Leisure Motivation Scale

In 1983, Beard and Raghob developed a model called the Leisure Motivation Scale, which sought to clarify motivators into four types, based on the work of Maslow. The four types were:

(a) The *intellectual* component, which assesses the extent to which individuals are motivated to engage in leisure activities which involve . . . mental activities such as learning, exploring, discovery, thought or imagery.

(b) The *social* component which assesses the extent to which individuals engage in leisure activities for social reasons. This component includes two basic needs . . . the need for friendship and inter-personal relationships, while the second is the need for the esteem of others.

(c) The *competence-mastery* component which assesses the extent to which individuals engage in leisure activities in order to achieve, master, challenge, and compete. The activities are usually physical in nature.

(d) The *stimulus-avoidance* component which assesses the desire to escape and get away from over-stimulating life situations. It is the need for some individuals to avoid social contact, to seek solitude and calm conditions; and for others it is to seek to rest and to unwind themselves.

We have to recognize, first, that the motivators which make people wish to take a holiday are not universally present. Some people appear to have little or no desire to take a holiday, for whatever reason.

Motivators and the individual tourist

Every tourist is different, and so are the factors which motivate them. The main factors which determine individual tourists' motivations are probably:

1 Their personality, in other words, are they:
   (a) gregarious or a loner?
   (b) adventurous or cautious?
   (c) confident or timid?
2 Their lifestyle which provides the context for their purchase decision. The motivations are likely to be different for people who are very concerned with being fashionable, or are preoccupied with their health, or live alone and want to make new friends, or enjoy partying.
3 Their past experience as a tourist and particular types of holiday, both positive and negative.
4 Their past life, for motivations such as most notably nostalgia, are a direct result of people's life to date. This may include where they took their honeymoon or military battles they have taken part in.
5 Their perceptions of their own strengths and weaknesses whether these relate to their wealth or their skills.
6 How they wish to be viewed by other people.

We must also recognize that motivators change over time for each individual in response to changes in their personal circumstances. These circumstances might include:

- having a child, or meeting a new partner
- an increase or reduction in income
- worsening health
- changing expectations or experiences as a tourist.

Multiple motivations

No tourist is likely to be influenced by just one motivator. They are more likely to be affected by a number of motivators at any one time.

Office workers staring out of their office windows in suburban London today may be motivated by a desire to take any holiday, anywhere to escape the monotony of their daily working life. However, they may have a number of other motivators that would influence the type of holiday they would like to take. They may, for example:

- want to escape a wet spell at home, and enjoy some sun and get a suntan
- desire a chance to take some physical exercise as a contrast to their sedentary lifestyle and to improve their health
- wish to pursue a hobby, whether it be surfing or eating Italian food
- want to widen their circle of friends or find a new partner
- wish see a particular church or museum
- want to relax.

Most people's holidays represent a compromise between their multiple motivators. Either one motivation becomes dominant or a holiday is purchased which ensures all of the motivators can be at least partly satisfied.

Shared motivators

We rarely take holidays alone, but who we take them with has an influence over the factors which influence our decisions.

Imagine a woman who is married and the mother or two young children, a member of a women's football team and a churchgoer. Her motivations may be different depending on which group she is intending to holiday with. If she is taking a trip with her children, then meeting their needs and keeping them happy may be her main motivation. On the other hand, she and her husband may be taking a trip on their own, to celebrate their wedding anniversary, in which case, romance may be the main motivator. When she takes a trip to play football with her team, it may be seen as escapism or a chance to indulge her passion for playing football. Finally, with her fellow churchgoers, she may be seeking spiritual fulfilment from a trip.

It is rare for every member of a holiday party to share exactly the same motivators. Differences in this respect undoubtedly account for much of the stressful side of holiday-making.

Many trips represent a compromise among those in a group which is travelling together, whereby:

- the views of a dominant member may prevail
- each member will go their own way for at least part of the time
- the group will stay together but each member will be allowed to choose what they will all do on one or two days.

Expressed and real motivators

We do not always express our true motivations because we:

- do not feel they will be seen by others as being acceptable. It can be difficulty to admit that you are only going on holiday to party and enjoy casual sex. It is far easier to talk about a more general desire to relax, unwind and 'have a good time'

- may not always recognize our motivations for they may be subconscious or unconscious
- may recognize that they are apparently conflicting. For example, we may want to relax by dancing and partying all night!
- can be aware of contradictions between our motivating factors and our actual behaviour. We may claim to want to improve our French when we go to France and meet French people. Then, because of our circumstances, and budget, and perhaps fear, we book a stay in an English-owned villa, in a village in the Dordogne where there seem to be few French people and everyone speaks English! This could be the result of an unfortunate chain of events or the outcome of the triumph of a subconscious motivator not to be humiliated in public, on holiday, because of our current lack of ability to speak French.

Perhaps we can best describe the points made in the past few sections of this chapter through a mini case study of a hypothetical family, the Browns.

Case study: the Brown family

In 1995, Mr and Mrs Brown married and took their honeymoon on the French Riviera. Both were keen sailors and chose this destination because they wanted to be able to go sailing together every day. They were besotted with each other, and every evening they sought the most romantic places they could for late candlelit dinners. Dancing and having sex were high on their list of priorities and they did not care if they never spoke to another person during the whole of their holiday. Both were young and adventurous and took part in a range of other activities like rock-climbing and ballooning. Mrs Brown would have also liked to look around the art museums but her husband was not interested, so she gave in because she did not want her husband to be unhappy.

By 2005 things had changed. The Browns now have two young daughters, and their relationship has deteriorated. Mr Brown is still obsessed with sailing but Mrs Brown has given it up. This year they are on holiday with friends at an old farmhouse on a Greek island. They say this is because they have not seen these friends for many years. However, their real motive is to minimize the need for them to have to talk to each other and to give them an opportunity to share the childcare and go off separately from time to time. The whole holiday has been planned around keeping the children happy, for they know that if the children are miserable everyone in the group will have an awful holiday. Mrs Brown secretly hopes to meet a new lover on the beach, while her husband is out sailing. Mr Brown wants to sail to help him relax. However, one evening they go together, at their friends' suggestion, to a romantic restaurant, they went to years ago, for a candlelit dinner, overlooking the harbour. The evening is a disaster – there is an icy atmosphere and they barely speak to each other.

Mrs Brown spends much of her time taking part in her new interest of horse-riding which she took up following last year's holiday in Majorca, when she tried riding for the first time. Mrs Brown chose the farmhouse because it has a swimming pool to keep the children happy, and all modern conveniences in the kitchen, to minimize the work involved in preparing meals and doing the dishes. This matters a lot because, these days, Mr Brown rarely helps out in the kitchen. Before coming away they told their neighbours they were taking a holiday to relax. The truth is that it was a last attempt to see if they could rescue their ailing marriage.

Hopefully, this mini case study has illustrated some of the points we have made so far in this chapter. It also shows the close link that exists between motivators and determinants. The latter subject will be taken up in Chapter 5 but let us now return to the question of motivators.

Motivators and different market segments

Not only are motivators different for each individual tourist but perhaps they also vary between different market segments. For example, the tourism industry seems convinced that segments are based on demographic criteria. They seem to assume that:

- young people want to party, relax, drink heavily, have sex, dance and make lots of new friends
- elderly people have a preference for sedate activities like bowls and bingo, and to be almost obsessed by nostalgia
- parents are preoccupied with the need to keep their children happy. They are also thought to want to escape from their parental responsibilities from time to time to spend time together.

There has been some research to test the motivating factors for different demographic groups. In 1996, Kaynak et al. published a study of Irish travellers' perceptions of salient attributes that led to their travel preferences of major foreign holiday destinations. This study found significant differences between tourists of different ages, sexes, educational attainment, income and marital status. Young people preferred vacations which gave opportunities for activity-based holidays, while older travellers sought restful destinations with sightseeing opportunities. The more highly educated respondents showed a preference for destinations which offered opportunities for nature-based or cultural activities. On the other hand, those people with a lower level of educational attainment stressed the importance of a vacation where they could try new and unfamiliar activities that were very different from their everyday life. Those on lower incomes saw their holiday as a chance to get away from the monotony of everyday life, and indulge in activities that built up their self-confidence. Higher-income earners wanted an intellectually stimulating holiday with excitement, and the chance to increase their knowledge of the destination area.

Motivators and gender

One aspect of demographics which the tourism industry seems to believe determines personal motivators, is gender. Different products such as golf trips or shopping trips seem to be based solely on a desire to match the perceived motivators of men and women respectively. However, when one looks at a range of personal motivators, there is some evidence to suggest that there is, in fact, relatively little difference between the sexes.

Research quoted by Ryan (1995) noted that in fourteen motivators there were significant differences in the weighting given to them by men and women in three cases. Women placed rather more value on trying to use a holiday to:

- avoid daily hustle and bustle
- relax physically
- relax emotionally.

National and cultural differences

As yet, relatively little research appears to have been done on national and cultural differences in relation to motivators. This is rather surprising at a time when more and more tourism organizations are seeking to sell their products to people in other countries.

We know that in some instances there are great similarities between groups of countries in terms of motivators. People in northern European countries and the northern states of the USA are often motivated by the desire to develop a suntan. However, in hot countries such as India and Saudi Arabia, the intention is to take trips to the cooler hilly areas to escape the intense heat at lower altitudes.

Some motivators are universal, such as nostalgia and romance, and the desire to see sights, although actual behaviour will be influenced by the nationality and culture of the tourist.

Many people around the world seek some form of spiritual fulfilment. However, the desire for such fulfilment and the wish to embark on a pilgrimage to gain it is more common generally among Muslims than Christians.

Motivators and different types of tourism product

Marketers clearly try to link the products they develop to the factors which motivate their target markets. Conventional wisdom certainly seems to indicate a belief that some motivators are closely associated with different types of tourism product. This is perhaps best illustrated in the visitor attractions sector. Figure 4.2 suggests some possible links between motivators and different types of visitor attraction.

We can see that there are some different motivators for different types of products, but there are also common ones such as status. Most

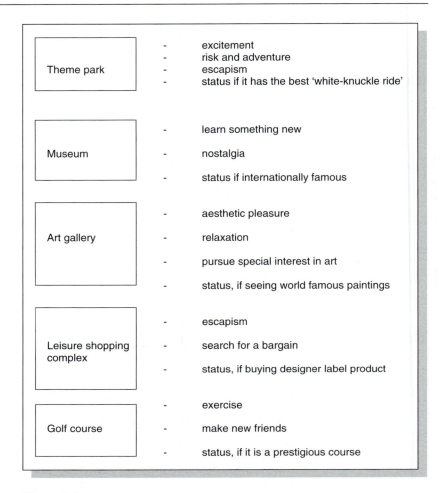

Figure 4.2
Major motivators and different types of visitor attractions

of us are interested in status, but its meaning varies from one type of attraction to another.

It is also important to recognize that the motivators listed in Figure 4.2 are highly generalized. They ignore the fact that attractions serve many markets which each have their own different motivators. Young people at a theme park may want excitement for themselves, but grandparents may go there with their grandchildren to please the children. Families may search out the gentler rides, while parents may want the nostalgic pleasure of revisiting a park they visited as children.

Motivators and the timing of purchase decisions

Motivators can also vary depending on when the decision to purchase a holiday is made. A last-minute booking may reflect a desire to obtain a discounted bargain or a wish to surprise a partner, or be a response to stress at work. Alternatively, a vacation booked many months in advance may be a result of a desire to:

- visit a famous annual event where early booking is essential to secure accommodation and flights
- enjoy the pleasure of looking forward in anticipation to the holiday.

Conclusions

It appears that the issue of motivation is highly complex and depends on a range of factors, including:

- the personality and lifestyle of the potential tourists
- their past experiences
- who they are planning to take a vacation with
- their demographic characteristics
- how far in advance they book their trip.

It will become clear that there are great similarities between motivators and determinants. There is a thin line, a grey area, between our desires and the factors that determine our actual behaviour.

Discussion points and essay questions

1 Examine the ways in which an individual's personality may affect their motivators in relation to taking a holiday.
2 Discuss those changes involved in suggesting that people with certain demographic characteristics will be motivated by particular factors.
3 Compare and contrast the likely motivators of people taking a 'sun, sea, sand and sex' holiday to a Greek island, with those on an upmarket cruise around the Caribbean.

Exercise

Design and implement a questionnaire survey of a small number of adults to try to ascertain the main motivating factors which influence their choice of holiday. Then produce a critical evaluation of your survey to highlight and account for its weaknesses.

Determinants

Types of determinants

There are two types of determinants:

- those factors which determine whether or not someone will be able to take a holiday or not
- those factors which determine the type of trip, if the first set of determinants allow a holiday to be taken.

In this chapter we will generally be considering the latter set of factors.

The type of trip taken can encompass a huge range of variables, including:

- the destination for the trip
- when the trip will be taken
- the mode of travel to be used
- the duration of the trip
- who will comprise the holiday party or group
- the type of accommodation that will be used
- the activities undertaken by the tourist during the holiday
- how much will be spent on the trip.

We can further subdivide determinants into:

- those which are personal to the tourist
- those which are external to the tourist.

These two types of factors are illustrated in Figures 5.1 and 5.2 respectively. Both are generalized pictures but they serve to illustrate the variety of determinants that exist.

Some of these determinants can preclude the individual from taking any trip. Health problems could be the best example of this phenomenon. Others will simply affect the type of trip which is taken.

It is clear that the determinants listed in Figure 5.1 will not carry equal weight with all tourists at all times. Different individuals will perceive certain determinants to be more important than others, based on their attitudes, personalities,

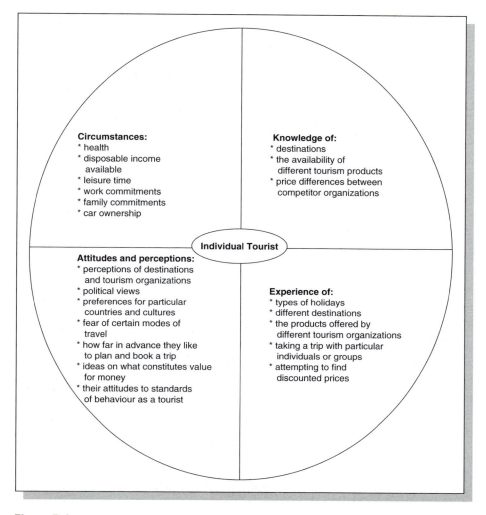

Figure 5.1
Personal determinants of tourist behaviour

principles, fears and past experiences. Even for the same individual the weighting given to each determinant will vary over time with changes in age, family situation and experience as a tourist. Personal determinants that are shared by a large proportion of the population may represent a market opportunity for the tourist industry.

As economies grow in the Pacific Rim, and European and American companies fight to compete in world markets, there are pressures on leisure time. Managers feel they need to be at work as much of the time as possible. This has been one of the reasons for the growth of intense short duration forms of vacation such as themed weekend breaks. These meet the needs of tourists looking for a short break from work, which will stimulate them.

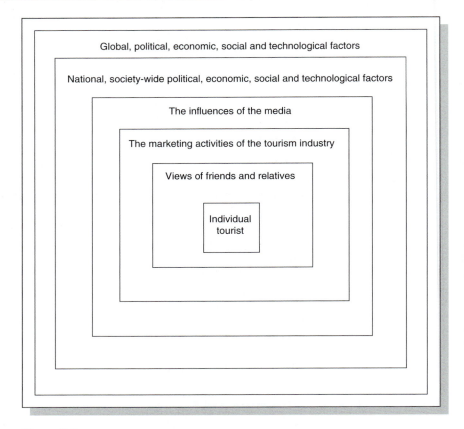

Figure 5.2
External determinants of tourist behaviour

At the same time, many airlines have seized upon the determinant which can stop some people taking any form of foreign holiday, namely, the fear of flying. This determinant clearly reduces their potential market. Therefore, they have begun to offer courses to help people overcome their fear of flying.

It is clear from these two brief examples, therefore, that the tourism industry can exploit certain determinants for their own benefit, or seek to influence them, again for their own benefit.

Perhaps the best example of the industry influencing and exploiting a determinant is the issue of price. Many tourists like to feel they have found a holiday at a discounted price. There is potentially considerable status value in being seen to have 'negotiated' a good deal for a tourism product. Therefore, the industry emphasizes the bargain dimension in its selling, with banner headlines in travel agencies and offers such as 'free child places', '20% off' and 'free insurance'.

The factors in Figure 5.2 can clearly be broken down into 'sub-factors' as the following examples demonstrate.

Political factors:

- government legislation and policy
- immigration restrictions and visa requirements
- civil disorder and terrorism
- the nature of the political system
- taxation policy, e.g. airport taxes
- tourist taxes.

The media:

- travel media, e.g. holiday features on television, in newspapers, and guidebooks
- non-travel media, e.g. news programmes and wildlife programmes on television

Tourism organization marketing:

- foreign destinations' advertising campaigns
- tour operator's brochures
- travel agent's special promotions.

The extent to which tourists' behaviour is determined by their own personal determinants or external determinants varies according to their own personality and lifestyle. Extrovert people may be more inclined to take account of external determinants, such as the views of their many friends and relatives. Introverts may rely more on their own experiences. Well-educated people who regularly watch news programmes and take an interest in worldwide social or environmental issues might be influenced by external factors such as the human rights record of a particular country's government. Those who either do not worry about such things, or do not even know of the situation in that country, might not even consider this factor.

It is also important to note that most determinants can be either facilitators or constraints upon tourists who wish to turn their motivations and desires into reality. For instance, high disposable income will be a facilitator while limited and low disposable income would be a constraint. Likewise, a guidebook which painted a rosy picture of a resort would be likely to persuade a potential tourist to visit it, in contrast to a negative portrayal which would normally have the opposite effect.

The determinants of group travel

In the case of group travel, whether it be a family or a party of friends, the issue of determinants is particularly complex. Each individual has his or her own determinants but the group has a set of determinants of its own. Each individual's determinants must be satisfied in a way that keeps the group as a whole content. This means compromise on behalf of every group member.

Alternatively, a strong group member may impose his or her own determinants, such as a fear of flying, on every other group member. The others would have preferred to fly to their holiday destination, but find themselves taking a ferry instead to meet the needs of the dominant group member.

The myth of rational decision-making

Tourists do not make wholly rational decisions based on perfect information. They may be ignorant of many of the determinants listed in Figures 5.1 and 5.2. Alternatively, they may be well aware of the determinants but choose to ignore them. For example, a young couple with two small children and stressful jobs may know they cannot afford a holiday, but they feel so desperate for a break from the daily routine that they decide to take a trip anyway. This is not rational behaviour, although to anyone in their situation it is wholly understandable! As in other aspects of life, pressure and emotion often overwhelm logic.

The role of unforeseen circumstances and opportunism

Following on from the issue of rational decision-making, are the twin matters of unforeseen circumstances and opportunism. Plans based on a tourist's current situation may become obsolete literally overnight owing to unforeseen changes in their personal circumstances. An obvious example relates to the tourist's health, where a decision to take a skiing holiday based on good previous experiences of such holidays would need to be rethought if the prospective tourist broke a leg!

Unforeseen circumstances can have a positive effect on tourist behaviour. A family may have decided that they cannot afford to take a trip from the UK to France this year. Then the value of the pound against the euro rises dramatically and newspapers start offering cheap ferry tickets. This persuades the family to change its mind and take a short trip to northern France.

The last minute discounted purchase phenomenon

The concept of determinants is geared to the idea of a relatively long period spent by the tourist planning the vacation, gathering information and evaluating alternatives. However, one of the growing phenomena of the tourist industry is the 'last-minute purchase' decision. Here the determinant is a desire to escape at short notice and a willingness to accept a less than ideal product if the price is low enough.

The role of the tourism industry

The tourism industry plays a major role in effecting the determinants of tourist behaviour. For example, it:

- develops products specifically to match the determinants of some tourist behaviour; for example, it can offer packages designed for tourists who have particular health problems such as mobility difficulties
- provides information to prospective tourists on everything from health problems to visa requirements, destination climate data to the destination's cultural attractions
- designs its promotional messages to fit the key determinants of the behaviour of different groups of tourists. This might include emphasis on discount deals for those with limited incomes or those who like to search for bargains, reassurance about the safety of a destination or selling the resort as one which has good facilities for children
- influences determinants such as offering people with limited budgets the opportunity to purchase tourism products on credit with repayments over a period of time.

A key role is played in this respect by the travel agent who is the intermediary between producers in the tourism industry and their clients. As Ryan (1997) says: 'The information provided becomes part of the information that determines a holiday-maker's expectations. The travel agent possesses the means to create the antecedents of success or failure of the holiday.'

Poor or inappropriate advice from an agent that leads to the tourist having an unsatisfactory holiday may well determine their future behaviour. It might make them:

- avoid using the same agent in the future
- decide not to buy the products of the same tourism organization again
- give a negative view of their holiday destination to friends and relatives.

Time lapses and determinants

Many tourists probably make purchasing decisions under the influence of determinants, or perceptions of determinants, which are outdated. They might have perceptions of destinations and tourism organizations which are no longer accurate.

For example, someone might still have an image of a quiet unspoilt Greek island as it was twenty years ago, when they last visited it. This may persuade them to make a return trip to the island, which is now highly developed and crowded. Or a business traveller may avoid booking with an airline because of its reputation gained a few years ago for being unreliable and having old aircraft. However, in the intervening period this problem might have been eliminated by the purchase of new aircraft.

Tourism organizations must be aware of these time lapses and outdated determinants of tourist behaviour when planning their marketing activities.

One-off experiences of determinants of tourism behaviour

The industry should not underestimate the impact of one-off bad experiences as determinants of future tourist behaviour. A delayed flight or a failure of the airline to deliver a pre-ordered special diet meal on one flight can result in tourists:

- boycotting the airline in future
- giving negative views about the airline to friends and relatives.

Conclusions

The determinants of tourist behaviour are complex and diverse. They include personal determinants which are different for each tourist. There are also external determinants, which will be interpreted in different ways by individual tourists. Finally, we have also seen that the issue of determinants is linked to other matters, such as the actions of the tourism industry, the idea of rational decision-making, last-minute purchases and the composition of holiday parties.

In the next chapter, we will see how motivators and determinants combine in the purchase decision process.

Discussion points and essay questions

1 Describe the ways in which personal circumstances such as health, family commitments, and work commitments could influence the type of trip taken by tourists.
2 Discuss the range of media that might influence tourist behaviour and the ways in which they might affect purchase decisions.
3 Explore the reasons why tourists' perceptions may not accurately reflect the main determinants that are, in reality, affecting them at a particular time.

Exercise

Carry out a survey among a small group of your friends/colleagues/ fellow students to try to identify which of the determinants in Figures 5.1 and 5.2 were the most influential when they last booked a holiday. Then produce a report, outlining your results, and noting any difficulties you experienced in collecting and interpreting the data.

Models of the purchase decision-making process

Introduction

Having considered the motivators and determinants of tourist behaviour in the previous two chapters, it is now time for us to look at the purchase decision-making process as a whole. Before that, we need to spend a little time looking at the characteristics of the product that tourists purchase. Tourism products are complex because they exist at two different levels:

- the package holiday which is a combination of the products of individual sectors such as accommodation, transport, destinations and visitor attractions
- the products of these individual sectors which can be sold as stand-alone products such as an air ticket or a theme park visit as part of a day trip.

In this chapter, we focus on the former, as it is the product which distinguishes the tourism industry from other industries such as transport and the hotel industry.

Tourism product and services

Tourism products are largely services. Marketing theorists have attempted to define services in relation to their intangibility and the fact that purchase of a service never results in the ownership of anything. They have attempted to clarify the differences between products and services by stating the characteristics of services:

- *Intangibility* – services have the characteristics of being intangible in that they cannot be seen, tasted or smelled before purchase. Tourism companies have tried to overcome this problem by offering the consumer videos of the holiday locations to make the experience seem more 'real'. The use of advanced technology such as Virtual Reality is also predicted to overcome the problem. Despite these advances, the consumer still has to take considerable risks when choosing their tourism product because of the intangible nature.
- *Inseparability* – services have the characteristic of overlap between the production and performance of the service and the consumption of it. A service in its purest sense has the provider and customer face to face. This will influence consumer buying behaviour and mean that consumers may change their behaviour patterns, according to their experiences.
- *Heterogeneity* – it is very difficult for the tourism provider to give the same level of service at every consumption time. The mood that the consumer is in will also affect their appraisal of the service. It will never be the same twice. This means that it is very difficult for the consumer to judge the potential quality of experience they will gain when they purchase the tourism product. It also means that it is dangerous for them, when considering a repeat purchase, to rely on past experiences. What was a happy experience in the past may turn out to be the complete opposite this time. The consumer may have changed and have different perceptions and expectations. Similarly, the service may have changed over time.
- *Lack of ownership* – the consumer only has access to the activity or facility when he or she buys the service. The consumer never owns anything at the end of the transaction. Service often leads to feelings of satisfaction rather than the ownership of a tangible item. This means that the purchase of a service will have a considerable emotional significance for the consumer.

Convenience versus shopping goods

The characteristics of services are only one aspect in relation to tourism products. General marketing theorists have also separated out convenience and shopping goods as having different characteristics (Middleton and Clarke, 2001) A convenience good is a manufactured item which typically has a low price and is bought frequently. A shopping good typically has a high price and is bought less frequently. Shopping goods generally satisfy higher-order needs in Maslow's hierarchy of needs. Howard and Sheth (1969) noted that the purchase of convenience-type goods involves the consumer in routine problem-solving behaviour,

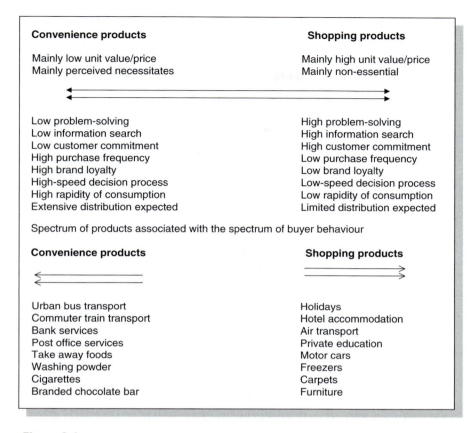

Figure 6.1
Spectrum of buyer behaviour characteristics – goods or services
Source: adapted from Middleton and Clarke (2001).

whereas the purchase of shopping goods involved the consumer in extensive problem-solving.

The spectrum of buyer behaviour for these two types of goods or services is explored in more depth in Figure 6.1. This figure shows that the characteristics of services which fit into the shopping products category have a considerable effect on consumer buying behaviour. From this it can be seen that a much more complex set of issues is involved in the purchase process for tourism products, than it is for fast-moving consumer goods (fmcg) products. The process involves the consumer in a more difficult set of decisions, a lengthier decision time and a higher level of commitment. Middleton and Clarke (2001) suggested that this results in lower brand loyalty and the expectation of a more limited distribution chain.

Let us now consider some of the other complexities in consumer behaviour involved in the purchase of tourism products. These complexities are shown in Figure 6.2 and are summarized below.

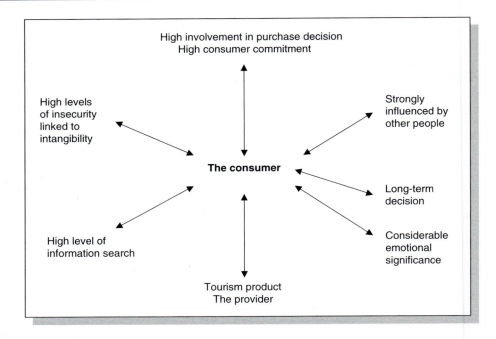

Figure 6.2
The complexity of consumer behaviour in tourism: the demand side

High involvement in purchase decision and high consumer commitment

The behaviour of consumers when they are purchasing tourism products and services demonstrates a high involvement in the process and high levels of commitment because of the nature of the products and services. This means that the behaviour patterns during purchase are not routine and every purchase occasion will show different approaches. The consumer will be actively involved in the buying process and will 'shop around' before coming to a decision. Therefore, the decision process will take longer.

Consumers will also change their behaviour patterns according to the type of holiday to be taken, their motives for the particular purchase occasion and their position in the family life cycle.

High levels of insecurity linked to intangibility

The intangible nature of tourism products and services means that the consumer can often have high levels of insecurity during purchase. They cannot try out the product or service before purchase and will therefore be looking for reassurance about their choices. This will mean that their behaviour patterns will be complex and will probably involve many people and agencies. The individual might take advice from friends, family, travel agents and television holiday programmes, for example, before making a choice of annual holiday.

Considerable emotional significance

The purchase of a holiday will be a major event in an individual's life. It is the holiday which is going to let the individual escape from the work environment and grey skies to renew his or her flagging spirits. The choice of holiday may also affect other close members of the family and compromises might have to be made during the decision-making process. The consumer might also be considering other substitute products and services in place of a holiday. They might, for example, be thinking about the purchase of other major items such as a car or home, rather than spending money on a holiday. This type of decision has particular emotional significance for individuals and their close associates.

Strongly influenced by other people

Individuals are likely to be strongly influenced by other people during the decision-making process for tourism products. If we take an example of individuals choosing a holiday product, they are likely to be influenced by other members of their family, and members of other reference groups. This makes their behaviour patterns very complex and difficult to study. The people who influence their decision will also change their views over time.

Long-term decisions

Despite the growth in the last-minute holiday bargain, most decisions that individuals make about tourism products are made a long way in advance. This means that individuals might be in a completely different frame of mind when they make their purchase decision than when they actually go on holiday. It also means that individuals will be trying to predict what they want to do in the future. This means that the decision itself may have an immediate effect on them. We all know the hope and anticipation felt when, in the depths of winter, we book a holiday in sunny climes!

High level of information search

We have already seen that the choice of tourism products usually has considerable emotional significance for the individual. This will mean that individuals will usually carry out an extensive information search before making their final choice. This will involve consultation with individuals, groups, organizations and media reports before a decision is made. This process of research and reflection means that the behaviour patterns are very complex.

From the above, we can see that the purchase of tourism products and services does not involve the consumer in routine behaviour patterns. This is completely different from their behaviour patterns when they are purchasing fmcg, which is more mechanized and predictable.

The tourist decision-making process

The decision to purchase a tourism product is the outcome of a complex process. This is the result of a number of factors, which we consider in this chapter, which relate to the consumer and to the external influences that act upon them.

However, it is also true that the diverse and interdependent characteristics of many tourism products make the purchase decision in tourism a complex phenomenon in its own right. This fact can be illustrated by thinking about the range of decisions a tourist has to make when choosing a holiday. These can be seen in Figure 6.3.

There are myriad factors that affect the holiday purchase decision, some of which are illustrated in Figure 6.4. Clearly these relate strongly to the motivators and determinants outlined in Chapters 4 and 5.

While Figure 6.4 is only a selection of the relevant factors, it does give a good idea of both the number and scope of such factors.

It is also important to recognize that the complexity of tourist decision-making is heightened by the fact that choosing their holiday

---

*   Which destination (country, region, resort) ?

*   Which mode of travel (scheduled air, charter air, ferry, rail, coach, car, bus) ?

*   Which type of accommodation (serviced or non-serviced) ?

*   How long will the holiday be (days / weeks) ?

*   At which time of the year will the holiday be taken
       (season, month, specific date) ?

*   Package holiday or independent travel ?

*   Which tour operator (if package holiday) ?

Figure 6.3
Decisions involved in choosing a holiday

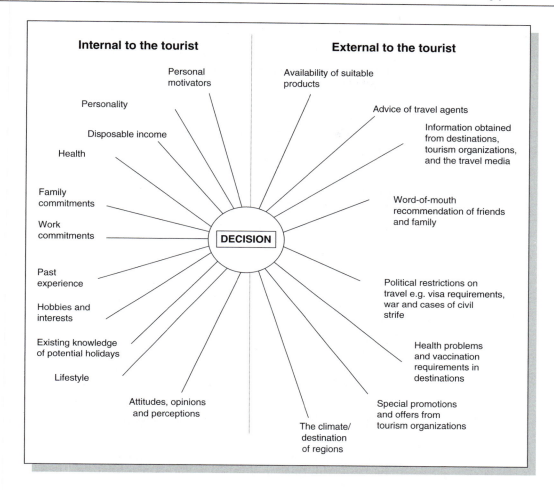

Figure 6.4
Factors influencing the holiday decision
Source: adapted from Horner and Swarbrooke (1996).

is not the last decision tourists have to make. Once on holiday they have to make a further set of decisions about what to do when they arrive at their holiday destination. They have to decide how to spend each day in terms of excursions and leisure activities as well as where to eat and drink, and so on. Each of these apparently simple decisions is the result of a complex decision-making process.

Models of purchase decision-making in tourism

We have already considered models of consumer behaviour for tourism in Chapter 3. Cooper et al. (2005) have identified three stages in the development of general consumer behaviour theory in relation to purchase behaviour, as follows:

1 The early empiricist phase covering the years between 1930 and the late 1940s was dominated by empirical commercial research and industry attempted to identify the effects of distribution advertising and promotion decisions.
2 The motivational research phase of the 1950s placed a greater emphasis upon in-depth interviews, focus groups themselves as a perception test and other projective techniques. There was a great deal of activity directed at uncovering real motives for action which were perceived to lie in the deeper recesses of the consumer's mind.
3 The formative phase from the 1960s provided the first general consumer behaviour textbook (Engel, Kollat and Blackwell, 1968) and other influential books (such as Howard and Sheth, 1969) followed soon after.

However, the early interest in consumer behaviour tended to focus on manufacturing industries, and later on general service industries. It was only in the 1970s that academics began to develop purchase decision models in tourism. It is important to recognize that these purchase decision models were being developed simultaneously with the work of writers like Cohen and Plog on the related subject of tourist typologies.

We have already considered models such as those developed by Wahab, Crompton and Rothfield (1976) and Mathieson and Wall (1982) in Chapter 3. These models all seem to see the decision as a linear process, and no distinctions are made about which factors might weigh heavier than others when decisions are being made.

In 1987, Moutinho published a vacation tourist behaviour model which differed from most previous markets in two respects:

1 It recognized that there are three distinctly different stages in the decision-making process:
   (a) pre-decision stage and decision process
   (b) post-purchase evaluation
   (c) future decision-making.

The model recognized that the last of these stages would feed back to the first, through a loop in the system.

2 It explicitly noted that purchase decisions are a result of three behavioural concepts:
   (a) motivation
   (b) cognition
   (c) learning.

There are many other models, although this brief section has highlighted the most widely discussed 'classic' models.

A critique of purchase decision models in tourism

Most of the models we have discussed so far have some common weaknesses that:

- limit their value in explaining the complex way in which purchase decisions are made in tourism, and
- make it difficult for tourism marketers to make use of them when developing their marketing strategies.

The main weaknesses are as follows:

1 In general they are based on little or no empirical research, and there is little evidence that they represent the reality of how decisions are actually made.

2 A large number of the best known models are now at least fifteen years old. This is a significant weakness in an industry where consumer behaviour is believed to be constantly evolving. Thus most of the major models predate recent developments in tourist behaviour, including:
   (a) the rapid rise of the Internet as a means of purchasing airline tickets and hotel beds
   (b) the impact of the 'no-frills' budget airlines
   (c) the rise of the all-inclusive resort holiday
   (d) the growth of direct marketing
   (e) the increasing popularity of last-minute spontaneous purchases of tourism products.

3 Most of the models developed to date have originated from work carried out by academics in North America, Australia and Northern Europe. Few, therefore, reflect the nature of consumer behaviour in the main emerging markets of South East Asia and Eastern Europe.

Another major criticism is that these models tend to view tourists as a homogenous group. Clearly this is not the case. Every tourist is different and it is possible to segment tourists on the basis of a range of factors that will influence their own individual process of making a purchase decision. Some of these factors have been explored in Chapters 4 and 5, and include, for example:

- whether tourists are travelling alone or if they are members of a family group or party
- how experienced tourists are and their past experiences as tourists
- their personality, in that some tourists make spontaneous last-minute decisions about their holiday plans, while others might enjoy spending months planning their trip.

Many models also fail to recognize the impact that motivators and determinants have on the purchase decision. Some motivators and determinants may be so powerful that they totally dominate the purchase decision, to the exclusion of all other factors. These could be as diverse as an obsessive hobby such as steam railways or rock climbing, to a health problem.

The majority of models also presume a high degree of rationality in the decision-making process, which is not always evident. Rational decision-making in tourism is limited both by the imperfect information which is available to most tourists and the fact that many consumers will be influenced by their own opinions and prejudices which may be irrational.

Most models also seem to assume that purchase behaviour and the process of making a decision remains constant regardless of the nature of the holiday being purchased. This is questionable, as the following contrasting examples show.

1 The purchase of a twenty-eight night tailor-made round-the-world package by a couple, valued at £5000, which includes stopovers with pre-booked airport transfers and accommodation in Dubai, Hong Kong, Tahiti, Sydney, Los Angeles and New York. A range of alternative airline offers have to be studied and bookings made to ensure seats on all the relevant flights. Pre-planning is also required in terms of pre-trip vaccinations. The consumer has a definite start and finish date for the tour, dictated by available annual leave from his or her job, so there is no flexibility about departure and return dates.

2 The purchase of a heavily discounted last-minute fourteen-night holiday by young students who simply want the cheapest summer sun holiday available. The destination is irrelevant and departure dates are fairly flexible, as the tourists have seven weeks off college in which to take the two-week long trip. However, they cannot make a decision until they have found out whether or not they will be required to re-sit any examinations. Once they know they are able to travel, they want to be on the beach, as soon as possible!

Clearly, in these cases, the nature of the purchase decision and the effort put into making it will vary significantly. Similar differences would exist if we were to examine other types of holidays.

Purchase decision-making and marketing in tourism

Marketing professionals in tourism are increasingly aware of the need to understand how their consumers make their decisions to purchase a particular product. Currently, the research conducted by tourism organizations about consumer behaviour is only beginning to tackle this subject seriously. It would therefore be fortuitous if the academic models could be used by marketers.

An appreciation of how consumers make decisions would help marketers develop their marketing plans in relation to the following, for example:

- when to attempt to influence consumers, in other words, focusing marketing activities at the time when most consumers are making decisions to buy a particular product
- the choice of advertising media based on which media the majority of consumers use to gain information about tourism products
- the selection of appropriate distribution channels or marketing intermediaries.

Therefore, we have to ask ourselves, are the models reliable enough so they could be used in this way. Perhaps not, for, as we noted previously, we must remember that many of the models are at least fifteen years old.

Marketing professionals who want to see if they can put these models into practice to guide their activities, need to see if there is any link between them and the technique of market segmentation. For, in a sense, these techniques represent an attempt to explain purchase decisions by reference to various characteristics of the tourist.

In other words, segmentation splits the population into subgroups who share the same purchase characteristics. It suggests that the decision of everyone in the subgroup is primarily determined by one set of influences. These influences, in classic marketing theory, are divided into four criteria:

1 Demographic, e.g. age, sex, race, stage in the family life cycle.
2 Geographical, e.g. where the tourist lives.
3 Psychographical, e.g. the personality and lifestyle of the tourist
4 Behaviouristic, that is, the relationship of the tourist to the product, e.g. the benefits they expect to receive from the purchase and whether or not they are first-time purchasers or regular purchasers of the product.

Tourism marketing traditionally relies heavily on segmentation, yet of these four sets of characteristics, only the psychographic plays a significant role in current purchase decision models in tourism. Yet marketers are also aware of the limitations of the four segmentation criteria outlined above. It is widely recognized that purchase behaviour is a result of the combination of two or more of these criteria, not just one.

The models do not help us to identify or predict the behaviour of individual tourists. It is very difficult to operationalize such general models at a time when marketing is increasingly a matter of targeting individual tourists, using computer databases. Nevertheless, there seems little doubt that, in spite of their weaknesses, these models have a role to play in tourism marketing.

Conclusions

We have looked at the process by which tourists make their purchase decisions, to buy a vacation, and how this process has been modelled by academics. These models appear to have some significant weaknesses in terms of describing, let alone explaining, the process by which tourists decide to buy a holiday. This chapter has also briefly highlighted the potential links which exist between purchase decision models and market segmentation techniques. The last thought on this subject must be that we still have a long way to go before we understand the ways in which tourists choose their vacations.

Discussion points and essay questions

1 Outline the factors which make the study of the purchase decision-making in tourism such a complex activity.
2 Evaluate the main strengths and weaknesses of one of models of consumer behaviour, as ways of explaining how tourists make purchase decisions.
3 Discuss the problems which marketing professionals might experience in trying to put into practice the models of purchase decision behaviour outlined in this chapter.

Exercise

Think about the last holiday you purchased, and produce a simple model to illustrate the process you followed to make the decision and the factors which you took into account. Then ask a group of friends, fellow students or colleagues to do the same, independently, without talking to each other. Compare the models and identify and try to explain both the similarities and the differences. Finally, note the difficulties experienced in carrying out this task. What do they tell you about the problems of studying purchase decision behaviour in tourism?

P A R T 3

Typologies of Tourist Behaviour

In Part Two we looked at how individual tourists make their purchasing decisions. It is now time to look at ways in which academics and marketers have sought to group tourists together on the basis of shared characteristics. This has resulted in typologies of tourists and methods of segmentation. Part 3 considers both of these.

These typologies are important for a number of reasons. They:

- represent an attempt to increase our knowledge of consumer behaviour in tourism
- can help marketers make important decisions on product development, pricing, promotional media and distribution channels
- may form the basis of market segmentation techniques
- might potentially, help to predict future trends in tourist behaviour.

In the following chapter, we consider both the typologies academics have produced and the application of classic segmentation techniques to tourism.

Typologies of tourist behaviour and segmentation of the tourism market

For over two decades, academics have sought to produce meaningful typologies of tourists and their behaviour. At the same time, practitioners have tried to apply and adapt classic market segmentation techniques to the tourism industry. In this chapter, we consider both of these approaches separately, although clearly there are links between them.

Academic typologies

The most fundamental debate, perhaps, is that about whether people are tourists or travellers. Although the term 'tourist' dates back two centuries, it has only become a word in popular usage in recent decades. Sharpley suggested that the terms 'tourist' and 'traveller' were, until recently, used interchangeably to describe 'a person who was touring' (Sharpley, 1994).

However, nowadays, the two words mean different things.

There is the idea that a tourist is someone who buys a package from a tour operator, while the traveller is the person who makes their own independent arrangements for their vacation. The idea has grown up that somehow the latter type of behaviour is somehow superior or better than the former. Therefore, many people who buy tourist packages want to still see themselves as travellers. (Horner and Swarbrooke, 1996)

As Sharpley noted, the term 'traveller',

> is usually applied to someone who is travelling/touring for an extended period of time, particularly back-packing on a limited budget. It contains a spirit of freedom, adventure, and individuality.
> The word tourist on the other hand, is frequently used in a rather derogatory sense to describe those who participate in mass produced, package tourism. (Sharpley, 1994)

Boorstin illustrated that the debate over this issue is full of subjective judgements when he wrote about the 'lost art of travel' in the following terms: 'The traveller, then, was working at something; the tourist was a pleasure seeker. The traveller was active; he went strenuously in search of people, of adventure, of experience. The tourist is passive; he expects interesting things to happen to him . . . he expects everything to be done to him and for him' (Boorstin, 1992).

As the quote shows, the debate is not new but it has come back into focus in recent years as status-conscious tourists have sought to differentiate themselves from other tourists and their experiences. As Sharpley (1994) noted, 'disliking and trying to avoid other tourists at the same time as trying to convince oneself that one is not a tourist is, in fact, all part of being a tourist'.

Culler (1981) put it succinctly when he wrote that, 'all tourists can always find someone more touristy than themselves to sneer at'.

The tourism industry has, in recent years, recognized the implications of this whole debate and has begun to emphasize more and more the 'non-touristy', 'unspoilt' nature of destinations. It has also sought to massage the egos of customers by convincing them that the product they are buying means they are travellers not tourists.

Having discussed this general issue about the classification of tourists, it is now time for us to turn our attention to a consideration of some well-known academic typologies of tourists. It will be interesting if we look at these typologies in a chronological order to see if we can see any trends in the classification of tourists.

Cohen (1972)

The influential sociologist, Cohen, identified four types of tourists, in 1972.

- *The organized mass tourist* who buys a package holiday to a popular destination and largely prefers to travel around with a large group of other tourists, following an inflexible predetermined itinerary. In general such tourists tend not to stray far from the beach or their hotel.

- *The individual mass tourist* buys a looser package that allows more freedom, for example, a fly-drive holiday. Individual mass tourists are more likely, than the organized mass tourist, to look for the occasional novel experience. However, they still tend to stay on the beaten track and rely on the formal tourist industry.
- *The explorer* makes his or her own travel arrangements and sets out, consciously, to avoid contact with other tourists. Explorers set out to meet local people but they will expect a certain level of comfort and security.
- *The drifter* tries to become accepted, albeit temporarily, as part of the local community. Drifters have no planned itinerary and choose destinations and accommodation on a whim. As far as possible, drifters shun all contact with the formal tourism industry.

Cohen described the former two types of tourist as institutionalized tourists, and the latter two as non-institutionalized. The latter are, Cohen agreed, the people who are the pioneers who explore new destinations. The institutionalized travellers then follow later when it has become less adventurous and more comfortable to travel there because of the development of a tourist industry and infrastructure. Sharpley (1994) quotes Goa in India as an example of this phenomenon.

Richard Sharpley criticizes Cohen's typology on the grounds that the institutionalized and non-institutionalized types are not entirely distinct from each other. He argues that even 'explorers' make use of specialist guidebooks to choose their transport routes and accommodation.

Plog (1977)

In 1977 Plog sought to directly link personality traits with tourist behaviour, and divided people into psychocentrics and allocentrics. He argued that the former were less adventurous, inward-looking people. They tend to prefer the familiar and have a preference for resorts which are already popular. Allocentrics, on the other hand, are outward-looking people who like to take risks and seek more adventurous holidays. Plog believed such people would prefer exotic destinations and individual travel. Between these two extremes, Plog suggested a number of intermediate categories such as near-psychocentrics, mod-centrics and near-allocentrics. He suggested that psychocentric American tourists would holiday at Coney Island while allocentrics take their vacation in Africa, for example.

Sharpley quite rightly criticizes this idea of linking types of tourists with specific destinations. He wrote: 'Destinations change and develop over time; as a resort is discovered and attracts growing numbers of visitors, it will evolve from an allocentric to a psychocentric destination' (Sharpley, 1994).

Perreault, Dorden and Dorden (1979)

Based on a survey of 2000 householders, these authors produced a five-group classification of tourists:

- *budget travellers*, who had medium incomes, but sought low-cost vacations
- *adventurous* tourists, who were well educated and affluent and showed a preference for adventurous holidays
- *homebody* tourists, who were cautious people who took holidays but did not discuss their vacation with other people, and spent relatively little time planning it
- *vacationers*, who were a small group who spent lots of time thinking about their next holiday and tended to be active people in lower paid jobs
- *moderates*, who had a high predisposition to travel but were not interested in weekend breaks or sports.

Cohen (1979)

Cohen, in 1979, suggested a five-group classification of tourists, based on the type of experience they were seeking:

- the *recreational* tourist, for whom the emphasis is on physical recreation
- the *diversionary* tourist, who seeks ways of forgetting their everyday life at home
- the *experiential* tourist, who looks for authentic experiences
- the *experimental* tourist, whose the main desire is to be in contact with local people
- the *existential* tourist, who wants to become totally immerse in the culture and lifestyles of the vacation destination.

Sharpley (1994) noted that this classification was not 'based on any empirical research: it is a mechanical categorisation'.

Westvlaams Ekonomisch Studiebureau (1986)

A survey of 3000 Belgians produced the following typology which identified seven types of tourists:

- *active sea lovers*, who want to take a holiday by the sea, with a beach close by
- *contact-minded holiday-makers*, who value making new friends on holiday and being hospitably received by local people
- *nature viewers*, who want to be well received by the host population while enjoying very beautiful landscapes
- *rest-seekers*, who want a chance to relax and rest while on holiday
- *discoverers*, who like cultural holidays and some adventure, but they also like to meet new people

- *family-orientated sun and sea lovers*, who were the largest group and like to do things together as a family and seek 'child-friendly' activities
- *traditionalists*, who value safety and security and try to avoid surprises by sticking with familiar destinations and types of holiday.

Dalen (1989)

A Norwegian survey of 3000 individuals led to a four-group classification:

- *Modern materialists* want to get a tan to impress people when they get home. They like partying and are more concerned with drink than food. Hedonism is their main motivation.
- *Modern idealists* also seek excitement and entertainment but want both to be more intellectual than the modern materialists. They do not, however, want mass tourism or fixed itineraries.
- *Traditional idealists* demand quality, culture, heritage, famous places, peace and security.
- *Traditional materialists* always look for special offers and low prices, and have a strong concern with personal security.

Gallup and American Express (1989)

American Express commissioned a survey of 6500 people in the USA, the UK, West Germany and Japan, which resulted in the following five-type classification:

- *adventurers*, who are independent and confident and like to try new activities
- *worriers*, who worry about the stress of travel and their safety and security while on holiday
- *dreamers*, who are fascinated by the idea of travel and they read and talk a lot about their travel experiences and different destinations
- *economizers*, who simply see travel as a routine opportunity for relaxation rather than as a special part of their life, and as such they want to enjoy holidays at the lowest possible price
- *indulgers*, who want to be pampered when they are on holiday.

Smith (1989)

Smith identified seven types of tourists:

- *Explorers* are a small group who travel almost as anthropologists.
- *Elite* tourists are experienced frequent travellers who like expensive tailor-made tours.
- *Off-beat* tourists aim to get away from other tourists.
- *Unusual* tourists make side trips from organized tours to experience local culture.
- *Incipient* mass tourists travel to established destinations where tourism is not yet totally dominant.

- *Mass* tourists expect the same things they are used to at home.
- *Charter* tourists have little or no interest in the destination itself providing that the holiday gives them the entertainment and standards of food and accommodation they expect.

Urry (2002)

Urry, in the UK at least, popularized the term the 'post-tourist' in the early 1990s that had earlier been mentioned by writers such as Feifer. These tourists are a product of the so-called 'postmodern' age. They recognize that there is no such thing as an authentic tourism product or experience and accept pseudo events for what they are. To the post-tourist, tourism is just a game and they feel free to move between different types of holiday. Today they may take an eco-tourism trip to Belize, while next year they may lie on a beach in Benidorm.

As Feifer (1985) said, the post-tourist is conscious of being a tourist, an outsider, 'not a time traveller when he goes somewhere historic; not an instant noble savage when he stays on a tropical beach; not an invisible observer when he visits a native compound'.

If such a tourist is now a reality, then as Sharpley suggested in 1994: 'For the post-tourist, then, the traveller/tourist dichotomy is irrelevant. The traveller has matured and evolved into an individual who experiences and enjoys all kinds of tourism, who takes each at face value and who is in control at all times. In effect, the post-tourist renders tourist typologies meaningless!'

Wood and House (1991)

The debate about sustainable tourism has, in recent years, led to some moralistic and judgemental approaches to the classification of tourists. For example, there is the idea of the Good Tourist, put forward by Wood and House in 1991. Such tourists behave in a responsible manner towards the environment and the host community in their holiday destination. It is argued that all tourists can aspire to join this group if they modify their behaviour in particular ways. Horner and Swarbrooke (1996) have suggested that, for tourism organizations, 'this group may represent a potentially lucrative niche market, which must be sold products it can feel good about buying'.

Wickens (1994) (in Seaton et al., 1994)

Relatively few writers have attempted to produce typologies of tourists visiting a particular destination. One recent exception to this situation is that produced by Wickens in 1994 in relation to a resort on the Chalkidiki peninsula in Greece. She based her research on Cohen's typology of 1972, and produced a five-group typology:

- *Cultural heritage* tourists are interested in the natural beauty, history and culture of Greece. They long to experience the 'traditional Greek village life' portrayed in the holiday brochures. They use the seaside resort as a base from which to tour the attractions in the region. This group tends to be made up of family groups and older holiday-makers.

- *Ravers* are attracted by the nightlife and the cheapness and availability of alcohol. They also enjoy the sun and the beach. They tend to swim and sunbathe in the day, and go 'clubbing' at night. These are mostly young males.
- *'Shirley Valentines'* are women on holiday with other women who hope for romance and sexual encounters with Greek men. For these women their holiday represents an opportunity to get away from their everyday lives of domesticity.
- *'Heliolatrous'* tourists are sun-worshippers whose main aim is to get a tan. They spend much of their holiday in the open air.
- *'Lord Byrons'* tend to return year after year to the same destination and even the same hotel or accommodation unit. They are in love with Greece, particularly its perceived relaxed, 'laid back' lifestyle. They want to be treated as a guest not as a tourist. They are after nostalgia and lament the impact of mass tourism on their favourite destination.

We have just looked at a brief selection of typologies which have been produced over the past thirty-five or so years. Many others have been omitted because of limitations of space. However, we have tried to offer a range of influential and less well-known typologies from authors of different nationalities. It is now time to see if we can identify some common threads in those which we have discussed.

A comparison of typologies

Most of the typologies attempt to group tourists together on the basis of their preference for particular vacation experiences in terms of:

- destinations
- activities while on holiday
- independent travel versus package holidays.

Some recognize that the motivations of tourists are tempered in reality by the determinants that contribute to their choice of vacation, such as disposable income.

A number of influential early typologies were not based on empirical research but as we have seen, many of the recent typologists – Perreault, Dorden and Dorden, Dalen, and American Express, for example – have arisen out of empirical studies. In 1987 Plog attempted to produce a typology of typologies. He wrote:

> researchers may actually come up with fairly similar dimensions but may label them differently. As it turns out, there possibly are

a very limited number of psychographic/personality dimensions . . . These dimensions may be more clearly defined, or combined in various ways, but they are covered by about eight broad categories. (Plog, 1987)

These categories were 'venturesomeness', 'pleasure-seeking', 'impassivity', 'self-confidence', 'playfulness', 'masculinity', 'intellectualism' and 'people orientation' (Plog 1987).

A critique of typologies

Not surprisingly, the attempts to classify tourists which we have discussed, and others, have attracted criticism, on a number of fronts:

1 'Broad brush' typologies based on simplistic, stereotypes cannot hope to encompass the complex patterns of behaviour we see in the real world.
2 Almost all the typologies do not allow for the fact that individual consumers can move between types in response to the impact of different determinants over time, including changes in health, income, leisure time, and family and work commitments.
3 They also tend not to recognize that many holiday-makers do not have autonomy over their choice of holiday destination and vacation activities. The decision is often the result of a compromise between the tourist and the other members of the holiday party, whether they be friends or relatives. Therefore what someone does on holiday may not reflect their true desires or personality.
4 Many of the most influential typologies are at least ten years old and therefore cannot represent the many changes in consumer behaviour which have taken place in recent years. They often predate newer developments such as mass long-haul holiday markets, budget cruises and the Internet, for example.
5 There is still a bias towards Europe and the USA in the vast majority of typologies. Far less has been published on the types of tourists found in Asia, Africa and the Middle East, for example, which might yield very different results.
6 On the other hand, some typologies are generally used as if they can be applied to people in all countries. They appear to ignore national and cultural differences, which surely weakens their validity.
7 Researchers have sometimes attempted to develop generally applicable typologies from surveys with small samples, which is, at best, questionable.
8 Many typologies are descriptive and, as such, do not greatly help us to increase our understanding of tourist behaviour.
9 They often ignore the fact that people may mature as tourists as they become more experienced as travellers. As Lowyck, Van Langenhave and Bollaert (1992) argue, it must be debatable 'whether it makes sense at all to divide people into different types without taking into account their full life spans'.

10 Too many typologies ignore the gap between professed preferences and actual behaviour, which is an important phenomenon in the tourism market. The gap can be caused by a number of factors, for example social conventions, ego and, even, self-delusion.

11 There are methodological criticisms of the typologies too. For example, some commentators argue that some researchers have allowed their own value judgements to influence their work.

12 There are still many gaps in the typology literature. For example, little has been written about the business tourist.

These criticisms are not intended to decry the idea of typologies but, rather, to illustrate how difficult it is to develop convincing typologies. Perhaps it also proves that there will never be one typology that reflects the behaviour of all tourists. Instead we may need as many typologies as there are tourism products, tourism markets, countries and cultures!

The marketing applications of typologies

Notwithstanding their considerable limitations, these typologies, while not developed with marketing in mind, have a potential role to play in tourism marketing. This could clearly contribute to decisions over product development, price and distribution.

However, their main role could well be in the field of promotion, particularly in the design of the messages which tourism organizations attach to their products, for different groups of potential customers. For example:

- 'travellers' want to be convinced that the holiday they may buy is not the type of 'package' bought by 'tourists'
- Perreault, Dorden and Dorden's 'budget travellers' need to be told that their prospective holiday package represents good value for money
- Plog's 'allocentrics' need to have the adventurous aspect of a product highlighted for them
- Dalen's 'traditional idealists' must be persuaded that their desired destination is safe.

On the other hand, practitioners would find it difficult to do these things, as current methodologies would make it very difficult and expensive for them to identify each of these groups and target different messages to different groups.

Therefore, it is perhaps time for us to move on to consider ways of classifying tourists that are devised specifically to make marketing more effective.

Market segmentation

Market segmentation has been well defined by Dibb et al. (2001) as: 'The process of dividing a total market into groups of people with relatively similar product needs, for the purpose of designing a marketing mix that precisely matches the needs of individuals in a segment.'

This clearly illustrates the fact that market segmentation is a form of consumer classification designed specifically to serve the marketing function. This is one difference between segmentation and the typologies we discussed earlier, which were largely developed by academics who were generally not concerned with their potential role in marketing. The second key difference is that whereas the typologies have been devised specifically in relation to tourism, segmentation is a concept derived from general marketing across all industries.

Classic segmentation criteria and their application in tourism

There are five classic ways of segmenting markets, in other words, the consumer population can be subdivided on the basis of five different criteria, into groups which share similar characteristics as buyers. We will now discuss each of these in turn, in terms of their use in the tourism industry.

Geographical segmentation

This method categorizes market groups on the basis of geographical factors, and is widely used in tourism as the following examples illustrate:

1 Theme park markets are often described in terms of catchment areas, expressed in geographical terms. In other words, Disneyland Paris is said to have an international catchment area and Alton Towers a national market, while most others in the UK have a regional catchment area.
2 Tour operators consider where their clients live when deciding which departure airports to offer flights from.
3 Airlines develop their routes on the basis of geographical patterns of demand.
4 An assumption is made that people from cool northern climates will often show a preference for warmer southern climates when selecting their holiday destinations.
5 The desire of urban dwellers to visit rural locations for leisure, as a contrast with their everyday environment.

Socioeconomic segmentation

This technique seeks to subdivide markets on the basis of socioeconomic variables. In the UK this is really another term for socioeconomic class as the British approach to socioeconomic segmentation is largely based on the JICNAR's classification. This splits society into six groups, based on occupation, represented by the letters A, B, C^1, C^2, D and E. While this is an apparently crude approach to segmentation it is widely used, with tourism organizations describing their markets in terms of classes A and B or C^2D. For example, the case of the UK theme park

market is an example of the latter, with museums and opera performances being typical of the former.

Demographic segmentation

This form of segmentation, based on subdividing the population on the
basis of demographic factors, has proved particularly popular in
tourism, as the following examples illustrate:

1 Age – some tour operators, notably SAGA and Club 18–30 in the UK,
   segment their potential market, purely in terms of age.
2 Sex – many weekend break packages and conference partner programmes base their market on gendered stereotypes. For instance,
   golf is usually seen as a male activity while it is argued that women
   will prefer shopping.
3 Religion – this is clearly at the heart of the pilgrimage market.

One demographic factor that has always been heavily used in
tourism is the idea of family status. The assumption is that a consumer's behaviour is determined by where they are in the family life
cycle. Figure 7.1 illustrates the way this model might be used in relation to the market for visitor attractions.

This family life cycle model is based on the approach used by the
tourism industry. However, there are other forms of the life cycle model.

This approach is also used by tour operators, including:

• holidays for teenagers who are holidaying separately from their parents and wanting independence and an active holiday, for example,
  PGL in the UK
• so-called family holidays where free child places are offered to make
  holidays more affordable for growing families
• products which have been traditionally aimed at 'empty nesters' to
  take advantage of their disposable income and leisure time, such as
  cruises and painting holidays.

Other demographic factors have also been used by tourism organizations including language. Destination marketing agencies have to
produce literature in the different languages spoken by their key markets, for instance.

Two criteria which have rarely been used are race and nationality. The
former is very sensitive but perhaps it will become increasingly utilized
as Europe becomes more of a multicultural society. Already race is a very
relevant criteria in the USA, with the rise of the African American market. At the same time, the rise of transnational companies in tourism, like
Accor and TUI, may make national differences an ever more important
way of segmenting the market for an organization's product.

The three methods we have discussed so far are rather crude, but
they are relatively easy to measure. The next approach is more sophisticated but is also more difficult to identify and measure.

Stage in Family Life-Cycle	Likely Preferences and Needs of Consumers
Child	Stimulation. Other Children to play with. Parental guidance and support.
Teenagers	New experiences. Excitement. Status. More independence from parents. Opportunities for active participation. Social interaction with other teenagers.
Young adult	New experiences. Freedom of action. Opportunities for active participation. Social interaction with other young adults.
Young couple	New experiences. Romance.
Young couple with baby	Facilities for babies. Economy. Ease of access for pushchairs and prams.
Growing families	Economy, eg. a family ticket. Something for all the family to do.
'Empty nesters'	Chance to learn something new. Passive rather than active participant most of the time.
Elderly	Watching rather than doing. Economy. Company of other older people. Easy accessibility for people with mobility problems.

Figure 7.1
The family life-cycle and visitor attractions
Source: adapted from Swarbrooke (1994).

Psychographic segmentation

This technique is based on the idea that the lifestyles, attitudes, opinions and personalities of people determine their behaviour as consumers. This is a more modern approach than the other three we have considered, and it has already begun to influence a wide range of industries, including clothing, food, drink, perfume and cars. It is also beginning to be seen in tourism as the following examples show:

• health farms and spas target their marketing at consumers who aspire to lead a healthy lifestyle
• people who are environmentally aware and whose lifestyle is influenced by environmental concerns are a good target market for conservation holidays
• hedonistic sun, sand, sea and sex holidays are usually targeted at extrovert people
• people who seek thrills are the target market for bungee-jumping or 'white-knuckle rides' at theme parks.

This method of segmentation is, as we said, the most modern and it is the most fashionable with marketers at the moment.

Behaviouristic segmentation

This technique groups consumers according to their relationship with a particular product. The range of variations in this approach are illustrated in Figure 7.2. This diagram is clearly selective but it shows both the number of approaches and the links between them.

Behaviouristic segmentation is used widely in tourism as we can see from the following examples:

1 Airline frequent flyer programmes (FFPs) are aimed at regular users to increase loyalty to the product and make people more enthusiastic purchasers of the product.
2 Hotels and airlines stress the quality of their service.
3 Budget tour operators, airlines and hotel chains promote services to consumers whose main 'benefit sought' is economy.

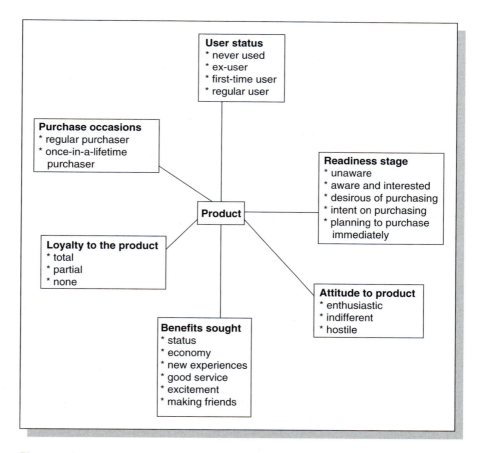

Figure 7.2
Different forms of behaviouristic segmentation

A critique of the classic methods of segmentation

There are three major criticisms of the application of the classic segmentation techniques to tourism, as follows:

1 Some of the techniques are dated and have not kept pace with changes in society; for example, the traditional family life-cycle looks increasingly inappropriate, with the rise of divorce and single parent families, non-related group household, and couples who choose not to have children.
2 It can be argued, too, that some techniques fail to recognize that tourist behaviour changes over time in response to changes in the circumstances of each tourist. Therefore, they will move between segments from time to time, as their income grows, their health deteriorates or they start using the Internet to gain tourist information.
3 Much of the market research in tourism is too poor and unreliable to allow us to accurately implement any of these methods.

In general, therefore, all we can do, perhaps, is segment general behaviour or motivations, rather than individual people. Marketers must then try to identify and target who is in their particular segment at a specific time when they are seeking to sell a certain product.

Tourism-specific methods of segmentation

While the five classic methods come from general marketing, some tourism academics and practitioners have sought to suggest other techniques which are especially relevant to tourism. For example, Middleton and Clarke (2001) suggested there are six ways of segmenting markets in travel and tourism:

1 Purpose of travel.
2 Buyer needs, motivations, and benefits sought.
3 Buyer and user characteristics.
4 Demographic, economic and geographic characteristics.
5 Psychographic characteristics.
6 Price.

While four of these are similar to the classic methods, they are worded differently. More fundamentally, Middleton and Clarke add two others – purpose of travel and price.

Other authors have suggested different methods of segmentation for individual sectors within tourism. Swarbrooke (1999) has suggested three extra criteria in relation to the visitor attraction market:

• visitor party composition, including individual, family group or groups of friends
• visit type and purpose, such as educational trips and corporate hospitality
• method of travel to attractions, for instance, private car or public transport.

Likewise, Shaw (1999) offered a range of appropriate ways of segmenting the airline market, including:

- journey purpose – business, holiday, visiting friends or relatives
- length of journey – short-haul or long-haul traveller.

Shaw believed that these were important criteria in determining the kinds of product a consumer would wish to purchase.

The special case of business tourism

Business tourism is unusual in terms of segmentation in that the market can be segmented into two types of buyer or user:

- the business traveller, who is the consumer of the product, the user of the service but who usually does not pay the bill
- their employer, who is the customer, the purchaser who pays the bill.

Tourists' response to perceived and real threats: a new approach to typologies and segmentation

In the early years of the twenty-first century the global tourism industry has been rocked by a series of major threats that have fundamentally affected tourist behaviour, including:

- the events of 11 September 2001 (9/11) in the USA, but also the terrorist attacks that have specifically targeted tourists since 2002 in countries such as Egypt, Kenya and Indonesia
- health scares including SARS and Asian flu
- natural disasters such as the tsunami in South East Asia and hurricanes in the Caribbean and the USA.

As yet, little research has been done on this subject but if such phenomena are going to be a major issue for tourism in the future, we need to understand more about how different types of tourist react to these threats, which is as much to do with their attitudes as it is to do with the reality of the threat.

Taking terrorism as an example, we can already see potential typologies/methods of association, as any terrorist attack or threat seems to elicit the following responses from different types of people:

- stop travelling anywhere altogether
- still travel but avoid certain types of transport
- still travel but avoid certain types of destination
- go ahead with their plans to visit destinations even if there is a perceived terrorist threat, but avoid places which are seen as high risk such as Western-owned hotel chains or tourist bars
- go ahead with their travel plans to visit places with a perceived threat and make no concessions to the fear of terrorism
- after a terrorist attack, decide to visit the place that has been attacked as a show of 'solidarity' with its residents

- after a terrorist attack, decide to visit destinations that are attacked because of a belief that 'terrorists' never strike twice in the same place
- after a terrorist attack, decide to visit the destination because in the immediate post-attack period prices will be very low.

Perhaps we should do more research on this approach to typologies/segmentation in the future.

This distinction becomes important when one considers airline FFPs, for example. Traditionally the employer (customer) has paid the bill but it has been the business traveller (consumer) who has enjoyed the benefits of the FFP, such as free flights for partners. Now airlines are realizing that it is the customers who really need to be wooed and are tying to appeal to them with discounted fares.

Marketing applications and segmentation in tourism

We noted earlier that segmentation is designed to serve the need of marketers. It is not surprising therefore, that writers like Middleton and Clarke (2001) believe that: 'Market segmentation and product formulation, are mirror images if they are correctly matched.'

Indeed, segmentation is designed to help with all four Ps of the marketing mix, namely, Product, Price, Place and Promotion. This link is discussed in more detail in Chapter 11, so at this stage we simply need to make two brief points.

First, successful marketing is not based on one method of segmentation alone; instead it makes use of a blend of different techniques that will be different on every occasion. We might link personality with geographical place of residence, or we might focus on benefits sought in relation to different demographic factors. A combination of socioeconomic geographical and demographic factors underpins the use of the ACORN residential neighbourhood classification system in tourism marketing.

Secondly, tourism organizations have to deal with, what Middleton and Clarke (2001) have called, 'Multiple segments'. For example they say that hotels serve at least five segments, namely, corporate/business clients, group tours, independent vacationers, weekend/midweek package clients and conference delegates: 'most (tourism) businesses deal with not one but several segments'.

Conclusions

While we have considered the so-called 'academic typologies' separately from segmentation techniques, there are clearly links between them. According to Horner and Swarbrooke (1996):

> The typology of Plog (1977) is based firmly on the principles of psycographic segmentation in that it is based on the personality of the tourist . . . Concepts such as the 'Post-Tourist' are closely linked to another element of psychographic

segmentation, namely lifestyles. For the post-tourist, tourism is just another aspect of their post-modern lifestyle.

We have seen how difficult it is to produce convincing typologies and segmentation methods and how all the existing approaches have attracted criticism.

Hopefully, the reader appreciates the importance of continually updating both the typologies and our approaches to segmentation to reflect changes in society and consumer behaviour. Finally, perhaps, we should not focus on how academics or marketers see tourist behaviour but, rather, try to find out how the tourists themselves evaluate their own behaviour. It is, after all, the perceptions that consumers hold that shape their real behaviour.

Discussion points and essay questions

1 Discuss the potential application of the following typologies of tourists' behaviour to the marketing of tourism products:
   (a) Cohen (1972)
   (b) Plog (1977)
   (c) Dalen (1989).
2 Evaluate the concept of the 'post-tourist' and examine its potential impact on the tourism market.
3 Discuss the extent to which the twofold typology, published by Gray in 1970, is still relevant today, in the light of changes in consumer behaviour and the tourism market.
4 Develop your own typology of tourists for a destination of your choice, like that produced by Wickens in 1994 (in Seaton et al., 1994), for a resort in the Chalkidiki region of Greece.

Exercise

Write a report examining the application of the five classic methods of market segmentation to *one* of the following markets:

- mass package tours
- scheduled airlines
- theme parks
- country house hotels
- cruises
- health spas.

Suggest which method or methods are most relevant and which combination of methods would be most appropriate.

PART 4

Tourism Demand and Markets

Having looked at the theoretical dimension of tourist behaviour in Parts 2 and 3, we now turn our attention to the current facts and figures relating to tourism demand and markets worldwide.

In four chapters we will explore:

- the global pattern of tourism demand
- national differences in demand in relation to domestic, outbound and inbound tourist flow
- the nature of demand in different market segments
- the markets for different sectors of tourism.

The global pattern of tourism demand

Introduction

In this chapter, we consider the patterns of tourism demand, divided by global regions. We start our analysis by considering the factors that influence tourism demand and continue by considering some of these key factors in more detail. These include the economic position of the regions or countries, the degree of urbanization and the overall quality of life. The chapter will finish with an analysis of tourism demand for regions of the world and we will draw comparisons between the different regions.

Factors that influence tourism demand

The factors that influence the levels of global tourism were explored by the World Tourism Organization (WTO) in 1995. These factors are shown in Figure 8.1.

Tourism arrivals and receipts

There was a growth of international tourist arrivals from 565 million in 1995 to 636.6 million in 1998, and the WTO predict that this will grow to 101.56 billion by 2020. The WTO have also explored the influences and determinants that affect the choices that individuals make when choosing a tourism product. These are shown below in Figure 8.2.

It can be seen from Figures 8.1 and 8.2 that many issues have an effect on levels of tourism demand. Demographic and

Figure 8.1
Factors shaping the development of tourism
Source: WTO (1995).

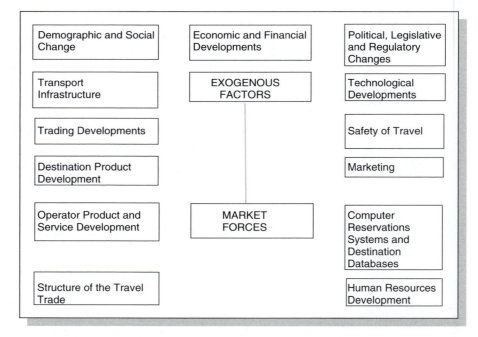

Figure 8.2
Influences and determinants
Source: WTO (1995).

social changes affect the patterns of tourism demand. One example of this is the ageing demographic profile in Europe, which is having an effect on the development of tourism products specifically aimed at third age sections of the population. Consumer knowledge of available tourism products also influences tourism demand. This is particularly important in developed countries, where individuals will generally be eager to learn about the opportunities for travel, particularly where political or economic factors have affected their decisions in the past. The growth of television programmes and specialist magazines on tourism has been a reflection of the growing interest in tourism. These programmes have also fuelled tourism demand, as has the growth and development of tourism companies offering more choice to consumers. The development of large aircraft that can travel long distances and carry large numbers of passengers has helped in the development of new long-haul destinations. Computer reservation systems and destination databases have made it easier for consumers to book travel packages.

The reduction in prices of tourism holidays has also increased the demand for tourism products. The development of good value for money holiday packages by the UK package holiday operators, for example, has been the main reason for the large numbers of British people travelling overseas on holiday packages, resulting in strong outbound tourism from the UK.

Key determining factors influencing tourism demand

We now consider some of the factors that influence tourism demand in more detail.

The economic position of the region or country has a direct effect on the levels of tourism demand. There are various ways of measuring economic activity of individual countries or regions. It can be anticipated that the world's biggest economies will provide a large proportion of tourism demand. It is interesting to look at the gross domestic product (GDP) per capita for different regions of the world, and a summary of these is shown in Table 8.1 for Europe and Table 8.2 for the rest of the world.

Income distributions have changed in different areas of the world owing to three major factors – economic reasons, demographic reasons and policy considerations (Euromonitor, 2004). Tables 8.1 and 8.2 show that changes in income distribution over the past ten years have been much more pronounced in some countries than others. A brief overview of the changes that have occurred across the world are given next.

Asia Pacific

There are extreme variations between different areas of the Asia Pacific region. Income is distributed across all the Asia Pacific regions according to regional dimensions, education levels, ethnic groups and the division of urban and rural areas. Japan, Hong Kong and Singapore

Table 8.1 GDP per capita: Europe, 1997–2003

	1997	1998	1999	2000	2001	2002	2003
Luxembourg	35 577	38 593	41 348	44 600	44 855	43 761	44 625
Denmark	28 151	28 496	28 948	29 743	29 989	30 024	30 163
Sweden	23 519	24 611	25 813	27 039	27 265	27 614	28 120
Ireland	19 421	20 418	23 082	24 858	26 197	27 467	27 605
UK	21 955	22 831	23 597	24 555	25 293	26 143	27 087
Finland	20 434	21 467	22 017	23 149	23 439	23 771	24.131
Netherlands	20 978	21 440	22 359	23.311	23 674	23 558	23 449
Austria	21 530	22 123	22 975	23 511	23 506	23 732	23 525
Germany	21 584	21 906	22 486	22 731	22 745	22 818	22 759
France	20 073	20 789	21 494	22 088	22 447	22 707	22 567
Belgium	20 463	20 948	21 796	22 291	22 231	22 319	22 530
Italy	17 552	17 860	18 196	18 678	18 986	19 186	19 309
Spain	12 259	12 649	13 261	13 792	14 205	14 651	15 156
Portugal	9 054	9 268	10 240	10 624	10 827	10 964	10 705
Greece	11 497	10 663	10 918	10 396	10 207	10 074	10 134

Source: World Advertising Research Centre (2005).

have the highest GDP per capita of the whole region. There are very big differences within countries according to the concentration of urban areas. In China, for example, there are huge divergences between the prosperous coastal regions and the relatively poor interior.

Africa and the Middle East

The income inequality between households in the Middle Eastern and African countries is relatively low. Gender inequality is however high, with economic share of the income being on average less than a fifth of that of men's average in the Arab countries, for example (Euromonitor, 2004).

South Africa has an uneven distribution of household income and this difference can largely be explained by race, with white-headed households having higher average incomes compared with black-headed households.

Western Europe

There has been rising inequality of incomes in Western Europe starting during the 1990s. This developed as a result of the demographic changes that the region experienced. The increase in the number of old people and smaller households has meant that the distribution of

Table 8.2 GDP per capital: rest of the world, 1995–2001

	1995	1996	1997	1998	1999	2000	2001
Asia							
Japan	38.6	35.0	31.9	35.3	39.5	35.2	30.0
Hong Kong	23.0	24.3	26.8	25.3	24.3	24.8	24.4
Singapore	23.7	25.0	22.1	21.1	21.3	22.4	20.1
Taiwan	12.0	13.0	11.8	12.7	13.4	13.1	—
Korea (South)	10.8	10.9	5.8	7.9	9.1	8.7	8.8
Malaysia	4.2	4.7	3.3	3.4	3.5	3.9	3.9
Thailand	2.8	3.0	1.7	2.1	2.0	1.8	1.8
Philippines	1.0	1.1	0.8	0.9	1.0	0.9	0.9
China	0.6	0.7	0.7	0.8	0.8	0.8	0.9
Indonesia	1.0	1.1	0.7	0.6	0.7	0.6	0.7
India	0.4	0.4	0.4	0.4	0.4	0.4	—
Pakistan	0.4	0.4	0.4	0.4	0.4	0.4	0.4
Pacific							
Australia	20.0	22.5	19.2	18.9	21.0	18.9	18.2
New Zealand	16.5	18.4	15.5	14.0	14.3	12.7	13.0
Africa							
South Africa	3.6	3.3	3.4	3.0	3.0	2.7	1.8
Egypt	1.0	1.1	1.3	1.3	1.4	1.4	—
Zimbabwe	0.6	0.7	0.4	0.3	0.4	—	—
Zambia	0.3	0.3	0.4	—	—	—	—
Kenya	0.3	0.3	0.4	0.4	0.3	0.3	—
Ghana	0.3	0.4	0.3	—	—	—	—
Tanzania	0.2	0.2	0.3	0.3	0.2	—	—
Uganda	0.3	0.3	—	—	—	—	—
Middle East							
Qatar	16.0	17.4	21.3	19.0	21.8	28.9	—
UAE	17.3	18.3	18.8	16.7	—	—	—
Israel	15.6	16.9	17.1	15.6	16.0	17.4	16.9
Kuwait	14.7	16.4	15.0	12.5	13.8	16.4	16.6
Bahrain	10.1	10.2	10.2	9.7	9.9	11.8	12.2
Saudi Arabia	7.5	9.0	9.0	7.7	8.1	9.3	8.9
Oman	6.5	6.9	7.0	6.2	6.4	8.3	—
Lebanon	3.6	4.0	4.5	5.1	—	—	—
Syria	3.6	4.2	4.4	4.5	4.5	4.9	—
Jordan	1.2	1.2	1.2	1.3	1.2	—	—

Source: World Advertising Research Centre (2003).

income has polarized between the lower-income households and the households where both partners work and have a relatively higher household income. The households with two partners who are working, whether or not they have children, are an obvious target for the tourism industry.

Eastern Europe

There have been two patterns of income distribution that have occurred in Eastern Europe. In Central and Eastern European countries, where welfare systems have been preserved, the distribution of income has remained fairly static. In Russia, however, there has been a rising inequality in income distribution owing to a rise in earnings among professionals and the self-employed. This emerging high-income group is an obvious target for the tourism industry.

North America

The USA has experienced increasing income inequality since the late 1960s. The highly skilled professional workers at the top of their professions have experienced real wage gains, whereas at the other end of the spectrum the poor have got poorer. Increases in divorces, separations and a trend towards later marriages have also contributed to a decline in the traditional higher-income household composed of two working adults.

We have only looked at a small sample of regions of the world but this has demonstrated that the distribution of income is undergoing significant change in certain areas of the world. It is also important to look at the distribution of income in relation to other factors; for example:

- Sex – this will be determined by the role of women in the total workforce of a country and the equality of incomes between the sexes.
- Education – the increase in education of a particular population will have an affect on the income distribution among the population. It is argued that a more unusual tertiary education system, for instance, will lead in the longer term to a fairer distribution of income from the privileged few.
- Age – there are major differences between countries and regions regarding the distribution of income among older people. Generally, elderly people living alone and elderly couples constitute a large proportion of households with low incomes. It is important to remember, however, that there are also an increasing number of affluent one-person and two-person households that can be targeted with tourism products.

We can also consider figures for disposable income for a range of countries to give us some clues as to the country that will generate tourism spend.

It can be seen from Table 8.3 that there has been a significant growth in the purchasing power of the average household in a number of countries over the past decade. Hong Kong and the United Arab Emirates remain high in the table, with Singapore showing rapid growth during the same period. Many European countries have also shown growth during the same period. It is interesting to note that

Table 8.3 Disposable income (purchasing power parity) 2003 in the top twenty countries of the world (International $ per household at current prices)

		PPP	% growth 1995–2003
1	Hong Kong China	69 155.5	20.7
2	United Arab Emirates	64 063.6	6.6
3	Singapore	63 789.1	57.2
4	USA	61 872.8	30.2
5	Kuwait	58 238.0	11.4
6	Taiwan	50 936.8	27.4
7	Ireland	48 238.4	50.7
8	Canada	45 569.8	25.7
9	Italy	44 642.5	16.1
10	Japan	44 544.5	13.6
11	Austria	43 830.6	19.7
12	UK	41 490.0	23.7
13	Australia	41 267.0	32.4
14	France	41 068.5	26.2
15	Norway	40 103.2	21.1
16	Belgium	39 717.4	18.9
17	Germany	37 143.4	28.0
18	Netherlands	37 143.4	28.0
19	Spain	34 857.5	11.7
20	South Korea	34 308.1	46.1

Source: adapted from Euromonitor (2004).

South Korea appears in the top twenty countries because of large growth in average household income over the past decade.

International tourism demand

The WTO has made predictions about the levels of inbound and out-bound tourism that will be experienced over the next decade. Their predictions for the levels of inbound tourism is shown in Table 8.4. It can be seen from these predictions that Europe will lose market share in the amount of international tourist arrivals, with the East Asia and the Pacific region growing in importance. The predictions for the world's top destinations by 2020 are shown in Table 8.5. It can be seen that countries such as China, Hong Kong and the Russian Federation move into the top ten. Other countries that are predicted to grow in popularity include Asian destinations, such as Thailand and Singapore, along with South Africa (WTO, 2005b).

New and existing tourism destinations are beginning to grow in importance, and the growth in the popularity of long-haul travel will continue to fuel these developments.

Table 8.4 WTO *Tourism 2020 Vision*: forecast of inbound tourism, world by regions (millions international tourist arrivals by tourist receiving region)

	Base year 1995	Forecasts 2010	2020	Average annual growth rate (%) 1995–2000	Market share (%) 1995	2020
Total	**565.4**	**1006**	**1561**	**4.1**	**100**	**100**
Africa	20.2	47	77	5.5	3.6	5.0
Americas	108.9	190	282	3.9	19.3	18.1
East Asia and the Pacific	81.4	195	397	6.5	14.4	25.4
Europe	338.4	527	717	3.0	59.8	45.9
Middle East	12.4	36	69	7.1	2.2	4.4
South Asia	4.2	11	19	6.2	0.7	1.2
Intra-regional (a)	464.1	791	1183	3.8	82.1	75.8
Long-haul (b)	101.3	216	378	5.4	17.9	24.2

Source: WTO (2005b).

Table 8.5 World's top destinations 2020

	Base year 1995 (million)	Forecast 2020 (million)	Average annual growth rate (%) 1995–2000	Market share (%) 1995	2020
1. China	20.0	130.0	7.8	3.5	8.3
2. France	60.0	106.1	2.3	10.6	6.8
3. USA	43.3	102.4	3.5	7.7	6.6
4. Spain	38.8	73.9	2.6	6.9	4.7
5. Hong Kong (China)	10.2	56.6	7.1	1.8	3.6
6. Italy	31.1	52.5	2.1	5.5	3.4
7. UK	23.5	53.8	3.4	4.2	3.4
8. Mexico	20.2	48.9	3.6	3.6	3.1
9. Russian Federation	9.3	48.0	6.8	1.6	3.1
10. Czech Republic	16.5	44.0	4.0	2.9	2.8
Total (1–10)	**273.0**	**716.2**	**3.9**	**48.3**	**45.9**

Source: WTO (2005b).

Table 8.6 World's top outbound countries 2020

	Base year 1995 (million)	Forecast 2020 (million)	Average annual growth rate (%) 1995–2000	Market share (%) 1995	2020
1. Germany	75	153	2.9	13.3	9.8
2. Japan	23	142	7.5	4.1	9.1
3. USA	63	123	2.7	11.1	7.9
4. China	5	100	12.8	0.9	6.4
5. UK	42	95	3.3	7.4	6.1
6. France	21	55	3.9	3.7	3.5
7. Netherlands	22	46	3.0	3.8	2.9
8. Italy	16	35	3.1	2.9	2.3
9. Canada	19	31	2.0	3.4	2.0
10. Russian Federation	12	31	4.0	2.1	2.0
Total (1–10)	**298**	**810**	**4.1**	**52.7**	**51.9**

Source: WTO (2005b).

Tourism departures and expenditures

The major industrialized countries will remain the leaders in the countries that are the producers of tourists who go abroad. Table 8.6 shows the predictions for 2020 of the world's top outbound countries.

It can be seen that there are two important newcomers to the list which tourism marketers will have to think very hard about in their planning for future business. These two new countries are China entering at fourth place, and Russia entering at tenth place.

Conclusions

We have considered the factors that affect world tourism demand figures. Inbound and outbound tourism are predicted to grow in importance over the next decade. Outbound tourism is predicted to grow rapidly from countries within the Asian regions. The Asian, African and Middle Eastern outbound markets are in their introductory or growth stages and there will be a great potential for developments from these regions in the future.

The nature of demand may alter as increasing numbers of outbound tourists travel from these regions. Increasing interest in beach holidays and environmental issues are examples of trends which are predicted for outbound tourists from Japan and Asia in general.

We now turn our attention to the national differences in tourism demand, which are explored in Chapter 9.

Discussion points and essay questions

1 Explain the reasons for the development in the levels of inbound and outbound tourism from East Asia and the Pacific regions of the world.

2 Explore the relationship between consumer knowledge of tourism opportunities and demand for tourism products. Discuss the ways in which a consumer can gain knowledge about tourism opportunities.

3 Evaluate the reasons for the Japanese tourists showing a growing interest in a beach-type holiday, rather than a city-based holiday.

Exercise

Design and conduct a small-scale survey of tourists to discover their interest in visiting the East Asia and Pacific area of the world. Do they envisage any problems involved in visiting areas such as these?

National differences: domestic, outbound and inbound

Introduction

In the previous chapter, we have looked at the pattern of world demands divided by regions of the world. It has been shown that certain areas of the world such as the Asia Pacific and Far East are growing in their levels of tourism. In this chapter, we consider the differences between individual countries in more depth. We start by considering the outbound and inbound tourism figures for a range of countries, and then we consider individual countries in more depth. This will enable us to look at particular issues related to tourism demand on a country by country basis. The chapter concludes with a discussion on the similarities and differences between individual countries in relation to their tourism figures.

Inbound and outbound tourism receipts

Table 9.1 illustrates outbound tourist expenditure for the main regions of the world with forecasts up to 2020.

Table 9.1 WTO *Tourism 2020 Vision*: forecast of outbound tourism, world by region

	Actual		Forecasts		
	1985	**1995**	**2000**	**2010**	**2020**
Total	**327.1**	**565.4**	**667.7**	**1006.4**	**1561.1**
Africa	6.3	13.9	20.3	36.4	62.3
Americas	82.3	107.8	127.3	172.7	232.1
East Asia/Pacific	30.5	84.3	88.5	193.2	404.9
Europe	174.3	312.6	373.5	519.9	728.7
Middle East	4.4	8.6	12.1	20.6	35.1
South Asia	3.7	4.3	5.8	9.9	16.9
Not specified	25.7	33.9	40.1	53.8	81.2
Intra-regional	266.3	464.1	544.1	790.9	1183.3
Long-haul	60.8	101.3	123.7	215.5	377.9

Market share (%)

Total	**100**	**100**	**100**	**100**	**100**
Africa	1.9	2.5	3.0	3.6	4.0
Americas	25.1	19.1	19.1	17.2	14.9
East Asia/Pacific	9.3	14.9	13.3	19.2	25.9
Europe	53.3	55.3	55.9	51.7	46.7
Middle East	1.4	1.5	1.8	2.0	2.2
South Asia	1.1	0.8	0.9	1.0	1.1
Not specified	7.9	6.0	6.0	5.3	5.2
Intra-regional	81.4	82.1	81.5	78.6	75.8
Long-haul	18.6	17.9	18.5	21.4	24.2

Average annual growth rate (%)

	Actual	Overall forecast	Forecasts		
	1985–1995	**1995–2020**	**1995–2000**	**2000–2010**	**2010–2020**
Total	**5.6**	**4.1**	**3.4**	**4.2**	**4.5**
Africa	8.3	6.2	7.9	6.0	5.5
Americas	2.7	3.1	3.4	3.1	3.0
East Asia/Pacific	10.7	6.5	1.0	8.1	7.7
Europe	6.0	3.4	3.6	3.4	3.4
Middle East	6.9	5.8	7.0	5.4	5.5
South Asia	1.7	5.6	6.2	5.4	5.5
Not specified	2.8	3.6	3.5	3.0	4.2
Intra-regional	5.7	3.8	3.2	3.8	4.1
Long-haul	5.2	5.4	4.1	5.7	5.8

Source: WTO (2005b).

On the basis of this data, a number of points can be made:

1 There will be a continued growth of outbound tourism from Europe.
2 There will be a significant growth in outbound tourism from the East Asia/Pacific region.
3 Other regions such as the Middle East, Africa and South Asia will experience growth in outbound tourism.

Table 9.2 shows inbound tourism receipts for a range of world regions with predictions until 2020. On the basis of this table a number of points can be made:

1 There will continue to be a growth of inbound tourism into Europe and the Americas.
2 The East Asia/Pacific region of the world will experience the largest growth in inbound tourism, leading to an overall market share of approximately 25 per cent in 2020 (WTO, 2005b).
3 The Middle East and South Asia will experience a steady growth in tourism over the next decade.

We can see from Tables 9.1 and 9.2 that the most important trend that is predicted to happen to inbound and outbound tourism over the next decade is the growth of business both from and into the East Asia/Pacific region.

Let us now turn our attention to considering individual countries in more detail.

The USA

The USA is one of the most important countries in the world in relation to inbound and outbound tourism receipts. The market for outbound tourism from the USA has the greatest potential for growth.

International travel has never been appealing to Americans, and less than 20 per cent of Americans currently own a passport (Euromonitor, 1996). Economic growth and competitive prices, however, fuelled the growth in tourism over the period 1990–95. There was a growth in outbound tourism during 1993 despite the fact that there were unfavourable currency values. The growth in inbound tourism grew slowly over the period 1990–95 because of the well-developed market and problems with the economy in some adjoining countries such as Mexico.

The overall volumes of inbound and outbound tourism in the USA for the period 1999–2003 are shown in Table 9.3.

The market for inbound tourism is predicted to decline slowly over the next ten years. The largest share of visitors to the USA come from Europe, but these are predicted to decline. The predictions for other inbound tourism to the USA shows a picture of steady decline from all major markets.

Table 9.2 WTO *Tourism 2020 Vision*: forecast of inbound tourism, world by region

	Actual		Forecasts			
	1985	**1995**	**1995**	**2000**	**2010**	**2020**
Total	**327.1**	**457.2**	**565.4**	**667.7**	**1006.4**	**1561.1**
Africa	9.7	15.0	20.2	27.4	47.0	77.3
Americas	64.3	92.8	108.9	130.2	190.4	282.3
East Asia/Pacific	31.1	54.6	81.4	92.9	195.2	397.2
Europe	212.0	282.7	338.4	393.4	527.3	717.0
Middle East	7.5	9.0	12.4	18.3	35.9	68.5
South Asia	2.5	3.2	4.2	5.5	10.6	18.8
Intra-regional	266.3	377.5	464.1	544.1	790.9	1183.3
Long-haul	60.8	79.8	101.3	123.7	215.5	377.9

	Market share (%)					
Total	**100**	**100**	**100**	**100**	**100**	**100**
Africa	3.0	3.3	3.6	4.1	4.7	5.0
Americas	19.7	20.3	19.3	19.5	18.9	18.1
East Asia/Pacific	9.5	11.9	14.4	13.9	19.4	25.4
Europe	64.8	61.8	59.8	58.9	52.4	45.9
Middle East	2.3	2.0	2.2	2.7	3.6	4.4
South Asia	0.8	0.7	0.7	0.8	1.1	1.2
Intra-regional	81.4	82.6	82.1	81.5	78.6	75.8
Long-haul	18.6	17.4	17.9	18.5	21.4	24.2

	Average annual growth rate (%)					
	Actual	**Actual**	**Overall forecast**		**Forecasts**	
	1985–1990	**1990–1995**	**1995–2020**	**1995–2000**	**2000–2010**	**2010–2020**
Total	**6.9**	**4.3**	**4.1**	**3.4**	**4.2**	**4.5**
Africa	9.0	6.1	5.5	6.3	5.6	5.1
Americas	7.6	3.3	3.9	3.6	3.9	4.0
East Asia/Pacific	11.9	8.3	6.5	2.7	7.7	7.4
Europe	5.9	3.7	3.0	3.1	3.0	3.1
Middle East	3.7	6.6	7.1	8.1	7.0	6.7
South Asia	4.8	5.9	6.2	5.7	6.7	5.8
Intra-regional	7.2	4.2	3.8	3.2	3.8	4.1
Long-Haul	5.6	4.9	5.4	4.1	5.7	5.8

Source: WTO (2005b).

Germany

Germany is an important country in relation to inbound and outbound tourism receipts. Table 9.4 shows the predictions for both inbound and outbound tourism for Germany over the next decade.

Table 9.3 Tourism Statistics: USA

	1999	2000	2001	2002	2003
Inbound Arrivals					
Tourists (overnight visitor)	48 505	51 219	46 907	43 525	41 212
Arrivals by region					
Africa	274	295	287	241	236
Americas	28 760	30 338	29 578	27 980	26 362
Europe	11 634	12 052	9 907	8 964	8 982
East Asia and the Pacific	7 302	7 921	6 535	5 889	5 192
South Asia	301	363	363	324	330
Middle East	234	249	237	127	110
Outbound					
Departures	57 318	61 327	59 433	58 050	56 175
Tourism expenditure in other countries (US$)	82 373	91 317	85 405	80 798	80 621

Source: adapted from WTO (2004).

Table 9.4 Tourism statistics: Germany

	1999	2000	2001	2002	2003
Inbound Arrivals					
Tourists (overnight visitor)	17 116	58 983	17 861	17 969	18 399
Arrivals by region					
Africa	142	160	147	144	143
Americas	2 400	2 865	2 334	2 151	2 049
Europe	12 497	13 516	13 093	13 289	13 878
East Asia and the Pacific	1 567	1 799	1 651	1 716	1 605
South Asia	—	—	—	—	—
Middle East	93	106	117	128	143
Outbound					
Departures	73 400	74 400	76 400	73 300	74 600
Tourism expenditure in other countries (US$)	61 504	57 888	56 709	61 581	73 652

Source: Euromonitor (2004).

The following points can be made about the state of tourism in Germany:

1 Tourism is one of the most important economic activities in Germany.
2 Inbound tourism is predicted to rise steadily over the next decade with the most arrivals still originating in Europe. The eastern European Union will play a major part in this growth.
3 Japan is an important Asian market for the German tourism industry.
4 Outbound tourism will continue to rise steadily over the next decade.

Japan

The appreciating value of the yen has encouraged overseas travel by the Japanese but has had a negative effect on the numbers of incoming visitors. Declining visitor numbers have also been accompanied by a reduction in spending by foreign tourists. The market for inbound and outbound tourism for Japan is shown in Table 9.5.

The following points can be made with reference to the inbound and outbound tourism for Japan.

Table 9.5 Tourism statistics: Japan

	1999	2000	2001	2002	2003
Inbound Arrivals					
Tourists (overnight visitor)	4 438	4 757	4 772	5 239	5 212
Arrivals by region					
Africa	13	15	15	17	16
Americas	853	899	866	928	824
Europe	580	625	630	688	665
East Asia and the Pacific	2 925	3 149	3 189	3 528	3 625
South Asia	60	64	66	73	76
Middle East	3	3	3	3	3
Outbound					
Departures	16 358	17 819	16 216	16 523	13 296
Tourism expenditure in other countries (US$)	41 213	42 643	35 526	34 977	36 506

Source: Euromonitor (2004).

1 Inbound tourism will continue to grow in Japan with the majority of the growth coming from the East Asia and Pacific regions.
2 Outbound tourism is predicted to grow over the next decade, although a slight decline was experienced in 2003 owing to adverse economic conditions. The growth in the popularity of package tours, the opening of the new Kansai International airport in 1994 and the growing interest among the Japanese for international travel has fuelled this growth.

The UK

The UK has a considerable tourism market in world terms. The inbound and outbound tourism figures are shown in Table 9.6.

The following points can be made in relation to the inbound and outbound tourism statistics for the UK.

1 The outbound travel market has grown at a quicker rate than the inbound market.
2 Inbound tourism has declined slightly over the past five years.
3 Arrivals from Europe continue to grow but arrivals from the USA have continued to decline over the past five years. This can be explained by the worries of travel because of the terrorist threat/Iraq situation.

Table 9.6 Tourism statistics: the UK

	1999	2000	2001	2002	2003
Inbound Arrivals Tourists (overnight visitor)	25 394	25 209	22 835	24 180	24 715
Arrivals by region					
Africa	588	618	630	631	569
Americas	5 000	5 287	4 582	4 619	4 326
Europe	17 046	16 307	15 059	16 409	17 371
East Asia and the Pacific	2 062	2 256	1 834	1 854	1 809
South Asia	291	314	326	308	294
Middle East	409	429	402	360	346
Outbound					
Departures	53 881	56 837	58 281	59 377	61 424
Tourism expenditure in other countries (US$)	45 536	47 009	46 096	50 606	58 602

Source: Euromonitor (2004).

France

France has always been a major destination for foreign tourists, largely owing to the range of scenery and attractions that the country can offer the foreign visitor. The country also has an excellent climate for tourism, ranging from the sunny Mediterranean climate of the south to the snowy climate of the French Alps. This has led to the development of tourism both in the summer and winter months. Revenue from inbound tourism more than doubled during the 1990s despite the worldwide recession and a strong French currency.

France did, however, experience problems in their tourism market during 1995 when there was a sharp decline in the size of foreign receipts from tourism as well as the number of visitors going to France because of a combination of political and economic factors.

Table 9.7 gives an overview of the inbound and outbound tourism statistics for France.

We can make the following points about French tourism:

1 There has been a steady increase in the market of outbound tourism from France, despite the many holiday opportunities which France offers to the French, although there was a decline in outbound tourism during 2002/03.

Table 9.7 Tourism statistics: France

	1999	2000	2001	2002	2003
Inbound Arrivals					
Tourists (overnight visitor)	73 147	77 190	75 202	77 012	75 048
Arrivals by region					
Africa	981	1 074	921	924	889
Americas	5 029	5 698	5 291	4 639	3 954
Europe	64 453	67 580	66 491	69 078	68 073
East Asia and the Pacific	2 261	2 353	2 114	2 080	1 890
South Asia	—	—	—	—	—
Middle East	233	399	325	249	210
Outbound					
Departures	16 709	19 886	19 265	17 404	17 426
Tourism expenditure in other countries (US$)	18 710	17 906	18 109	19 708	23 576

Source: Euromonitor (2004).

2 The French have easy access to bordering European countries such as Spain, Switzerland, Italy and Germany. Despite this, a large proportion of the French still prefer to remain at home for their holidays.

3 Inbound tourism which originated from Europe continued to rise during the past five years.

Spain

Spain is a major European holiday destination. It offers a wide range of scenery and an excellent climate, which has allowed the country to develop substantial tourism receipts, particularly in the package holiday business. Outbound tourism for Spain is shown in Table 9.8.

The following issues can be highlighted:

1 It can be seen that Spain has experienced a steady increase in arrivals during the last decade. There are increasing numbers of East Germans and Russians visiting Spain. The European visitor constitutes the majority of the inbound tourism business for Spain with a large majority originating from the UK and Germany.

2 Outbound tourism showed a slight overall increase during the period 1999–2003.

Table 9.8 Tourism statistics: Spain

	1999	2000	2001	2002	2003
Inbound Arrivals Tourists (overnight visitor)	72 060	74 462	75 678	80 024	81 944
Arrivals by region Africa	—	—	—	—	—
Americas	2 238	2 519	2 174	2 080	1 941
Europe	43 587	44 499	46 827	49 304	49 005
East Asia and the Pacific	2 261	2 353	2 114	2 080	1 890
South Asia	359	301	265	241	248
Middle East	—	—	—	—	—
Outbound Departures	3 519	4 100	4 139	3 871	4 094
Tourism expenditure in other countries US$	7 430	7 264	7 897	8 733	10 544

Source: Euromonitor (1994).

3 The market for outgoing tourism from Spain is still a young market which offers substantial potential for growth. The Spanish like to go to other European countries and France is the most popular destination. Other cheaper destinations such as Turkey, Tunisia and Morocco are also becoming popular with Spaniards

4 Spain has developed its tourism offering over the last decades with a new emphasis placed on cultural tourism, sport tourism (including golf and water sports), and conference business.

Newly emerging tourism-generating countries

We have already considered the increasing importance of countries which are experiencing a dynamic growth of the outbound market. Two countries which are at a dynamic stage of their development are India and China. Many destinations are experiencing a strong increase in visitor numbers from these two countries, and this trend seems set to continue and intensify.

Other countries experiencing a strong growth in outbound travel during the last decade are Singapore and Hong Kong, with Thailand and Indonesia beginning to emerge as important growth areas. China is also a country which is expected to show a considerable growth in outbound tourism statistics.

The growth in Europe continues to emanate from Eastern Europe, with Poland and Hungary also showing strong growth. European and Asian economies, however, are experiencing increasing numbers of Russian visitors. Brazil is expected to show considerable growth in the European market in the near future.

National differences in tourism markets

Figure 9.1 illustrates the relative scale of domestic, inbound and outbound tourism in ten selected countries. The allocation of 'high', 'medium' and 'low' takes into account the geographical size of the country and its resident population, for example.

A deeper investigation of the factors behind these differences shows that:

- there are many different factors that account for different scales of domestic, inbound and outbound tourism
- even where the scale of the market is relatively similar, the markets themselves can be very different.

Let us now illustrate this by considering each country in turn.

Australia

Australia, as a developed economy where people have relatively high amounts of leisure time, has a reasonably highly developed domestic

Country	Domestic	Inbound	Outbound
Australia	Medium	Medium	High
Dominican Republic	Low	High	Low
France	High	High	Medium
Germany	Medium	Low	High
Japan	Medium	Low	Low
Netherlands	Medium	Medium	High
Nigeria	Medium	Low	Low
Russia	Medium	Low	Medium
Spain	High	High	Medium
USA	High	Medium	Low

Figure 9.1
Suggested relative levels of domestic, inbound and outbound tourism in ten selected countries

tourism market. Its inbound market has been traditionally related to in-migration from Europe but has now grown to include leisure tourists from Asia and Europeans who do not have relations in the country.

However, its geographical isolation ensures that it will never be a mass market destination for people from other continents. A large proportion of Australians travel abroad for holidays, reflecting both Australia's geographical isolation, which creates a desire to see other places, and the availability of time and disposable income. However, the isolation influences the market in that the major outbound segment is young people who travel abroad for one month up to a year. If you live thousands of miles from most potential destinations, a short trip hardly seems worthwhile. The young people and their parents often see a journey to Asia, Europe or North America almost as completing their education, and opening their eyes to the wider world. It could thus almost be seen as the modern version of the 'Grand Tour'.

The Dominican Republic

The Dominican Republic, on the other hand, is a poor, developing country with low levels of domestic and outbound tourism as a result. However, it has become a major destination in recent years for:

- Europeans looking for inexpensive, all-inclusive, sun, sand, and sea holidays in an exotic location
- gamblers from Caribbean countries and South America who come to play the casinos.

In the latter case, the local language of Spanish is the lingua franca of the visitors so there is no language problem.

France

France is the world's top tourist destination because of:

- its generally attractive climate
- its diversity of attractions, from the culture and romance of Paris to the chic of the Riviera, from the friendly villages of Brittany to the vineyards of Burgundy, from the beaches of the West Coast to the Alpine ski resorts
- government investment in the tourism product from the 1960s such as new resorts of the Languedoc-Rousillon coast
- its strong image for food and wine
- its accommodation establishments and restaurants offer relatively good value (outside Paris!)
- effective marketing of the product by the government.

These factors also help to explain the country's high level of domestic tourism and the medium level of outbound tourism. However, there are other reasons. A high proportion of French people own second homes in their own country, which encourages them to take trips in their own country. Furthermore, while it could be seen as an issue of 'chicken or egg' the outbound tourism sector is not highly developed, which means foreign holidays remain quite expensive for French people. Furthermore, language problems further constrain their ability to take holidays abroad.

Germany

Conversely, in Germany, outbound tourism is very high, reflecting both the highly developed state of the economy and the statutory holiday entitlement enjoyed by employees, together with a lack of domestic attractions. The climate is not good for summer sun holidays and there is a lack of stylish coastal resorts and attractive cities. The same reasons also explain the medium only level of domestic tourism and the low inbound demand. For foreign tourists, Germany is also an expensive destination, again, reflecting the highly developed state of its economy.

Japan

Japan, perhaps surprisingly in view of the stereotypes of the Japanese tourist, generates, in reality, relatively low levels of outbound demand. This is largely the result of the high cost of living in Japan and the long hours worked there. Indeed, the Japanese government is so worried about the latter fact that they are now encouraging their citizens to take more holidays! The main segment which does travel from Japan are young women travelling together, the so-called 'office ladies', and other segments rarely found elsewhere such as the 'working soldiers'. As a developed economy, Japan has medium levels of domestic tourism but receives only a low level of inbound tourism. This may be due to its high cost of living, language difficulties or its isolation from traditional tourist trip generating countries. With the help of Asian tourist markets, which are actually closer to Japan in some cases, it might become more widely visited in the future.

The Netherlands

As an affluent country, the Netherlands generates large numbers of outbound tourist trips. Outbound tourism is also stimulated by the small size and lack of diversity of the Netherlands itself, which limits domestic tourism opportunities. The highly unbalanced nature of the Netherlands and its flat terrain leads Dutch people to seek foreign destinations that are more rural and hilly. They are major players in the camping and caravanning and eco-tourism markets. The lack of diversity and hills also reduces inbound tourism to the Netherlands, which is restricted to the city of Amsterdam and the bulb fields in spring.

Nigeria

As a developing country with a large population, Nigeria has a medium level of domestic tourism, largely related to visiting friends and relatives. Its relatively low level of economic development also resists outbound tourism although there is an annual inflow of Muslim pilgrims to Mecca and an inflow of business tourists. Because of its unstable political history and poor infrastructure, it also attracts relatively few tourists.

Russia

Domestic tourism in Russia is at the medium level reflecting the well-developed domestic tourism industry which grew up under Communism. Subsidized social tourism at Black Sea resorts created a large domestic market but this has shrunk since the end of Communism. Domestic tourism is probably lower than it was ten years ago because of the reduction in subsidies and the drastic reduction in the living standards of most Russians. Inbound tourism was always low because of political restrictions on such tourism, but it is now being constrained by political instability, crime and the weakening of the transport infrastructure. Outbound tourism is growing but is still restricted to a small wealthy elite. However, this small market is high spending and is very attractive, as shopping tourists and even second home owners travel to a variety of destinations from Benidorm to Cyprus, Dubai to New York.

Spain

Spain has a well-developed domestic tourism market based on the variety of attractions in the industry, both in the countryside and on the coast.

Family-owned second homes in the country also stimulate domestic tourism as does the large-scale provision of social tourism schemes in the country. The breadth of attractions also account for the high inbound tourism situation, albeit most of it gravitating to the coast. In recent years, the emphasis has switched to other aspects of the product, notably the cities and the coast. This began in 1992 with the Olympics in Barcelona, Madrid being designated as the European City of Culture, and Expo '92 in Seville. Spanish outbound tourism is still only at a medium level but is growing, particularly among young people who are travelling abroad for education and culture in ever greater numbers.

The USA

Finally, we turn to the USA, where domestic tourism is high owing to:

- range of attractions available and the diversity of its landscapes
- the well-developed transport infrastructure
- the highly developed tourism industry which is a world leader in theme parks, for example.

These same reasons attract a growing number of inbound tourists, from Europe and Asia, as well as from Canada. At the same time, outbound tourism from the USA is lower than one might expect, partly because of the attractions of holidaying at home.

However, the lack of outbound trips taken by American tourists also reflects other factors, such as:

- their general lack of skills in speaking foreign languages
- their fear of terrorist attacks
- the fact that many people in the USA are too poor to afford the cost of travelling outside the USA.

We can see therefore that the scale of domestic inbound and outbound tourism reflects a range of different factors – some general and some specific to particular countries.

Conclusions

It was expected that 1995 would signal a period of recovery for many of the world's leading economies, which in turn would lead to an increase in tourism. The recessionary tendencies have however persisted and increased levels of unemployment in many Organization for Economic Co-operation and Development (OECD) countries has meant that consumer confidence and spending on leisure travel has been slow to recover. The purchasing power of individual countries' currencies abroad also has a considerable effect on leisure travel. Germany and Japan both had disappointing economic performances, but the strength of their currencies means they will continue to experience large travel markets.

The largest growth in tourism in the next decade will originate from the emerging markets of Asia, rather than from the mature industrialized countries of the Western world.

We can consider the differences between countries to begin to understand the reasons for the variations. The French, for example, have a beautiful country with a favourable climate and well-developed infrastructure for tourism. They also have considerable variations in geographic and climatic conditions, so it is possible to ski and worship the sun in beautiful surroundings at different times of the year. These factors have encouraged the French to stay at home for holidays, which has meant that figures for outbound tourism are lower than for other industrialized countries.

The UK, in comparison, has experienced a long-term trend of high outbound tourism figures. Many factors have contributed to this – not least the poor summer weather that the UK traditionally experiences. The most important influence, however, on the growth of outbound travel, has been the development of the package holiday companies in the UK, over a long period of time. This has made the package holiday to sunny climes accessible to people from all social backgrounds.

This theme will be considered again in Chapter 15 when we consider whether there is a rise of the global/Euro tourist in the postmodern world.

Discussion points and essay questions

1 'The development of inbound tourism by a country is much more dependent on natural features than marketing activity' (Horner and Swarbrooke, 1996). Discuss this statement, with reference to individual countries.
2 Discuss the importance of the inclusive tour in the development of international tourism.
3 Explore the reasons for industrialized countries having different levels of inbound and outbound tourism.

Exercise

Select one of the countries of the world that is experiencing a growth in inbound and outbound tourism. Quantify the growth figures over the past ten years and suggest reasons for this trend.

The nature of demand in different segments of the tourism market

Until now, we have tended to focus on the traditional vacation as the core tourism product and the conventional holiday-maker as the tourist. However, we know that the tourism market is very diverse and the product far from homogenous. Therefore, in this chapter we will look at the nature of demand in a number of the different segments of the tourism market. This is not an attempt to produce a comprehensive typology of market segments in tourism but, rather, is to illustrate the diversity of market segments in tourism, which each have their own demand characteristics:

- family market
- hedonistic tourists
- the backpacker market
- visiting friends and relatives (VFR)
- excursionists or day-trippers
- educational tourists
- religious tourists
- the 'snowbird' market
- ethnic minority tourists
- tourists with disabilities
- social tourism
- the short-break market.

The family market

The first point to make is that the nature of the family varies dramatically from one country to another. In the USA and Northern Europe, the family usually means the 'nuclear family' with two parents and between one and three children. However, in Southern Europe, the Middle East and many Asian countries, there is the phenomenon of the 'extended family' with a higher number of children and the inclusion of other relatives in the holiday party and/or their involvement in the purchase decisions.

At the same time we must note that in the so-called developed world there is also the growing phenomenon of the single-parent family, where owing primarily to divorce, the family unit consists of one parent and the children.

However, in this section we will focus upon the nuclear family of Northern Europe. This segment represents the core market for many tour operators and types of products, including camping and caravanning trips, self-catering holidays and theme parks.

The core determinant in the family market is the existence of children. Many families choose holidays that meet the needs of their children. These needs will vary depending on the age of the children:

1 *Babies*. Here the need is to choose a holiday where the baby's safety and comfort will be the primary concern. This could mean avoiding countries with poor hygiene standards and choosing airlines and hotels which offer special services for babies such as free baby food.
2 *Infants*, from two to five years old, where a short journey to the destination can be a priority as the child may get bored on long journeys. Safety in this case may mean ensuring that young children who are keen to practise their walking cannot get into danger on balconies or near swimming pools.
3 *Early school-age children*, from around five to twelve years old, often want to play with children of a similar age and may be content with the simple pleasures of play areas and swimming pools.
4 *Teenagers*, aged from thirteen to eighteen, will usually want to be independent and enjoy more adult activities.

The point eventually comes when the young person wants to take a holiday separately from their parents. This could take the form of:

- an educational trip organized by their school
- an organized children's camp such as BUNAC or Camp America
- an activity-based trip such as a PGL canoeing holiday in the UK or a farm-based vacation, for example, the Gîtes d'Enfants in France
- a single-sex group holiday with a group of friends.

On the other hand, many children may continue into early adult life to take at least some holidays with their parents, particularly if they cannot afford a holiday because they are on a low income.

The number of children in a family also has an impact on demand. Families with several children may need to look for an economically priced holiday owing to the high cost of raising children. This explains why they are a major component of the market for camping and caravanning holidays, for example.

The preference of many families for self-catering holidays is partly explained by the desire to minimize holiday costs. However, it is also a result of the desire of some families not to be bound by the formality and etiquette involved in staying in a hotel and eating at particular times. Children tend not to fit well into such rigid regimes and self-catering has the advantage of being less regimented.

The tourism industry works hard to attract the lucrative family market, particularly through discounts for children and free child places. However, often, such offers are of little value to single-parent families as they are usually based on the stereotypical nuclear family of two adults and several children. Thus, the industry is failing fully to come to terms with a rapidly growing variation in the traditional family market.

Hedonistic tourists

A very different market is that of the hedonistic tourist, the pleasure-seeker. This market is traditionally associated with younger people and brand names such as Club 18–30 in the UK. It is a development of the original four Ss concept of sun, sand, sea and sex tourism, with perhaps the addition of the fifth 'S' of sangria to represent the consumption of alcohol.

Increasingly the hedonistic tourist in recent years has also driven the growth of a distinctive style of nightlife and partying in destinations like Ibiza. For the hedonistic tourist, the main motivator is the desire for physical pleasure and social life. At the same time there is a fashion dimension with different resorts coming in and out of fashion, depending on the perceived quality of the local nightlife.

The hedonistic tourist's day often looks very different to that of the family on holiday we have just been considering. They tend to wake late and then spend their time round the swimming pool or on the beach. They will then usually go out partying and not get to bed until the following morning.

Hedonistic tourists often travel in single-sex groups of friends and prefer the freedom and economy offered by simple, self-catering accommodation. This phenomenon of hedonistic tourism is particularly associated with Northern Europe and has been criticized on two main grounds:

- the heavy drinking can lead to fights and problematic relations with the local host community – the so-called 'lager lout' phenomena
- the fear that much of the casual sex on such holidays is unprotected and therefore carries the risk of spreading HIV or AIDS.

However, we should note that hedonistic tourism is not a new phenomenon in tourism. As we saw in Chapter 3, the Romans visited spas for largely hedonistic reasons, and in the late nineteenth century and early twentieth century young men travelled to Paris to gamble and visit brothels. The only difference, really, is that modern hedonistic tourism is a mass market and the tourism industry promotes this form of tourism overtly, as in the Club 18–30 advertising campaigns of the mid-1990s onwards.

There are some forms of 'hedonistic' tourism, on the other hand, which are either illicit or illegal, notably the phenomenon of sex tourism in destinations like Bangkok and the Philippines. Increasingly children are being drawn into this activity. The key difference, of course, with the hedonistic tourism we discussed earlier is that in this case payment may be involved and one of the partners may well be an unwilling participant. The main sex tourism client tends to be male and older than the 'sun, sea, sand, sex and sangria' tourist we discussed above. They can be of any nationality but this market appears to be well developed in Japan and Northern Europe. However, in countries such as Australia and Sweden it is illegal for residents to take sex tourism trips. This is an example of governments regulating tourist behaviour and it demonstrates that the old marketing cliché of 'the customer is always right' is wrong!

The backpacker market

Another form of tourism which appears to appeal mainly to a younger market is backpacking, whereby tourists use a rucksack or backpack rather than a suitcase to carry all they need for their trip. However, the term has come to signify more than simply the type of luggage used by this type of tourist. It also implies:

- independent rather than packaged travel
- a desire to keep expenditure to a minimum
- a tendency to try to get off the beaten tourist track
- a trip that might extend beyond the usual duration of one to two weeks of a normal holiday.

This latter point is very important because it is linked to the fact that most backpackers are usually students, who have long vacations. Or it can involve people taking a year out from education before they begin college or taking a year out after completing a college course. It is therefore a form of travel based on the idea of spending a longer period over a vacation than is the norm for most people.

Backpacking is a truly international market that is popular with young people from every developed country, particularly the USA, the UK, the Netherlands, Germany, Australia and Japan. It could be argued that this is an early example of the truly global tourist, for the behaviour of backpackers tends to be similar regardless of their nationality. This is partly because backpacking has its own parallel travel media consisting of guides such as the 'Lonely Planet' and 'Rough Guide' series. These tourists read the same guides and therefore often stay in the same accommodation and visit the same attractions.

Backpacking is very popular currently in long-haul destinations such as South East Asia and South America. Within Europe there is the well-known phenomenon of the 'inter-railer', backpackers who travel across Europe by rail, utilizing discounted rail-fare packages offered to young people.

Backpacking is likely to grow as the numbers of students around the world grow. However, it is unlikely to become popular with other groups in society because there seems no prospect of most people in employment gaining much more paid holiday. However, it could begin to appeal more to early retired people who have the time and want to be a little more adventurous in their holiday-making activities.

Visiting friends and relatives (VFR)

The VFR market is one for which there is little reliable data. Because such people do not stay in commercial accommodation and are usually domestic tourists, they are rarely recorded by tourism statisticians. While this market is of no real interest to the accommodation sector it is very important for the visitor attraction market. Friends and relatives usually feel obliged to take their visitors out during their stay, which brings business for local attractions.

For some people, particularly those on lower incomes, visiting friends and relatives can be an inexpensive alternative to a normal holiday.

The VFR market clearly involves a strong social motivation or it can be driven by a sense of family duty. Visiting friends and relatives tourism can also be related to more formal occasions such as weddings and funerals.

Students tend to be heavily involved in the VFR market in two main ways:

1 They make many new friends at college who they may visit during their vacation and/or after their course has ended.
2 They are visited by their parents in most cases and feel obliged to show them around the area.

Although most VFR tourism is domestic, there is an international dimension. This is particularly the case in relation to people whose relatives have emigrated to another country. Some notable tourist flows as a result of this phenomenon are:

• Turkish workers travelling home from Germany to Turkey and their relatives visiting them in Turkey

- relatives travelling between the UK and India or Pakistan
- British people travelling to visit relatives in Australia and New Zealand
- tourist flows between North African countries and France.

Visiting friends and family, notably the latter, is particularly highly developed in Middle Eastern and Asian countries, where the extended family is the norm.

In Europe the VFR market is also being driven up by the huge increase in second home purchases by British people and other Northern Europeans. They are then inviting their friends and relatives to join them at their second homes for their holidays. Also we have more people retiring to a foreign country and, again, inviting their friends and relatives to visit them.

Excursionists and day-trippers

The day tripper or excursionist is generally a domestic tourist and is the core market for most visitor attractions, many seaside resorts and some rural areas.

In general, the excursionist does not wish to travel too far, given that they only have one day or less available for their leisure activities. This often results in the day-trip market for an attraction being limited to those who live within one and a half hours' driving time, although in larger countries such as the USA excursionists may be willing to travel further than this for a day-trip. While the duration of a trip is generally the whole day, they can be as short as three to four hours.

Some day-trips require preplanning and booking but the majority do not. They can therefore be a spontaneous decision. Day-trippers have a spare day and will decide in the morning where to go. Their decision may well be influenced by the weather. If it is sunny a theme park trip might be selected, while rain could well result in the selection of an indoor attraction such as a museum.

The day-trip market is largely a car-based market, although coach excursions also play a significant role in the market, particularly among other day-trippers. Day trippers are also major consumers of food and drink services and tend to make considerable use of leisure shopping facilities.

While day-trips are normally domestic, they can be international. For example, shopping trips by Britons to France and Malaysian people to Singapore. At the same time, there has been a growth in longer-distance trips. For example, UK tour operators currently offer winter season day-trips by air from UK airports to destinations such as Paris, Prague and Reykjavik from £99 upwards. Tourists can even take a ten-hour trip to Tromso, beyond the Arctic Circle, from Heathrow airport, for around £200.

Educational tourists

There has been a massive growth in the broad field of educational tourism in recent years. This has been fuelled by both the growth in higher and further education worldwide and the desire of many older tourists to learn something new during their annual vacation.

Travelling for education is not a new phenomenon. In the UK in the seventeenth and eighteenth centuries, the sons of the aristocracy undertook the 'Grand Tour' to complete their education. Since the 1980s, in Europe, there has also been a growth in school student exchange schemes.

Educational tourism today has a number of dimensions, including:

1 Student exchanges between universities where students may travel for periods ranging from two or three months to a year. In some cases, in Europe, these have been subsidized by European Union initiatives such as the ERASMUS and SOCRATES programmes.
2 Young people attending language classes in a foreign country, which can last from a week to several months. Part of these courses may be trips to see local attractions and students may well live with local families for the duration of their course.
3 Themed holidays where tourists travel with like-minded people to pursue a common interest which could be archaeology, a foreign culture, painting or cooking.

In the first two cases the consumer, i.e. the tourist, may not be the actual customer who makes the decision or pays the bill. In these cases, the customer might be the college or the parents.

Religious tourists

Religious tourism is one of the oldest forms of tourism. It is unique, perhaps, in that it is driven by a sense of duty and obligation rather than a search for pleasure and leisure.

The Haj pilgrimage by Muslims to Mecca in Saudi Arabia, is undoubtedly the greatest single flow of religious tourists in the world today. It is estimated that in 1996, around 200 000 Muslims made this pilgrimage from Indonesia alone! Every able-bodied Muslim with the financial means is expected to make this pilgrimage at least once during their lifetime. The Haj takes place during a set period each year, namely, the twelfth month of the Islamic calendar. However, there are pilgrimages which can take place at any time of the year such as Umroh.

The Christian pilgrimage phenomenon inspired classic literature such as Chaucer's Canterbury Tales. However it is now much less important than it once was owing to the decline in the number of active worshippers, particularly in Europe. However, there are still pilgrimages to Rome, Jerusalem, Santiago de Compstella and Lourdes.

Pilgrimages and visits to holy sites are also a major motivator of religious tourism trips for Hindus and other religions.

In general, the phenomenon of the pilgrimage is a highly restricted market, being only available to believers in a particular faith. However the traditional infrastructure of religious tourism has also become an attraction for the non-religious tourist, most notably visiting cathedrals and churches.

At the same time, owing to the growing pressures of life, many non-believers are taking short trips to religious establishments for relaxation and spiritual enlightenment. For instance, men (only) can visit Orthodox Greek monasteries in Mount Athos in Greece, for a short period, free of charge, providing they abide by the regime of the monastery.

The 'snowbird' market

The first international mass tourism market was based on the 'summer sun' holiday, where Northern Europeans travelled to Southern Europe in the summer to get a suntan. One of the latest major growth markets in the USA and Northern Europe is also inspired by climatic motivators. In the USA this involves 'snowbirds' from the cold, snowy Northern States of the USA travelling to Southern States such as Florida and California for their mild winter climates. In Northern Europe it involves people travelling to Southern European destinations to escape the winter climate at home.

On both continents this phenomena has two interrelated characteristics:

1 The trips are of long duration, from four weeks to four months.
2 They are normally taken by retired people who have the time to take such a long vacation.

The motivations of older people to take such trips are not so much related to the desire to get a suntan but, rather, by a wish to:

- escape the cold weather in their own state/country
- reduce their expenditure on heating at home
- improve their health given that they may suffer from illnesses like arthritis which may be exacerbated by the damp, cold weather in their home state/country
- make new friends and have a less lonely life than they might in their own community.

Ethnic minority tourists

Many countries contain ethnic minority communities, many of which may have been in the country for generations. Often people in these communities will have maintained contact with their original country, and will have their own patterns of tourism and tourism infrastructure.

In many developed countries few people from ethnic minorities are regular purchasers of the products of the mainstream tourism industry. Few of the customers of the major UK tour operators, for example, come from the Asian, Afro-Caribbean or Chinese communities.

However, that is not to say that many people from ethnic minority groups are not making leisure trips; as we saw in the section on VFR tourists. In some cases, though, lack of disposable income in ethnic minority groups, which suffer above average rates of unemployment, is probably a factor in the low take-up of the holidays offered by tour operators.

Nevertheless, as yet it is only really in the USA, in the case of the Black American market that an outbound and domestic distinctive ethnic market has developed, served by specialist travel agents. What is more, this parallel market relates to both leisure tourism and business tourism. In the latter case there is, for instance, an organization of black convention organizers.

It remains to be seen whether, as ethnic minority communities grow in various countries, and become more integrated and gain greater economic power, they will enter the mainstream market or represent a parallel marketplace.

Tourists with disabilities

One of the most controversial areas within tourism is the issue of tourists with disabilities and their opportunities to take tourist trips. In many cases tourists with disabilities are denied equal access to tourist products.

However, we need to recognize that there are many kinds of disability and degrees of disability, including:

- mobility problems, ranging from elderly people who may have difficulty climbing stairs to people who are confined to a wheelchair
- sight difficulties ranging from minor impairment to a complete lack of vision
- hearing difficulties, ranging from minor impairment to complete hearing loss

These are the most widely recognized disabilities which affect travel, but there are many others.

Clearly, the needs of such tourists may dictate every aspect of their holiday choice and may even determine whether they are able to take a holiday at all. The situation is further complicated if their condition is such that they need someone to accompany them, for this person may not be easy to find, and will normally have to pay as much as the traveller with disabilities.

It has to be recognized that the situation for travellers with disabilities varies from country to country, being more sympathetic in the USA and Scandinavia than in most other countries. An American person with disabilities wishing to travel to Scandinavia, for example, should be able to do so with the minimum of inconvenience. However, a Greek or Turkish traveller with disabilities wishing to visit South America may find it an impossible dream.

Social tourism

Social tourism is a largely European phenomenon that is based on the idea that tourism is a social right of the citizen and/or tourism brings social benefits to the individual, so that some form of subsidy or state support is justified.

In the current climate of deregulation, privatization and reduced public expenditure in Europe, social tourism is under threat. Nevertheless, it is still significant in countries such as Germany, France and Spain. It takes a number of forms, including:

- subsidized visits to health spas for people with particular illnesses, in France
- the state and employer supported Chèques Vacances scheme in France which helps workers on lower incomes to be able to afford to take a holiday
- non-profit-making holiday centres owned and operated by trade unions or voluntary sector organizations in a wide range of European countries, notably in Germany, France, or Spain.

Social tourism reached its peak, perhaps, in the former Soviet Union, where it encompassed every worker and was the core of the Soviet domestic tourism industry. It also had an international dimension within the old Eastern bloc nations, where tourists used subsidized resort facilities and accommodation in other Eastern European countries.

The short-break market

The growth of the five-day week with a full two-day weekend, and the rise of car ownership and faster aircraft, have helped stimulate the development of the short weekend break market since the 1960s in the developed world. It is also now a growing phenomenon in the newly developing economies of Asia. In most cases, the short break is an additional holiday rather than a substitute for the main annual holiday.

Short breaks exist in a number of forms, including:

- romantic weekends for a couple in a city such as Rome or Paris, or for an American couple in an old New England inn
- shopping trips, for example, a group of women friends in the UK going to London or a party of Russian tourists flying to Paris to buy luxury goods or a visit to Indonesia by a group of Singaporean tourists who want to buy authentic craft products
- visiting friends and relatives trips

- health farm or health spa breaks, designed to relieve stress or improve the health of the tourist
- special interest and activity breaks such as fishing trips, painting, horse-riding or golf
- breaks built around a special event whether it be a theatre performance or a football match
- unwinding, relaxing breaks in country house hotels in the UK or Gîtes d'Interludes in France, for example.

While not comprehensive, this list of types of breaks illustrates that they are both domestic and international. One of the fastest growing sectors in tourism is the international city-break market. Furthermore, tourists are prepared to travel further and further for a short break. In 2004–05, breaks of four and five nights were being offered by UK tour operators to Montreal, Dubai, Cape Town or even Hong Kong!

Although it is difficult to generalize, short breaks tend to be either:

- planned and booked well in advance, to heighten the sense of anticipation, or
- purchased at the last minute as a reaction to stress or a particularly difficult week at work or as a spontaneous celebration of a happy event or good news.

In the developed world, the short break is likely to grow in importance as work pressures arising from the competitive situation in all industries increase.

Conclusions

We have seen that there are a number of different sub-markets within tourism, some of which are interrelated. For example, the VFR phenomenon is a submarket but it is often also a form of short break market. Furthermore, it is a significant element of the day-trip market when the VFR tourist is taken to visitor attractions by their hosts. It would have been possible to identify a number of other such submarkets.

For tourism marketers it is important to realize that the tourism market is not a homogenous whole but rather a collection of overlapping submarkets each with their own characteristics.

Discussion points and essay questions

1 Discuss the likely problems that might arise from the presence at the same time in a resort, of both hedonistic tourists and families.
2 Evaluate which sectors of tourism benefit most *and* least from *both* VFR tourists and backpackers.
3 Explore the possible motivators and determinants of a day trip to an art gallery *and* a seaside resort *and* a craft workshop.

Exercise

Make contact with a local or national group which represents people with any type of disability. Ask them what difficulties their members experience, as a result of their disability, when they are choosing and taking a holiday. Finally, suggest what the tourism industry could do to make it easier and more enjoyable for their members to take a holiday.

Consumer behaviour and markets in the different sectors of tourism

Introduction

One of the problems of writing a book on consumer behaviour in tourism is that tourism is not a single homogenous activity or market. It is a complex web of interrelated sectors each of which has its own characteristics in terms of consumer behaviour. In this chapter we endeavour to demonstrate the diversity of forms of consumer behaviour and markets found within tourism.

Before we go any further we must stress that in this chapter we are concerned with the behaviour of the tourists who are the final consumers of the various markets and consumer organizations. However, within the complex structure outlined in Figure 11.1 it is clear that there are other producer–customer relationships, namely, those between suppliers and producers and producers and intermediaries. This is true, for example, of the vitally important relationship between hoteliers (supplier) and tour operators (customer) and between airlines (customer) and travel agents (intermediary).

We should also point out that most of this chapter is concerned with leisure tourism, but we should not ignore the massively important 'parallel world' of business tourism.

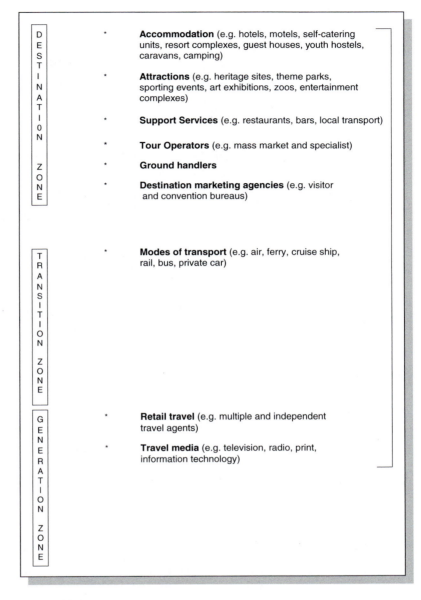

Figure 11.1
The sectors of tourism

Later in this chapter, therefore, we devote some space to discussing the unique nature of consumer behaviour in business tourism.

Finally, by way of introductory comments, it is clear that, in addition to differences between behaviour in different sectors, there are also significant differences within sectors. Towards the end of this chapter we illustrate this point through examples drawn from the tour operations and accommodation sectors.

We now look at some of the different sectors of tourism in terms of differences and similarities in relation to several key demand characteristics.

Factors taken into account when making a purchase decision

Price, in almost all cases, seems to be a constant factor regardless of which sector of tourism we consider. Location is another standard factor, whether we are talking about the area of a city in which a hotel is located, the departure airport offered by tour operator or how far an attraction is from the visitor's home. We can also assume that the tourist's previous experience of an organization's services and the reputation of the organization will also be relevant to purchase decisions in all sectors of tourism.

By contrast, there are also some differences, for example:

- safety is a major issue for choosing airlines in some parts of the world, or selecting a holiday destination, but would rarely be an explicit factor taken into account when choosing a hotel
- fashionability can be a major consideration when choosing a holiday destination, but is rarely relevant when choosing airlines or accommodation units.

Seasonality

Most sectors have peak and off-peak seasons, although these differ from one country to another. Often peak seasons will be the same for different sectors in any particular country. School holidays will usually be the peak time of demand for tour operators, charter airlines and visitor attractions. However, for city-centre hotels and scheduled airlines school holidays are their off-peak season, because that is when business people usually take their holidays with their families.

Distance travelled to use tourism product and services

Owing to the nature of the tourism product, tourists always have to travel to the location where the tourism product or service is delivered. This distance can vary from a few hundred metres in the case of travel agent to hundreds of kilometres in the case of a hotel bed.

Frequency of purchase

We might find that in the UK, for instance, the average person makes the following number of purchases of different tourism products in a typical year.

- twelve visitor attractions (two museums, a zoo, two theme parks, two historic houses, a factory shop, an art gallery, two festivals or

special events, and a waterfront development like the Albert Dock, in Liverpool)
- two inclusive tours offered by a tour operator (a summer sun two-week package and an off-peak weekend city break)
- one airline seat purchased independently not as part of a package holiday (a flight to visit a relative in the USA)
- one accommodation purchased independently not as part of a package holiday (hotel stopover on the way to a family wedding in another part of the country
- four retail travel outlet (to book the holidays, plus an air ticket, and a hotel).

Methods of segmenting the market

In most sections of tourism there are some common methods of segmenting the market which appear to work well. These include:

- geographical (where consumers live)
- demographic (age, sex and family status)
- business versus leisure travellers
- frequent travellers versus infrequent travellers
- independent tourists versus organized groups.

Alternatively, there seem to be a few approaches to segmentation which appear largely to be applicable to one sector only. For example, in the visitor attraction sector, the tourists' personality can be an important way of segmenting the market. Introvert, studious people may prefer to visit museums while extrovert adventurous risk-takers may form the core of the market for theme parks where 'white-knuckle rides' are the main attraction.

Price paid for the product or service

The products offered by tourism organizations vary dramatically in price. The typical range of prices for the products of different sectors is as follows:

- destinations – usually no direct fee or price is paid by the tourist to enter a destination
- retail travel – no direct price is charged to the customer although the retail travel outlet receives from the tour operator a proportion of the price paid by the tourist, as commission
- visitor attractions – many are free but even the most expensive rarely charge more than £20 for admission
- restaurants – meals can vary in price, from £1 to over £100
- accommodation – can be free (e.g. monasteries) or around £10 per night (youth hostels) at one extreme or, at the other end of the spectrum, a luxury hotel or resort could charge several thousand pounds per night

- transport – coach fares can cost as little as £5 to £10, while long-distance journeys first class by air cost thousands of pounds
- tour operators – weekend breaks, self-catering holidays, and last-minute discounted holidays can cost less than £100 per person, while a fully inclusive escorted tour around the world may cost over £10 000.

Clearly the price charged also varies dramatically between countries. One night in a hotel room in a good quality hotel may cost more than £150 in Hong Kong, £150 in France, but only £50 in Thailand.

Methods of booking or reserving

In the visitor attraction sector, pre-booking is rare, whereas in sectors such as airlines, hardly anyone would consider not pre-booking and just turning up at an airport in the hope that a seat will be available to their chosen destination. The accommodation sector falls somewhere between these two extremes in that some people pre-book while others wait until they arrive in a place and then walk around to find a suitable hotel.

Where pre-booking is the norm, the choice is between using intermediaries or agents, or booking directly with the producer. Most of the products of tour operators are sold via intermediaries, as are the majority of flights and ferry trips. However, the trend in all sectors seems to be towards direct booking.

So as we can see, there are both similarities and significant differences between the sectors of tourism in terms of aspects of consumer behaviour.

Special cases

The picture presented so far is very generalized and there are three special cases which we will discuss next:

- retail travel
- destinations
- business tourism.

Retail travel

Retail travel is a unique sector in tourism in that it does not have a product of its own. Instead it exists to provide a service, namely, giving consumers access to the products of the other sectors of tourism.

Its different function in the tourism system means that it differs from the demand for other sectors in a number of respects. For example, the peak season is not when people travel but, rather, when they book their trips. In the UK, for example, this can mean the period immediately after Christmas when many people book their summer holidays.

Destinations

From consumers' point of view, it is perhaps better to see the destination as a do-it-yourself (DIY) kit, rather than as a finished product. It offers tourists a range of opportunities from which they can produce their own product or experience. The choice of possible permutations are virtually limitless, subject only to constraints such as money, and information, and tourists can use the destination in many different ways. This is illustrated in Figure 11.2, where we look at how different tourists might use the destination of Crete.

The varying ways in which different tourists will use the same destination will depend on the characteristics of these tourists, for example, their age, sex, past experience, hobbies and interests, lifestyle and personality.

Finally, as we noted earlier, destinations are also unique among the sectors of tourism, in that no direct charge is made for using them. It is possible for tourists to use a range of services, for example, beaches, parties and free museums, without incurring any expenditure. They can also window-shop and enjoy walking around historic streets absolutely free of charge.

Tourist A.	Stays in a large modern resort hotel, in a quiet resort, eats in the hotel, and spends most of the day sun-bathing by the hotel pool, and then drinking in the hotel bar at night.
Tourist B.	Stays in a simple apartment complex on the coast, wakes late, sunbathes and then goes partying in the night-clubs of Aghios Nikolaos in the evening.
Tourist C.	Makes their base in a small traditional pension, relaxes over long meals in local tavernas and attempts to make contact with Cretan people.
Tourist D.	Uses a modern resort hotel as a base, but spends all day visiting cultural sites including the Temple at Knossos and the archaeological museum in Heraklion
Tourist E.	Stays in the cheapest accommodation they can find because they want to spend all their time and money indulging their interest in watersports such as diving and windsurfing.
Tourist F.	Tours Crete by hire car, staying a few nights in each place they like the look of; they have no pre-planned itinerary.
Tourist G.	Takes a cruise around the Mediterranean which includes a one-day port call to Heraklion and an optional excursion to the Samarian Gorge.

Figure 11.2
Different potential uses of Crete as a destination

The parallel world of business travel

Business tourism is a very different activity to leisure tourism and the business traveller is a fundamentally different consumer to the leisure traveller. The world of business tourism exists in parallel to that of leisure tourism. Sometimes business tourists use similar services to leisure tourists, such as hotel bedrooms and airline seats. At other times they use services which are uniquely offered to business travellers, such as convention centres. Even where they use the same hotels and airlines as leisure tourists, special provision may be made to meet business travellers' needs, such as in-bedroom computer access points in hotels and onboard fax machines on aircraft. They also have their own infrastructure of business travel agents and incentive travel organizations.

Figure 11.3 illustrates the differences between consumer behaviour in business tourism and leisure tourism. The first item in this figure

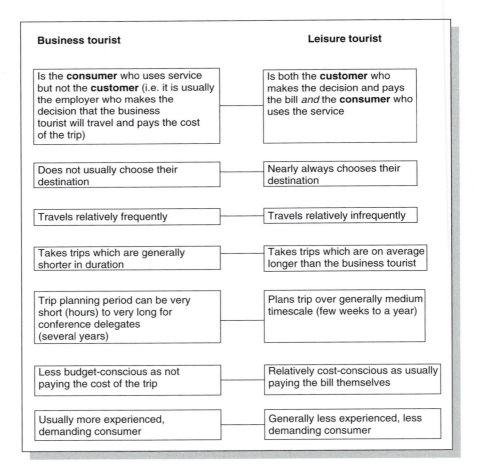

Figure 11.3
Differences in consumer behaviour between business tourists and leisure tourists

is particularly important because in recent years there has been tension in the relationship among employers (customers), business travellers (consumers) and the tourism industry, most notably airlines. Companies looking to reduce their travel budgets and arrange them more effectively have often been irritated to see airlines offering their employees who travel on business, perks such as Air Miles. The companies believe that as the customer who pays the bill, it is they who should receive any benefit that may be offered by airlines. Many of them would prefer lower fares instead of perks for their employees.

Taking the final element in Figure 11.3 further, the expectations of business tourists tend to be higher than the average leisure traveller. This may be because:

- they are more experienced travellers and therefore have a more comprehensive understanding of general standards in the tourism industry, against which to judge the performance of an individual tourism organization
- they are often travelling on a higher daily budget than the average leisure traveller
- the airlines and hotel sectors have recognized the lucrative nature of the business tourist and have therefore focused their promotional efforts on impressing the business tourist, thus raising their expectations.

However, before we take this point too far let us remember that many leisure tourists today are also business tourists in their working lives. This brings us to a further interesting point, namely the links which exist between business tourism and leisure tourism, in terms of consumer behaviour. These include the following four examples:

1 When the working day is over the business tourist becomes a leisure tourist, eating out in restaurants, drinking in bars and watching entertainment performances.
2 Conference programmes often have social programmes for delegates, which will probably feature attractions that are predominantly aimed at leisure tourists such as folklore shows and museums.
3 When business tourists have finished the business they have to conduct, they may choose to stay on for a few days as a leisure tourist. This is more likely to be the case if the destination is a long way from their home or is a well-known leisure tourism destination. They may well use this extra time to take 'add-on' trips. For instance, a trip to mainland China could be added on to a business trip to Hong Kong island.
4 Business tourists may take their partner with them; while they are working, their partner will be behaving as a leisure tourist.

Finally, we should note that in the longer term the demand for business travel may decline as the need for trips is substituted by the use of communication technologies such as video-conferencing. The market for training courses that involve students or tutors travelling to meet each other could also be reduced by the development of virtual reality simulations, which allow training to be conducted at the trainee's usual place of work. This is already playing a part in the training of surgeons in new techniques.

However, it seems likely that there will be business tourism for the foreseeable future, for as long as personal face-to-face contact is either thought to be essential or desirable.

Differences within individual sectors of tourism

In this chapter, we have focused on similarities and differences in consumer behaviour between the different sectors of tourism. However, it would be wrong not to look at the differences in behaviour which can exist within the same sector. We will illustrate this point through four examples drawn from the accommodation and tour operation sectors respectively.

Luxury hotels and budget motels

There are clearly different motivators for guests at five-star hotels than would be the case for budget motels. The luxury hotel client seeks a special experience, status and a high level of personal service. The budget motel user is motivated by a desire for a functional experience, a convenient location and economy.

Serviced and non-serviced accommodation units

Consumers who prefer to use non-serviced or self-catering accommodation for their holidays may well make this choice because they:

- have children and find self-catering more flexible than staying in hotels
- are on a limited budget and by taking food with them, or buying cheaply from local supermarkets, they should be able to enjoy a holiday in the same destination at a lower cost than would be the case if they were to stay in a hotel
- prefer to buy and cook fresh local food products rather than eat hotel meals, based on imported ingredients and international menus
- could be suspicious of hygiene standards in the local hospitality industry.

Mass-market and specialist tour operators

Tourists who buy mass-market package tours and those buying the products offered by specialist operators are often seeking different benefits from their purchase. The mass-market customer may well be motivated by a desire for:

- a low-cost product
- visiting destinations which are clearly popular and have a well-developed infrastructure for tourists
- the company of other tourists
- a more passive, resort-based holiday.

Conversely, the tourist who buys a specialist tour operator's package may well be motivated by their wish to:

- appear to be a sophisticated consumer
- pursue a particular personal interest whether it be a sport like diving or a hobby like bird-watching
- visit less popular destinations that are 'off the beaten track'
- mix with relatively few other tourists.

Long-term plans and last-minute purchases

The tour-operating field also sees significant differences in consumer behaviour in terms of when people plan and book their holidays. Some customers like to plan and book their holiday months before they travel. This might be because they fear that if they do not they might not find the exact product or be able to arrange the itinerary, they want. Therefore, this type of behaviour is more commonly found among tourists who wish to take more unusual or exotic holidays or have definite views on which accommodation establishment they wish to use.

Other tourists prefer not to plan or book their vacation trip until very late, perhaps a few days before their departure. This could be for a number of reasons, for example:

- a belief that they may be able to take advantage of last-minute discounting by tour operators
- the excitement of making a late decision in that one does not know one's destination until the last minute
- a late unforeseen opportunity to take time off work.

Commonly, last-minute purchase is associated with consumers who are less concerned with where they go and specific hotels, than with price and departure dates.

Conclusions

We have seen that there are similarities and differences in demand characteristics between the different sectors of tourism. However, as we have just seen, there are also significant differences within individual sectors of tourism.

Finally, it is important to recognize that there are differences in the structure and nature of tourism industries in different countries, so some of the points made in this chapter would vary in their application dependent on the country being visited.

Discussion points and essay questions

1 Discuss the marketing implications of the differences between business tourism and leisure tourism, for airlines and hotel chains.
2 Compare and contrast the main ways of segmenting the market in the different sectors of tourism.
3 Examine the differences in consumer behaviour within an individual sector of tourism of your choice.

Exercise

Design and conduct a small survey of tourists to identify similarities and differences in the way they purchase:

- accommodation services
- package holidays
- visits to attractions.

PART 5

Consumer Behaviour and Marketing

Clearly, consumer behaviour in tourism is a subject worthy of academic study in its own right. However, it is also a matter of growing interest to tourism practitioners as organizations seek to keep ahead of changes in consumer tastes so that they can ensure they offer what the customer wants. Modern tourism marketing, we are told, must be customer centred if it is to be successful.

In this part, therefore, we briefly explore two of the most important areas in which consumer behaviour and marketing are linked together:

- Chapter 12 discusses the applied side of consumer behaviour research, in other words, marketing research
- Chapter 13 covers the relationship between the marketing mix, or four Ps, and consumer behaviour in tourism. This means looking at how tourism organizations might manipulate their product, price, place and promotion to reflect the characteristics and desires of their customers.

Researching tourist behaviour: marketing research

Most tourism practitioners and students will be aware of the lack of reliable, up-to-date statistics for tourism in most countries of the world. We seem to know even less about why tourists do what they do or, alternatively, do not do what the industry would like them to do. Yet, we are talking about arguably the world's largest industry and the mainstay of many national economies across the globe. At the same time, modern marketing is predicated on the idea that knowing your customers, and then anticipating and meeting their needs, is the key to success.

There seems to be an apparent contradiction here in that we know how important consumer behaviour research is for the tourism industry but we are not doing as much of it as we should. Is this because we are ignoring this issue or is it a reflection of how difficult it is to carry out consumer research in the tourism field.

In this chapter, we look at:

- the data on consumer behaviour, both qualitative and quantitative, which tourism marketers require
- the problems involved in collecting and interpreting this data.

In this chapter, we are focusing on marketing research rather than market research. Marketing research is the collection of data with the single intention of using it to make an organization's marketing activities more effective. In other words, in contrast to market research, it is applied, action-based research.

The tourism industry needs research data for a variety of purposes. It helps to:

- identify opportunities for product development
- set prices in relation to those of competitors and to what consumers are willing to pay
- ensure that the distribution network is working effectively
- select the best combination of promotional techniques and the most appropriate advertising media
- subdivide the total market into segments which can be targeted by the organization
- make adjustments to customer service in the light of customer comments
- review and change brands and logos
- make decisions about investment in new facilities
- choose locations for new hotels and theme parks, for instance
- suggest opportunities for diversification.

Tourism organizations require a wide variety of data on tourist behaviour, both qualitative and quantitative, including the following:

1 *Statistical profiles of tourists.* Many research projects collect information on the profile of tourists visiting everything from a country to a visitor attraction, over a particular period. This data might typically include:
   (a) the age and sex of tourists
   (b) their stage in the family life cycle
   (c) where they live
   (d) their occupation and income.
2 *Statistical records of tourist behaviour.* Here we are concerned with data about:
   (a) where tourists like their holidays
   (b) at what time of the year people take their main vacation
   (c) how much they spend on their holiday
   (d) how many trips they take each year.
3 *How tourists make purchasing decisions.* We saw in Chapter 6 that the process by which tourists make purchase decisions is very complex. It is clear that the process is different for each tourist, as are the motivators and determinants which shape the final decision.
4 *Who makes the purchase decision.* Within a family or group who are travelling together, marketers need to know who makes the decision so that they know whom they should target with their promotional messages.
5 *When the purchase decision is made.* This too is important because it should influence when a tourism organization plans its promotional campaigns. An organization needs to know at what time of the year most decisions about the main holiday are taken and

how far ahead of taking the holiday, purchase decisions are made.

6 *Consumer perceptions*. It is tourists' perceptions that really matter because it is these perceptions which determine their actual behaviour. Organizations, therefore, need to understand consumer's perceptions about individual products, destinations, types of holiday and particular tourism organizations. When interpreting these perceptions it is important to recognize that perceptions are often based on factors which are beyond the control of tourism organizations. At the same time, the perceptions can often be based on an old experience which is no longer relevant to the reality of the current situation.

7 *Tourist satisfaction*. Chapter 17 explores the complexities of measuring tourist satisfaction. However it is clear that the industry must understand what determines whether or not customers will be satisfied with the products it offers. We need longitudinal research which helps us to see how the expectations of tourists rise over time so that we can keep ahead of those expectations.

8 *The identification of trends in tourist behaviour*. We need to be able to identify trends in tourist demands so that tourism organizations can anticipate them and develop new products accordingly.

9 *Segmentation criteria*. As more organizations adopt the technique of segmentation there is a great need for research that identifies the characteristics of different segments, and allows organizations to place individual tourists into the appropriate segments.

10 *Product positioning in relation to competitors*. We need to know how tourists perceive the similar product of different organizations and how they decide which one to purchase.

11 *The attitude of non-users*. It is important, if an organization is to gain new customers, that it knows why tourists are not currently purchasing its products. It can then try to attract some of these people by modifying its product range.

12 *Cultural and national differences in tourist behaviour*. At a time when more tourism organizations are seeking to sell their products internationally, it is vital that we understand cultural and national differences in marketing and tourist behaviour. There are two types of differences:

   (a) 'hard' differences such as variations in the main holiday season dates
   (b) 'soft' differences such as attitudes towards service and the desire for particular types of facilities.

   This issue is dealt with in Chapter 9.

13 *The link between the consumer behaviour of tourists and their purchase of other products*. People do not buy vacations in isolation from how they purchase other products. They are an extension of people's everyday lifestyles. A knowledge of this link helps tourism organizations to plan joint promotions, for instance those between a supermarket and an airline.

There are clearly many different types of qualitative and quantitative data required by tourist organizations.

Current weaknesses in consumer behaviour research in tourism

While there have been improvements in recent years, there are still some general weaknesses in consumer behaviour research in tourism. Some of the major weaknesses are illustrated in Figure 12.1.

Perhaps some of these weaknesses are avoidable, given the inherent problems involved in the collection and interpretation of research data in tourism.

Problems involved in the collection and interpretation of research data in tourism

We can identify a number of problems involved in the collection and interpretation of tourism research data:

1 There are difficulties in identifying and measuring tourism where the tourists do not cross any national boundaries, i.e. domestic tourism. No records are usually kept of such movements even though they may represent the majority of tourist trips taken to destinations within a country.

2 There are disagreements over how long one has to stay away from home before one is a tourist. The standard definition involves

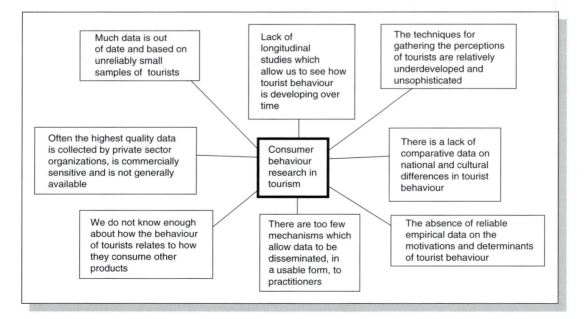

Figure 12.1
Main weaknesses in consumer behaviour research in tourism

spending at least one night away from home. In other words it excludes day-trips, which make up the overwhelming proportion of most theme park visits.

3 Tourists, when questioned, can provide inaccurate information either deliberately or accidentally. They might, for example:
   (a) Mislead the interviewer because they do not wish to offend by saying they have not enjoyed the company's product.
   (b) Lie about their activities on holiday because they are ashamed of them.
   (c) Genuinely not remember how much they spent on holiday or exaggerate the amount they spent to give the impression that they are wealthier than they really are.

4 It is also very difficult for tourists to answer some of the standard questions they are often asked, such as:
   (a) Where and when did you first hear about this destination?
   (b) Are you likely to use this airline again in the future?
   Many organizations ask this type of question but could you answer them? They first ask you to analyse something which may have happened up to fifty or more years earlier. In any event, how do you know when you first heard about a destination and what does it mean anyway. I may have heard the word 'Venice' and seen a picture of it on a postcard when I was five years old, but may not have visited the place until I was fifty years old. When I answer the interviewer's question about where and when I first heard about Venice, what will he or she learn that can possibly help them with their marketing. The second question is too hypothetical to elicit a useful reply or it could lead to me giving them the answer I think they want to hear, rather than the real one!

5 The problem of when to ask people questions. Should you ask them about:
   (a) Their plans, before their holiday starts?
   (b) Their experience, while they are on holiday?
   (c) Their memories, after they return from their holiday?
   This choice will greatly affect the results and the easy answer of saying 'ask all three' is usually not practical or cost-effective.

6 It is very difficult to find a sample of tourists that is representative of tourists as a whole, for a variety of reasons, including:
   (a) The problem of seasonality of demand in tourism means that different types of tourists and nationalities will use tourism products at different times of the year, so surveys conducted at one time of the year may miss whole market segments.
   (b) Tourists are all individual and so are the decisions they make, so how can any sample be representative?
   (c) Interviewers will often prefer to interview people they think look friendly or they find sexually attractive, or who speak the same language. All of these can lead to a biased sample.

If we move on to consider the more sophisticated fields of qualitative research, the problems become even greater. One needs to be a trained psychologist perhaps to effectively elicit answers to complex questions such as 'Why did you choose this holiday?'

Usually such a question simply receives a reply which reflects only the conscious thinking, e.g. price. However, there may be many deep-seated subconscious reasons for the choice of a holiday that are very important but likely to be missed.

There are a range of other problems involved in marketing research in tourism:

1 The fact that perhaps the most valuable marketing data is never made public. It is collected by organizations, for their own pur-poses, and is kept secret because of its commercial value to the organization.
2 Some public sector research, while publicly available, is flawed per-haps because it has often been collected for 'political' purposes, such as to justify an increase in departmental budgets.
3 Where marketing professionals carry out research they may be in-clined either to:
   (a) word questions so that the results cannot imply that they have not been doing their job well, or word it to prove that they have been doing a good job, or
   (b) suppress the results or discredit the research if the outcome is critical of current marketing practices.
4 Good marketing research is expensive and when budgets are under pressure it is often the first item to be cut. While this may have little short-term impact, its long-term effects may be, literally, immeas-urable.

We can see, therefore, that marketing research is a vital aspect of tourism marketing but it is fraught with problems.

The future of consumer behaviour research in tourism

Increasing numbers of academics and practitioners are working to im-prove the quality and quantity of consumer behaviour research in tourism. Perhaps this is an indication that tourism is at last maturing as an industry.

The authors believe that over the coming years, consumer behaviour research in tourism will need to develop in the following ways if it is to become more effective:

1 *The development of more sophisticated techniques for collecting qualita-tive data in tourism*, possibly including:
   (a) Focus groups – groups of consumers who are similar in terms of age, sex and income, for example. These groups are then used to elicit new attitudes and perceptions. They could be shown a draft brochure, for example, and asked their opinion of a desti-nation that a tour operator is intending to offer to its customers.
   (b) Observation – to overcome the problem where tourists prefer to do one thing but in reality do another.

(c) User diaries – where consumers are asked to recount their activities and impressions as they go through their holiday.

(d) Informal conversations with tourists – Chris Ryan has advocated the use of informal conversations with tourists as a way of gauging their views and perceptions, in spite of the subjectivity of the technique. He argues that:

> Conversations are an excellent research methodology for revealing the confines and ambiguities involved in holiday-taking, and illustrates this with a discussion about the importance of (the) friendliness (of the people towards the tourists) . . . Free-ranging conversations are an important resource for researchers. They confirm the nature of the tourist experience, and whether the concerns identified by researchers (involved in the) project are indeed the concerns of those questioned . . . Research that denies the opportunity for holidaymakers to speak of their own experience in their own words is itself limited. (Ryan, 1995)

2 *Making greater use of secondary and individual sources*. More use should be made of a range of indirect and secondary sources, including:

(a) Wider dissemination of the work of academic researchers and the report produced by organizations such as MINTEL and the Economist Intelligence Unit. There is a clear role here for state-owned tourist boards. The English Tourist Board Marketing Intelligence journal, *Insights*, is a good example of such a dissemination mechanism.

(b) Using feedback on consumer behaviour and perceptions from intermediaries such as travel agents.

(c) Organizations undertaking more systematic scanning of their business environment in terms of those political, economic, social and technological factors which influence tourist behaviour.

3 *Satisfaction-related research*. In this era of buzz words such as 'quality and customer-led marketing' increasing attention will be focused on the issue of tourist satisfaction. This is dealt with in more depth in Chapter 17. In terms of marketing research, the implications of this concern with tourist satisfaction mean a greater role for:

(a) Research which helps us identify where 'critical incidents' occur in tourism and consumer's responses to them. These incidents might include employers responding when the service delivery system fails, employee responses to complaints or special requests from customers, and spontaneous unsolicited employer actions. The results of this research would help organizations enhance their service delivery.

(b) Interviews with consumers before, during, and after their consumption of the product. These interviews would highlight how the product measured up to the customers' expectations, and how their experience is likely to affect their future purchase behaviour.

Conclusions

We have seen that tourist behaviour research is a complex field. However, it is a vital activity if the industry is to satisfy its customers and flourish. Consumer research needs to cease to be the Cinderella of the tourism industry and to become, instead, the cornerstone of decision-making in the industry.

In the next chapter we will see how the marketing mix is manipulated by tourism organizations in response to patterns of consumer behaviour. Research has a vital role to play in determining the appropriate marketing mix at a particular time.

Discussion points and essay questions

1 Discuss some of the main problems involved in carrying out customer questionnaire surveys.
2 Evaluate the ways in which tourism organizations can use the results of marketing research to improve their marketing.
3 Discuss the advantages and disadvantages of qualitative and quantitative research in tourism.

Exercise

Think about a tourism organization of your choice. Imagine that the organization has decided that it needs to know more about its existing customers to help it improve the effectiveness of its marketing activities. However, it can only afford a survey with ten questions. You should therefore devise a questionnaire that contains the ten best questions you can think of to gain valuable information that will help the organization improve its marketing.

CHAPTER 13

The marketing mix and tourist behaviour

Introduction

Once they have obtained their research data on consumer behaviour, tourism organizations have to manipulate their marketing mix or four Ps, to reflect the nature of their target markets. In this chapter, we explore the ways in which tourist behaviour influences the four Ps and the ways in which tourism organizations seek to exploit market trends through the use of the marketing mix variables.

This will mean covering a range of issues relating to the four Ps, including, for example:

- Product – tangible aspects, service element, branding
- Price – discounting, value for money
- Place – the role of intermediaries, direct sell
- Promotion – advertising, brochures, sales promotions.

When a tourism organization has identified its target customers, it must try to understand their behaviour and try and reflect this in its marketing programmes. The marketing mix is the set of variables which the organization can alter in the short term and the long term in order to satisfy their customer requirements. The four components, as listed above, can be amended separately or in combination with one or more of the other components. The marketing mix is therefore like a set of levers that the organization can adjust to meet their aims.

This chapter looks at each of the elements of the marketing mix and discusses the important aspects of each in relation to consumer behaviour for tourism organizations. We commence our analysis with the product.

Product

The tourism product must be designed or amended to reflect consumer needs and wants. One of the key objectives for any tourism organization is *product positioning* which was defined by Kotler and Armstrong (2004) as: 'The way in which the product is defined by consumers on important attributes – the place the product occupies in the consumers' minds.'

The correct positioning of a product will mean that the consumer can recognize it as being distinct from competitors' product because theirs will be unique, often intangible, elements associated with the product, which will allow the organization to differentiate its offerings.

The organization must understand its consumers' needs and wants before it can correctly position its products and services in relation to competitors' products. It will also have to study the market and the competition before it can effectively spot a gap in the marketplace to exploit. Organizations often use positioning maps to help them spot an opportunity in a particular marketplace. An example of a positioning map for the hospitality industry prior to the development of the budget hotels is shown in Figure 13.1.

Consumer preferences were moving towards being more budget conscious as a result of the recession which had gripped the country during the early 1990s. Consumers wanted better value-for-money products and were prepared to sacrifice high levels of service to achieve this. The hospitality organizations developed their ranges

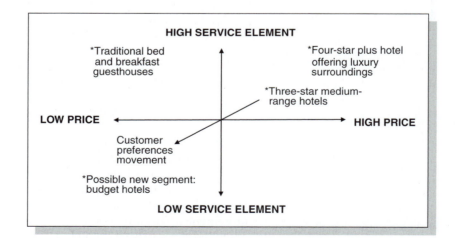

Figure 13.1
Positioning map of the UK hospitality industry prior to the development of the budget market
Source: Horner and Swarbrooke (1996).

of budget hotels under various brand names to reflect this demand (Horner and Swarbrooke, 1996). The correct positioning of the product to reflect consumer behaviour is therefore vital for the organization.

The position of the product in the product life-cycle will also mean that a particular type of consumer will be attracted to the product, and that the marketing programme will have to reflect the consumers' needs and wants. The product life-cycle incorporates four main stages, which are shown in Figure 13.2.

The product life-cycle model has been criticized as a forecasting model. It does, however, allow the organization to identify different types of consumers who are attracted to their products, according to where they are in the life-cycle.

The tourism organization will probably have products and services in different parts of the product life-cycle. They will be attracting different types of consumers to each of its products, and the marketing mix will have to be designed around their needs. This concept is illustrated in Figure 13.3, which refers to a tour operator that markets products at three different stages in the product life-cycle. The marketing programme for each product is different because it has to reflect the need and wants of the particular group of consumer in the market segment. It can be seen from Figure 13.3 that each product requires a particular marketing strategy to reflect the target group's needs and wants.

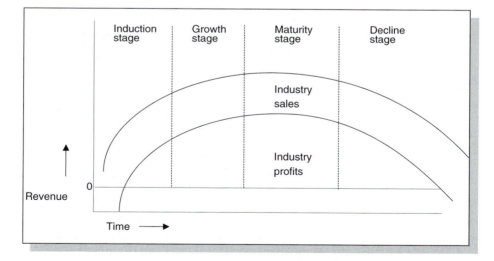

Figure 13.2
The four stages of the product life-cycle
Source: Kotler and Armstrong (2004).

Product	PLC stage	Consumer	Marketing programme
Summer sun holidays or FIT's	Maturity	Middle majority family clientele	Reassuring promotion emphasizing brand Relaunching activity with new destination
Long haul holidays or FIT's	Introduction	Innovators Outer directed individual	Promotion to build awareness Sales promotion (with distributors) Emphasis on product excitement
Flydrive holidays to the USA	Growth	Families in middle-income bracket seeking new experiences	Brand building promotion Work on distribution Reassurance on safety in brochure

Figure 13.3
The tour operator's product portfolio, the target consumer and the marketing programme
Source: adapted from Horner and Swarbrooke (1996).

Branding

One of the key aspects of differentiation for a product or service is branding. Kotler and Armstrong (2004) defined branding as: 'a name, term, symbol or design or combination of them, intended to identify goods or services of one seller or group of sellers and to differentiate them from those of their competitors'.

Brand names, logos or trademarks encourage consumers to buy products and services because they give them the benefits that they are seeking. These benefits range from familiarity and safety, to status and self-esteem (Horner and Swarbrooke, 1996).

Tourism organizations find branding particularly useful because a brand adds tangible cues to a service which is largely intangible in nature. This idea is explored in more depth in Figure 13.4. This figure explores the benefits that a strong brand name brings to an organization which is marketing a fully inclusive tour (FIT) product.

The strong brand identity allows the organization to give the right type of messages to their target consumer. A powerful brand will also allow the organization to develop their product or service on an international basis since a strong brand will give messages of quality. The major airlines have used powerful brands to develop their business, appealing to international consumers. The use of branding by tourism organizations, to appeal to an international tourism consumer and reflect their needs and wants is explored in Figure 13.5.

We have considered some of the important aspects of the product in relation to consumer behaviour. We will now turn our attention to the price.

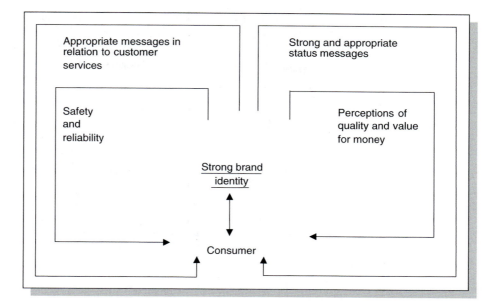

Figure 13.4
The importance of a strong brand name on consumer choice for a FIT

Sector	Example	Comments
1. Destinations	Spain – 'España Passion for Life' 'Smile, you're in Spain'	To attract new up-market customer seeking cultural experience and to promote an image of Spain as a fun destination
2. Transport	British Airways	To attract international customer seeking reliability and customer service
3. Attractions	Disneyland Europe The Magic Kingdom	To attract children interested in the Magic of Disney
4. Tour operator	TUI – Sustainable Programme	To attract environmentally conscious post-modern tourist
5. Accommodation	MGM – Las Vegas	To attract the customer interested in combining entertainment and gambling

Figure 13.5
The use of branding to appeal to international consumers in tourism

Price

Pricing is a key principle for any organization when it is marketing products and services. The price that an organization charges for its products and services must strike a balance between what the organization is trying to achieve in financial terms and, most importantly, the needs and wants of consumers from the target group. The pricing decisions of organizations will be affected by a number of factors including the pricing objectives, legal and regulatory issues, the competition and costs. The most important factor in terms of this book, however, is the consumer's perception of price in relation to quality and value for money. For non-profit-making organizations, the objectives are often to encourage new users. This is can be achieved by using *differential pricing strategies,* where different prices are charged for different market segments.

The consumer must see a link between the price charged and the product quality. Many tourism organizations charge a high price which is a reflection of the special features of the product in terms of design or service delivery. Small specialist tour operators can charge relatively high prices for the special features of the holiday on offer, their attention to detail and their high levels of personal service.

The airlines charge different prices for different levels of service. This relationship is explored in Figure 13.6. It can be seen from this diagram that the price of each product in the airline industry links to the perceptions of the market segments, and is reflected in the levels of service and product offerings. The most important issue here, for the airline, is whether customers perceive that the price they are paying represents good value for money in relation to the service delivery.

Tourism is a service industry, which means that it sells products that are, by their very nature, perishable. This means that organizations must work hard to obtain maximum usage or occupancy. The airline or train that departs when it is only half full will be losing valuable revenue. The tour operator that is relying on high volumes to maximize profits will have to work hard to gain sales. Pricing is often used as a competitive advantage tool in tourism in a number of ways to try to influence consumers in their purchasing patterns. A summary of some of these ways of using price to influence consumer behaviour is shown in Figure 13.7.

Product	Customer	Customer expectations
First class Highest price	High socioeconomic group Customers with high status	* High levels of personal service * Rapid check-in * Large amount of space on board
Business class Medium price	Business traveller Medium/high socioeconomic class	* Some personal service * Reliable and quick check-in * Good space allocation on board * Business services on board
Economy class Lower prices	Families Low/medium socioeconomic class Students/single people	* Little personal service * Limited menus * Little space on board * Services for children

Figure 13.6
The relationship of price to consumer perception of quality for a major airline

Technique	Example	Effects on consumer behaviour
Low introductory pricing	FIT – Tour Operator	Lures consumer in to new market
Low prices across the board	Economy – air travel	Encourages consumer who is interested primarily in economy
Last-minute discounting	Middle-range hotel	Encourages consumer to impulse purchase at last minute
Discounting to particular market segments	Museums	Encourages underprivileged groups to visit
Premium pricing	Luxury hotels	Encourages consumer who is looking for status, value and exclusivity

Figure 13.7
The ways in which price is used in tourism to influence consumer behaviour

It can be seen from Figure 13.7 that different pricing strategies will encourage consumers to enter the market or, in certain circumstances, remain loyal to an organization. Pricing strategies can also encourage consumers to enter a market and can be used to discourage consumers from abusing natural resources or facilities.

We have considered some of the important aspects of price. We now turn our attention to place (or distribution).

Place (or distribution)

A distribution channel (or place) has been defined by Kotler and Armstrong (2004) as: 'the set of firms and individuals that take title or assist in transferring title, to the particular good or service as it moves from the producer to the final consumer'.

Place is of great significance to consumers because they might like the product and be able and willing to pay the price asked, but if they are unable to gain access to it no sale will result. Consumers are affected by the intermediaries in the distribution chain. It is often the retailer who has the most powerful effect on consumers when they are making their purchase decisions. The retail travel agent, for example, has a primary function in the relationship with consumers on behalf of the package holiday operator. This function was summarized by Horner and Swarbrooke (1996) and is shown in Figure 13.8.

It can be seen from this diagram that travel agents perform an important function in relation to the consumer. They can act as powerful persuaders in relation to consumer choice. They also act as points of contact for customer complaints if problems occurs with holidays.

The special nature of tourism has led organizations to develop special distribution systems including consortia, central reservation systems, affiliations and specialist operators such as tour operators and travel agents.

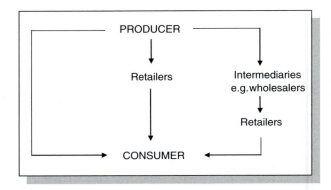

Figure 13.8
The function of the retail travel agent
Source: Horner and Swarbrooke (1996).

The tourism industry has been very active in the development of direct sell operations. Computerized reservation systems have allowed service organizations such as airlines and hotels to communicate directly with the customer and cut out the intermediaries. This brings the organization distinct advantages with regard to the consumer because it is able to negotiate a sale directly with the consumer. It also allows the development of a relationship between the supplier and the consumer and facilitates sales promotion activity.

However, tourism organizations do tend to use direct sell methods, encouraged by the development of multimedia systems which will be increasingly important in the industry. Point of information (POI) systems are multimedia computers which stand alone and provide the customer with interactive services. Point of sale (POS) systems allow customers to buy their tickets and use electronic fund transfer (EFT POS) systems to make direct payments. These systems increasingly will be linked to POI systems and will mean that the customer can purchase tickets in shops, departure points or, even, in the home. Innovations such as multimedia systems and CD-ROMs will allow tourism organizations to develop a more sophisticated direct marketing business and travel agents will become increasingly redundant.

All these developments will, however, depend on the attitude of the consumer. Consumers may resist the new technology and still feel happier being sold tourism products in a face-to-face experience within a retail shop. Their attitudes may well be determined by the market segment into which they fit.

A good example of organizations that use a combination of different sorts of distribution systems are the international airlines. This is explored in Figure 13.9.

The airlines sell directly to the customer using telephone or interactive systems such as Minitel in France, or the Internet. They also rely on their own retail outlets, other intermediaries such as travel agents and on-line distributors. The airlines are able to build different relationships

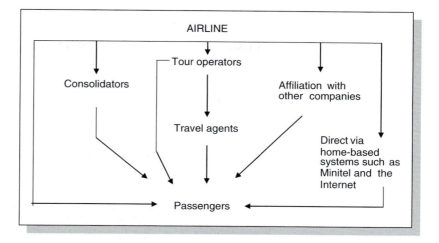

Figure 13.9
The distribution channels for airline seats

with customers via the different distribution systems. The airlines may negotiate discounts by using their direct sell network, whereas they offer a full-cost business service to business people via a travel agent.

The distribution of tourism products is being revolutionized by the development of new electronic databases which can be incorporated into telecommunication systems. These include computer reservation systems (CRS), global distribution systems (GDS) and Viewdata.

Many tourism organizations see the development of global sales and distribution systems as a key strategic objective. These systems will allow organizations to communicate directly with customers on a worldwide basis. These developments have allowed many tourism organizations the opportunity to develop direct marketing distribution channels.

In recent years tourism distribution has been revolutionized by the growing use of the Internet. It has reinforced, and acted as a catalyst for, the trend towards direct sales and the removal of travel agents from the distribution chain. It is now easy for tourists in many countries to buy airline seats and hotel beds on-line, as well as hire cars and even book excursions.

However, while the Internet has allowed tourists to bypass high street travel agents, it has created new types of travel agents, the on-line travel agent. These include brand names such as Expedia, Lastminute.com, Travelocity, and so on. These on-line travel agents have helped stimulate the rise of the independent do-it-yourself traveller. At the same time, some of these on-line agents, such as Expedia, have almost become tour operators because they enable tourists to create their own tailor-made package, including flights, hotel, transfers and excursions.

Meanwhile many traditional tour operators and travel agents have struggled to come to terms with the Internet and their sites are often inferior to those of companies like Expedia. This might be because they are rather 'schizophrenic' about the Internet, as they also own a lot of high street travel agency outlets.

We have considered the major aspects of distribution in relation to consumer behaviour for tourism organizations. We now consider the final part of the marketing mix – promotion.

Promotion

The final part of the marketing mix – promotion – is the way in which the tourism organization communicates in an effective way with its target customers. Promotion is used by organizations to affect the way in which consumers behave and it is therefore a vital motivator for any tourism organization. Tourism organizations use a variety of methods for marketing communication which are summarized in Figure 13.10.

The methods of marketing communication that a tourist organization uses depend on the type of product, the aims of the campaign and the market characteristics. The definition and aims of the main types of promotion are explored in Figure 13.11.

It can be seen from Figure 13.11 that there are a variety of marketing communication techniques, which will have different effects on consumer behaviour. The tourism organization will use press or public relation techniques when it wants to create a favourable impression of the organization in the consumer's mind. An example of this type of

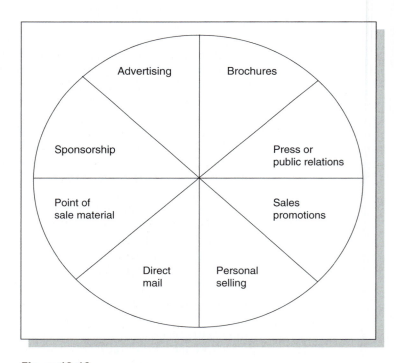

Figure 13.10
Methods of marketing communication

Type of marketing communication	Definition	Comments on consumer behaviour
Advertising	Any paid form of non-personal communication and promotion of ideas about goods or services by an identified sponsor (Kotler, 1994)	* Targets large consumer groups with strong visual images * Effective for mass-market high-volume products * The consumers and potential consumer can be targeted with repeat message
Brochures	A catalogue or video to show the images of the holiday destination or hotel (Horner and Swarbrooke, 1996)	* Reassures consumer of what to expect * Allows the consumer to differentiate and discriminate between different offering
Press or public relations	Non-personal stimulation of demand for a product, service or business unit by planting commercially significant news about it in a published medium or obtaining favourable presentation of it on radio, television, or stage, that is not paid for by the sponsor (Kotler and Armstrong, 2004)	* Gives consumers or stakeholders favourable impression of the organization or product * A high profile image is lodged in the consumer's mind * Raises awareness of new products and services in potential consumer's minds
Sales promotion	Short term incentives to encourage purchase or sale of a product or service (Kotler and Armstrong, 2004)	* Encourages the consumer to try the product/service for the first time * Encourages consumer loyalty
Personal selling	Oral presentation in a conversation with one or more prospective purchasers for the purpose of making sales (Kotler and Armstrong, 2004)	* Persuades or coerces potential consumers, or existing consumers to buy more * Give consumers favourable impression linked to customer services
Direct mail	Communicating directly with customers without the aid of marketing inter-mediaries such as retailer or agents (Horner and Swarbrooke, 1996)	* To bring potential consumers into the market * To encourage past consumers to repeat purchase * To appeal to consumers using customized offering
Point of sale material	A sales promotion method that uses items such as outside signs, window displays, and display rails to attract attention to inform customers, and to encourage retailers to carry particular products (Dibb et al., 2001)	* To encourage consumers to purchase a product/service * To encourage the consumer to purchase more within a particular setting * To raise awareness in the consumer's mind of product/services
Sponsorship	The financial or materials support of an event activity person, organization, or product, by an unrelated organization or donor. Generally funds will be made available to the recipient of the sponsorship deal in return for the prominent exposure of the sponsor's name or brand (Dibb et al., 2001)	* To gain positive images of an organization in potential consumer's minds * To raise awareness of a product in consumer's mind when restrictions apply elsewhere * To associate products with popular individuals in the consumer's mind

Figure 13.11

The definitions and aims of the main types of marketing communication in relation to consumer behaviour activity is the long-running public relations campaign for British Airways as the 'World's Favourite Airline'.

A brochure is used by tourism organizations when they are trying to initiate sales. The brochure should be used to reassure consumers about the product offering, which is particularly important in a market where there is a high spend feature. A very good example of a tourism organization using a brochure to inform and reassure potential customers of their products is the technique used by Thomson, the tour operator in the UK, where they show customer ratings for every aspect of the holiday, e.g. food, accommodation and location, based on market research with returning customers from the previous year.

Advertising is used by tourism organizations when they want to reach large audiences in an efficient manner. Television advertising is often used by tourism companies at the beginning of the booking season to encourage early interest and bookings. Advertising is often used to repeat the marketing communication messages in an attractive and appealing manner. The logic here is that repetition of messages will have a greater positive effect on the consumer.

Sales promotion is often used by tourism organizations to try to encourage the potential consumer to buy the product for the first time, or to repeat purchases. The package holiday companies in the UK have used sales promotion technique extensively in their marketing programmes to influence consumer behaviour. Sales promotions such as 'free child places' target certain market segments at the beginning of the season and produce frenzied purchasing behaviour because places are strictly limited.

Personal selling is very important in tourism because services, by their very nature, involve a high degree of face-to-face selling activity. Personal selling is used by tourism organizations either directly or indirectly to initiate sales or encourage consumers to buy more. The large exclusive hotels, for example, use personal selling at reception and throughout the hotel to sell the guest more products and services during their stay.

Point of sale material will help the tourism organization to encourage consumers to enter the market or to buy more of the particular product or service. It is very important that the point of sale material and merchandising material in general meets consumer expectations. Styling and colouring of the material should be attractive to the consumer and should reflect the organization's image and brand identity. It is also important that the styling of materials should be updated with new themes and colours according to customer perceptions. The theming of public houses in the UK by the big breweries on an Irish theme is one example of point of sale and merchandising activity. It is likely that the Irish theme will become unfashionable over time, and re-styling along another theme will be necessary.

Direct mail is the final technique which organizations can use to communicate with consumers. This is being developed extensively by tourism organizations because the use of sophisticated databases will allow the development of customized promotional offerings. The large hotel chains, for example, can talk directly to their corporate clients. They may even communicate directly with individual business clients to inform them of new products and services on offer within their operation.

The intangibility of services means that the promotional techniques which tourism organizations use often have special characteristics. Tourism organizations often use symbols to stress the nature of the service to the consumer. This makes it easier for the consumer to identify with the organization and to recognize its products and services. The symbols developed by organizations are often linked to strong brand identities. The holiday company Thomson, for example, uses the brand name and the bird in flight symbol to help the consumer to identify with feelings of freedom associated with their holiday products.

The link of promotion to lifestyle has been extensively developed in markets such as alcoholic drinks and the car industry. There are signs that the tourism industry is beginning to develop similar styles of advertising to reflect consumer lifestyles. The tour operator brochures, for example, are becoming more like designer lifestyle magazines. The authors predict that this type of development will continue in the future. The development of niche tourism products designed to appeal to distinct market segments will mean that these types of selective promotional literature based on consumer lifestyle will become increasingly popular.

However, the Internet is now also a crucial part of the promotional mix, as even people who will not buy products on-line see it as a major source of information. Destination websites are a popular source of information for tourists, but they are often very weak, being static and with little concrete information or links to sites where tourists can actively buy products.

Company websites again can also often be rather static without moving images or sound, or updated information, which negates the advantages the Internet has as a promotional tool. Many tourism organization sites also lack a reservations facility so that tourists can book on-line.

At the same time, tourism organizations need to be aware that their product will also be featured on other people's websites over which they have no control. For example, sites like this have customer reviews of hotels and Skytrax for airlines. These are well used by travellers but are largely beyond the control of tourism organizations and their marketing departments.

Conclusions

In this chapter we have looked at the key issues involved in the development of each part of the marketing mix in relation to consumer behaviour. It is important to remember that there are some general points which can be made about the design and subsequent manipulation of the marketing mix:

1 Tourism organizations should consider each element of the marketing mix separately and evaluate the relationship of each part to consumer behaviour.

2 The tourism organization should ensure that the different components of the marketing mix interact effectively to produce the desired effect on the target consumers and their behaviour patterns.

3 The tourism organization should consider how its total portfolio of products has an effect on its consumer's behaviour patterns. Construction and manipulation of an effective marketing mix to reflect consumer behaviour patterns is vital for tourism organizations.

Tourism organizations need to recognize the importance of the Internet, which by potentially combining promotion and distribution in one transaction, theoretically turns the four Ps into two Ps, and a combined Internet category which combines 'place' and 'promotion'. However, it is also important to recognize that the use of the Internet is not the same all over the world. In many countries, people are still concerned about on-line security while in others they simply do not have access to the Internet.

Nevertheless, there is no doubt that the Internet will become an increasingly important part of the marketing mix for tourism organizations.

Discussion points and essay questions

1 'Customers purchase benefits not products.' Discuss this statement in relation to the design and implementation of effective marketing mixes for tourism organizations.

2 Outline the role of promotion within tourism marketing, particularly in relation to consumer behaviour.

Exercise

Choose one tourism product or service. Consider how each element of the marketing mix for the chosen product or service has been designed to reflect consumer wants and needs. Are there any improvements that could be made to any element of the marketing mix, in your opinion?

PART 6

Topical Issues in Consumer Behaviour

In this part the authors highlight four issues in consumer behaviour in the tourism field which are very topical. All these subjects are currently exercising the minds of academics and practitioners alike. The subjects are as follows:

- the debate about the 'green tourist' and the extent to which such a market segment exists
- the concepts of the 'Euro-tourist' and the 'global tourist', in other words, types of tourists and tourist behaviour that are relatively homogeneous, with few national differences; we will examine whether or not this phenomenon exists currently or may develop in the future
- the emergence of new markets and types of demand, and the reasons which underpin their growth
- the whole issue of quality and tourist satisfaction, given that we are always being told that only organizations that satisfy tourists with quality products and services will flourish in the future.

In all four cases we endeavour to present the reader with a balanced discussion that makes the key issues clear.

At a time when the tourism industry and tourist behaviour is changing so rapidly, it is vital that all those involved in tourism are aware of these topical issues.

The green tourist: myth or reality?

Since this book was first published, in 1999, there have been major developments in the debate about ethical issues in tourism and their relationship with tourist behaviour. In this chapter we revisit the concept of the 'green tourist', which was a major topic of debate in the 1990s, particularly among academics. We then go on to look at other developments that have taken place in the field of ethical tourism in the past few years.

But let us begin, back in the 1990s, with the concept of the 'green tourist' that was in vogue in that decade.

The green tourist?

In a debate where terms are used frequently, but are rarely defined, we should perhaps begin by talking briefly about what we mean by the term 'green'. Most definitions of the term focus on the natural physical environment. This is in contrast to the now more fashionable term, sustainable, which tends to be concerned with the future and with the balance between the environment, society and the economic system. In recent years, environmental or 'green' issues have come to the forefront of public debate in many countries. These have included 'global warming', animal welfare and wildlife conservation, organic food, pollution and the recycling of waste products. In the late 1980s and early 1990s a view developed that there was now a green consumer, who considered environmental issues when deciding which product to buy or not to buy. One of the first illustrations of this was a consumer boycott of aerosol-based products that contained chlorofluorocarbons (CFCs) in the late 1980s, after the media and pressure groups alerted consumers to the environmental impact of these CFCs. This led to companies replacing CFCs with other ingredients.

Another example of the so-called 'green consumer' was seen to be the growing concern with food safety and quality and an increase in demand for organic food. Politicians, too, recognized the rise of the 'green consumer' in the late 1980s and early 1990s, and rushed to endorse policies that were seen to be environmentally friendly. In its most extreme manifestation, this development in public opinion led to the growth of 'green' political parties in the UK and France, for example. Since the 1990s, however, in the UK at least, public concern with environmental issues appears to have lessened.

It is important to recognize that most of what we have been discussing has been largely viewed from a UK perspective. Consumers have been interested in a range of environmental issues for many years in Germany, for instance, and the general level of public concern with these issues there is consistently higher.

Tourism, green issues and sustainability

While there has been relatively little explicit evidence of concern over green issues on the part of tourists, that is not to say that there has been no interest in the subject from anyone. In the 1980s and 1990s there was considerable debate worldwide on the environmental impacts of tourism and on the links between green issues and tourism. It became a high-profile subject in these years because of a number of factors:

- the writings of academics about the impacts of tourism, including the highly influential book by Mathieson and Wall, *Tourism: Economic, Physical and Social Impacts*, published in 1982
- popular, if rather subjective, books that have set out to influence the behaviour of tourists themselves, including:
  - Wood and House, The Good Tourist: *A Worldwide Guide for the Green Traveller* (1991)
  - Elkington and Hailes, *Holidays that Don't Cost the Earth* (1992)
- proactive action on behalf of North American hospitality organizations such as Intercontinental and Canadian Pacific, designed to make their activities more environmentally friendly
- the work of pressure groups, notably Tourism Concern
- high-profile policy statements and initiatives by government agencies such as those made in the UK in the early 1990s.

One thing is clear, as the debate developed, the term 'green tourist' did not achieve the acceptance that the phrase 'green consumer' has in general. The whole debate became complex with a series of different terms being used.

Figure 14.1 shows some of the other words and phrases that were often used instead of the term 'green' in relation to both tourists and tourism.

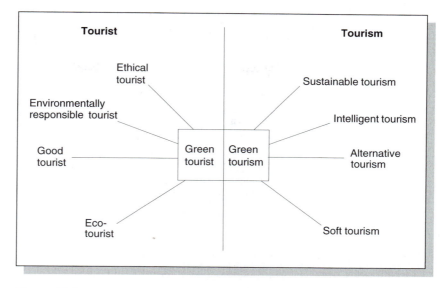

Figure 14.1
Alternative terms for green tourists and green tourism

Although these words are used, apparently, interchangeably with the term 'green', some of them are different in subtle ways:

- *Eco-tourists* are largely motivated by a desire to see the natural history of a destination. In addition they may or may not be interested in protecting the environment of the area, but it is certainly not their main concern.
- *Alternative tourism* usually means tourism that is less packaged and is smaller scale. It is assumed that this will mean it is 'greener' than mass market package tourism, but this is not necessarily the case.
- *Intelligent tourism* is related to the growing desire of some tourists to learn something new while they are on vacation. It is thus associated with particular forms of tourism which might be seen as educational, including cultural tourism and study holidays. Again, there is nothing inherently green about such holidays.
- *Sustainable tourism* is concerned with social justice and economic viability as well as the physical environment, and is also about the future. Both of these differentiate it from mainstream green issues and green concerns.
- *Ethical tourists* will be concerned with a broader range of issues that the archetypal green tourist. For example, they may be interested in human resource policies in the tourism industry, such as pay levels and the employment of local labour, as well as the way in which the economic benefits of tourism are distributed throughout the economy. It is this term, 'ethical tourist' which is now the most commonly used.

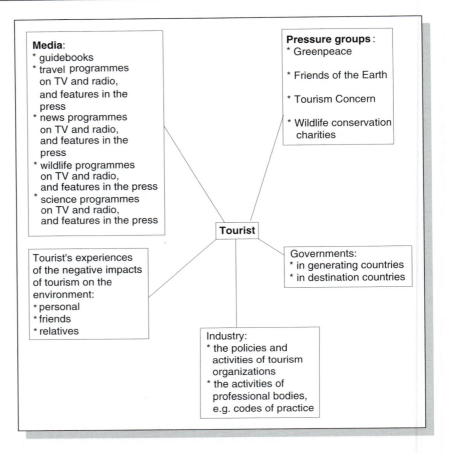

Media:
* guidebooks
* travel programmes on TV and radio, and features in the press
* news programmes on TV and radio, and features in the press
* wildlife programmes on TV and radio, and features in the press
* science programmes on TV and radio, and features in the press

Pressure groups:
* Greenpeace
* Friends of the Earth
* Tourism Concern
* Wildlife conservation charities

Tourist

Tourist's experiences of the negative impacts of tourism on the environment:
* personal
* friends
* relatives

Governments:
* in generating countries
* in destination countries

Industry:
* the policies and activities of tourism organizations
* the activities of professional bodies, e.g. codes of practice

Figure 14.2
Influences on tourists that may have increased their interest in green issues in the 1990s

Figure 14:2 shows some of the influences which informed and interested tourists about green issues, in the 1990s.

Issues of concern to green tourists

Figure 14.3 identifies a selection of issues that might be expected to be of concern to green tourists.

Clearly, many of these are interrelated, e.g., transport and pollution, and wildlife and conservation. However, it is important to recognize that they can be seen from different perspectives and they can exist in more than one 'box' at a time.

'Shades of green tourists'?

As in any complex market, one cannot really talk about green tourists as if they were a homogenous group. Tourists will each have their own

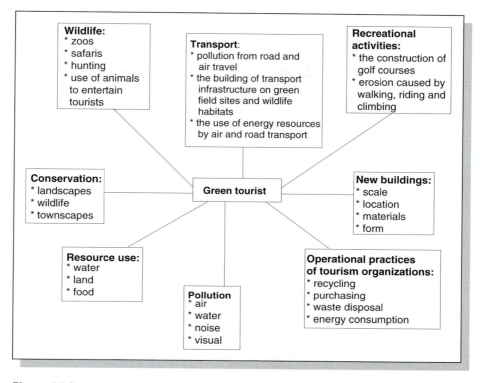

Figure 14.3
Issues that may concern the green tourist

views and these will determine their behaviour and differentiate them from other tourists. It is therefore perhaps better to talk in terms of 'shades of green tourist', from dark green tourists to those with no hint of green whatsoever!

Figure 14.4 offers a representation of this concept and suggests some hypothetical examples of what it might mean in practice, in relation to tourist behaviour.

The different shades of green may reflect differences between consumers in terms of their:

- awareness and knowledge of the issues
- attitudes towards the environment in general
- other priorities in life such as making a living
- their health, family commitments and housing.

The motivation of the green tourist

Green tourists might be influenced by a number of motivators, including:

- an altruistic belief in the need to protect the environment
- a desire to feel good about their behaviour as tourists

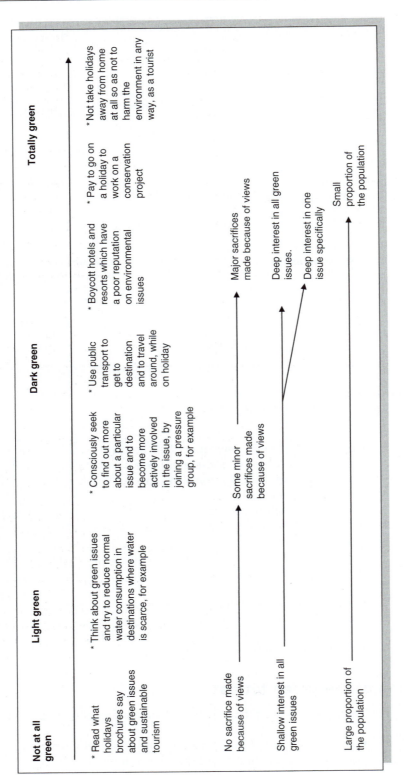

Figure 14.4
'Shades of green consumer' in tourism

- a wish to improve their image among friends and relatives by being seen to be concerned with environmental issues.

Whatever, the motivation to be a green tourist it may not always be converted into actual behaviour, because of the influence of a range of determinants.

Key determinants of behaviour

The main determinants that may prevent tourists from being able to behave in a greener manner, include:

- information obtained from the media and pressure groups
- amount of disposable income and other concerns such as poor housing or unemployment
- personal previous experience or that of friends and relatives
- ownership or non-ownership of a private car
- interest in particular issues such as animal welfare or activities such as riding and climbing
- preferences for particular types of holiday – beach, sightseeing, touring – and different destinations
- membership of particular environmental pressure groups and conservation organizations such as Greenpeace and the Worldwide Fund for Nature
- advice received from the industry, notably tour operators.

It is now time to see how these motivators and determinants are, or are not, reflected in actual tourism demand.

Evidence of the existence of the green tourist

Although much was written about the green tourist in the 1990s, there was relatively little empirical research to establish the existence of this market segment. However, there seems little doubt that tourists have been interested in the environmental quality of the destination areas where they spend their holidays, since the early 1990s.

A report by BAT Leisure Research Institute in 1993 for example, claimed that, 'of ten criteria for a quality holiday listed by consumers, seven related to the environment' (Horner and Swarbrooke, 1996). Guest surveys, conducted by the German tour operator TUI, also showed that, for German tourists at least, environmental quality did affect their satisfaction with their holiday. Figure 14.5 clearly demonstrates this fact in relation to five ecological criteria, which were identified by TUI, in relation to Cyprus. However, this was more about consumers' vested interest in the environment as a key determinant of the quality of their holiday experience than about tourists' concerns with the impact of tourism on destinations in general. The green tourist should surely be interested in tourism in all destinations, not just where they are holidaying that year.

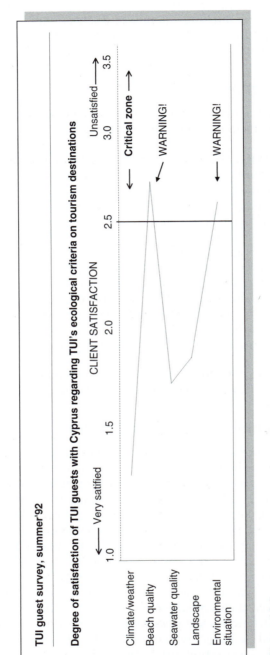

Figure 14.5
Guests' views on the environmental quality of their resort in Cyprus, 1992 (Reproduced by kind permission of TUI)

If this latter definition is used then there would appear to be relatively little explicit evidence of the existence of the green tourist. In most cases, tourists either seemed unaware of the issues, or had some awareness but did not seem to modify their behaviour or demands as a result. In general, there appeared little evidence of consumers boycotting certain pursuits in tourism because of their concerns over environmental issues. Few visitors to Spain, Greece or Turkey appeared willing to forgo the pleasure of a swimming pool, for instance, to reduce pressure on scarce local water resources.

Likewise, relatively few tourists seemed to make decisions based on environmental concerns. For example, very few tourists appeared to:

- choose an airline based on the effectiveness of its environmental management practices
- boycott hotels which did not recycle waste or which provided complementary toiletries in their bathrooms, which had been tested on animals
- campaign against the building of new theme parks and accommodation units that destroyed wildlife habitats.

By the end of the 1990s, the only real examples of tourists' concern with environmental issues, among British tourists at least, related to wildlife. Tourists responded, to some extent, to appeals to:

- not buy souvenirs made from parts of animals
- not be photographed with monkeys and bears which are kept in captivity and 'exploited' by resort photographers
- not attend bullfights or festivals which are alleged to involve cruelty to animals.

Interestingly, these issues to which tourists responded to some degree were ones which had been highlighted by the media and animal welfare pressure groups.

However, at the other extreme, we can recognize the growth of a small distinct niche of 'dark green' tourists. One manifestation of this development was the growth of conservation holidays, where tourists spend their holiday doing voluntary work on environmental projects. This trend began to develop in the early 1990s and continued to grow.

Writing in 1996, the well-known guidebook author, Arthur Frommer, identified a number of such holidays including:

- the Sierra Club in the USA, and its projects to protect wilderness areas in areas such as the Adirondack Forest Preserve in New York State
- the American-based La Sabranenque Restoration Project organization which operates in Europe to restore decaying villages
- Earthwatch, based in Massachusetts, USA which organizes holidays whose volunteers work on environmental research projects.

Such projects also existed in the UK, for both adults and children, run by organizations such as the British Trust for Conservation Volunteers and the National Trust.

Some commentators also seemed to view the growth of eco-tourism as evidence of the rise of the 'green tourist'. However, while there is no doubt that eco-tourism has been growing rapidly, it is questionable whether those who take such trips can be viewed as 'green tourists'.

They are motivated, mainly, by a desire to experience the ecology of destinations at close quarters and to get 'off the beaten track'. This is different, in the view of the author, from being committed to taking holidays that are environmentally friendly. In some ways, one could argue that, by going off the normal tourist routes, eco-tourists are responsible for spreading the negative environmental impacts of tourism to new areas. Therefore their activities may be harmful even though their intentions are good.

It appears that, we can say that there seemed to be little interest in green tourism among most tourists in the 1990s, but that there is a small niche market of dark green tourists.

The tourism industry and the 'green challenge' in the 1990s

It is interesting that, while there is little evidence of widespread environmental concern among tourists in the 1990s, the tourism industry sought to take initiatives on the environment in recent years. This interest dates in most cases from the late 1980s or early 1990s when the general debate on the environment reached its zenith with the consumer boycott of CFC-based aerosols and the highly publicized concerns over global warming.

Governments, keen to appear responsive to the concerns of voters sought to show that they too were concerned about the environment. This is the context in which many tourism organizations began to take an active interest in the environment. They were responding to the perceived threat of potential government regulation of the tourism industry.

Industry action took a number of forms:

1 Tour operators began to include information on environmental issues for their clients and have started to encourage them to become more concerned about the environment.
2 Hotel chains like Grecotel adopted environmental management policies and devised campaigns to raise tourist awareness of environmental issues in destinations in Greece.
3 Sponsoring award schemes for environmentally friendly tourism, such as the sponsorship of the 'Tourism for Tomorrow' awards by British Airways.

Many people criticized the tokenistic approach to the environment which was taken by many tourism organizations. For example, the planting of a new tree for every guest who stayed at a hotel or giving a few pennies to an environmental charity for each tourist who booked a holiday, can certainly be viewed as cosmetic. However, perhaps it could be argued that in taking such action the industry was just reflecting the general lack of in-depth interest in environmental issues of most tourists.

At the other end of the spectrum, new organizations sprung up which targeted 'dark green tourists' and tried to sell them 'green holidays', such as eco-tourism packages.

From green tourism to ethical tourism

Since the 1990s there has been a fundamental change in the debate about so-called 'sustainable tourism'. The change has been so profound that one rarely hears anyone talking about 'green tourism' or 'green tourists' and those who do are seen as odd and not as tourists.

The terms used in Figure 14.1, which were so trendy in the 1990s, now look outdated. In the debate over ethics in tourism, the new in terms and buzz words are as follows:

- *ethical tourism* which focuses on the impacts and the behaviour of tourists, and attempts to apply moral values and concepts more to the practices of tourism
- *responsible tourism*, which implies restraint and a sense of responsibility on behalf of both tourists and the tourism industry and its activities and impacts
- *fair trade tourism* and the idea that tourists should pay a fair price for the vacation they enjoy and that their vacation should not be enjoyed at the expense of local people; this has mirrored the growing concept of fair trade in relation to commodities such as coffee and tea
- *pro-poor tourism* where the emphasis is on using tourism as a vehicle to reduce poverty and stimulate social and economic development.

These developments in terminology reflect a fundamental shift in the debate over the ethics of tourism and tourist behaviour, notably:

- a move away from being concerned just about the physical environment, towards a broader interest in the social and economic impacts of tourism
- a switch from seeing tourism as something with negative impacts that have to be managed to something which can also have positive impacts
- a reduced reliance on government action and regulation and greater emphasis on the potential role of the industry and tourists themselves as positive agents of the change. This idea is underpaid by the rise of the concept of corporate social responsibility, which is now so fashionable in the business world.

These changes in thinking in tourism mirror developments in industry and society as a whole, which have seen:

- pressure groups changing, from outright opposition to companies and their actions, to engaging in partnerships with these companies in an endeavour to influence their behaviour
- a loss of faith and confidence in governments and their ability to achieve positive changes in the impacts of tourism in destinations
- greater emphasis on the behaviour of tourists themselves, particularly in terms of where they are seen to behave unethically.

Conclusions

In Figure 14.3 we identified the main issues that were being debated. Of course, these issues are still relevant but in the past few years we have seen a major change from a concern with 'green tourism' to debates about 'ethical' tourist behaviour. However, whatever the term, it seems to be embraced only by a minority of the market, albeit a growing minority.

Discussion points and essay questions

1 Discuss the implications of the concept of 'shades of green' in relation to tourist behaviour for *either* the tour operation sector *or* the hotel industry.
2 Critically evaluate the idea that eco-tourists are practising a form of 'green tourism'.
3 Discuss whether the tourism industry is leading tourist opinion on environmental issues, or vice versa.

Exercise

Devise and carry out a survey of *either* tourists in a destination *or* people in your local area who take holidays, to establish the extent to which the 'green tourist' is a reality.

Your survey must be methodologically sound and your report will cover:

- how you selected the sample of people you surveyed
- how you selected the questions you asked the results
- your interpretation of the results
- any problems you experienced that you feel made your results less reliable than they might otherwise have been
- advice for researchers who may want to carry out similar projects in the future.

CHAPTER 15

The rise of the global/Euro tourist?

Introduction

This chapter considers whether there has been an emergence of a global or Euro tourist. The implications of this would be that organizations could target groups of consumers who have similar wants and needs on a global or European basis, without the need to refer to national differences. This would open up new opportunities for the marketing of tourism products and would bring potential economies. The chapter also considers the emergence of the postmodern tourist and the implications of this for tourism organizations.

Globalization

We must recognize that many tourism organizations are global corporations operating across national boundaries. There is a trend in the tourism sector towards globalization, which is being fuelled by a variety of factors. But what is globalization and does it affect consumer behaviour in tourism? The term 'globalization' refers to the fact that companies are increasingly selling their products and services to a worldwide market, which is itself becoming more homogenous.

The position in Europe, of course, tends to be viewed in relation to the rest of the world. There are three interrelated aspects of globalization that we can now consider: the business environment, consumer behaviour (the demand side) and the industry structure (the supply side).

The business environment

There are a series of major forces that are present in the business environment of tourism organizations that are fuelling the globalization trend. These are summarized in Table 15.1.

It can be seen from Table 15.1 that there are many factors that are drawing the process of globalization. There are changes being exercised by the industry, changes in technology and changes in the political environment in many regions of the world.

Table 15.1 The forces that are fuelling globalization in the macro- and micro-environment

1 Technological developments such as global distribution systems which are allowing companies to operate on a truly global basis. Likewise, increasingly sophisticated types of media technology such as the Internet are making it easier for consumers to gain access to products from all over the world.
2 Political change in a number of regions of the world such as Southern Africa, the Middle East, Eastern Europe, North America and Mexico (with the trade treaty between the USA, Canada and Mexico). In general, these changes are making it easier for companies to set up operations in these regions, and for investors to invest in new projects in such countries.
3 Trade treaties such as the GATT Agreement are slowly creating a 'level playing field' on a global scale where companies from other parts of the world can compete with local companies on equal terms.
4 Economic development in many countries outside the so-called 'developed world' is taking place often at great speed. These countries, such as those of South East Asia, for example, are thus becoming more attractive markets for foreign companies. They are also developing their own leisure industries as their economies grow, and their companies are proving increasing competition for those from the older industrialized countries.
5 The media is also becoming more globalized and that in turn is leading to some globalization of social and cultural factors in the business environment. For example, interest in environmental issues is growing in many countries and the media has played a major role in this. The same is true in relation to health, for example. Likewise, the globalization of the media has also helped create some globalized social phenomena such as the international teenage culture.
6 The growth of competition within individual countries and the impact of domestic economic recessions in the early 1980s has led to companies looking abroad for their future growth. Globalization through joint ventures, franchises, strategic alliances, takeovers and mergers has become the way in which many organizations have sought to achieve competitive advantage.
7 Management theorists, particularly those from the USA and Japan have had their ideas widely disseminated around the world and many have been highly influential. Many companies are therefore now being managed in terms of standardized management theories, from Bradford to Bogota, and Boston to Bangkok. In theory, at least, this should make it easier for companies to undertake transnational expansion.

Source: Horner and Swarbrooke (2005).

Consumer behaviour

Some commentators have suggested that we are moving towards a day when we will see the birth of a Euro or global consumer, whose behaviour will differ in relation to their nationality. Global consumers, it is argued, are becoming more standardized in their lifestyle and approach, particularly as they are increasingly exposed to the international mass media.

The emergence of the Euro consumer or the global consumer was explored originally by Halliburton and Hünerberg (1993), when they discussed the factors on the supply side and the demand side which had fostered the development of this new type of consumer. These factors they termed 'global efficiency' and 'customer convergence':

- *Global efficiency* suggested that organizations would try to exploit the common characteristics of consumers to active efficiencies in production marketing and distribution.
- *Customer convergence* explored the idea that customers from different countries of the world are becoming increasingly similar in their habits and purchase patterns. If customers are converging in their habits and buying patterns then the Euro consumer or global-consumer could exist.

Does the Euro or global consumer exist?

The idea that consumers are becoming increasingly similar in their behaviour patterns, despite their national characteristics, is an idea that has been explored for over a decade. An early attempt at identifying multinational target groups across Europe shown in Table 15.2, for example, was completed by Sinus GmbH of Germany in 1990.

There have been conflicting ideas expressed by academics over the years on the idea of globalization of products and services. Levitt (1983) was one of the first academics to support the move to globalization. A number of academics and commentators have supported this view (Guido, 1991; Ohmae, 1982).

Kotler (1984), on the other hand, argued against the logic of globalization and suggested that it would only be relevant for large multinational organizations such as McDonald's and Coca-Cola. Other commentators have also argued against the logic of globalization (Kashani, 1989). It has been argued that there will be a continued relevance of cultural diversity and that markets will move increasingly from the mass-market approach to markets which offer highly differentiated products to meet highly differentiated consumer needs in a variety of cultural settings (Homma, 1991).

This model, developed by Sinus GmbH of Germany, tried to develop an international approach to consumer research, describing the so-called social milieus in West Germany, France, the UK and Italy. A comparison was made between the values, attitudes and beliefs in each social milieu across the four countries. The research showed that certain segments of the population had a similar structure and attitudes in all four countries that were studied. This seemed to indicate

Table 15.2 Multinational target groups

UK	France	Italy	West Germany	Target group
* The upper class	* Les héritiers	* Neo-conser-vatori	* Konservatives-gehobenes Milieu	* Upper conservative mileus
* Traditional middle-class milieu	* Les conser-vateurs installés	* Piccola borghesia	* Kleinbürger-liches Milieu	* Traditional mainstream
* Traditional working-class milieu	* Les laborieux traditionnels	* Cultura operaia	* Traditionsloses Arbeitermilieu	* Traditional working-class milieus
* Social climbers * Progressive working-class milieu	* Les noveaux ambitieux	* Rampanti * Crisaldi	* Aufstiegs-orientiertes Milieu	* Modern mainstream
* Progressive middle-class milieu	* Les managers modernes	* Borghesia illuminata	* Technokratisch-liberales Milieu	* Trendsetter milieus
* Thatcher's children	* Les post-modernistes	* Edonisti	* Hedonistisches	* Avant-garde milieus
* Socially concerned	* Les néo-moralistes	* Critica sociale	* Alternatives Milieu	* Socio-critical milieus
* British poor	* Les oubliés * Les rebelles hédonistes	* Sottoprole-tariato urbano	* Traditionsloses Arbeitermilieu	* Underprivi-leged milieus

Note: The model takes into account all social milieus in those four countries except for the Italian *cultura rurale tradizionale* which has no comparable counterpart in the UK, France and West Germany.

Note: The model takes into account all social milieus in those four countries except for the Italian *cultura rural tradizionale* which has no comparable counterpart in the United Kingdom, France and West Germany.

Source: Adapted from Sinus GmbH, Germany (1990).

that certain segments of the population could be selected and targeted by organizations without reference to national characteristics.

There have been researchers more recently who have suggested that there is in fact a Euro consumer who shares particular features as a result of amounts of income, age and a growing interest in environmental concerns (Leeflang and van Raaij, 1995).

There are other academics, however, who have suggested that the differences in lifestyles at the local, regional and national levels across Europe mean that there is no such thing as a Euro consumer (Tordjman 1995).

Despite this, there is still a tendency among tourism businesses and their market research/advertising agencies to try to increasingly group consumers together across national boundaries.

The global consumer

We can now consider the debate that has taken place over the past twenty years on the emergence of the global consumer. There is evidence to suggest that there are an increasing number of global products beginning to emerge. These have been developed primarily by large multinational enterprises. The debate still rages about whether the global consumer does in fact exist. Advertising agencies which design campaigns for products that are sold in more than one country have been aware of the subtle changes in message which have had to be made so that their advertisements are acceptable to individual nationalities. Clark (1987) of J. Walter Thomson, for example, argued that consumers exhibit national and cultural variances which are significant. Usunier (1993) suggested that consumers always 'construct' the identity of brands when the brand represents a global product. It appears that the global product is pushed on to consumers rather than consumers demanding it. There has been some discussion about the false 'global' consumer and the fact that their resistance to global products will be hidden from global marketers (Clark, 1987). One important issue is knowing whether there are intellectual, ethical and practical reasons for protecting local cultures and consumers from globalization (Usunier, 1993). It was suggested quite early on, however, that organizations would find difficulties in creating global standardized approaches in marketing programmes owing to natural entry barriers related to culture (Buzzell, 1968).

Since then there have been a number of texts which have sought to advise practitioners how to gauge their decisions regarding standardization and globalization (Ghoshal, 1987; Hampton and Buske, 1987). It was suggested that the levels of standardization that can be achieved will depend on the nature of the product and the links the product has to the individual's national culture.

It can be assumed that tourism products are eminently suitable for globalization because tourism has been described as 'the single largest peaceful movement of people across cultural boundaries' (Lett, 1989).

Tourism is arguably one of the most visible global and influential factors in global, social and economic development (Vellas and Bécherel 1995). The movement of individuals across cultural boundaries widens their experiences and makes them more aware of other cultural influences and products. Student travellers, for example, gain an educational experience which widens their perspective and develops their attitudes. International business travellers similarly experience the world and buy global brands from a wide range of duty free shops in the increasingly standardized world of international air travel. These two groups, alone, represent an opportunity to organizations which are seeking to standardize their products in global offerings.

It is the very young, however, who are the most likely to become the global customer of tomorrow. The desire to be associated with global products, whether McDonald's or Disney, has never been better developed. Young children, who have been sensitized to global products at an early age, are then exposed to multinational satellite television channels such as MTV, the satellite music channel. It will be interesting to see whether these children continue in their global desires when they become older or start to show renewed interest in their local national environment and demand products which are strongly linked to their national identity.

We have considered the general philosophical question of whether there is such a thing as a global consumer or Euro consumer in the general sense. We have also suggested that the nature of tourism could lend itself to a global approach in marketing programmes. In Chapter 9, we saw that consumers from different countries of the world exhibit different patterns of spending on tourism. We can now turn our attention to consumer behaviour in relation to the tourism industry in more depth to investigate whether there are any common patterns which emerge.

Industry structures

Globalization is an opportunity for European organizations because it means that there are opportunities for expansion and new markets to exploit. Globalization has not just been seen in the commercial sector but in government-funded destination marketing agencies as well, which have been putting effort into marketing their products on a truly global scale. However, globalization can also be a threat to Europe's tourism industry. It is predicted, for example, that Europe will lose its share of the worldwide international tourism market as new destinations outside Europe come to the market. The ways in which the European tourism industry can react to this threat are explained in Table 15.3.

Table 15.3   Ways in which the European tourism industry can react to the threat of globalization

- Concentrating on higher-quality, premium priced products rather than competing purely on price
- Working on improving the service element of the product which is often compared unfavourably to those offered in other parts of the world, most notably South East Asia
- Becoming better at marketing in terms of research, new product development, promotion, distribution and selling
- Anticipating changes in consumer behaviour better and adapting products quicker to meet changes in demand
- Utilizing technology to improve both efficiency of operation and the service which is offered to customers
- The coming together of European businesses in particular sectors so that their combined strength allows them to compete with non-European companies

Source: Horner and Swarbrooke (2005).

Behaviour patterns and tourism

The purchase of tourism products by consumers is inherently linked to the economy. Many developed economies are reaching maturity in terms of the free time and personal income which consumers spend on tourism. The number of people in the world that are able to engage in tourist activity grows as the economic situation of each country improves and becomes integrated into international economic networks. Tourist activity is therefore growing in areas such as Asia, Latin America and Eastern Europe (WTO, 2005a).

Very little research has been carried out to look at consumer behaviour in tourism in relation to nationality. The only clear link established on a global basis is that as an individual's income rises, so their spending on tourism increases.

We now provide a short review of some of the research that has been carried out to investigate cross-cultural behaviour patterns in relation to tourism demand.

Empirical research carried out by Reisinger and Turner (1999) has shown the similarities and differences between tourists as a result of their cultural differences. A research programme carried out in 1998 indicated that there was a distinct difference between Japanese and Australian tourists. Three cultural dimensions were identified as being critical to the Japanese tourists – courtesy responsiveness, competence and interaction. The research suggested that tourism marketers should target Japanese tourists by emphasizing certain aspects of service provision such as service punctuality, professional competence, apologetic attitude, social etiquette, customer differentiation based on social status and age, sense of order, politeness and respect, accuracy and adequacy of information, concern about the collectivist needs of Japanese tourists, and binding personal relationships.

This work suggested that Japanese tourists, who are a growing market segment, wanted particular service levels that were distinct from the demands placed on the industry by other groups from different countries. This research supported the view that there is no such thing as a global consumer since Japanese tourists seem to want particular levels of service delivery that are not demanded by tourists from other countries in the world.

Research carried out by Weirmair (2000) suggested that it was necessary to devise a differentiated approach to tourism marketing which distinguishes between global, national and subnational cultures for the following three reasons:

1 There is theoretical evidence that supports the view that cultural norms affect consumer/tourism behaviour
2 The majority of studies fail to clearly demonstrate the ability of only broad-based segmentation schemes.
3 The researchers' own work showed that culture had an impact on quality evaluation and satisfaction scores of different alpine tourists holidaying in Austria.

Weirmair (2000) suggested that the tourists' various cultures and subcultures should be reflected in the product/service design and the communication of these to different tourists should be on the basis of their culture and subculture.

Research carried out by Crotts and Erdmann (2000) considered a range of overseas visitors who visited the USA. The research showed that national culture influences how customers evaluate travel services and their willingness to repeat purchase and recommend a service to others. They also suggest that national cultural differences are one of the many forces that influence consumer decision-making process. They also found that gender and socioeconomic class also have an affect on how consumers interact with others and the researchers suggested that these should be taken into account by travel service providers.

Research carried out by Ahmed et al. in 2002 considered the effect of the country of origin of the consumer and the brand effect on a range of tourists who had purchased an international cruise package in Singapore. The research showed that the country of origin of the tourist did determine the tourist's views on quality and attitude ratings for the cruise provider.

A strong brand identity, however, overcame these attitudes and was more powerful than the attitude formed in the country of origin. We can conclude from this piece of work, that the development of a strong international brand identity may well overcome differences of opinion that are formed on the basis of a tourist's national and cultural setting.

The targeting of a global consumer may well require the tourism provider to reflect on cultural differences but, if the organization has developed an internationally recognized brand that has high quality associations, this may alleviate differences in behaviour patterns on the basis of country of origin of the consumer.

Post-modernism and tourist behaviour

We can now consider the history of the academic debate that underpins the concept of postmodernism and its relationship to consumer behaviour. The traditional view of the relationship between consumer and producer was that of the consumer demanding mass-produced goods and services at a low price. This led the producers into mass production of products and services which had universal appeal. This has been described as a process of 'McDonaldisation' (Ritzer, 2000). The closest the tourism industry has come to this phenomenon has been in the development of mass-market package holiday companies, which have developed products based on the premise that the transportation of large numbers of tourists would produce economies of scale. These companies developed fairly standardized, good value products, and quality was often sacrificed for price (Sharpley, 1996).

The emergence of the postmodern consumer is predicted to have a major affect on the tourism industry (Sharpley, 1996). Postmodernism represents the end of the structured and ordered state of society and signifies the replacement of the belief in progress based on scientific rationality by an emphasis on choice, a plurality of ideas and view-points, and 'the ecletic borrowing and mixing of images from other cultures' (Voase, 1995).

It is a replacement of modernism which emerged from scientific and technological advances, and which occurred in the eighteenth and nineteenth centuries and led to mass production and the belief in the development of homogenous mass markets, where everybody would have similar attitudes and tastes. Postmodernist consumers however, are showing different behaviour patterns. They find it diffi-cult to separate reality from image, particularly as simulated experi-ences are increasingly developed. The postmodern tourist will seek out new experiences. The heritage tourism industry, for example, has been described largely as a postmodern phenomenon (Walsh, 1992). The development of green tourism, or eco-tourism, has also been attributed to the postmodern phenomenon (Sharpley, 1996). Concern for the environment and sustainability are, according to Munt (1994), the 'highest order discourse of post-modernisation'.

Postmodern consumers may well remove the impetus from the glob-alization of tourism products. They will require more individualistic and highly developed products. It is likely that greater choice and variety of tourism products will be demanded. They will be seeking environmentally friendly tourist experiences and increasingly looking for authentic and realistic tourist experiences. The desire for perceived quality and good value for money will, however, still force the tourism organization to seek more economies of scale.

There is evidence to suggest that the mass market and standardized approach to tourism will become increasingly out of date by 2010. The postmodern tourist will require more individualistic approaches with more variety and quality. One group which has emerged is the 'petit bourgeois' who are a new group of consumers seeking experiences previously on offer to the upper classes, but at a more affordable price (Sharpley, 1996).

The targeting of this group has been demonstrated in tourism by the development of the mass market cruise. The Carnival Cruise Lines case study in Part Eight does show, however, that the cruise product cannot be translated directly from one market to another, because of different behaviour patterns of consumers in different countries. It is necessary to try to change consumer perceptions about the cruise product when transferring it to other markets. It is also often neces-sary to use more traditional distribution channels, such as the tour operator, so that this new group of consumers accepts the new style of product more readily.

Despite these problems, the development of cruise market within a broader market is an example of the development of a product which appeals to the new postmodern petit bourgeois who is seeking a new social status and identity, and is increasingly rejecting the lowest com-mon denominator of tourism products.

Conclusions

In this chapter we have discussed whether the Euro tourist or global tourist does in fact exist. We have seen that there is much evidence to suggest that they do not exist, although we have recognized that the very nature of tourism could allow tourist organizations to target groups of consumers on a European or worldwide basis.

Very different people live in different countries of the world. They have different cultures and behaviour patterns. We have only to look at the difference between the Australians and Asians, which has been discussed in this chapter, to see the differences which do exist.

It is possible, however, to select particular market segments on a European or worldwide basis for tourism products. Consumers who fit into these market segments can then be targeted with products of a similar nature. Airlines have developed brands which target business travellers on an international basis. They do, however, have to subtly change particular aspects of the marketing mix to suit the national characteristics of the consumer.

Table 15.4 explores four market segments which could be targeted on a worldwide or European basis. It can be seen that these segments have very similar behaviour patterns and therefore seek similar benefits.

Table 15.4 Possible global consumers or Euro consumers of the future

Market segment	Benefits sought
The European or international business traveller	* Reliable service * Good quality surroundings * Flexible booking opportunities * Reliable connecting services
The young student traveller	* Good value for money products * Discounts * Flexible co-ordinated packages, e.g. round Europe, round the world * Educational experiences
The environmentally conscious tourist	* Sustainable tourism products * The opportunity to travel to remote and underdeveloped areas of the world * Reassurance of environmental features of the products
The middle-class family group tourist	* Good value for money * Discounted products * Reliability of service * Safety features

Business travellers want a good quality and reliable service with flexible booking arrangements and good quality products and services. British Airways have tried to target this market segment by developing a strong brand image in association with a long-term public relations campaign using the logo 'The World's Favourite Airline'. They have also added extra features to their products to appeal to the business traveller. One example of such a development has been the introduction of more roomy seats in Business Class which recline fully for long-haul flights.

The major international airlines have started to target the international business traveller directly by the use of in-flight magazines which are often printed in different languages. These magazines carry features which appeal to the business traveller and carry advertisements for other organizations, such as prestigious hotels and car hire companies, which also target this group.

Young student travellers represent another group which has similar behaviour patterns on a European or worldwide basis. This group have often experienced an advanced level of education and have the ability to understand and converse in foreign languages. They are increasingly exposed to satellite advertising, such as MTV – the satellite music channel. They are looking for good value holiday packages which take them to new out-of-the way destinations for new and exciting experiences.

The environmentally conscious traveller is a market segment which has been growing in size during the postmodern period. The group is generally still restricted to a small minority, and there are differences in numbers depending on the country. The WTO (1996) predicts that this group of consumers will continue to grow in the foreseeable future. It is likely that new tourism organizations will develop products targeted at this group. Existing tourism organizations will try to adapt their products to incorporate more environmentally friendly features (see the TUI case study in Part Eight as an example of this).

We have seen in this chapter that models are being developed to suggest that there is the development of the middle class which crosses national boundaries. The postmodern period has seen the development of the petit bourgeois. This has meant that there is the emergence of the middle-class family group tourist. This group is looking for new tourism experiences which mimic their bourgeois predecessors.

They want to see new places and allow their children to have the tourism experiences they never had. The tourism organizations which target this group must offer exciting destinations but with the added benefits of good value-for-money discounts, reliability of service and re-assurance about safety. Mass-market package holiday companies have been very effective at targeting this group, and most have developed brands specifically for this purpose. Tourism organizations have also tried to take products which have successfully targeted the middle-classes in certain countries and transfer these to other countries.

The development of large multinational tourism organizations and the maturity of markets will encourage these organizations increasingly to move across national boundaries with their products and services.

The academic debate of whether a global consumer or Euro consumer exists may be quickly overtaken by the budgets of these organizations as they forge ahead with their marketing programmes.

Discussion points and essay questions

1 'The emergence of the global consumer or Euro consumer can be attributed to the marketing activities of large multi-national organizations rather than changes in consumer behaviour' (Horner and Swarbrooke, 2005). Discuss the relevance of this statement.
2 Evaluate the importance of whether a global consumer or Euro consumer exists for the development of tourism products.
3 'The very nature of tourism could allow tourism organizations to target groups of consumers on a European or world-wide basis' (Horner and Swarbrooke, 2005). Discuss this statement.

Exercise

Collect statistical evidence to evaluate whether a Euro consumer does exist for tourism products.

CHAPTER 16

The emergence of new markets and changes in tourist demand

The tourism market worldwide is going through a period of great change in the current era in terms of:

- the demand for new types of tourism product
- the rejuvenation of some older established forms of tourism
- changes in the ways in which tourists purchase tourism product
- the growth of outbound tourism from countries which traditionally have generated few international tourist trips.

In this chapter we highlight a number of such trends in the global tourism market. It is important to recognize that some trends are the result of a complex three-way relationship between the tourism industry, the media and tourists. One also needs to understand that it is difficult to generalize about such trends, for there are great differences in demand between different market segments.

Figure 16.1 illustrates thirteen major emerging markets and changes in demand which we will be considering in this chapter.

The all-inclusive vacation concept

In the early days of package tourism, the all-inclusive package was the norm. It provided security for travellers unused to travelling to other countries. However, in recent years we

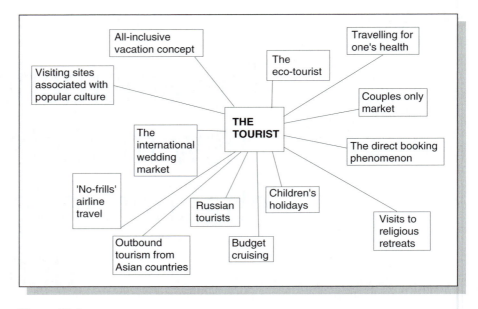

Figure 16.1
Thirteen major emerging markets and changes in demand

have seen a trend towards more flexible packages, which allow tourists to buy meals outside their hotel and to plan their own excursions. However, in the 1990s we saw the growth of all-inclusive vacations across the world. For example, many packages to the Caribbean from Europe are based on the all-inclusive principle. They tend to include travel, all needs, drinks, excursions, leisure activities and entertainment. They are popular with those tourists who know exactly how much their holiday will cost when they book it, and enjoy the fact that they will only need to take a small amount of spending money with them.

The all-inclusive concept has proved particularly popular in developing destinations such as the Dominican Republic. This may reflect the fact that:

- in some destinations there is only a very limited choice of restaurants and a poorly developed tourism infrastructure outside the main resort hotels
- because of a fear of crime and language difficulties, many tourists do not feel confident enough to travel away from their accommodation.

All-inclusive holidays tend to flourish at both ends of the tourism market:

- at the luxury end where leading players are the Sandals organization in the Caribbean and Club Med on a global scale
- at the budget end where many two- and three-star hotels in the Mediterranean are offering two week all-inclusive packages from a little over £300 per person!

Children's holidays

Children are now tourism consumers in their own right. As well as influencing the choice of family holiday destinations, the industry is now offering holidays for children that are for children only, i.e. without their parents.

This market is already well developed in the USA via the summer camp movement, with brand names like Camp America. However, it is also developing in Europe, as we can see from the examples outlined here:

1 In the UK, the operator PGL has over a period of years, developed a range of activity holidays aimed at young people, such as canoeing on the Ardeche river in France. For more destinations from PGL you should consult the case study on the company in Part Eight.
2 Young people in France can spend time in a Gîte d'Enfants, usually farm-based accommodation where the visitors learn about life and work on a farm.

Sometimes, these two products can be purchased by schools and group trip organizers on behalf of children. However, often they are purchased directly by the family on an individual basis. For the child or young person the motivator for such a holiday is probably the chance to make new friends and the feeling of being independent and 'grown up'. However, while the young person is the consumer, the parent is usually the customer, making the final purchase decision and paying the bill. For parents, safety and security is probably the major determinant of the product they choose to purchase. They may also feel better disposed towards products that they feel will make their children healthier or that are educational.

As children become increasingly targeted as consumers in their own right, with all kinds of interests, it seems likely that this market will grow, and that the young people themselves will play an even greater role in deciding which product their parents should buy.

The international wedding market

Some people have always travelled abroad for their honeymoon. We see in the case study of the Japanese tourism market, in Part Eight, that many Japanese couples travel as far as Europe for their honeymoon. However, in recent years, there has been a growing number of people travelling abroad to get married, and the industry has quickly sought to exploit this growth market.

For UK couples, popular wedding destinations include:

- the USA, particularly Las Vegas and New England
- Caribbean islands, including St Lucia, the Cayman Islands and Barbados
- Cyprus.

The package offered to couples can include not only the ceremony but also videos, flowers and music, as well as the food and drink.

In many cases the only real restriction on where a couple can get married are residence restrictions before a couple can legally marry in a particular place. In some destinations, there can also be other legal requirements such as blood tests.

As well as 'conventional' weddings in exotic locations there has also been a growth in unconventional weddings, where the couple 'tie the knot' while:

- they are under water
- they drift down under a shared parachute
- they bungee jump off a tall bridge
- sitting in an ice cave.

There is clearly a status value to being wed abroad, particularly if the location is perceived to be particularly exclusive or exotic.

Visiting sites associated with popular culture

In recent years, there has been a growing trend for tourists to visit places associated with aspects of popular culture. This can include locations where films and television programmes are made, the homes of major figures in popular culture and the settings for best-selling books.

As popular culture has become increasingly global, this phenomenon has become truly a worldwide market. Examples are the Hollywood film studios such as Warner Brothers, which encourage visitors to see where their favourite programmes are filmed.

Other examples of this phenomenon of tourists visiting popular culture sites, include:

- the coach parties visiting the areas where television series such as *Heartbeat* were filmed in the UK
- the *Sex and the City Tour* in New York
- film locations such as used in the Harry Potter films and *The Da Vinci Code*.

In the UK there is even the *Archers* phenomenon where tourists visit a fictional village which is the setting for a radio programme. Many tourists who visit television and radio programme locations are older, while those who visit film locations tend to be younger. A large number of destinations have built their local tourism industry around a chance association with a television programme such as Holmfirth in West Yorkshire, where *Last of the Summer Wine* is filmed. Trails may be developed to allow tourists to visit places associated with a programme or film. Weekend breaks may also be offered that allow fans to meet characters from the programme. In the area of popular music, we have already seen that fans are keen to visit sites associated with their heroes. Hence the popularity of Elvis Presley's home at Graceland, and

Jim Morrison's grave in Paris. If we take our definition of popular culture further we can surely include popular sports such as soccer, where for many overseas fans a visit to the trophy room at Old Trafford or Anfield would be a lifetime's ambition. As popular culture becomes ever more commercialized and global, and tourists seem ever more willing to travel to popular culture sites, this market seems set to grow.

Budget cruising

For many years the cruise market was the preserve of a small elite enjoying an exclusive leisure pursuit. However, in the 1990s, the emergence of tour operators offering cruises at budget prices has changed all that. Pioneered in Europe by the UK operator Airtours and Thomson, British people were offered the chance to enjoy a week's cruise in the Mediterranean from around £300. This product innovation has brought a whole new segment into the cruise market. It has also helped fuel the renaissance in the cruise market as a whole, which was already under way. Cruise companies are using new on-board leisure facilities and themed cruises to attract new younger market segments.

And it is not just cruise companies that are trying to promote the idea of budget cruises. Many ferry companies on longer routes are endeavouring to sell their ferry services as cruise products with similar on-board entertainment and facilities. Brittany Ferries, for example, encourages passengers to cruise to Santander as a start to their holiday in Europe.

The rise of budget cruises has also made the upmarket operators review their prices and offer more discounts. At the same time the luxury end of the market is also flourishing, as are the specialist markets of Antarctic voyages and river cruises, for example.

'No-frills' airline travel

In the global recession of the early 1990s, leisure and business travellers looked for bargains in air travel. As we emerge from the recession, there is evidence that the desire for a good deal has become a permanent feature of the market.

This demand has been accommodated by a range of new 'no-frills' airlines, including South West in the USA. In the UK the best examples are easyJet, and Ryanair. Such airlines have taken advantage of the move towards the liberalization of air transport in Europe to offer new services. The emphasis is on informality and basic service. As far as possible, such carriers keep down costs by being paperless organizations. They also offer no 'complementary' in-flight services. In return they can offer low prices.

These airlines have become fashionable with customers, and not just those on limited incomes. They are also popular with better-off travellers who simply resent paying a higher price for a short journey.

'No frills' airlines are also beginning to extend other travel related markets. easyJet, for example, has recently entered the budget cruise and the hire car market.

The direct booking phenomenon

The growth of technologies such as the Internet, smart cards and multimedia systems, and the Internet has made direct booking easier both for tourists and the industry. For the client, direct booking holds out the prospect of lower prices because there is no travel agency commission and/or better service is offered.

Many tour operators have founded their own direct booking brand, but at the same time, more airlines are offering direct booking links for clients. The same is true of ferry companies. In the hotel sector, major chains have set up central reservations systems to give customers direct access to any of their hotels, anywhere in the world.

The rise of the small specialist tour operator has fuelled the rise of direct booking. These small specialists cannot guarantee a high enough volume of sales to interest most travel agents. Therefore, they have to sell direct to their clients. Direct sell is better in some ways for it should ensure that the tourist should receive more detailed information about the product. It also gives the organization the chance to receive direct feedback about its products, and their appeal, from prospective clients.

The rise of the Internet as a holiday booking system has allowed global companies such as Expedia and Travelocity to sell holiday components individually or as a package. This trend of direct bookings is predicted to grow.

The couples-only market

For many years the industry has focused on the family holiday and on holidays for single activities, such as Club 18–30. But what about holidays for couples without children?

In recent years, this segment has been taken more seriously for several reasons:

- the growing number of couples that are making a conscious decision not to have children
- the relatively high disposable income of this segment and its tendency to take several holidays per year.

For this market, romance and shared interests are major motivators, as is the desire to be in an adult-only environment, without other people's children. Some tour operators have launched brands to attract this market specifically, or else have included in their brochures the suitability of particular hotels and resorts for such people. Many country house hotels are also trying to tempt this market by either banning children or restricting the access of children in the evening. However, in hotels which also want to attract the family market this can be a sensitive issue. It is important to recognize that even people with children can temporarily enter the couples-only market when they take breaks away from their children, where romance is usually the main motivator.

Travelling for one's health

Travelling for one's health is one of the oldest motivators in tourism. But, today, the range of health tourism products is greater than ever before. Travelling for health covers a multitude of types of demand, including:

- visits to health resorts or 'health farms' which provide a holistic product often designed to relieve stress or put right the effect of overindulgence in people's everyday lives
- activity holidays designed to enhance the tourist's overall level of physical fitness
- seaside-resort based sea-water treatments or thalassotherapy, in France, for example
- natural mud treatments in the Dead Sea area or Iceland, for instance
- mineral water treatments designed to cure or alleviate particular conditions.

Even on holiday, where health is not the main concern, it is often still a consideration. Guests may demand healthy menus in hotels, for example, and leisure facilities such as gyms and swimming pools. In the increasingly stressful world of work, it seems likely that in future health tourism will grow, and the concept of health may increasingly encompass mental as well as physical health.

Visits to religious retreats

The pressures of everyday life and the search for new spiritual values appears to have stimulated the demand for trips to religious retreats in two main ways:

- visits to the homes of modern religious cults, and sects, notably in the UK, the USA, and Asia
- visits by non-believers or agnostics to conventional religious retreats, not only for religious enlightenment, but also for relaxation and spiritual enrichment. Examples of such retreats are Mount Athos in Greece which only admits men, for a limited period of time, and the Taizé community near Cluny in the Burgundy region of France.

At the same time, religious retreats are still attracting considerable number of believers as well as visitors. In most retreats, life is simple and the comforts are few. Personal, private contemplation is often the core experience. The 'customer' is not paying for the services they receive but rather for peace and the space to think. There appears to be no reason why the demand for religious retreats will not continue to grow.

The eco-tourist

Eco-tourism is a global growth phenomenon of the tourism market in the 1990s. The eco-tourist is someone whose main motivation for taking a trip is to see wildlife and communities in their natural habitat. It is linked with other phenomena such as the desire to learn something new while on holiday. Eco-tourism is also being put forward by some people as being synonymous with sustainable tourism. It is seen as a less exploitative, soft form of small-scale tourism that has a relatively low impact. It is now difficult to separate the hype from the reality but there is no doubt that seeing themselves as eco-tourists can give them a feel-good factor, a feeling that their holiday is somehow better than the mass-market beach holiday.

The growth of eco-tourism seems to stem from two main sources:

- the growing concern over green issues which has focused attention on the plight of rainforests and endangered wildlife
- media wildlife and travelogue programmes which have increased awareness of destinations.

Demand has also been stimulated by destinations such as Costa Rica or Belize, which are selling themselves as eco-tourism destinations. Eco-tourism holidays exist at all price levels from budget overland 'expeditions' to luxury safaris and continent-wide tours.

Eco-tourism products are highly diverse and may include:

- wildlife safaris in East Africa
- journeys up the rivers of Borneo to see native villagers
- visits to endangered rainforests
- natural history walking holidays in the mountains of Europe
- outback trips in Australia
- whale-watching holidays to New England or New Zealand.

For some people, eco-tourism packages constitute their whole vacation. However, in other cases, they are just a day trip while on a beach holiday.

At the same time, people on an eco-tourism holiday may also want to use the environment for sporting activities such as white-water rafting. If they do, then is it still an eco-tourism holiday?

There is a controversial dimension to eco-tourism, in that:

- some potentially authentic, wildlife-based activities that should be seen as eco-tourism, such as hunting, may be seen as socially unacceptable
- where eco-tourism grows it can begin to cause major environmental problems, such as is the case with the mass safari market in Kenya.

When all is said and done, eco-tourism is not an altruistic form of tourism. It is as self-indulgent as all forms of tourism. It is about tourists spending their leisure time in the way that gives them the benefits they seek.

Russian tourists

Since the demise of old-style communism and the rise of the market economy in Russia, there has been a noticeable increase in outbound tourism from Russia. As the new Russian middle class has become wealthy, it has found it difficult to find outlets for this new-found wealth in Russia itself. These Russians have therefore used tourism as a way of improving their status in their own community. It sometimes seems that in every destination of the world which is famous for shopping – Dubai, Paris, London and Hong Kong – there are Russian tourists spending heavily in the shops. The most graphic evidence of this phenomenon is the huge pile of luggage that seems to be a feature of every Aeroflot check-in around the world!

At the same time, Russian tourists are becoming a vitally important market segment for traditional Mediterranean destinations such as the 'Costas' in Spain. Not only are they visiting these resorts but they are also buying property as second homes. This phenomenon is well developed that there are even property magazines produced in Russian in resorts such as Benidorm.

In a country of some 200 million people, where only a fraction is currently travelling abroad, there is clearly great potential for future growth.

Outbound tourism from Asian countries

Traditionally, the only Asian country which has generated considerable outbound tourism has been Japan. However, today, with the growth of economies in the region, we are seeing a rapid growth in outbound tourism from other countries, notably from South Korea and Taiwan.

Tourists from these two countries are increasingly travelling to worldwide destinations, including Europe and the USA. At the same time, tourists from Hong Kong, Malaysia, Singapore and Indonesia, are increasingly travelling within South East Asia, particularly for short-duration shopping trips. This growing phenomenon is being aided by the relatively short distances between these places, and the highly developed airline network in the region.

There are two other markets which offer potential for massive growth in coming years:

- China, where rapid-economic growth and the growth of a capitalist economy will create a new affluent class who will want to travel abroad for pleasure
- India, which has the world's largest middle class of any country.

As Asian people travel further, it will be important for the tourism industry at their destinations to recognize how their culture and the nature of their demand differ from other markets. They must also be careful to recognize that Korean or Taiwanese or Chinese tourists are not like Japanese people. They must guard against stereotyping all Asian tourists as being like the Japanese.

Many South Koreans already visit Las Vegas. However, according to the Las Vegas Convention and Visitors Authority, their behaviour is very different to that of other foreign visitors. For example, they:

- book later than most other tourists
- use packages more than many other national markets
- often visit friends and relatives while in the USA
- stay in the USA for longer than most other visitors
- dine out less than other tourists, but are more likely to visit the national parks than other nationalities
- spend significantly less than tourists from many other countries
- rely heavily on travel agents for advice.

The growth of outbound tourism from Asia seems set to be one of the main characteristics of the changing nature of tourism over the next few decades.

Conclusions

In this chapter, we have looked at a number of different emerging markets and changes in the nature of tourist demand. We have seen how some regions of the world are becoming major generators of foreign trips for the first time, while in traditional markets we have noted new trends. These trends will probably continue into the future but they will evolve and be joined by new, as yet unforeseen, developments in demand.

Discussion points and essay questions

1 Select three of the emerging markets and changes in demand outlined in this chapter, and explain their growth.
2 Discuss the extent to which the rise of 'no-frills' airlines, budget hotels and low-priced cruise products is likely to continue.
3 Evaluate the likely impact of the growth of outbound tourism from Asia on the global tourism industry.

Exercise

Choose one of the following markets:

- scheduled airline
- hotel
- mass-market tour operator
- visitor attraction
- retail travel.

For your chosen market produce a report, supported by statistical and qualitative evidence, highlighting current trends in the market and emerging types of demand.

Quality and tourist satisfaction

The concept of quality

Quality is a buzz word in all modern industries, and is seen as being the key to achieving customer satisfaction. In this chapter we explore what the concepts of quality and satisfaction mean in tourism. First, we begin by looking at some standard definitions of quality.

Gummesson, writing in 1988, divided definitions of quality into two types:

- technology-driven and product-orientated definitions which defined quality in terms of conformance to requirements based on company specifications
- fitness-for-purpose definitions, that are market driven and customer orientated, and which focus upon customer utility and satisfaction.

In general, the first type of definition tends to be used in manufacturing industries where the main aim is usually standardization and reliability. The second type, with its emphasis on customers and their satisfaction, is more commonly used in service industries.

Service quality is a more complex concept than manufacturing industry quality because of the unique characteristics of service products, or what Frochot in 1996 described as the 'intrinsic services nature of heterogeneity, inseparability of production and consumption and intangibility'.

Because of these characteristics, the standardization of product that is the aim of manufacturing companies is impossible to achieve in tourism. In any event, in tourism the customer wants to feel that their experience will be different to other people's and tailor-made to match their tastes.

In many people's minds quality is an absolute that is either present or absent from a product. It either is or is not a quality product. However, in reality, it is more of a continuum from little or no apparent quality to high or even, in theory at least, total quality.

Furthermore, it has often been assumed that quality means premium-priced products, at the top end of the market. This is clearly not true if we take the fitness-for-purpose view of quality, where any product can be seen as a quality product if it meets the needs of the purchaser. Therefore, a simple youth hostel could be a quality product for a young walker on a limited budget looking for an inexpensive bed for the night. At the other end of the scale, for the tourist who enjoys being pampered, only a five-star hotel with a high staff to guest ratio will meet their desires.

This brings us to the crucial issue at the heart of quality in service industries and the fitness-for-purpose definitions. They are customer orientated and every customer is different. Quality is not a fact or a reality in such industries; it is a perception in the minds of the customer. In other words, quality is in the eye of the beholder. Whether or not a tourist will perceive a product as a quality product, or not, will depend on:

- their individual attitudes, expectations and previous experiences as a consumer
- the benefits they are looking for from the particular purchase in question.

These needs and desires are closely linked to motivators and determinants. In terms of a holiday they might include:

- looking for a low-cost vacation because of a lack of disposable income
- a desire to gain status from purchasing a particular holiday
- searching for a destination where the tourist will feel safe and secure
- a wish to take a type of holiday that will make it easier for the tourist to make new friends
- a deeply held desire to meet local people, see the 'real' country, and 'get off the beaten track'
- a need for relaxation and the reduction of stress levels.

Tourists might be seeking more than one benefit from a holiday, and these might be conflicting or even contradictory.

The quality jigsaw in tourism

Because of the complex nature of tourism, product quality can be seen as a jigsaw, with many equally important, but different-sized, pieces that must all fit together perfectly in order to satisfy the tourist. The jigsaw is illustrated in Figure 17.1 in relation to the purchase of a family's annual summer holiday in a resort hotel.

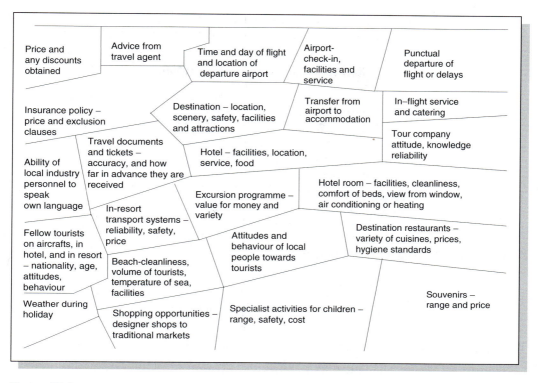

Figure 17.1
The quality jigsaw

The importance of tourist satisfaction

Satisfying the consumer in tourism is important for three main reasons:

1 It leads to positive word-of-mouth recommendation of the product to friends and relatives, which in turn brings in new customers.
2 Creating a repeat customer by satisfying them with their first use of the product brings a steady source of income with no need for extra marketing expenditure.
3 Dealing with complaints is expensive, time-consuming and bad for the organization's reputation. Furthermore, it can bring direct costs through compensation payments.

The tourist satisfaction process

Figure 17.2 illustrates a simplified view of the process by which tourists are satisfied or not.

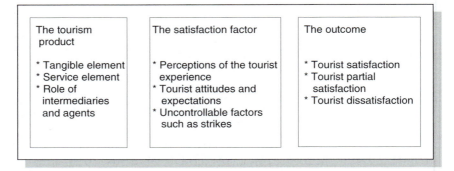

Figure 17.2
The tourist satisfaction process

Key models and techniques

There a number of models and techniques used in service industries in relation to quality and customer satisfaction. Several of these have been applied to tourism by various authors.

The SERVQUAL technique

The SERVQUAL scale was first introduced by Parasuraman, Zeithaml and Berry in 1985. They attempted to develop an instrument that would measure service quality across a range of service industries. It was based on empirical research, albeit not in the tourism industry. They stated that service quality has five dimensions:

1 Tangibles: physical facilities, equipment and appearance of personnel
2 Reliability: the ability to perform the promised service dependably and accurately
3 Responsiveness: willingness to help consumers and provide consumers with prompt service
4 Assurance: knowledge and courtesy of employees and their ability to convey trust and confidence
5 Empathy: caring individualized attention the firm provides to its customers. (Quoted in Frochet, 1996)

Based on this idea they developed this technique whereby customers are asked questions and on the basis of their answers a score is calculated for each of the five criteria, and sub-criteria within these five groups. However, the model has been criticized on various methodological grounds.

A number of writers have attempted to apply the SERVQUAL technique to tourism services. One such particularly interesting attempt was made in 1996 by Frochot, who was studying its application to heritage sites.

The service gap concept

This concept is based on the idea that dissatisfaction in services such as tourism is caused by gaps between expectations and perceived outcomes. Parasuraman, Zeithaml and Berry identified five such potential service gaps:

1 Differences between consumer expectations and management perceptions of consumer expectations.
2 Differences between management perceptions of consumer expectations and service quality specifications.
3 Differences between service quality specifications and the service actually delivered.
4 Differences between service delivery and what is communicated about the service to consumers.
5 Differences between consumer expectations and perceptions of the quality of the service received. (Parasuraman, Zeithaml and Berry, 1985)

Laws has applied this concept to the airline business:

In airline advertising, passengers are often shown seated, or reclining in relaxed comfort in spacious cabins. They are attended by elegant and calm stewardesses (more rarely by stewards) and are featured enjoying delicious, carefully presented meals and fine wines. The reality is often very different. The point is that marketing communications are educating passengers to expect a level of service which it is beyond the ability of a carrier to deliver in all but the most favourable conditions. These might occur when there were no strikes, no mechanical failures, the cabin crew were on their peak performance, the plane was less than full, and all passengers were relaxed. (Laws, 1991)

The aim therefore, must be to use our marketing activities to create realistic expectations in the minds of our customers or else dissatisfaction may well result, however 'good' we feel our product is.

The critical incident approach

The critical incident approach to quality and consumer satisfaction is based on the idea that a tourist's satisfaction or otherwise with their experience of a product or service is a result of so-called 'critical incidents'. These incidents are concerned with the interaction of the organization's employees and customers, which can be termed the 'moment of truth' or 'the service encounter'. It assumes that there is a 'zone of tolerance' (Parasuraman, Zeithaml and Berry, 1985). In other words, customers will not notice a situation where the perceived experiences deviate only slightly from their expectations. Critical incidents are those which go beyond this zone of tolerance. 'A critical incident is one that can be described in detail and that deviates significantly, either positively or negatively, from what is normal or expected' (Bejou, Edvardsson and Rakowski, 1996).

Clearly an organization will wish to rectify the problems which caused a negative incident and pacify the customer, while at the same time building on the strengths which contributed to a positive incident.

In 1996, Bejou, Edvardsson and Rakowski published an interesting study of negative critical incidents in the airline industry in Sweden and the USA. In the hotel sector, such critical incidents could include:

- whether or not the check-in process goes smoothly
- if a meal ordered via room service appears quickly and meets the customer's expectations
- whether or not the concierge can provide an item which the guest has forgotten to pack.

These three models or techniques are largely based on an organization's perspective of service quality. This leads us to the issue of the service staff themselves.

The human resource management dimension

In a service industry such as tourism, human resource management is clearly of great significance in relation to quality and tourist satisfaction. Tom Baum has described the role of staff as 'making or breaking the tourist experience' (quoted in Ryan, 1997).

Tourist satisfaction depends on effective human resource management. This will only occur if staff:

- have the technical skills to carry out their job effectively
- have a positive attitude towards their job and seem committed to pleasing their customers
- operate as a team and there are good working relations between front-line staff and managers
- are reliable in terms of attendance at work
- deal with complaints promptly, sympathetically and effectively.

However, in tourism, clients often complain about the quality of service and staff performance, particularly waiting staff and tour operator representatives. This is probably not surprising as such staff are often employed as poorly paid temporary staff, with little training and working long hours.

Nevertheless, many tourism organizations have sought to put in place customer care programmes and other measures designed to improve the quality of service for customers. The fashionable technique of 'empowerment' has been used by companies such as the hotel chain, Marriott, to encourage staff to take more responsibility for satisfying customers' needs.

The role of marketing intermediaries

In tourism, a vital role is performed by the marketing intermediaries, most notably, travel agents. Their service is of great importance to most tourists and has a major influence on their ultimate satisfaction or dissatisfaction because they:

- provide advice on destinations and hotels, and their suitability for the client
- handle bookings and the issue of tickets
- advise the tourist on health issues and immigration formalities in the destinations
- take the client's money on behalf of the tour operator
- deal with complaints on behalf of the client.

Each of these factors can either enhance or diminish the quality of the tourist experience.

Work carried out in New Zealand by Cliff and Ryan in 1994 (quoted in Ryan, 1997) outlined consumer concerns about the reliability and performance of travel agents. They identify three dimensions to the travel agent's service quality:

1 Tangible elements, e.g. the decor of the premises and the dress of the staff. If these do not satisfy the potential client they will not even think of using that travel agent.
2 Reassurance that the agent is reliable, and competent. If this reassurance is not given to the client, they may enter the premises but they will not book via the agent.
3 After the travel, if the tourist is not satisfied with the arrangements made by the agent, they are unlikely to use them again.

Furthermore, inadequate performance by the marketing intermediary also affects the reputation and custom of the tour operator. If an agent recommended a family to visit a particular resort and apartment complex in a certain resort that is lively, loud and not suitable for people with young children, the tourists would be dissatisfied with the holiday they had purchased from a particular operator. Yet, it could have been a perfectly good holiday package, ideal for a young single person. It was just that the agent recommended it to clients for whom it was not designed.

The importance of problem-solving

The test of any quality management system is what happens when something inevitably goes wrong and the customer complains. Tourists do not expect perfection, but they do expect prompt action when problems occur.

Indeed, dealing effectively with difficulties and complaints can actively enhance tourist satisfaction. If everything on a holiday goes to plan, tourists tend not to notice. However, if something goes wrong and the organization handles the situation well, then the organization's reputation can be enhanced in the mind of the tourist. However, for this to happen, some basic guidelines need to be followed:

1 Problems have to be put right as soon as possible. On a two-week holiday, the whole experience can be ruined if clients are not moved from inadequate to satisfactory accommodation within the first day or two.
2 Make it easy for clients to contact resort representatives so they do not spend hours of their precious holiday trying to locate the person who is supposed to be there to help them.
3 Ensure that any offer of compensation is fair and reflects the gravity of the problem.

Personal factors and satisfaction

There are two important personal factors which affect a consumer's satisfaction or otherwise, notably stress and arousal, and we will now briefly consider both of these.

Stress and tourist dissatisfaction

Stress caused by any aspect of the vacation experience tends to lead to tourist dissatisfaction. This stress can result from a variety of sources, as we can see from Figure 17.3.

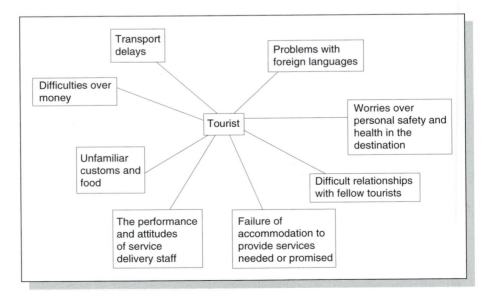

Figure 17.3
Sources of stress for tourists

We could have listed many others but those shown in Figure 17.3 give a good indication of the range of such factors. The tourist industry is constantly seeking to ameliorate these stresses, particularly at the higher end of the market.

Tourist satisfaction and arousal

In tourism, satisfaction is clearly connected to the concept of arousal. Too little arousal can cause boredom and dissatisfaction. According to Ryan (1997): 'The distinction between relaxation, a common motivation for holidays, and boredom is, from this viewpoint, dependent upon a level of arousal that is sufficient for relaxation, but is not so low as to induce boredom.'

At the other extreme, there is the concept of 'hyper-arousal, producing panic, frenzy and possible collapse' (Yerkes-Dodson Law, quoted in Ryan, 1997). A classic case of this in tourism might be the fear of flying experienced by some travellers. Hyper-arousal is likely to cause dissatisfaction in general.

However, interestingly, in recent years the growth of so-called adventure tourism – white-water rafting and bungee-jumping, for example, has been based on hyper-arousal. This search for hyper-arousal is the exception though for hyper-arousal in tourism normally arises when something goes wrong or there is an unforeseen occurrence such as an aircraft delay, and is seen as negative. Hyper-arousal is closely related to the concept of stress in tourism.

Changing expectations of quality over time

Tourists' expectations, in general, have risen over time in response to two influences:

- an improvement in their everyday standard of living and housing amenities which make them always demand something extra when they are on holiday
- product innovations by organizations that are then copied by competitors and become the norm.

We can see the way in which the consumer expectations of the accommodation product have developed over the years in response to both these factors.

At one time, hot and cold running water and shaving points in bedrooms were the height of sophistication. Then in-room radios were introduced and interior-sprung mattresses. After that came televisions, en-suite bathrooms, minibars and automatic alarms. These were followed by cable movie systems and, eventually, satellite television, jacuzzi baths and in-room computer links. Each of these was state of the art when first introduced but have now become the norm.

The interesting point is that while established generating markets such as the UK have passed slowly through all these stages, the recently developed markets such as Korea and Russia have demanded the latest state-of-the-art facilities from the beginning. At the same time, there are still consumers who are satisfied with less sophisticated in-room facilities or, rather, they are willing to accept them in return for a low price.

The importance of uncontrollable factors

The factors which influence product quality or customer satisfaction, yet are outside their control, are a major problem for the tourism industry. These include:

- weather such as unseasonal rain in Mediterranean resorts in the summer, or lack of snow in Alpine ski resorts in the winter
- strikes that affect tourists such as air traffic controllers and ferry crews
- harassment of tourists by beggars and traders
- poor transport infrastructure in the destination country
- poor hygiene and sanitation standards and disease
- the perhaps unrealistic expectations of tourists; for instance, some people hope that a romantic weekend in Paris will put life back into a failing and doomed marriage
- the behaviour of other tourists in the resort or accommodation establishment
- government bureaucracy and bureaucratic factors such as visa restrictions and departure taxes.

Any of these may cause tourist dissatisfaction with a holiday experience but they are outside the control of the tour operator that sold the holiday.

A good example of uncontrollable factors and tourist dissatisfaction comes from Las Vegas. The 1996 *Las Vegas Visitor Profile Study* showed that 5 per cent of visitors were dissatisfied because they did not win enough money in the casino! There is absolutely nothing the tour operator can do to solve this problem.

Subjective factors

Another difficulty in relation to quality and tourist satisfaction is that tourists have different attitudes, standards and prejudices. Often their satisfaction or otherwise is based on subjective views about an issue which is important to them, and which they judge in their own unique way.

Again the 1996 Las Vegas Visitor Profile Study shows that:

10% of visitors found the people in Las Vegas rude and unfriendly
8% thought it too expensive
7% said it was too hard to get to
4% felt it was too intense
3% claimed Las Vegas was dirty.

All these factors are subjective opinions based on individual interpretations of experiences as tourists. It is difficult to see how the tourism industry can effectively respond in concrete terms to such views.

National differences in quality standards and tourist satisfaction

There is clear evidence that there are national differences in tourist expectations in relation to quality standards. It is widely recognized for example, that German tourists are more concerned with the environmental quality of resorts than their British counterparts.

The authors' discussions with airline marketing executives also show that passengers from different nationalities have different quality standards. The consensus appears to be that passengers from countries like Japan and the USA have higher expectations than those from more recently industrialized countries. These national differences in tourist expectations are obviously of great significance to organizations which operate transnationally, such as hotel chains and major airlines.

There are also national differences in the supply side, in terms of the quality of the product offered. These can lead tourists to modify their expectations if they are planning to visit a particular country, or even to decide not to visit a country. The different quality standards can cover elements of the product such as:

- food hygiene in restaurants
- fire safety in hotels
- public transport in destinations
- interpretation techniques in museums
- technical competence and attitudes of guides at heritage sites.

When considering the issue of national differences in product quality and tourist expectations, it is important to distinguish facts from the clichés and stereotypes which exist.

Conclusions

We have seen that quality and tourist satisfaction are inextricably linked. However, they are both subjects about which we still have much to learn. In many cases we find airlines trying to apply models and techniques to tourism which were developed for service industries in general. We have yet to develop convincing models and techniques based on large-scale empirical research in tourism. This will not be easy, for we have also seen that many of the factors which affect satisfaction are uncontrollable, and quality is a highly personal and subjective concept.

Discussion points and essay questions

1 Discuss the idea that the most important factors which determine whether tourists will be satisfied or not are beyond the control of tourism organizations.

2 Critically evaluate the SERVQUAL technique and its potential use to tourism organizations.
3 Discuss the suggestion that quality means high price.

Exercise

Select a small sample of people, perhaps ten, who have recently taken a holiday. You should then interview them to see:

- how satisfied they had been with their holiday
- which factors influenced their satisfaction or otherwise.

Produce a report of your findings, indicating what you have learnt from the survey about quality and tourist satisfaction while recognizing the limitations of your survey.

PART 7

Conclusions and Future

At the end of a long text dealing with a complex and only partially understood concept, the time has come for the authors to attempt to draw some conclusions and make predictions about the future.

In this part of the book we:

- identify the main conclusions which have arisen from the previous seventeen chapters
- highlight the need for further research and the development of new consumer behaviour models in tourism
- compare tourist behaviour to that of consumers in general
- suggest some ways in which tourist behaviour may evolve in the future.

Conclusions

At the end of such a lengthy book on a very complex subject, it is difficult to try to draw some general conclusions. Nevertheless, the authors now highlight some key points which they believe have emerged from the preceding chapters.

1 *Tourist behaviour has a long history*, dating back over 2000 years. Many 'modern' forms of tourism such as health tourism, are simply a continuation of a tradition that dates back to Roman times. At the same time, some early forms of mass tourism such as Christian pilgrimages are now specialist niche markets.

2 *Many existing models of consumer behaviour in tourism are generally much simpler than general consumer behaviour models.* Yet, tourism is a particularly complex aspect of our modern consumer society, so perhaps they are too simplistic.

3 *Most of the motivations that make tourists want to take a particular holiday can be divided into six distinct, but related, groups*:
   (a) physical
   (b) emotional
   (c) personal
   (d) personal development
   (e) status
   (f) cultural.

4 *The motivations of any individual tourist are influenced by their*:
   (a) personality
   (b) lifestyle
   (c) past experiences
   (d) personal circumstances, including family situation and disposable income.

5 *Tourists may well have more than one motivator* at any one time.

6 *Tourists may admit to a socially acceptable motivator while in reality they may be driven by a motivator which is less socially acceptable*. They may be conscious or unconscious of this important destination.

7 *Different types of tourism product are associated with different motivating factors*, e.g. museums and theme park visits are stimulated by different motivations generally.

8 *There are two types of determinants of tourist behaviour*:
  (a) those which are personal to the tourist
  (b) those which are external to the tourist.

9 *Those determinants which are personal to the tourist are of four types*:
  (a) their personal circumstances
  (b) their knowledge
  (c) their experiences
  (d) their attitudes and perceptions.

10 *The external determinants include the following five types*:
  (a) the views of friends and family
  (b) the marketing activities of the tourism industry
  (c) the influence of the media
  (d) national political, economic, social and technological factors
  (e) global political, economic, social and technological factors.

11 *The main purchase decision-making models used in tourism, as outlined in Chapter 6, tend to have a number of weaknesses*, including that:
  (a) they are often based on little or no empirical research
  (b) many are now at least fifteen years old and do not take account of recent changes in patterns of purchase behaviour such as the growth of last-minute purchases
  (c) most are based on experiences in the traditional markets such as Europe and the USA, not the new markets such as South East Asia
  (d) they are too simplistic to explain the complex process of purchasing a tourist product.

12 *Many academic typologies of tourists are flawed* in that they:
  (a) rarely differentiate between different nationalities and cultures
  (b) tend not to recognize that tourists can move between categories and rarely always remain in one category
  (c) do not usually recognize that holiday choice is often a compromise rather than an expression of the true desires of the tourist
  (d) often have methodological weaknesses such as being based on small samples, for example.

13 *Typologies of tourists are clearly similar to the concept of market segmentation*, although the former are theoretical while the latter is concerned with applications and practice in marketing.

14 *In the global tourism market, the major growth in tourist arrivals is being seen in Asia and the Pacific, while Europe is experiencing relative decline in its share of world tourism.*

15 *There are significant differences between countries in terms of tourist behaviour* in domestic, outbound, and inbound tourism.

16 *Tourism is not a single market but is rather a series of submarkets, all of which have their own characteristics.* These submarkets include:
  (a) the family market
  (b) the backpacker market
  (c) hedonistic tourists
  (d) those visiting friends and relatives
  (e) day-trippers or excursionists
  (f) educational tourists

(g) religious tourists

(h) The 'snowbird' market

(i) ethnic minority tourists

(j) tourists with disabilities

(k) retired people

(l) short-break takers.

17 *There are also variations in consumer behaviour within the different sectors of tourism*, namely:

(a) accommodation

(b) visitor attractions

(c) destinations

(d) transport operators

(e) tour operators

(f) retail travel.

18 *Business tourism is very different in terms of consumer behaviour from leisure tourism*, in terms of:

(a) frequency of trips

(b) duration of trips

(c) when purchase decisions are made

(d) who makes purchase decisions.

19 *In business tourism, we see the difference between customers and consumers*. The former tend to be the companies which pay the bills, while the latter are the employees, usually the business travellers themselves.

20 *Research on tourist behaviour is weak in a number of respects*, most notably:

(a) the fact that much quantitative data is outdated and based on small samples, which mean the results are open to question

(b) the relative lack of sophistication in terms of qualitative research on how and why tourists make their decisions.

21 *Consumer behaviour affects every aspect of marketing, in that it should influence*:

(a) product development

(b) pricing strategies

(c) distributive channels

(d) promotional campaigns.

22 *There is no such thing as a 'green tourist'*; there are instead, 'shades of green consumers' in tourism and, indeed, there are some tourists who are not at all green.

23 *There are significant differences between nationalities in terms of tourists' attitudes towards the environment.*

24 *The current era is seeing the growth of a number of emerging markets in tourism*, including:

- eco-tourism
- the phenomenon of direct booking
- children-only holidays
- all-inclusive vacations
- budget cruising
- outbound tourism from Asia and Russia

- 'no-frills' airline travel
- the international wedding market
- couples-only holidays
- visiting sites associated with popular culture such as films and television programmes
- visits to religious retreats
- taking trips designed to improve the health of the tourist.

25 *There is no apparent evidence for the idea that we are seeing the emergence of the 'global tourist' or even the 'Euro tourist'.*

26 *Quality in tourism is a jigsaw where, if any piece is missing, the customer will be dissatisfied.*

27 *Tourist dissatisfaction is largely a result of gaps between expectations and perceived outcomes, viewed from the perspective of the tourist.*

28 *The concept of quality and the expectations of tourists change overtime.*

29 *There are many uncontrollable factors which influence tourist satisfaction, namely:*
   (a) weather
   (b) strikes
   (c) harassment of tourists by beggars and traders
   (d) difficulties within the destination such as hygiene problems, poor infrastructure, and crime
   (e) the behaviour of other tourists.

Hopefully, this book has helped, in a small way, to focus attention on this important field in the study of tourism. As well as the main text we hope that the discussion points, exercises and the following case studies have helped you to deepen your understanding of this crucial area of tourism management.

In the era of so-called 'consumer-led marketing', where organizations are told they must meet the demands of their consumers if they are to thrive, it is vital that we understand tourists and what makes them 'tick'.

In the final chapter, we gaze into our crystal ball and attempt to predict what might happen in the future. This is a risky activity at a time when consumer factors appear to be changing at an ever greater pace and new forms of tourism are continually emerging.

The future of tourist behaviour

In this chapter, we consider how tourist behaviour might evolve in the future in terms of who will be travelling, what tourists will buy and how they will buy tourism products.

It is likely that future tourist behaviour will be influenced by a range of factors including those illustrated in Figure 19.1.

The impact of these factors and others, will lead to:

- the growth of outbound tourism from countries which have previously not been major generators of international tourist trips
- the expansion of tourism demand from certain groups in society
- the development of new types of tourism product changes in the way in which we purchase tourism products.

We now look at each of these in a little more detail.

New-generating countries

There are economic, political and social reasons why the major growth in outbound tourism in future years will be seen largely in countries which until recently have generated relatively few international tourist trips. These countries include:

- Eastern Europe, where political and economic change is slowly creating a growth in outbound trips
- Asia and the Pacific where economic growth is rapidly expanding the market for outbound trips by the residents of those countries. For example, outbound trips from South Korea rose between 1986 and 1995 from 455 500 to 3 819 000, an increase of some 850 per cent in just ten years.

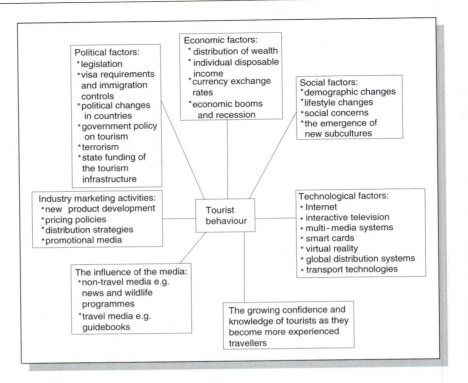

Figure 19.1
Factors that will influence the future of tourist behaviour

However, in both cases, the growth in outbound tourism will only continue if there is political stability and economic growth in both regions of the world. Past events seem to indicate that this may not be the case, with uncertainty over the future of Russia after Yeltsin left power and turmoil in the currency markets of South East Asia.

As yet, there is little outbound tourism from most countries in Africa and South America. This may change, however, as:

- some economies, such as Brazil, are growing rapidly
- political change in some countries may lead to a more equal distribution of wealth which may make more of the population able to take a trip abroad.

Market segments which will grow in importance

Social change, the influence of the media and the actions of the tourist industry seem likely to have the following effects on segmentation in tourism:

1 Demographic change in Northern Europe, the USA and Japan will lead to growth in the importance of the elderly or 'third age' market.

Conversely in countries where the population is becoming more youthful – Southern Europe, South America and South East Asia – there will be a growth in the 18–30 market segment.

2 As children become ever more consumers in their own right, an increasing number of them will take holidays separately from their parents.

3 There will be more non-Christians travelling internationally in future which will have implications for the tourism industry worldwide.

4 We may see the growth of segments which share similar characteristics, regardless of their nationality. Students may be the first example of such a segment.

5 As attitudes towards people with disabilities change over time, there should be a growth in the number of travellers who have disabilities. They will become a major market which the industry will not be able to neglect.

New types of tourism products

The development of any new types of tourism products will result from:

- the changing tastes of tourists
- whatever the industry chooses to make available to tourists
- technological innovations
- social concerns.

In Chapter 16 we looked at some of the current trends in tourist demand and the products that are now in fashion.

The veteran travel writer, Arthur Frommer, writing in 1996, identified a number of types of tourism products that may grow in popularity in the future. These included:

- 'vacation resorts that stretch the mind and change your life'
- 'political travel' which allows tourists to visit countries which are often in the news and see for themselves what everyday life is like there
- 'volunteer vacations' where tourists work for nothing on projects which are good causes, such as conservation work or building a school in a poor country
- taking holidays that involve staying with an ordinary family in another country
- searching for new modes of travel, such as freighter ships and sailing vessels
- 'ethical holidays' where tourists are concerned about the impact of their trip on the host community and the staff who look after them
- health-enhancing holidays.

Frommer also talks about finding 'new ways to visit old destinations', where, he argues, tourists visiting well-known destinations, perhaps for the third or fourth time, will look for new, more off-beat experiences. For example, visitors to London may seek out less touristy neighbourhoods and 'fringe' arts events.

It is also likely that the growing pressures of modern life will lead more people to use their holidays to reduce stress and/or gain spiritual enlightenment as an antidote to the materialism of modern life. This will increase demand for trips to 'retreats', even among those who do not have strong religious beliefs.

As well as the development of new products, many tourists will be encouraged by the industry to take similar types of holidays as they have before, but in new locations. This might include:

- European tourists taking short city breaks to places further afield, such as Cape Town, Samarkand, Tbilisi, Havana and Teheran
- beach holidays being taken in Namibia and Brazil
- skiing trips to Japan, Argentina and Chile
- cultural holidays in Myanmar, Laos, and Nigeria.

In general, it seems likely that tourists will travel longer distances for their main vacations, even though their main holiday activity or motivation may be little different from the past.

Virtual reality and fantasy tourism

One of the major current debates in tourism revolves around virtual reality technologies, and the ability to create synthetic substitutes for real tourism experiences. The question is, will virtual reality (VR) reduce the demand for conventional tourism or increase it by stimulating even more people to want to take particular trips.

The *potential* application of VR in tourism, once the technologies themselves have become more sophisticated, is virtually unlimited. We could let people:

- feel the sun on their face, hear waves lapping on the shore, as they lie on a deserted beach on a Pacific Island, all in their own home
- experience a visit to the greatest of the pyramids in Egypt, without the fear of terrorist activities, stomach upsets or overbooked flights, because they would not need to leave home
- enjoy a romantic *bateaux-mouches* cruise on the Seine in Paris, with the love of their life, all from the comfort of their bed at home.

At the same time, virtual reality technologies, and other technological innovations, could help us to develop new forms of escapist tourism, by allowing people to live out their fantasies. Already, the Russians are allowing tourists to experience what it is like to:

- be a cosmonaut training for their first space flight
- be a fighter pilot, on a sophisticated flight simulator.

In this case, it is a result of economic necessity and the desire to attract foreign currency, through the use of well-established VR technologies.

Ultimately, development in VR and related technologies could allow the creation of new fantasy-based resorts. For example, just as in the film *Westworld*, whole themed resorts could be built where tourists could totally immerse themselves in a fantasy experience. The tourist could be a Roman gladiator, a medieval knight, a Wild West gunslinger or a Chicago gangster. They could enjoy playing these roles in a safe environment.

Alternatively, one day we will be able to create artificial environments, where tourists can experience holidays under the sea, or in gravity-less environments. Or perhaps, one day, tourism will be a wholly mental activity, with no need to travel; an activity which takes place purely within the tourist's own home and is limited only by the imagination of the tourist.

Will tourism demand turn full circle?

It is often assumed that the evolution of tourism demand is a linear process of stages which are passed through in a sequence. Figure 19.2 illustrates the widely accepted conventional wisdom about how the behaviour of many British tourists has changed over time.

There are several reasons why this apparent linear process may become more circular in future. It could perhaps turn full circle if:

- diseases such as malaria discourage tourists from taking trips to long-haul destinations, where the threat of infection is perceived to be high
- the Earth's resources become depleted and it either becomes difficult to justify long-haul trips or the cost of fuel makes such trips too expensive
- the tourism industry makes the coastal resorts of Britain and Spain attractive to tourists for their main holiday. This could involve cleaning up beaches and making more water-based activities available or offering non-beach-dependent attractions such as theme parks, casinos and shopping. Resorts such as Benidorm are already setting a good example in this respect.

At the same time, the coastal resorts of Britain and Spain, for example, may begin to be seen as attractive as heritage tourism destinations, given that mass tourism is now part of our modern heritage.

We already have examples of how tourism demand can turn full circle. Spa tourism reached its peak in Europe in the eighteenth and nineteenth centuries and then declined early in the twentieth century. Now, however, the spa resorts of Europe are experiencing a boom. Likewise, cruising which went into decline after the Second World War is currently experiencing a real renaissance. In both cases, the change has resulted from social factors and the activities of the tourism industry.

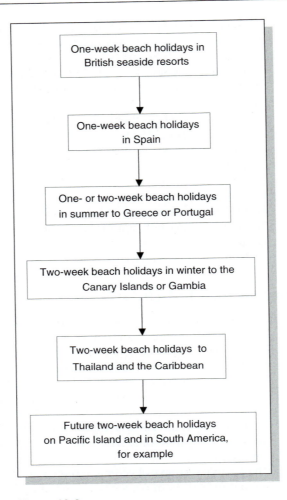

Figure 19.2
The evolution of beach holiday demand among
British tourists

The number of holidays per annum

In many countries, a large number of tourists now take more than one holiday per year, and this trend looks set to continue. This has a number of implications for tourist behaviour:

1 The main holiday will be the longest, and may well be used for relaxation, stress relief, and 'recharging the tourist's batteries'.
2 The extra holidays might normally be shorter, more active and more specialist in nature.

The extra holiday might be used for intense, short leisure experiences, as an antidote to the route of everyday life, including day trips to cities in other countries or twenty-four hour visits to a foreign mountain range to climb a particular peak.

The unchanging tourist

Before we get carried away by the idea that tourism demand is constantly changing, let us briefly remember that there are some tourists whose behaviour is not following the trends we have been discussing in this book. These are tourists who:

- are doing the same on holiday as they did twenty years ago, for instance, relaxing on a beach or by the hotel pool
- are taking their holidays in the same type of destination or, even, in exactly the same place as they were two decades ago.

British seaside resorts are still packed with tourists on summer holidays, as are those of all Northern European countries.

There will continue to be a group of tourists who do not wish, or are not able, to change their behaviour, regardless of what other tourists are doing.

Changes in the way we purchase tourism products

Technological innovations are going to continue to change the way in which we purchase tourism products, in several ways:

1 The development of the Internet and interactive television will stimulate the growth of direct marketing and direct booking. People will increasingly be able to access information and make bookings from their own home or office. Tour operators, airlines and hotels will help encourage this trend as the Internet is a relatively inexpensive promotional tool and direct selling takes away the need to pay commission to travel agents.
2 The growth of ever more sophisticated global distribution systems will help tourists put together individual, tailor-made itineraries, by giving them access to the detailed product information which they require.
3 Smart-card technologies will bring with them the benefits of ticketless travel which will stimulate the growth of last-minute purchases of tourism products.

Developments in technology such as multimedia systems and the Internet are blurring the dividing line between promotion and distribution in tourism. In other words, tourists, through these systems, can both gain information and make bookings at the same time, in the same place.

We might also see changes in the future in terms of who we buy holidays from, as the role of travel agents declines and other organizations take their place. These could be:

- high street retailers who will combine selling holidays with the sale of goods needed by tourists, such as clothes, sun protection creams and luggage

- tele-shopping networks that may simply add holidays to the portfolio of products they sell
- banks who provide loans for holidays and sell currency, might go on to sell the holidays themselves
- telecommunications companies which may become involved in selling holidays as their systems play more and more of a role in the distribution of the tourism product.

So far in this chapter we have looked at how the consumer behaviour of tourists might change in the years to come. However, we do need to recognize how important it is for us to become better at researching tourist behaviour so we can identify any changes in behaviour and explain them. Therefore, we now turn our attention to the issue of researching consumer behaviour in tourism.

Towards a new agenda for consumer behaviour research in tourism

In Chapter 12, the authors provided a critique of current consumer behaviour research in tourism. If we are to better understand tourist behaviour and use this knowledge to improve marketing within the industry, we need to adopt a new agenda for research. This agenda should contain the following points:

1 Focus on the process by which tourists make their purchase decisions.
2 Recognize the importance of tourists' perceptions and endeavour to find out more about where these perceptions come from.
3 Pay attention to the need for us to improve our techniques for conducting qualitative research, including the use of focus groups, observation and informal conversations with tourists.
4 Give a high priority to the issue of quality and tourist satisfaction. We need to better understand how tourists perceive quality and what makes them satisfied or dissatisfied with a particular tourist experience
5 Be concerned with the need to conduct longitudinal research that will help us to identify trends in tourist behaviour.
6 Explore the link between consumer behaviour research and the criteria on which we segment tourism markets, to make segmentation more closely mirror the realities of actual tourist behaviour.
7 Look at how tourists evaluate the offers of different tourism organizations and decide which one to purchase.
8 Concentrate some effort on developing techniques that help us to understand why people choose *not* to purchase particular products.
9 Place great emphasis on the need to recognize and research variations in tourist behaviour between different nationalities and different cultures.
10 Explore the links between consumer behaviour in tourism and that in other industries, for people's purchase of tourist products is clearly related to their purchase of other products.

In general, a new approach to research in consumer behaviour would also involve:

- academics producing techniques and models which have practical applications, and disseminating them as widely as possible, and in as easily comprehensible a form as possible
- practitioners making more use of consumer behaviour research when taking marketing decisions.

Government tourism agencies have a key role to play in bringing both groups together and helping them work together for their mutual benefit, in terms of both:

- the research they themselves commission
- how consumer behaviour data is presented and disseminated.

Summary

We have seen that a range of factors will lead, in the future, to changes in who the tourists are, what they buy and how they buy it. However, the authors have also noted that the behaviour of some individual tourists will not change noticeably.

At the same time, even within the global tourism market as a whole, we will find that changes in behaviour will be evolutionary rather than revolutionary. We will also see variations in the power of change between different:

- countries
- market segments
- sectors of the tourism industry.

Nevertheless, there is little doubt that tourist behaviour will change in fundamental ways in the years to come. That is why it is so important that we become better at researching consumer behaviour in tourism.

PART **8**
• • • •

Case Studies

Introduction

This book has used many tourism examples to illustrate the points made in individual chapters. It is useful, however, to consider longer and broader case studies to evaluate some of the main issues in relation to consumer behaviour in more depth.

The case studies that follow show a number of tourism organizations from a variety of countries. These organizations range from small to large, and operate in one or more than one country. Some case studies are short and have been written to explore one particular issue. Others are much longer and give an overview of whole organizations and how they relate to consumers.

The case studies have been grouped together under particular headings to allow the reader to examine issues in relation to consumer behaviour and compare and contrast the approaches of the different organizations. The case studies were researched in 2006 and therefore, as for all published case studies, are only snapshots at that particular time. We are aware that the material in the case studies will date but this does not make the lessons that can be learned from them any less valuable.

We hope that you enjoy reading the case studies and exploring in more depth some of the issues related to consumer behaviour.

Case studies

Targeting different market segments
1 PGL
2 Thomas Cook's Club 18–30
3 The segmentation of the outbound Japanese market
4 Segmenting the leisure shopping market

Customer service
  5 The Savoy Hotel, London

New emerging tourism markets
  6 First Choice Holidays' all-inclusive package
  7 The cruise market: Carnival Cruise Lines

Industrial tourism
  8 Wensleydale Creamery, Hawes, North Yorkshire
  9 Société Roquefort
 10 Industrial tourism in France

Environmental initiatives
 11 British Airways' environmental policy
 12 TUI – Germany's environmental policy

Hedonistic tourism
 13 Ragdale Hall: health hydro
 14 The international spa market

Leisure and tourism
 15 Adventure tourism in New Zealand
 16 Gay and lesbian tourism in Australia

Budget tourism
 17 easyJet

Destination marketing and the consumer
 18 Las Vegas, Nevada, USA
 19 Taiwan: the emergence of a new major outbound tourism market
 20 The inbound market to the Republic of Cyprus

Activity holidays
 21 Susi Madron's cycling for softies

PGL adventure holidays

Introduction

PGL Travel Limited is the leading British company that provides adventure holidays for young people. The holidays are designed around holiday centres which the company has bought or leased, and developed. Young people go on the holidays without their parents and it is often the first time that they have been away from their family for any length of time. The holidays incorporate a selection of outdoor and indoor activities, and accommodation can range from tents to dormitories. The company has also developed substantial business in the school holidays market.

Background

The company takes its name from the initials of the man who started it in the 1950s – Peter Gordon Lawrence. The idea for the company came to Peter when he went on holiday to Austria in 1950 and sailed down the Danube in a folding canvas canoe. In 1957 he started to organize canoe camping trips for young adults down the River Wye. Peter led the groups himself and called his new venture, PGL Voyages. Peter expanded the business to Wales and the Brecon Beacons National Park.

In the 1960s and 1970s PGL's holidays were based on canoeing, sailing and pony trekking, with the accommodation in tents. During the early years, the company developed holidays for school groups, and expanded these holidays to include the Ardeche Gorge in the South of France. The company now has permanently staffed headquarters in France and the UK.

The company gradually grew during the 1980s to become the leading UK provider of adventure holidays. Properties were bought by the company and converted to permanent centres. This development included the acquisition of a mansion house in Perthshire and the flagship 250-acre estate of Boreatton Park in Shropshire.

During the 1990s the company gradually diversified into other markets, including educational tours for schools, and field study courses. There was a considerable expansion into the school's adventure market in 1991/92, when the company acquired the Quest Outdoor Adventure programme from a failed competitor.

Peter Lawrence, the founder of the company, sadly died in August 2004, but left behind the solid foundation of a company that provides countless opportunities for young people to have fun, adventure and gain personal development.

The company today

The company now has over forty years' experience and is recognized as being Britain's leading operator of activity holidays for children and teenagers. PGL has twenty-three centres in the UK and France. The company offers a full range of activities including archery, pony trekking, motor sports, abseiling, canoeing, orienteering, assault courses, sailing, windsurfing, climbing and others. Specialist holidays include mountain biking, Dordogne adventure, driver awareness, 'Indiana Jones' theme holiday, farming, beach life-guarding, French language, and tennis coaching.

The company has twenty UK centres which are listed in Exhibit 1.1. A full range of the company's products are described in Exhibit 1.2.

All holidays include care and tuition by well-trained staff, use of specialist equipment and clothing, evening entertainments and full-board accommodation.

The adventure centres and activities require the professional help of 100 head office staff. The company also own the Alton Court head office complex which includes over 100 000 cubic feet of warehouse capacity for its storage of all the specialist equipment required for the organization of the holidays.

PGL Travel Limited is recognized by major activity organizations including the Royal Yachting Association, and the British Canoe Union.

Customers of PGL Travel Limited

The holidays are designed for young people of ages six to eighteen years inclusive. Customers can choose a range of holidays designed for different age ranges. These include holidays designed for the six to nine, eight to eleven and eleven to thirteen-year-old age groups. The activities on offer are geared to this particular age group. The young people who go on the holidays are often experiencing time spent away from their families for the first time. This means that the safety and security of the young people is a major priority for the company and these aspects are stressed in the promotional literature for the holidays.

Exhibit 1.1 Summary of the products and centres

Locations: 20 UK centres
2 in Scotland
4 in Wales
2 in Herefordshire
1 in North Devon
1 in South Devon
1 in Dorset
3 on Isle of Wight
1 in Sussex
2 in Surrey
1 in Shropshire
1 in Suffolk
1 in Buckinghamshire
10 European centres
1 in Austria
9 in France
1 in Spain

Source: PGL Travel Limited.

Exhibit 1.2 Product range

PGL Activity Holidays – With over 47 years' experience, the initials 'PGL' are synonymous with fun and adventure for children. In many families, several generations have now enjoyed the challenge and thrills of a PGL activity holiday. Thousands of children have learnt a little independence, made lots of friends and developed social and activity skills thanks to PGL.

Our brochure features 16 centres throughout the UK and in France from our 240 acre site in Shropshire to our Chateau near Paris. There are multi activity holidays with up to 60 different activities and holidays where children can concentrate on a chosen activity such as Pony Trekking, Motorsports, Football, Mountain Biking, Drama or Surfing. There are also themed holidays like Spellbound and Secret Agent as well as Watersports holidays in the Mediterranean and Ski holidays in Austria.

PGL Family Active – PGL has been operating activity holidays for children for nearly 50 years and we know what makes for happy children. Now parents too can join in the action and be there to share in their child's happiness and achievements. Surprise your children by being the first one down the Zip Wire, lead the way on the bike trail and of course, embarrass them at the disco – it's

(Continued)

Exhibit 1.2 *(Continued)*

about time parents got their own back! As well as longer holidays many of our centres also offer weekends and mini-breaks for families in centres as diverse as a chateau near Paris, redwood lodges in Scotland and a hamlet in the Dordogne.

PGL Adventure UK – Over the years PGL has become a leading provider of outdoor activity courses for school and youth groups. Thirteen of our centres operate in term time and offer special group rates. Safety has always been our number one priority and this is reflected in our impressive record. All of our UK centres are subject to inspection by the Adventure Activities Licensing Authority or the British Activity Holiday Association, as appropriate to the activities on offer. A PGL activity course provides children with the opportunity for personal and social development as they learn new skills and interact with others.

PGL Adventure UK also incorporates:

PGL Exploring ICT – With the growing importance of ICT across the school curriculum, PGL has created an exciting state of the art course which brings ICT out of the home and classroom to help pupils understand its practical uses in everyday situations. Using the very latest in computer hardware and software combined with the experience of thrilling outdoor activities, pupils can create, control and monitor real life situations.

PGL Mission Earth! – Our new Mission Earth! course delivers environmental education as an all-embracing mission combined with superb outdoor activities. Pupils learn about key ecological concepts and apply this to a real-life scenario to gain an understanding of the relevance of environmental principles in their own lives. Specifically written for primary school children, it is a cross curricular course covering key elements of a wide range of National Curriculum subjects.

PGL Overseas Adventure – PGL operates 8 activity centres in the South of France and Spain. These centres are predominantly watersports based, taking advantage of the natural surroundings. Whether children experience the exhilaration of canoeing down the Ardeche or windsurfing on the Mediterranean [or even both], three PGL owned and run centres in France and Bethany House, our new centre near London, offer a unique combination of learning and leisure. As a low cost alternative to the traditional tour, we can offer flexible tailor-made camping tours to Northern France. Our experienced and knowledgeable office team is always on hand to guide you through every stage of your tour planning and arrangements.

PGL School Tours – PGL has arranged a comprehensive programme of educational tours to the most popular UK destinations

Exhibit 1.2 (*Continued*)

as well as many countries on the Continent. There are also specialist study courses to choose from including Language Detectives, Geography, Field Studies, History and Art Tours. Bethany House, near London, and four PGL owned and run centres in France, including Chateau de Grande Romaine – our new centre near Paris offer a unique combination of learning and leisure. As a low cost alternative to the traditional tour, we can offer flexible, tailor-made camping tours to Northern France. Our experienced and knowledgeable office team is always on hand to guide you through every stage of your tour planning and arrangements.

PGL Ski – PGL has been active in the schools' ski market for many years and runs an extensive programme of ski courses by coach and air to Austria, Andorra, France, Italy, Switzerland and the USA. We have a wide range of destinations to suit groups of all abilities. We have also placed a PGL Ski Representative at each of our hotels to help with the day to day running of your ski course, to ski with your group and to help organize an exciting programme of evening entertainment.

PGL Loch Ranza – Situated on the Isle of Arran, this purpose built centre at Loch Ranza offers a wide programme of field study courses, including Geography, Geology, Biology and Environmental Science. The rugged landscape of Scotland provides a magnificent study area and Arran has a tremendous variety of features in a compact area.

Source: PGL Travel Limited

The ages of the UK guests for the 1996 season are shown in Exhibit 1.3.

The young people who go on a PGL holiday gain many experiences from their time at the centre. They may be away from home for the first time and are learning about leading a more independent life. They may be looking for excitement and adventure in a range of different activities. They may also be looking for new friends and new experiences. Some of the comments which were made by young people who went on PGL holidays are shown in Exhibit 1.4.

It is the parents of the young people who are the purchasers of the holidays. PGL Holidays commissioned a piece of market research in 1994 to discover the type of people who purchase their holidays. This market research was carried out by ICD Marketing Services and provided a full customer and prospect profile analysis for the company. ICD Marketing Services distributes consumer questionnaires throughout the UK and from these it gathers information relevant to their clients.

Customers of ICD Marketing Services can select their own particular information from a series of sources including the National Consumer

Exhibit 1.3   Age of UK guests, 1996 season

Age	Percentage
6	2
7	4
8	8
9	11
10	12
11	12
12	14
13	12
14	11
15	8
16	6
17	1
18	1

Source: PGL Travel Limited

Database, which has information on 38.5 million individuals and/or 22 million households, the British Investors Database, which has 6.1 million shareholders, and the Lifestyle Database, which is a survey carried out by ICD Marketing Services. The ICD Marketing Services research is designed to help clients improve their sales, usually by direct marketing methods.

The National Lifestyle Report which is completed by the company includes information on over 3 million individuals in the UK. The report covers a number of elements including:

Maps show the postal area and television area distribution of the client's present database and of the prospective target. This can have important implications for integrated national or regional campaigns.

Lifestyle Cell Clusters use principal component analysis and cluster analysis to allow the client to arrange individuals into groups which can then be targeted. The Lifestyle Database incorporates 100 different cell clusters utilizing the most significant lifestyle and demographic characteristics available. The numbers of individuals on the client's database is compared to the percentage on the Lifestyle Database to produce a Prospect Index. The logic behind this research is that individuals with similar lifestyle characteristics have similar purchasing intentions. The upper cell ranking comprises those prospects that fit the target best, and these can then be used to generate complex address details for the client.

The results of the survey carried out by ICD marketing for PGL Holidays Limited revealed some interesting facts about the customers for their holidays and prospective groups to target.

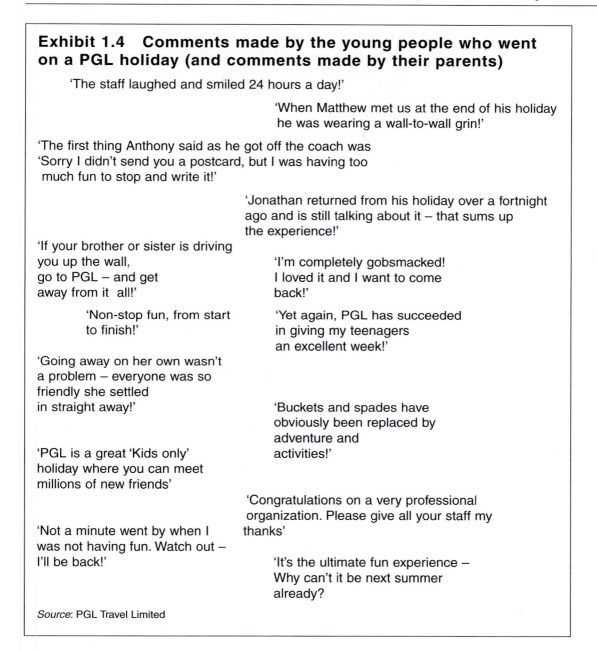

Exhibit 1.4   Comments made by the young people who went on a PGL holiday (and comments made by their parents)

'The staff laughed and smiled 24 hours a day!'

'When Matthew met us at the end of his holiday he was wearing a wall-to-wall grin!'

'The first thing Anthony said as he got off the coach was 'Sorry I didn't send you a postcard, but I was having too much fun to stop and write it!'

'Jonathan returned from his holiday over a fortnight ago and is still talking about it – that sums up the experience!'

'If your brother or sister is driving you up the wall, go to PGL – and get away from it all!'

'I'm completely gobsmacked! I loved it and I want to come back!'

'Non-stop fun, from start to finish!'

'Yet again, PGL has succeeded in giving my teenagers an excellent week!'

'Going away on her own wasn't a problem – everyone was so friendly she settled in straight away!'

'Buckets and spades have obviously been replaced by adventure and activities!'

'PGL is a great 'Kids only' holiday where you can meet millions of new friends'

'Congratulations on a very professional organization. Please give all your staff my thanks'

'Not a minute went by when I was not having fun. Watch out – I'll be back!'

'It's the ultimate fun experience – Why can't it be next summer already?

Source: PGL Travel Limited

Details of these are shown in Exhibit 1.5. It can be seen from this research that the customers for PGL holidays are largely from the ABC1 socioeconomic groups. They are professional people who read the quality newspapers and have a relatively high standard of living. They live in a good standard of owner-occupied accommodation and often own more than one car.

Promotion of PGL Holidays

The promotional strategy of PGL has helped to sustain the company as the market leader in the activity holidays market. A loyal following of party leaders and children has been built up through an emphasis on quality, safety, and value for money, all of which are highlighted in the promotional literature.

Exhibit 1.5   Lifestyle summary of the PGL customer

*	*Occupation*	Director, manager, professional people, self-employed, doctors, teachers, other professionals and housewives are particular targets
*	*Gender*	More females than males
*	*Marital status*	Married people are the predominant group
*	*Newspaper readership*	Daily Telegraph, Daily Mail, Sunday Times, Guardian readers
*	*Age*	35–54 years is the predominant age group
*	*Number of children*	2 children is most common followed by 1 child and 3 children, in that order
*	*Age of children*	Aged 11 to 15 and Aged 5 to 10 are the most important age groups
*	*Home ownership*	Most of the customers are owner occupiers
*	*Property types*	Over half of the customers live in detached houses. The rest live mainly in semi-detached or terraced properties
*	*House price*	The customers live in houses from a range of price brackets. A particular target in the range £100 K to £500 K was identified by the research
*	*Household income*	Household Income was found to be predominantly in the £20 000 plus bracket. A particular target was in the £40 000 plus bracket

---

Exhibit 1.5 (*Continued*)

*	*Hobbies and interests*	Customers were found to have a wide range of hobbies and interests. Particular reference was made to

- Further Education
- Gardening
- Theatre and Arts
- Wines
- Watching Videos

The most popular sporting activities included

- Swimming
- Aerobics/Keep Fit
- Badminton/Squash
- Tennis
- Cycling

* *Credit cards/ bank accounts*

Most of the customers were found to have bank accounts.
A high proportion also had credit cards and store cards

* *Holidays and travel*

A high proportion of the customers were found to holiday in the UK. Locations in decreasing order were shown to be:

- The UK
- Other European
- Canada
- Africa
- Asia/Far East
- Australia/New Zealand

Over half of the holidays are taken as weekend or short breaks. Self catering package holidays, or villa holidays are also popular.

* *Car ownership*

Over half of the customers own 2 cars, with saloons and estates being the most popular makes.

* *Residence*

Customers from the Central and Southern half of England were found to be of particular importance.

Source: Research report by ICD Marketing for PGL Travel Limited, 1996.

PGL focuses on six methods in their communication mix:

- direct mail
- personal selling
- advertising
- public relations
- word of mouth
- the Internet.

The mix of communication methods used is amended according to the product and the effectiveness of each tool relative to the market. Advertising, for example, is more effective for the marketing of holidays aimed at the individual unaccompanied child.

The promotional mix for PGL is shown in Exhibit 1.6.

Exhibit 1.6   Promotional mix

Direct mail – direct mail is the most cost-effective marketing tool for PGL's needs – it enables us to accurately target our customers and assess quantitatively the success of different campaigns. Underlying all PGL direct mail activity is the central database which encompasses all existing clients and enquirers plus details of potential customers. Specialist mailing lists are also purchased from external suppliers. Items mailed include brochures, newsletters and videos for use at home or parents' evenings.

Personal selling – PGL has a team of Group Travel Advisers covering the whole of the UK who not only promote our products to schools and groups, but build and maintain a personal rapport with party leaders. As the whole of the booking process can be carried out over the telephone or by correspondence, it is important to present the 'human face' of PGL to party leaders and to personalize the service we offer to individual needs.

Advertising – advertising features in varying degrees in most of PGL's campaigns depending upon the overall marketing mix for each product. It is mainly used in conjunction with individual holidays for children and teenagers. PGL adverts appear in the quality Sunday newspapers and supplements, educational supplements and children's publications to name but a few and are often timed to coincide with brochure launches and special offer mailings.

Public relations – PR activities include press releases, advertorials in newspapers and magazines, newsletters and the provision of holidays for competitions. Journalists are also encouraged to send their children on PGL holidays and report on their experiences.

Exhibit 1.6   (*Continued*)

PGL tries to work closely with the communities surrounding our centres, supporting local fetes, sporting events etc. Similar opportunities also exist for supporting school fetes, sports days and newsletters and PGL has sponsored a number of achievement awards at school prize-giving ceremonies.

Word of mouth – word of mouth is the most powerful promotional tool and PGL actively encourages positive word of mouth by rewarding existing clients when they introduce a new group or individual to PGL.

Internet – as you can see from all the above, communicating frequently with our customers is our key marketing strategy and the Internet provides us with an ideal, flexible method of getting our message into our customers' homes and schools. It will help us to provide up to date product and resort information, an alternative booking method, the opportunity for you to interact with other PGL customers (both individual and school) and even the facility to buy PGL T-shirts on-line before you leave for your holiday, course or tour.

Source: PGL Travel Limited

Conclusions

PGL Holidays have been developing their product to meet the growing interest in holidays for young people wanting to experience quality time away from their families. They offer well-run and secure holiday centres which are staffed by experts in their field. This gives parents the security of knowing that their children will be looked after in an appropriate environment. For the children, PGL offers exciting adventures and new experiences. Many of the children who go on a PGL holiday cannot wait to get back for their next one!

Discussion points

1 Evaluate the role of safety in the choice of outdoor pursuits by parents for children.
2 'Buckets and spades have been replaced by adventure and activities'. Explain the reasons for the change in the types of holidays which young people are demanding.

Thomas Cook's Club 18–30

Introduction

The Club 18–30 brand is owned by Thomas Cook Holdings Limited, London. The Club 18–30 unique holiday formula has remained more or less unchanged over the years and provides holidays for this specific age group of customers to the liveliest resorts in the central locations of major holiday regions. The company currently offers holidays to ten destinations across the Mediterranean and the Canaries, and flies from a number of UK airports. The company also offers a full range of accommodation from budget to all-inclusive packages.

History of the development of the Club 18–30 brand

Club 18–30 has been in existence for over thirty years, and was the first holiday company in the UK to specialize in holidays exclusively for young people.

Club 18–30 was, originally, part of the International Leisure Group (ILG), which collapsed in 1991. The collapse of ILG forced Club 18–30 into voluntary liquidation, despite the fact that it had been a profit-making division. Five weeks after the collapse, the existing directors of Club 18–30 bought the trade name and reformed the company. This move received enormous support from the travel trade and overseas suppliers. The company was prevented from trading under the Club 18–30 name owing to Association of British Agents (ABTA) legislation; hence the re-formed company became known as The Club.

The Club witnessed enormous growth during the 1990s from a small tour operator to a top ten UK operator. The ABTA granted the company permission to trade under the original branding, Club 18–30, in August 1994, and so The Club reverted back to the original name.

Thomas Cook AG is now one of the biggest European holiday companies. Some facts and figures about the company are shown in Exhibit 2.1. The company continues to offer a 'one-stop' holiday planning experience to its customers by using a strong portfolio of brands that it has acquired. The Club 18–30 brand is positioned in the UK market to target the young holidaymaker.

The Flying Colours Leisure Group became the owners of the Club 18–30 brand in 1995. This group was formed in November 1995 and was backed by a £40 million deal involving a major family tour operator, Sunset Holidays, and Club 18–30 were bought. The management team of the Flying Colours Leisure Group has extensive breadth and depth and, until March 1997, was headed by Jeremy Muller who was formerly Managing Director of Club 18–30. More recently Thomas Cook took over the company. The final chapter in the history of the brand was when the German tour company, NUR Touristic, and a new company, Thomas Cook NG, was formed in 2001.

The current business of Club 18–30

Thomas Cook aims to drive ambitious growth through successful market segmentation and positioning. The success of the Club 18–30 brand shows that well-targeted products using a portfolio of differentiated travel products can provide a successful business strategy in the competitive holiday market. The development of the Club 18–30 brand has been recognized as a dynamic response to the conservatism which has typified the UK market for overseas holidays.

Club 18–30 carried over 100 000 passengers in 1995. Some facts and figures about Club 18–30 are shown in Exhibit 2.2.

The Club 18–30 holiday concept

The Club 18–30 holiday formula was the first of its kind in the UK, and has remained unchanged over the years of development. The company

---

Exhibit 2.1   Thomas Cook AG: facts and figures

* Number two in the European leisure industry
* 7.5 billion euros in sales
* 24 600 employees
* 37 tour operator brands
* 75 aircraft
* 2400 travel agencies
* 75 000 controlled hotel beds
* operates in European and international markets
* offers the customer 'one-stop' holiday planning

Source: Thomas Cook web pages.

Exhibit 2.2   Club 18–30: facts and figures

Club 18–30 is the market leader in overseas summer-sun based youth holidays.

More than 100 000 passengers were carried in 1995.

The product is highly respected in the travel trade, and available from over 6000 travel agents.

Regional flying from a number of airports ensures high profile image is maintained throughout the UK.

Constant evaluation of resorts ensures that only the most 'happening' of places makes it into the company brochure.

Over 5000 applications are received annually for jobs as Clubreps. Less than 100 new Clubreps are required.

The company launched the idea of flexible booking in a 'pick and mix' approach with the launch of flexibletrips.com in 2004.

Source: Thomas Cook.

---

concentrates on attracting clients in the eighteen to thirty-year-old age bracket. Club 18–30 contracts hotels and apartments in the liveliest resorts and in central locations. The Club 18–30 accommodation is often used exclusively for the company's clients because it was recognized many years ago that it was preferable for the clients to have their own separate facilities and places to stay.

The holidays were originally marketed as 'a fortnight of Saturday nights' and entertainment is available twenty-four hours a day, seven days a week. Club 18–30 also offered its clients a range of unique excursions and club reps help make up an unrivalled fun holiday experience for their clients.

The range of countries on offer in the Club 18–30 range is shown in Exhibit 2.3.

The company selected resorts in an attempt to put together a Mediterranean party scene. They chose the best resorts that stayed awake twenty-four hours a day and selected accommodation which was near to the centre of the action.

San Antonio, in Ibiza, was selected because it is well known as the dance capital of Europe and the area offers blue zone beaches.

The twin fun-spots of Magaluf and Palma Nova on Majorca were selected for their range of bars, lots of pubs, English food and nightclubs. Resorts on Gran Canaria and Tenerife were selected for their bars, disco bars and clubs. Resorts on the Greek Islands of Corfu, Crete and Rhodes were selected for their around-the-clock entertainment. A recent addition to the product range is Cancun in Mexico.

The beach and pool are the main focal points of daytime activity, with a suntan the priority for most clients on a Club 18–30 holiday. The main action of the holiday, however, starts after dark. The resorts which the company picks have a good variety of local colour and generally have two or three major venues or attractions close at hand.

Exhibit 2.3   The Club 18–30 product range

* Ibiza
* Majorca
* Tenerife
* Gran Canaria
* Cyprus
* Corfu
* Crete
* Rhodes
* Kos

Source: Club 18–30.

The clients prefer to stay in self-catering or bed and breakfast accommodation, and so the company ensures that there is a good selection of well-priced restaurants and cafés close to the accommodation.

The Clubrep is an important aspect of the Club 18–30 holiday. He or she will be with the clients pretty well around the clock and will act as a party organizer, personally taking the clients to the best bars and nightspots. The ratio of Clubrep to clients is 1:25 because he or she is a social catalyst and the client's best friend. Many of the clients are travelling abroad for the first time, so the Clubrep provides a vital role in making sure the clients have an enjoyable time. The Clubrep concept became the focus for the *Club Reps* television programme based on Faliraki, Greece, in 2002. The company hoped that this programme would dispel misconceptions about the hedonistic image of the brand. The company subsequently withdrew 'bar crawls' from the product and tried to encourage customers to engage in more upmarket pursuits such as scuba diving and paintballing. The company is now trying to improve the image of the brand with the use of an advertising campaign that communicates the 'cool' nature of the Club 18–30 holiday. The campaign includes print advertising, radio advertising and the introduction of exclusive nightclub events across the country (Mintel, 2005). This campaign was developed by the advertising agency Saatchi and Saatchi in February 2005 based on the strapline 'be on the list', and encourages potential visitors to visit the website beonthelist.com. Since the introduction of the Club 18–30 concept there have been a number of competitors that have entered the market. These are shown in Exhibit 2.4.

The Club 18–30 client

A summary profile of the Club 18–30 client is shown in Exhibit 2.5.

The predominant age range for clients is eighteen to twenty-six, with an average age of twenty-one to twenty-two. Lower age limits are enforced fairly stringently, but the upper limits are fairly vague. If a client feels that the holiday would be suited to them, even if they are older, then they are welcome to go on the holidays. The company has a record

Exhibit 2.4   Competitors of Club 18–30 holidays in the UK

Brand	Company	Product range
2wentys	First Choice	Beach/resort holidays in the Mediterranean
Escapades	MyTravel	Beach/resort holidays in the Mediterranean plus Egypt, Dominican Republic and Mexico
Freestyle	TUI UK	Beach/resort holidays in the Mediterranean
Just – 'Just Chill' concept	TUI UK	Independent holiday to a range of Mediterranean resorts
Contiki	Travel Corporation	Adventure holidays across the world
Ibiza Trips	Avant Garde Travel	A variety of package holidays in Ibiza
EasyCruise	easyJet	Short cruises around the Mediterranean
Youthtravel.com	lastminute.com	On-line packages

Source: Mintel (2005).

Exhibit 2.5   The Club 18–30 client

Average age:	21/22
Male: female ratio:	50 : 50
Socioeconomic group	C1/C2/D/E
Marital status:	Single
Lifestyle:	In full time employment. Resident in parental home. Influenced by fashion, music, dance and entertainment (their spending patterns reflect this)

An 18–30 holiday is usually their first holiday abroad with friends, but without parents.

Source: Club 18–30.

of customers coming back, year after year, and some female clients even bring their mothers with them.

The male to female ratio is generally 50:50, but varies between 40:60 and 60:40. This is partly due to price as female clients tend to go when it is cheaper, and it is also fashionable for them to get an early suntan in May or June. Most of the clients go on a Club 18–30 holiday with a friend of the same sex. In low season, the average number of people per booking is two. In high season, this rises to three or four with groups of friends sharing apartments. Many customers go on a Club 18–30 holiday for their first holiday experience away from their parents.

The advertising campaign

The Saatchi and Saatchi advertising agency, London, were appointed by Club 18–30 in October 1994 to handle the above advertising campaign for the brand, and they have handled the advertising campaign since then. The original campaign objectives set by Club 18–30 were to increase bookings for summer 1995, raise the awareness of the Club 18–30 brand name and accurately reflect the nature of Club 18–30 holidays to the appropriate target market.

The campaign which the advertising agency developed, highlighted the fun of a Club 18–30 holiday in a 'tongue in cheek' way. It was designed to speak to the target market (seventeen to twenty-five year olds) via their type of media (forty-eight sheet posters) and in their style of language.

The advertising agency designed a series of posters which incorporated controversial and suggestive statements which were designed to appeal to the target audience. Examples of the poster copy are shown in Exhibit 2.6.

The initial campaign spend was £250 000 which allowed the company to concentrate a month-long, medium-weight campaign around the area where there was potential for growth. The campaign was

---

Exhibit 2.6   The 1995 Club 18–30 poster campaign poster copy

'It's not all sex, sex, sex'

'Girls. Can we interest you in a package holiday?'

'It's advisable not to drink the local water. As if . . .'

'Beaver España'

'You get two weeks for being drunk and disorderly'

'Discover your erogenous zone'

'The summer of 69'

Source: Flying Colours, 1995.

---

nationwide, other than Scotland and London, and was particularly concentrated in catchment areas of regional airports, such as Newcastle, Manchester, Birmingham, East Midlands, Cardiff, Belfast and Bristol. The posters were placed in major town centres where the largest population of young people in the 18–30 age range live and work. Research showed that the target group found the poster campaign humorous and appealing. The campaign also portrayed the products in a true light and consciously discouraged families, and other groups of people who would not enjoy this type of holiday, from booking a Club 18–30 holiday. The campaign commenced in January 1995 and for the 1995 season Club 18–30 enjoyed record bookings, 30 per cent higher than the previous year.

The company decided to run an amended version of the campaign in 1996. There had been criticism of the campaign and the Advertising Standards Authority (ASA) insisted that the Club 18–30 campaign should be vetted by themselves before it was run. The company decided to run a forty-eight sheet billboard campaign along the lines of the previous 'Jolly Japes' campaign, but the posters urged the reader to look for the real advertisements in magazines such as Sky, Loaded and Company. These magazines were chosen because they are read by the target audience. It also allowed the company to design press advertisements which were much more explicit, but similar to the first campaign.

The awareness and public relations gained from this campaign made an essentially small budget work very hard. The advertising campaign continued to make sure that the product remained at the forefront of youth culture. The brochure, which is produced on an annual basis, is a major part of this. The brochures are designed with this in mind, and there is a strong emphasis on style and fun.

Early brochure design caused comment in the trade. The brochure used 'Flo' and her 'pensioner pals' to introduce the products and it was designed to be humorous, but informative. The brochure also incorporated advertisements for other companies that sell products targeted at the same market segment.

The company were criticized for their product range and their controversial advertising campaigns by some pressure groups, in the light of HIV and AIDS. The company decided to take positive action about this and although they did not consider themselves as moral guardians, they thought it would be sensible to reiterate the 'safe sex' message wherever possible. Young people in the 1990s had been the first group to benefit from the government Health Education Authority's advice on sex education. Club 18–30 recognized that young people may have sex on holiday, and for that reason, the company reacted positively to the government Health Education Authority's initiative of 1991, which asked travel companies help educate young travellers in the dangers of casual sex overseas. Club 18–30 included information on safe sex and protection within every ticket wallet. The company also provided confidential supplies of condoms to clients for their Club 18–30 holiday.

The government Health Education Authority sought to address the problem of drug abuse among young people in 1997. Club 18–30 responded accordingly and offered realistic advice on drugs and the laws governing their use overseas to clients before they travel.

A statement by the Club 18–30 Managing Director, Stuart Howard, in February 1996 emphasized the point.

> We believe it is important to be proactive on these issues. Everybody knows that holidays are a time of romance and excitement, and we have 30 years of experience in dealing with this. Condoms are not as reliably available in many Mediterranean resorts, as they are here. Drugs, unfortunately are widely available everywhere. Although we have no wish to set ourselves up as moral guardians, we believe that it is only responsible to take up these initiatives on our client's behalf.

Club 18–30 was one of the first tour operators to respond positively to the government Health Education Authority's initiative on drugs.

More recent advertising campaigns have also been devised by Saatchi and Saatchi advertising agency.

The Future

It is predicted that the market for holidays aimed at the youth market will grow as disposable income continues to rise among the group. It is likely that the customer will start to demand more independently designed holiday packages with an increasing emphasis on adventure based activities.

The customer will also start to travel further afield as they become more experienced holidaymakers. An increase of bookings via the Internet is also predicted to be a feature of the market (Mintel, 2005).

Conclusions

Club 18–30 is one of the best examples of a UK brand which has aggressively targeted a particular market segment and positioned their products to suit the behaviour patterns of their clients. The company has repeatedly targeted the clients with effective and eye-catching advertising, which has been controversial enough to attract substantial media attention. The company also reacted positively to the government Health Education Authority's campaigns on safe sex and drug abuse. This has meant that the company are seen to be acting positively for their clients in the face of major health concerns.

The company is now having to react to increased competition and changing consumer behaviour.

Discussion points

1 Discuss the ways in which Club 18–30 has been very effective in designing holidays which suit the lifestyle of their target clients.

2 Explore the dilemma which a company, such as Club 18–30 can have when it is trying to design effective and appealing advertising campaigns without offending society at large. Discuss the ways in which Club 18–30 has overcome this potential problem.

The segmentation of the outbound Japanese market

The Japanese tourists are one of the classic stereotypes of the tourism world. Yet, it is still a market which is little understood by many businesses wishing to attract Japanese tourists.

There has been a steady growth in outbound tourism from Japan over the past twenty years. Details of this growth are shown in Exhibit 3.1. The reasons for the growth in outbound tourism from Japan have been attributed to a number of factors that are explored in Exhibit 3.2.

The destinations of Japanese outbound tourists are shown in Exhibit 3.3 and the reasons for travel in Exhibit 3.4.

For those accustomed to the Western European and North American markets, the Japanese market has very different characteristics based on Japanese culture.

Dace, in 1995, was one of the first authors to suggest different categories of Japanese tourists, including:

1 'Working Soldiers', who are male managers in the 30 to 50 age group, who have difficulty in finding time for a vacation because of their work commitments. They appear to want to enjoy 'meaningful experiences rather than just visual tours' (Beecham, quoted in Dace, 1995). They are also enthusiastic, discerning shoppers.
2 'The Silver Greys', are fifty to sixty-year-olds who have been influenced by growing up in the era of post-war austerity in Japan. They live frugal lives but when on vacation they like to 'let themselves go'. However, they want the familiar when on holiday, including Japanese food and guides who speak their language.

Exhibit 3.1   Trends in number of Japanese travelling abroad

Year	Outbound travellers (millions)
1980	3.91
1981	4.01
1982	4.09
1983	4.23
1984	4.66
1985	4.95
1986	5.52
1987	6.83
1988	8.43
1989	9.66
1990	11.00
1991	10.63
1992	11.79
1993	11.93
1994	13.58
1995	15.30
1996	16.69
1997	16.80
1998	15.81
1999	16.36
2000	17.82

Source: Japanese Tourist Board.

Exhibit 3.2   Reasons for the growth in outbound tourism from Japan

1. Steady population growth since 1980 with bulges in the 25–29 and 50–54 age groups

2. Japanese propensity for hard work has fuelled income growth

3. Increased demand to go abroad

4. Increased air capacity

5. Increased business travel

6. Increased interest in Asia as a tourism destination

Exhibit 3.3   Japanese outbound travel by purpose of visit and leading destination

Destination	Leisure	Business	Other	Total
USA	4 336 954	495 568	241 151	5 073 673
Korea	2 117 958	247 967	20 619	2 386 544
China	1 012 524	413 312	42 656	1 468 492
Thailand	734 546	132 389	19 003	885 938
Taiwan	554 901	278 034	12 042	844 977
Hong Kong	580 249	208 874	21 403	810 526
Australia	636 819	36 097	26 951	699 867
Singapore	461 250	104 252	19 657	585 159
Italy	402 630	39 198	10 016	451 844
Indonesia	386 599	49 334	8 180	444 113
UK	282 524	64 397	54 923	401 844
France	310 506	56 325	22 375	389 206

Source: Ministry of Justice, Weekly Travel Journal; Mintel (2002).

Exhibit 3.4   Japanese outbound travel by purpose of trip, 2000

Purpose of trip	Number of trips 2000	Percentage share 2000
Holiday	14 582 476	81.8
Business	2 599 173	14.6
Diplomat/official	55 857	0.3
Overseas assignment	55 119	0.3
Study/research	100 401	0.6
Technical training	193 779	1.1
Volunteer	14 691	0.1
Emigration	130 251	0.7
Accompany spouse	86 843	0.5
Total	**17 818 590**	**100.0**

Source: Ministry of Justice, *Weekly Travel Journal*; Mintel (2002).

3 'The Full Mooners', are mature married couples who prefer to take single centre holidays, and are very quality-conscious.

4 Technical Visits and Old Study Tours. Japanese companies use work-related study tours as a way of recruiting and rewarding staff. Most such tourists are men and many such trips are combined with leisure pursuits such as golf.

5 Student Travel. School, college and university students take, generally, short-duration trips, most popular in February. They tend to book flights and accommodation-only packages.

6 The 'Young Affluent' or 'Shinginsi'. This is a twenty to thirty-year-olds segment which has grown up in a period of affluence in Japan. They like to flaunt their money and are independently minded. They rarely take packaged vacations and are major participants in the short-break and activity holiday market.

7 The 'Office Ladies'. These are unmarried women in their early twenties. They have high disposable income and they tend to be living at home with their parents. They like Western countries and enjoy visiting capital cities, such as Paris and London, and shopping. They like organized tours, although there is a trend towards more independent travel.

8 The 'Honeymooners', are a segment defined by the fact that it goes overseas for its honeymoon. This is true for as many as 95 per cent of Japanese couples (Beecham, quoted in Dace, 1995), who choose Asian destinations, European cities or places in the USA.

The Japanese market does have a controversial dimension in terms of:

- the demand of some Japanese tourists that their destinations should offer Japanese food, service, guides, and so on. This can alienate some local communities as has been seen on the Queensland coast in Australia, for example
- Japanese male tourists are a significant proportion of the sex tourism market in many Asian destinations.

It can be seen that the USA is the major tourist destination for Japanese tourists. A large proportion of tourist trips are for leisure purposes with business travel being of secondary importance. A high proportion of female Japanese tourists in 2000 travelled for leisure (70 per cent), whereas 30 per cent of married men travelled for business, with a high percentage of business travellers visiting China and other Asian countries (Japanese Tourist Board, 2002).

Research has been conducted to investigate the special nature of Japanese tourists on the basis of their cultural identity. Ahmed and Krohn (1992) considered the special characteristics that the Japanese tourist requires when visiting the USA as a result of their cultural identity. These special characteristics are shown in Exhibit 3.5.

Discussion points and essay questions

1 Discuss the reasons for the growth in the outbound Japanese tourist market in the past twenty years.
2 Explore the motivations of the different market segments of Japanese tourists.

Exhibit 3.5 Special characteristics of Japanese culture that influence tourist behaviour

1. Belongingness (e.g. travelling with other)
2. Family influence (e.g. purchasing gifts for family)
3. Empathy (e.g. not expressing true personal feelings)
4. Dependency (e.g. being loyal and devoted)
5. Hierarchical acknowledgement (e.g. behave in relation to social status)
6. Propensity to save (e.g. saving to overcome insecurity)
7. The concept of Kinen (e.g. collecting evidence of travel to show others)
8. Tourist photography (e.g. the importance of photography)
9. Passivity (e.g. avoidance of physical activity)
10. Risk avoidance (e.g. avoiding adventurous pursuits)

Source: Ahmed and Krohn (1992).

---

3 Critically analyse the consumer behaviour of one of the market segments of outbound Japanese tourists. Explore what this will mean for destination marketers.

4 Evaluate the different activities that the typical Japanese leisure tourist will engage in during their holiday experiences. Discuss what your findings will mean for destination marketers who are trying to attract Japanese tourists.

Segmenting the leisure shopping market

Leisure shopping, in other words buying things for pleasure, rather than out of necessity, and enjoying the actual process of shopping, is a major element of the tourism market today. Indeed, for some destinations it is the core of their tourism product and many tourists now spend more on retailing than they do on their flight or their accommodation.

However, like all markets, the leisure shopping market is not a homogeneous market; it can be divided into different segments on the basis of different criteria. Let us now examine some of these criteria.

First, there is the issue of how far tourists are willing to travel for leisure shopping. This may vary from a few kilometres to thousands of kilometres. The distance travelled will, of course, also have an impact on the duration of the trip.

We could also segment the market on the basis of either ability to spend or willingness to spend, which are not the same thing at all. This segment could range from those willing to spend thousands of US dollars or euros on a trip to those unable or unwilling to spend more than a few dollars or euros. Indeed, for some 'window-shopping' may be as important a part of the experience as actually buying something.

As with all types of tourism the leisure shopping market may also be divided into domestic, inbound and outbound segments.

Leisure shopping can also be segmented in terms of its seasonality built around events such as sale periods or Christmas shopping or, even, specially organized shopping festivals.

It is also perhaps important to distinguish between trips where retailing is the main purpose of the trip and a general vacation where shopping will be undertaken on just one or two days.

We can also segment this market on the basis of who is taking the trip, namely a person on their own, a couple, a family or a group of friends. In the UK, for example, groups of women friends may well take a shopping trip together.

It is also interesting to split the market based on the kind of outlets people prefer to visit including:

- major shopping malls
- small independent shops
- factory outlets and warehouses that sell products directly from the manufacturers
- traditional markets or souks.

Some people will shop in all such outlets, while others will have particular preferences.

It is also interesting to see if we can divide the market into segments based on the products people like to buy. In other words, people may prefer to buy branded designer goods through to traditional local products.

At the same time, we also have people who are only really interested in particular types of product, which might include clothing, jewellery, CDs and DVDs, food and drink. Furthermore, while most people like to buy new products, some people really enjoy buying second-hand items from shops and flea markets.

Many people would argue that the market can be easily segmented by gender; in other words, women like leisure shopping more than men. However, while there may be some truth underpinning this view, it is far too stereotypical given that many men enjoy shopping, and some women hate shopping.

In tourist destinations, one always has the distinction, too, between those who are shopping for themselves and those who are buying for others.

Let us now look at some ethically questionable or unethical forms of leisure shopping, including people who:

- shop for profit, in other words, they buy things with the express intention of taking them home to sell. Sometimes such 'tourists' may exceed the legal limit on purchasing certain goods such as alcohol or tobacco, to the point where they are engaging in 'smuggling'
- buy illegal souvenirs, for example, ancient artefacts or items made from endangered animals.

Having looked at the different ways of segmenting, we might now briefly look at the role which leisure shopping plays in tourist destinations. This can perhaps best be illustrated through Exhibit 4.1.

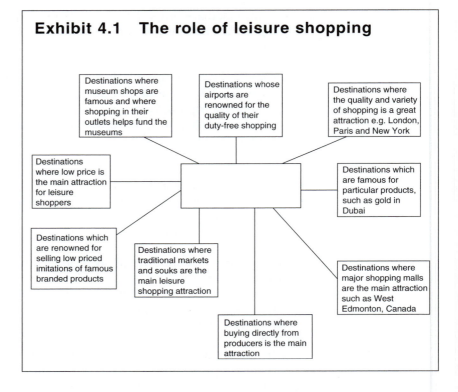

Exhibit 4.1 The role of leisure shopping

Destinations where museum shops are famous and where shopping in their outlets helps fund the museums

Destinations whose airports are renowned for the quality of their duty-free shopping

Destinations where the quality and variety of shopping is a great attraction e.g. London, Paris and New York

Destinations where low price is the main attraction for leisure shoppers

Destinations which are famous for particular products, such as gold in Dubai

Destinations which are renowned for selling low priced imitations of famous branded products

Destinations where traditional markets and souks are the main leisure shopping attraction

Destinations where major shopping malls are the main attraction such as West Edmonton, Canada

Destinations where buying directly from producers is the main attraction

As leisure tourism has grown, so too have the sources of advice available for tourists concerning leisure shopping opportunities, in destinations.

There are now specialist guidebooks on leisure shopping, in particular cities, often also giving advice on where to stay and eat. Most of these guides are 'mainstream' but very often include details of quirky and unusual retail outlets as well. More 'traditional' guidebooks to destinations as a whole, such as Fodor, Frommer, Lonely Planet, Time Out and so on, tend to offer a lot of advice about where to shop.

Travel features in magazines and newspapers also tend to focus a lot of attention on leisure shopping. Destinations often organize special shopping festivals in the off-peak season to boost demand, including examples in Dubai and Hong Kong.

In many cities, tourists can now take organized shopping tours. For example, in New York, tours are available to food shops and clothing shops, as well as trips to out of town shopping complexes such as the Woodbury Common Factory Outlet. Leisure shopping malls have almost developed into mini-destinations in their own right. Multi-development complexes and food courts in many countries have become day-trip destinations.

Leisure shopping is a global phenomenon, but it is particularly well established in the US domestic market, and is also a major factor influencing the destination choice of many outbound tourists from recently developed countries in Asia for example. It is also a major activity for tourists from former communist countries, for whom leisure shopping is a relatively new experience.

Conclusions

In the past twenty years leisure shopping has grown dramatically worldwide and is now a major component of the global tourism market. However, as we have seen, it is a very diverse market which has yet to be thoroughly researched. It seems likely to continue to grow and become an even more important phenomenon for tourist destinations.

Discussion points and essay questions

1 Discuss the reasons why leisure shopping has grown so dramatically over the past twenty years.
2 Discuss the ethical issues which are raised by certain aspects of leisure shopping.
3 Critically evaluate the suggestion made by some commentators that leisure shopping is fundamentally a female market.

Exercise

Select a destination and, using guidebooks, brochures, websites, etc., analyse the leisure shopping product. Then design a marketing strategy for the destination, identifying which potential leisure shopping market segments it should target and what it will need to do to attract these segments.

The Savoy Hotel, London

Introduction

The Savoy Hotel is located on The Strand in the heart of the West End theatre district of London. The Savoy has played host to eminent men and women and provided the setting for glittering social occasions for over a century.

The Savoy Hotel was built with every luxury in mind. It was sold in 2005 to the Fairmont Hotels and Resorts Company. The ownership of the other hotels in the Savoy Group – the Berkeley, Claridge's and The Connaught – remain unchanged.

The original Savoy Group of Hotels and Restaurants were located in the capital of England, London. The company also owned The Lygon Arms in Broadway, in the Cotswolds. The hotels in the Group were represented by 'The Leading Hotels of the World' group. In 1995 the Group embarked on a major programme of work to re-establish itself as the world's leading luxury hotel chain. This programme of work involved a major period of refurbishment which has tried to maintain the old charm of the hotels, but introduced new comfort and facilities. The programme also involved an extensive programme of management restructuring and training, and new approaches to sales and marketing.

A brief history of the Savoy Group

The Savoy Hotel was built by theatrical impresario, Richard D'Oyly Carte. He had built the first theatre with electric lights in the world – The Savoy Theatre, in 1881, and proceeded to commission operettas. Gilbert and Sullivan wrote the operetta *Trial by Jury* for Richard D'Oyly Carte, and it proved to be an instant smash hit when it was staged at the theatre.

Richard D'Oyly Carte began to realize that theatre customers often needed overnight accommodation, and in 1885 he began to resurrect the Savoy Hotel on the banks of the River Thames. He recognized that he needed people with considerable talent to run the hotel. He brought César Ritz from Switzerland and Escoffier from France to convert the cooking at the Savoy to an art form. Society flocked to the new creation, to try out the new dishes and soak up the luxurious ambience. The Savoy has been at the heart of the arts in London for over a century. It continues to be the home of leading artists and is a meeting place for journalists, captains of industry and politicians.

D'Oyly Carte quickly decided to expand his interest in hotels, and refurbished Claridge's in Mayfair in 1899. It opened with a flourish and quickly became a favourite hotel with royalty. Heads of state and royalty have stayed in the hotel ever since.

The Connaught was built in 1897 and rapidly became the hotel for the landed gentry. D'Oyly Carte also purchased The Berkeley which was located in Piccadilly. The area started to change after the Second World War, and the Managing Director, Hugh Wontner, was commissioned to seek out a new site. Land was found in Belgravia, a very elegant part of London, and the hotel was finally opened in 1972. The Berkeley has become a popular location for social, diplomatic and business gatherings.

The Group also purchased The Lygon Arms in the Cotswolds, and Simpson's in the Strand. The Savoy Group of Hotels that existed before the sale of the Savoy is shown in Exhibit 5.1.

Exhibit 5.1   The Savoy Group of Hotels and Restaurants prior to the sale of The Savoy in 2005

THE BERKELEY, Wilton Place, Knightsbridge, London SW1X 7RL
Tel: 0171 235 6000

CLARIDGE'S, Brook Street, Mayfair, London W1A 2JQ
Tel: 0171 629 8860

THE CONNAUGHT, Carlos Place, Mayfair, London W1Y 6AL
Tel: 0171 499 7070

THE SAVOY, The Strand, London WC2R 0EU
Tel: 0171 836 4343

THE LYGON ARMS, Broadway, Worcestershire WR12 7DU
Tel: 01386 852255

SIMPSON'S IN THE STRAND, 100 Strand, London WC2R 0EW
Tel: 0171 836 9112

EDWARD GOODYEAR Court Florist, 45 Brook Street,
London W1A 2JQ
Tel: 0171 629 1508

SAVOY THEATRE, The Stand, London WC2R 0ET
Tel: 0171 836 8888

Source : The Savoy Group Promotional Literature

The Savoy Group's collection of hotels and restaurants has always epitomized excellence in service, style, elegance and cuisine. The combination of the rich history, and the distinguished cast list of guests and staff make it unique. It has also encouraged and trained thousands of young, career-minded people – indeed, it is a 'school' for learning to deliver quality of service.

We have always been at the very heart of innovation, a characteristic of The Savoy Group, and I am delighted to be in a position to help continue this tradition. I enjoy working with the staff, maintaining the existing high standards and enhancing them where appropriate. In this industry, the hotel business and the needs of our guests are constantly evolving, and our job is to make sure that we keep abreast of every change.

We aim to offer the best of both worlds – maintaining respect for the past and an understanding of the future. We have the very latest in technology and efficiency, giving modern comfort, which is combined with the original interiors and traditional standards of service.

The Savoy Hotel plc comprises a group of luxury hotels that is independent and answerable only to its Board of Directors. The Group's key objective is to maintain all the elements of style and service that have made it famous and envied throughout the world. (Ramon Pajares – Managing Director, Savoy Group 1999)

The Savoy Group, under the leadership of Ramón Pajares began the painstaking process of restoring the hotels within the Group to be the most distinguished and individual hotels in England. The customer survey had noted some particular areas for attention such as general levels of comfort, improved business services and improved levels of personal service.

The Group spent £62 million on the refurbishment. The project affected all five hotels in the Group's portfolio and has combined careful restoration work with the installation of state-of-the-art technology. New bedrooms, penthouse suites, luxurious fitness facilities, meeting rooms and modern business amenities have all been incorporated in the ambitious programme. The programme was controlled by the Managing Director, Ramón Pajares and was summed up by his maxim: 'respecting the past and understanding the future'.

The refurbishment programme carried out at the Savoy and Claridge's is shown in Exhibit 5.2.

The Group paid particular attention to the needs of the business executive in their refurbishment project. Business amenities and meeting rooms were upgraded. The refurbished rooms incorporate ISDN lines, video cameras, projection screens, high-quality sound systems and sophisticated audiovisual systems. Dual-line telephones, dedicated fax

Exhibit 5.2   The refurbishment programme at the Savoy and Claridge's in the late 1990s

CLARIDGE'S

A London name to rank alongside Christie's, Harrods and the Victoria and Albert Museum, Claridge's has all the style, elegance and sophistication of an English stately home.

Business at theTop

A central element in the £32 million refurbishment programme at Claridge's has been the creation on the sixth floor of a self-contained conference suite, comprising four inter-connecting meeting and dining rooms.

Olympian Fitness

Claridge's magnificent new health and fitness centre. The Olympus Suite, is ideally suited for the international traveller.

Seventh Heaven

Pride of place in Claridge's hotel wide restoration programme is taken by the two new luxurious Penthouse suites, one traditional, one Art Deco style, and seven Art Deco de luxe double bedrooms on the seventh floor.

Double Award

In two separate readers' polls in 1996, Claridge's has been voted by Travel & Leisure magazine one of Europe's 25 best hotels and by Institutional Investor magazine, one of the world's 25 best hotels.

THE SAVOY

The Savoy is a London landmark whose history and location are entwined with the capital's vibrant cultural and commercial past. Rich, elegant and flamboyant, the hotel's unique atmosphere makes any visit an event in itself.

Restoring the Glory

The restoration of the famous Front Hall is just one element in an £18 million list of improvements which have brought a renewed sense of style to The Savoy.
Other public areas, including the American Bar, have been sympathetically restored to their former glory.

Big Business

The magnificent Abraham Lincoln and Manhattan meeting and banqueting rooms, have been carefully restored to maintain their classical style whilst also incorporating the latest technology.

Past and Future

Guest rooms have been redecorated, their architectural features painstakingly restored and bathrooms throughout upgraded.

Style Vote

The Savoy's stylish interiors and elegance remain as popular as ever with readers of Institutional Investor and Travel and Leisure magazines, who voted it one of the world's 100 best hotels in their respective 1996 polls.
It has just been named Egon Ronay's Hotel of the Year.

Source: The Savoy Group.

lines and modem points were incorporated. The rooms have individually controlled air-conditioning systems, a CD player and a CD library on demand, and the provision of US and European electrical points, voice mail and language facilities.

The refurbishment programme was followed by an extensive period of staff training including an intensive customer service training programme.

The Group also placed a new focus on sales and marketing. The first stage of this was to communicate the good news about the refurbishment programme across the world. The Group established a website and travelled to cities around the world, including Tokyo, Singapore and Hong Kong to tell the trade about the dramatic improvements in the refurbished hotels.

The Group reorganized the sales and marketing departments. Specialists were appointed who were given the responsibility of regaining market share by developing key geographic markets (the UK, the USA, Europe and Japan) and by focusing on individual business and leisure segments. It was hoped that this quality marketing would help to re-establish the company as the first choice for customers who were looking for a luxury hotel in London.

The Savoy Hotel was bought by an American hotel company, the Fairmont Hotels and Resorts Company, on the 19 January 2005. The philosophy, mission and service statements of the Fairmont Hotels and Resorts Group US are shown in Exhibit 5.3. The ownership of the other members of the group – Claridge's, The Berkeley and The Connaught remain as they were.

The Savoy today

The Savoy has a long history of development and has maintained the Art Deco touches that have made it so famous. The hotel now has an array of modern amenities that make the hotel attractive to the business and leisure traveller. The visitor to the Savoy comes from the UK and worldwide, with a large amount of the business being dependant on male business travellers. The Far East is an important market, with Japanese visitors being a particularly important segment of customers. Both business and leisure customers look for high levels of individual service, and business guests particularly look for conference facilities, individual meeting rooms and business technology. The challenge for the Savoy is how to keep updating these services without changing the ambience of the hotel. An important part of the Savoy's hotel customer base is the special treat visitors. An example of a package that seeks to attract this type of customer is shown in Exhibit 5.4.

Conclusions

The Savoy Group has had to respond to demands from its guests to see improved facilities and services. A major investment programme coupled with staff training programmes and renewed sales and marketing

---

Exhibit 5.3 The Fairmont Hotels and Resorts' approach

OUR PHILOSOPHY

We will earn the loyalty of our guests by exceeding their expectations and providing warm and personal service in distinctive surroundings.

At Fairmont Hotels & Resorts we are known for our warm and personal service, our elegant hotels and resorts, and the pride of our history. What began as one hotel in 1886 has grown into one of the leading hotel companies in the world with luxury properties in the most spectacular locations across North America and the Caribbean. We offer a century-long tradition of excellence in service and elegance in hospitality.

Our Mission

To provide our guests with:
− Places of Unrivalled Presence
− Experiences that are Authentically Local
− Service that is Engaging

Our Service

A century of experience as hoteliers has created a tradition of hospitality that is evident in everything we do. We know that even the best locations and offerings would be meaningless without outstanding guest service.

At Fairmont Hotels & Resorts, our employees are central to our operations philosophy. We believe that a well-trained, motivated workforce will naturally exceed guest expectations. Service Plus, our custom-designed service delivery programme, gives our people the tools they need to succeed. We then carefully monitor our progress through employee opinion surveys and guest feedback.

Fairmont Hotels & Resorts has an outstanding reputation for environmental stewardship, community involvement and innovative social programmes. Our award-winning initiatives enhance employee satisfaction, win guest loyalty and create a positive public profile for the brand as a whole.

Source: Fairmont Hotels and Resorts.

---

effort have attempted to reverse a downward trend in sales experienced in the 1990s. The initial results of the programme of work indicate that it has been successful. Particular emphasis was put on the use of new technology, improvements in public rooms, and, leisure and business facilities.

The focus on particular market segments, designing products to suit their needs and wants and communicating these developments to

---

Exhibit 5.4   Hotel packages – The Savoy

Deluxe Luxury Break Packages

Treat yourself to a getaway with our *Deluxe Luxury Break Package*

Package Includes:
Room accommodation including VAT
English Breakfast
Bottle of chilled Champagne
Basket of Fresh Fruit

Availability:
This offer is valid year-round, subject to availability

Rates – see web page link

Source: The Savoy.

---

them has been a major part of the continued strategy by the Fairmont Hotel Group.

Discussion points

1 The restoration programme at The Savoy Group was based on the maxim of: 'respecting the past and understanding the future'. Discuss the importance of this statement, in relation to the needs and wants of the customers of The Savoy.
2 The Savoy carried out marketing research with guests to inform their refurbishment programme. Prepare a detailed plan of the marketing research programme which you would carry out for the Savoy prior to another programme of redevelopment. Suggest an ongoing programme of marketing research with guests which you would implement at the hotel.
3 Explore the ways in which a hotel such as the Savoy can balance the different needs of the business and leisure customer.

First Choice Holidays' all-inclusive package

Introduction

First Choice Holidays was formed as a result of an extensive re-launch of the Owners Abroad company in 1994. The company offers a full range of package holidays and uses a range of sub-brands. It piloted the idea of an all-inclusive holiday during the 1995 season, which led to the successful introduction of the all-inclusive brochure for the 1996–97 season. The company still offers inclusive holidays in 2006.

The all-inclusive product

The all-inclusive holiday concept was developed in the 1990s to respond to a growing demand from consumers for a holiday which was priced to include all food, accommodation and activities for the duration of stay. The all-inclusive concept offers the customer all transport, accommodation, drinks and sporting activities included in the price. In 1996, First Choice Holidays was the first package holiday operator to introduce the all-inclusive holiday into the UK mainstream market with the introduction of a wide range of all-inclusive deals to popular summer Mediterranean destinations. During this period a National Opinion Poll (NOP) survey revealed that 40 per cent of people did not understand the concept of the all-inclusive holiday and thought that it was 'too good to be true'. A survey carried out in 1995 revealed that the majority of interviewees thought that 'all inclusive meant simply a standard package holiday, including only accommodation, flight and transfer.

It became apparent in 1996 that the all-inclusive package holiday had become one of the fastest growing types of holidays in the UK. At the same time, First Choice was voted Number One for all-inclusive holidays by travel agents in a Mori survey. A new NOP survey, commissioned by First Choice holidays in 1996, showed that people's awareness and support for the all-inclusive holiday had increased during the year.

The all-inclusive concept was well received by the British consumer who was keen to make their pound stretch further. In the 1996 survey 73 per cent of the interviewees stated that there were particular benefits to be gained from purchasing an all-inclusive type of holiday. They made such statements as:

- 'It would make financial planning easier.'
- 'It provides better value for money.'

Other respondents noted the advantages it would bring if they could eat and drink all they wanted every day, and the fact that they would be encouraged to be more active on holiday because there was no extra charge for sporting activities. A sceptical 13 per cent, however, remained to be convinced that such an attractive holiday option exists and think that it is 'too good to be true'.

It has been estimated by First Choice that a family of four, on a week's holiday in a Spanish resort, would spend on average £22.40 on ice cream for the children (if each child had a minimum of two ice creams per day) and that the parents would spend on average £103.60 on alcohol (based on each adult having an average of two glasses of wine, two bottles of beer, and a local spirit and mixer per day at local prices). If the extra costs such as those for snacks, soft drinks, teas, coffees, water sports and entertainment are added on, the savings are obvious. The all-inclusive holiday which is often only £100 per person per week more expensive than the similar half-board holiday, therefore offers extremely good value for money.

Kevin Ivie, the First Choice Group Marketing Director of First Choice Holidays in 1997, stated:

> First Choice is now a leading authority on Mediterranean all-inclusives. The concept was tested last summer in selected resorts and following its great success, a full range of all-inclusive holidays were launched for Summer '96. In fact, a MORI survey conducted in 1996 found that more than half of all travel agents advise customers that First Choice provides the best all-inclusive holidays. It has been a trump card this year for First Choice and, ever quick to adopt a good idea, we expect that some of the other leading tour operators may try to copy the all-inclusive theme for next summer.

The early growth in the all-inclusive package has continued since the 1990s, with a growing number of countries, regions and hospitality companies specializing in this type of product offering. The growth of the all-inclusive package has been attributed to a number of factors associated with patterns of consumer behaviour in relation to holiday purchases.

The all-inclusive customer

First Choice Holidays carried out some early research into the type of customer that was emerging for the all-inclusive product offering. Results from this early research are shown in Exhibits 6.1 and 6.2.

It can be seen from these two exhibits that the early customer in the UK for the all-inclusive packages tended to be married and largely from the thirty to fifty age group. A large proportion of the customers were from a higher socioeconomic group such as professional/senior manager. Single people also represented an important part of the target group.

The all-inclusive range of holiday also offer free child prices, discounts for children and groups, and special offers for tropical honeymooners.

First Choice has conducted limited market research on customers returning from all-inclusive holidays. Overall impressions of these holiday-makers seem to be very favourable. There is limited information regarding the demographic and lifestyle profile of the all-inclusive customer. Highlights of the limited data collected give some ideas of the

---

Exhibit 6.1   The First Choice all-inclusive target group

Age of all-inclusive guests

20 or under	6%
21–30	18%
31–40	29%
41–50	25%
51–65	13%
65+	2%

Marital status

Married	74%
Single	23%
Divorced/separated	5%
Widowed	1%

Source: First Choice Holidays.

Exhibit 6.2   The profiles of the all-inclusive customer

Age profile

20 or under	6%
21–30	18%
31–40	29%
41–50	25%
51–65	13%
65+	2%

Marital status

Married	74%
Single	23%
Divorced/separated	5%
Widowed	1%

Socio-economic groups

Professional or senior managers	24%
Middle/junior managers	12%
Administrators	11%
Self-employed	10%
Students	3%
Housewives	7%
Retired	5%

Favourite newspaper

Daily Mail
The Sun
Daily Mirror

Source: First Choice Holidays, 1997.

profiles of this group of holiday-makers. Details of this preliminary market research are shown in Exhibit 6.2.

The all-inclusive customer today comes from a range of market segments. These market segments are explored in Exhibit 6.3.

It can be seen from Exhibit 6.3 that there are some similarities between the all-inclusive customers of today compared with the early customers who showed an interest in the product. The increase in the number of niche holiday-makers – such as health, sport and naturism,

---

Exhibit 6.3　Market segments that are attracted to the all-inclusive product

SOCIOECONOMIC	– Middle/high income
FAMILY LIFE-CYCLE	– Singles – Couples without dependant children – Families
LIFESTYLE	– Health tourist – Naturism – Sport tourist
BEHAVIOURAL	– Weddings and honeymooners – Gay couples – Business traveller

Source: adapted from Mintel (2001a).

---

gay all-inclusive and the business traveller, is an increasingly important part of the market. It is important to consider the reasons for the growth in the all-inclusive product in relation to trends in consumer behaviour.

Why choose an all-inclusive package?

The choice of an all-inclusive holiday has been attributed to a number of factors that are associated with consumer behaviour. These factors are explored in Exhibit 6.4.

It can be seen that the growth in the interest of the all-inclusive type of package has been a result of changes in consumer lifestyles. Individuals, couples and families are increasingly finding themselves earning plenty of money but having very little time to spend it. There is also a desire to purchase easy and quick fixes in the holiday market with the desire to experience a hassle-free holiday of relaxation.

The all-inclusive holiday experience has been criticized for a lack of involvement in the local communities in which it is based. Recent research for First Choice by Mintel (2005), however, showed that only about a quarter of respondents were concerned about the impact of tourism on the local environment of countries.

The supply side of the all-inclusive product

The development of the all-inclusive package holiday has allowed countries, regions, tour operators and hospitality companies to develop business which targets the type of consumer from across the world.

Customers from the USA, Canada, Japan and European countries (Germany, the UK, France, Netherlands, Austria, Switzerland and

> ### Exhibit 6.4 Reasons for choosing all-inclusive package holiday
>
> * **Cash rich/time poor customers**
>   Consumers with decreasing amounts of leisure time but increasing income seek shorter/fuller experiences
>
> * **Security issues**
>   Worries about crime and the risks associated with more unknown destinations mean that all-inclusive is a safe option
>
> * **Relaxation**
>   Increased stress levels mean that the all-inclusive resort offers a quick fix experience with no hassle. The experience offers total relaxation
>
> * **Money worries**
>   The all-inclusive package allows the customer to have the security of paying for everything before departure and there are no worries associated with extra money or currency change
>
> *Source*: adapted from Mintel (2001a).

Italy) have continued to purchase all-inclusive packages across the world. We can now look at examples of a hotel chain, a tour operator and a country that has explored the all-inclusive holiday product.

Examples of all-inclusive initiatives

The tour operator: First Choice

First Choice Holidays is a leading international leisure travel company which operates in sixteen countries and employs 14 000 people. They were one of the first UK tour operators to offer an all-inclusive holiday product. The group had the original desire to develop and operate a high-quality, mass-market package holiday business in the UK and American markets, through the use of a portfolio of brands that have been developed over the last decade.

The current Chief Executive, Peter Long, recognized that the aim of the business is to target the leisure customer from a wide range of countries, including the UK, Ireland, Canada, France, Germany, Spain, Italy, the USA, Holland, Austria, Switzerland, Norway, Portugal, Belgium, Denmark, Sweden and Australia (First Choice web page, accessed 2005).

The group was one of the first in the UK to develop the all-inclusive package holiday and to recognize the potential for this type of product in the mainstream holiday sector. The current all-inclusive package on offer by First Choice Holidays is shown in Exhibit 6.5. The group has

---

Exhibit 6.5   All-inclusive – feel like a star with all your holiday essentials taken care of

Booking an all-inclusive holiday ensures that all holiday essentials, such as meals, drinks and snacks are included in the price. Not only does this represent excellent value for money, but it also helps you plan your budget. This means your spending money can be saved for optional excursions and those all-important holiday souvenirs.

We have many all-inclusive holidays in the Caribbean, the Canaries, Balearics and Turkey, to name but a few.
What's included in the price of my all-inclusive holiday?
– Buffet breakfast, lunch and dinner
– Snacks between meal times
– Unlimited locally produced alcohol drinks for adults
– Unlimited soft drinks, tea and coffee
– Sports and non-motorised watersports facilities in many hotels
– Daytime and evening activities programme
– Plus many of our all-inclusive accommodations offer 24 hour service, catering for you no matter what the time

Source: First Choice website, accessed 2005.

---

widened their range of all-inclusive destinations from their early development of the market in the 1990s.

New destinations such as Bulgaria, Cyprus and Turkey have now been added to the brochure, and the group intend to expand the range of destinations in the future.

The hotel group: Sandals, Jamaica

All-inclusive hotels and resorts in Jamaica have largely been developed by local entrepreneurs rather than international companies. This included Gordon 'Butch' Stewart who founded the Sandals company and the Issa family who founded the SuperClubs and the Issa Resorts Group (Mintel, 2001a).

The initial concept of the Sandals resort was to develop a hotel that catered for couples only and offered a full range of hospitality and leisure facilities. The group also developed wedding and honeymoon packages as part of the product offering.

A later development was carried out in 1999 when Sandals launched their new 'Beaches resort' which brought the all-inclusive idea to a wider range of market segments including singles, couples and families. The company has developed 'Kids Kamp' which caters for children and 'Ultra-Nannies' which offers a babysitting service to customers. This change in direction in 1999 has meant that the company can now target a wider customer base.

Jamaica relies on these chains to promote the island as a tourist destination and they are therefore critical to tourism receipts for the country as a whole.

The country: Cuba

The largest island in the Caribbean, Cuba, lies off the south coast of Florida and has used the development of the all-inclusive package as a major part of their tourism development strategy.

Fidel Castro took control of the island in 1959 and since then the island has been under communist rule. Cuba has a blend of cultural tourism and beach destinations and there has been a growth in the number of hotels on the island over the past decade. Much of this development has been in the form of three-, four- and five-star all-inclusive hotels in key beach destinations such as Varadero, Cayo Largo, Cayo Coco and Santa Lucia. International hotel chains such as Super Clubs, Club Med, Sandals, Sol Melia and Iberostar have been active in the development of the all-inclusive resort in these areas of the island. Specialist tour operators such as Captivating Cuba have been active in promoting all-inclusive trips to Cuba with the optional extra of a cultural visit to Havana, the island's capital.

It will be interesting to see whether this growth in all-inclusive tourism will continue to be the major source of tourism revenue for Cuba in the future. The all-inclusive resorts have provided an easy entry for Europeans into an island that has largely been inaccessible to the independent holiday-maker because of poor communications and infrastructures. It will be interesting to see whether this position changes once the elderly Fidel Castro dies.

The lifting of the US trade embargo, for example, could have a profound effect on tourism development. For the moment, the development of the all-inclusive resort has provided access to Cuba for a growing number of international tourists.

Conclusions

The growth of the all-inclusive holiday package has been as a result of a response by the tourism and hospitality sector to a changing pattern of consumer behaviour. It will be interesting to see whether this concept develops further or whether it is a passing fad.

Discussion points

1 Critically evaluate the reasons for the growth in interest by consumers for the all-inclusive type of package holiday.
2 Carry out an in-depth study of a destination, tour operator, or hotel chain that has used the all-inclusive concept as a major part of their strategic development. Assess the role of the all-inclusive concept in the future development of the chosen destination or organization.

The cruise market: Carnival Cruise Lines

Carnival Cruise Lines is an American company which was set up by shipowner, Ted Arison. He redesigned the concept of the cruise holiday from an up-market and luxury occasion, to a casual fun experience. He created Carnival to compete with the successful land resorts of Florida and the Caribbean, and to provide an alternative family holiday at sea, which was to be carefree and informal. The cruises were to be reasonably priced so that they would appeal to all generations and within an affordable budget.

The Carnival fleet today offers the customer all the attractions, entertainment, sports, activities and shops which they would find in a holiday complex. This allows the customer to be entertained in a resort-like atmosphere, while sailing around beautiful areas of the world, such as the Caribbean and the Mexican coast.

The Carnival concept is to offer customers an experience which is just as exciting as the destinations visited during the cruise. The cruises are excellent value for money for customers on a limited budget, since nearly everything – food, parties, shows, activities and entertainment – is included in the initial cruise price. The cabins have been designed to be spacious and feature private facilities, air conditioning, television, radio and telephone. Carnival's new superliners also have demi-suites with balconies and luxurious 28 square foot suites.

The 'Fun Ships' cruise ships currently go to over sixty destinations, and these are listed in Exhibit 7.1.

Exhibit 7.1 Destinations visited by Carnival 'Fun Ships'

Alaska – Glacier Bay: Northbound Alaska: Southbound Alaska. Experience the unmatched beauty and majesty of Alaska the grandest way possible.

Bahamas – visiting the Bahamas is the perfect antidote to life's everyday demands. Ever since the days of Blackbeard, this has been the ultimate tropical playground.

Canada/New England – our neighbours to the north greet you warmly as they invite you to spend time enjoying their hospitality, fall foliage and native delicacies.

Caribbean – Eastern Caribbean: Southern Caribbean: Western Caribbean – swim in the blue water and see the fascinating sites of the Caribbean.

Europe

Hawaii – with its lush tropical beauty, surfing-ready waves and welcoming warmth, Hawaii's natural attractions offer an irresistible lure.

Mexico – Baja Mexico: Mexican Riviera – discover the sandy beaches, renowned vineyards and open-air markets of Mexico.

Panama Canal – an engineering marvel and one of the most significant waterways on earth, the Canal is one of Panama's most amazing sights.

Special voyages – Bermuda: Cruise to Nowhere – get ready for two fun-filled days cruising aboard one of Carnival's floating resorts.

Transatlantic

Source: Carnival Cruise Lines.

History of Carnival Cruise Lines

The corporation was established in 1972 by Ted Arison who had the vision of establishing a different type of cruise company. A brief review of the development of the company can be seen in Exhibit 7.2. The development of the company has been rapid over the past twenty years, and often astonishing. The announcement by Micky Arison, the son of Ted Arison, that the company was to build three more ships in a short space of time was met by incredulity by commentators at the time, who wondered about the profitability of such a venture.

The decision to commission the biggest liner in the world in 1996 – the 100 000-tonne *Carnival Destiny*, was also a bold move in the

Exhibit 7.2 A brief history of Carnival Cruise Lines

1972 Ted Arison formed a new enterprise aimed at expanding the cruise market from Miami.
Bought *Empress of Canada*, renamed it the *Mardi Gras*.
Mardi Gras ran aground on first voyage with 300 travel agents aboard

1975 *Mardi Gras* operating at over 100 per cent occupancy as a 'Fun Ship'
The *Empress of Britain* is purchased and renamed the *Carnivale*.

1977 Purchase of the *S A Vaal*. $30 million facelift – renamed the *Festivale*.

1978 Announcement of construction of brand new passenger ship – the *Tropicale*.

1979 Micky Arison succeeds his father, Ted Arison, as Carnival's President.
Announces that company will build three more ships over next four years.

1984 Diversification into 3–4-day Bahamas Cruises.

1985 The first superliner, *Holiday*, is launched.
Mardi Gras' service (3–4 days) from Fort Lauderdale launched.

1986 *Jubilee* introduced into service.
Festivale sails out of San Juan.

1987 *Celebration* introduced into service.
Announcement of 70 000-ton *Fantasy* with a $200 million price tag.
Public offering of 20 per cent of stock, which netted the company $400 million.

1990 Inaugural voyage of the *Fantasy*.
Ecstasy joins the fleet in late 1990.
Purchase of Holland America Line.

1991 The *Sensation* joins the fleet.
Completion of $250 million, 1500-room mega-resort in the Bahamas.

1995 Investment in Airtours plc (29.5 per cent) – UK package holiday operation.
Fascination: *Inspiration*: *Imagination* introduced into service.

1996 Launch of the *Carnival Destiny* – 100 000 tonnes.

1998 Carnival Cruise Lines introduces seventh 'Fantasy-class' vessel, the *Elation*. the first new cruise ship deployed on the West Coast.
The eighth and last in the 'Fantasy-class' series, the *Paradise*, enters service.

1999 Debut of the 102 000-tonne *Carnival Triumph*, Carnival's second 'Destiny-class' vessel.

2000 A third 'Destiny-class' vessel, the 102 000-tonne *Carnival Victory*, is launched.

2001 Carnival introduces a new class of vessel with the launch of the 88 500, tonne *Carnival Spirit*, the first new 'Fun Ship' ever positioned in the Alaska and Hawaii markets.

(Continued)

Exhibit 7.2 *(Continued)*

2002 A second 'Spirit-class' vessel, the *Carnival Pride*, is launched
      Carnival's third 'Spirit-class' ship, *Carnival Legend*, enters service
      Debut of the 110 000-tonne *Carnival Conquest*, the largest 'Fun Ship'
      ever constructed

2003 Second 110 000-tonne 'Conquest-class' ship, the *Carnival Glory*, begins
      year-round seven-day cruises from Port Canaveral, Florida, 19 July

2004 *Carnival Miracle*, the fourth in Carnival's 'Spirit-class' begins a series of
      twelve voyages from Jacksonville, Florida – the first 'Fun Ship' sailings
      from that port – 27 February
      A third 110 000-tonne 'Conquest-class' ship, the *Carnival Valor*, begins
      year-round seven-day service from Miami, 19 December, becoming the
      largest 'Fun Ship' ever based at that port

2005 A fourth 110 000 tonne 'Conquest-class' vessel *Carnival Liberty*, is to
      debut 20 July, operating Carnival's first-ever Mediterranean cruises

2007 *Carnival Freedom*, the line's fifth 110 000-tonne vessel is scheduled to
      enter service in February

Source: Carnival Cruise Lines

company's development. The company has invested heavily in other holiday companies in the world to try and spread their interests into related areas. The purchase of the Holland America Line, for example, meant that the company gained substantial interest in the luxury cruise market.

The current Carnival Cruise Line fleet

The company now has a fleet of superliners including the *Fantasy, Ecstasy, Sensation, Inspiration, Imagination* and *Fascination*. The current Fun Ship fleet is listed in Exhibit 7.3.

The *Carnival Destiny* was one of the first superliners commissioned by the company and was launched in 1996. This superliner is the ultimate in cruise liners, with a full range of facilities and public rooms. The poolside entertainment area spans four decks and has four swimming pools, a 200-foot waterslide, two swim-up bars, seven whirlpools and an outdoor amphitheatre. The dining rooms have huge windows which give panoramic sea views. The liner has a two-level Nautica Spa with its own jogging track. The Millionaire's Club is the largest casino at sea and there are excellent shopping malls and nightclubs. The superliner is ten decks high and has a roofed Grand Atrium Plaza which embodies sophisticated modern design. The company has used the services of world-renowned designers and fitters to create a unique

Exhibit 7.3 Fun Ship fleet

Carnival Conquest
Carnival Glory
Carnival Liberty
Carnival Pride
Carnival Triumph
Carnival Victory
Ecstasy / Elation
Fantasy
Holiday
Inspiration
Sensation

Carnival Destiny
Carnival Legend
Carnival Miracle
Carnival Spirit
Carnival Valor
Celebration
Elation
Fascination
Imagination
Paradise

Source: Carnival Cruise Lines.

Exhibit 7.4 Carnival Destiny

Ship profile

Name:	Carnival Destiny
Company:	Carnival Cruise Lines
Originally Built:	1996
Refurbished/Built:	N/A
Formerly Named:	N/A
Country of Registry:	Panama
Normal Crew Size:	1100
Nationality of Crew:	International
Officers:	Italian
Hotel Cruise Staff:	International

Size/capacity
Gross Registered Tonnage: 101 000
Length: 893 feet   Beam: 116 feet
Total Capacity: 2642   (Dbl Occupancy)

Accommodation
Outside Cabins: 740
Inside Cabins: 519

Currency on Board: US Dollars

Facilities
Fully Air Conditioned and Stabilised
All Cabins with Private Facilities

Carnival Cruise Lines

Public rooms

Galaxy Dining Room
Universe Dining Room
The Trattoria
Happy Valley (Chinese)
Sun & Sea Restaurant
Palladium Showlounge
The Criterion Lounge
The Onyx Room
Millionaire's Club Casino
Point After Dance Club
Cheers Wine Bar
Downbeat
Apollo Bar
Destiny Bar
Cafe on the Way
All Star Bar
Virtual World (V. Reality)
Teen Club Disco

(Continued)

Exhibit 7.4 (*Continued*)

Three Swimming Pools & Whirlpools (5) + Children's Pool
Ship-to-Shore Telephone
'Camp Carnival' Facilities and Entertainment for Children
Children's Playroom and Teen Club
Closed Circuit TV
Shore Excursions Office
Dry Cleaning and Laundry Service
Duty Free Shops
Beauty Parlour/Barber Shop
Elevators (18)
Full Casino
Gymnasium
Golf Driving Platform
Infirmary
Sauna & Massage/Spas
Shuffleboard & Skeet Shooting
Table Tennis
Library
24 hour Free Room Service
24 hour Pizzeria

Source: Carnival Cruise Lines.

Exhibit 7.5 MS Carnival Liberty

Ship profile	**Carnival Cruise Lines**
Approximate cost	$500 million
Shipyard	Fincantieri Cantieri Navali, Italiani, S.p.A. Monfalcone, Italy
Inaugural cruise	July 2005
Country of registry	Panama
Speed	**22.5 Knots**
Approximate crew size	1160
Nationality of crew	
Officers	Italian
Hotel staff	International
Cruise staff	International
Size/capacity	
Gross registered tonnage	110 000
Length	952 feet

Exhibit 7.5 *(Continued)*

Beam	116 feet
Beam at pool decks	125 feet
Maximum draft	27 feet

Total guest capacity (including uppers)	3700
Normal cruise capacity (Basis 2)	2974
Number of guest decks	13
Space ratio	37

Accommodation

Penthouse suites	10
Suites	42
Ocean view with balcony	504
Ocean view without balcony	343
Ocean view with glass wall	18
Interior cabins	570
Total	**1487**

Public rooms and capacities

Name	Capacity
Venetian Palace (Main show lounge)	1400
Emile's (Lido/Poolside Restaurant)	1396
Sterling Restaurant (Aft Dining Room)	1122
Gilded Restaurant (Forward Dining Room)	744
Czar's Palace (Casino)	484
Victoria Lounge (Aft Show Lounge)	425
Hot & Cool (Dance Club)	211
The Stage (Live Music/Karaoke Bar)	88
Harry's (Supper Club)	108
Persian Room (Port Restaurant Annex)	28
Satin Room (Starboard Restaurant Annex)	36
Promenade Bar (Promenade Bar)	23
Jardin Cafe (Promenade Patisserie)	50
Flower Bar (Lobby Bar)	10
Piano Man (Piano Bar)	100
Gloves Bar (Sports Bar)	55
Antiquarian Library	17
Paparazzi (Wine Bar)	30
Empress Bar (Club Lounge)	40
The Cabinet (Grand Bar)	147
Tapestry Room (Multi-Function Room)	100
Spa, Health Club and Beauty Salon	13 300 sq ft

(Continued)

Exhibit 7.5 (*Continued*)

Facilities

Bars & Lounges (22)	Teen Dance Club
Photo shop	Whirlpools (7)
Beauty shop	Boutique
Shuffleboard	Game room
Duty-free shop	Infirmary
Jogging Track	Elevators (18)
Full Casino	Internet Cafe
Volleyball Court	Children's Playroom
Dining Rooms (2)	Sushi Bar
Closed-Circuit TV	Fully equipped Spa & Health Club
Tour Office	
Swimming pools (4)	

Equipment

Stabilizers	Diesel Electric
Bow Thrusters (3)	Propulsion System
Stern Thrusters (3)	6 medium-speed engines
Twin Rudders (Individually controlled)	Developing approx. 84 933 HP

Source: Carnival Cruise Lines.

and vibrant interior. Further details of the *Carnival Destiny* are shown in Exhibit 7.4.

More recently the company has commissioned the *Carnival Liberty*, which was introduced to enable the company to operate in the Mediterranean region. Details of the *Carnival Liberty* are shown in Exhibit 7.5.

Key personnel in the company

Ted Arison, the shipping informal entrepreneur had the initial idea of repositioning the cruise business into an informal fun occasion. A key part of the development of the Carnival Cruise Line, however, has been completed by Micky Arison, Ted's son, who grew up in the shipping business. Micky Arison led the company as Chairman and Chief Executive Officer (CEO) of the Carnival Corporation. It is his business acumen which has brought the company considerable financial success.

He oversaw diversified travel and tourism holdings including twenty-five cruise ships marketed under four different brand names, as well as the largest tour operator and hotel chain in Alaska and the Yukon territory in the late 1990s.

The company is now led by Carnival President and CEO Bob Dickinson. He is very proud of the rapid expansion of the business and the anticipated record-breaking year for guests carried in 2005: 'From new itinerary and homeport choices to expanded dining activity and entertainment options, Carnival has a variety of exciting developments on tap for the coming year. Consumers are encouraged to book early to not only get the best price but also the itinerary and stateroom of their choice' (Bob Dickinson, 2005).

Distribution of Carnival Cruise Line products

The company does sell cruises directly to the customer, particularly in the USA and Canada. However, the development of the overseas business for the company has been more difficult and reliance had to be placed on appropriate package holiday companies in different markets.

The most difficult problem for sales in the UK has been the perceptions by potential customers of what a cruise product is. Potential customers tend to think of cruises as being an up-market and luxury holiday, where they have to dress up in formal clothes for dinner and engage in intellectual conversations over cocktails. This perception has been built up by the more traditional and established cruises companies which have served the market. The main objective of Carnival Cruise Lines is to get over these perceptions, and convince potential customers that they are offering an informal and fun holiday which is similar to that which can be experienced in a traditional onshore resort. One of the ways that this has been achieved is to distribute the products, wherever possible, through mainstream package holiday companies which the customer has dealt with previously for other package holidays. The mainstream cruise businesses in the UK joined together in the late 1990s, and spent £80 000 per year to employ a public relations company, BGB Associates to manage an ongoing public relations campaign to try to get this message across to potential customers via the media.

Carnival Cruise Lines worked hard in the late 1990s to improve their sales in Europe. In the UK, for example, the company has worked with a series of major UK tour operators, such as Unijet, Airtours and Virgin Holidays, so that the cruises are featured in their packaged holidays programme. The company negotiated marketing agreements with major high street retailers to produce dedicated Unijet/Lunn Poly, Unijet/Co-op and Virgin/Lunn Poly Carnival brochures displayed under the banner of 'Florida and the Caribbean Cruise and Stay Holidays'. A large proportion of the UK bookings come via these tour operators, which are shown in Exhibit 7.6.

The company also targeted the UK in 1997 to increase their sales in the UK by a further 60 per cent. The company used two different marketing strategies in 1997. The first target was the tour operation business, which is aimed specifically at customers who are planning to take a holiday in Florida and view the Carnival Cruise as an add-on. The second market was the cruise market, which is being targeted with a new Carnival 'Sun Waves' brochure which features seven-night Caribbean cruises on board the *Inspiration* out of San Juan combined with non-stop British Airways flights from London Gatwick.

Exhibit 7.6   Distribution of the Carnival Cruises in the UK market, 1997

Product	Operator
Carnival Cruises – Baja and Mexican Riviera – Alaska – The Caribbean – Special Voyages – The Bahamas 3-11 days	Equity Group
Airtours - Florida and Caribbean (Carnival) Caribbean Cruises Florida and the Caribbean Celebration Sun Waves SM	Airtours plc
Carnival Sun Waves Caribbean San Juan	British Airways
Thomas Cook Holidays *Dominican Republic* *Cruise and Stay* Dominican Republic and Cruise	Thomas Cook Holidays
Florida and Caribbean plus *California and Mexico** Cruises to Caribbean and Mexico in combination with Orlando	Co-op Travel
Florida and Caribbean plus *California and Mexico** Cruises to Caribbean and Mexico in combination with Orlando	Lunn Poly
Virgin/Lunn Poly Carnival *Florida** and the Caribbean Cruise and Stay Holidays	Virgin Holidays

Source: Carnival Cruise Lines.

Note: *Agreements with High Street Retailer to produce dedicated brochures.

Customers of Carnival Cruise Line

Carnival Cruise Line carries approximately 6 million customers every year. An early profile of the customers in 1996 is shown in Exhibit 7.7.

It can be seen from this exhibit that the majority of the customers in the early days, originated from the USA and Canada. The company tried to increase their sales in overseas markets. The current customer

---

Exhibit 7.7 Customers of Carnival Cruise Line, 1996

1.	Numbers	Average numbers of passengers per year
	Worldwide of which –	6 million
	US/Canada nationals	4.5 million
	and overseas	1.5 million
	UK	15 000
	Numbers who gamble on board	500 000

2.	Demographic profile	Percentage
	Under 35	30
	Teenagers and under	10
	36–54	40
	Over 55	30

3. Socioeconomic groups

Target group is 'Middle American'
Socioeconomic groups B, C^1, C^2

Source: Carnival Cruise Lines.

Exhibit 7.8 Children's services on Carnival Cruise Line

Camp Carnival – Children's Club

Aim	To provide a similar atmosphere to American 'summer camps' To give parents the freedom to enjoy themselves
Staff	Each superliner has an Assistant Operations Director, Youth Director and over 50 qualified trained staff who are responsible for the Camp Carnival
Groups in Camp Carnival	– Toddlers 2–5 – Juniors 6–8 – Intermediates 9–11; 12–14
Facilities	Indoor children's playroom and video arcade Music and dancing Play area on deck on the *Carnival Destiny* Family accommodation in cabins

Source: Carnival Cruise Lines.

Exhibit 7.9   Romantic weddings with Carnival Cruise Lines

Weddings take place in the port of embarkation, on shore, or on board

Wedding locations are:

* Miami, Florida
* Port Canaveral, Florida
* Tampa, Florida
* Los Angeles, California
* New Orleans, Louisiana
* St Thomas, US VI
* San Juan, Puerto Rico
* Grand Cayman

Different wedding packages:

Just for the Bride and Groom
Welcome Aboard Wedding
Deluxe Romance Wedding

Puerto Rico –	On board
	On island
St Thomas –	On board
	On island
Grand Cayman –	On board
	On island

Wedding licences must be applied and paid for by the couple

Source: Carnival Cruise Lines.

---

tends to be older, on average, although the company is keen to develop the market for families and children.

The typical customer has a mid-range income and is probably used to taking resort-based holidays. The company has high levels of repeat purchase, particularly in the US market. The company is trying to target particular market segments with specifically designed products.

Children, for example, were targeted in the late 1990s with a Camp Carnival service, and a range of facilities designed particularly for them. These services are shown in Exhibit 7.8.

The company has also developed a substantial market in the weddings and honeymoon markets. Customers can now get married either on board or on shore at a selection of locations, and the company offers a wide range of wedding packages to suit different customer requirements. Details of these packages are shown in Exhibit 7.9.

The company has also targeted the health-conscious customer and offers first-class fitness and recreational facilities on all their

---

Exhibit 7.10   Spa Carnival

It has never been so easy to relax. Get your workout in and spend the day soaking in the jacuzzi, lounging on the sun-drenched deck or swimming in the crystal-clear pool. The options are endless, so spend the day doing what you want.

'Fun-Ship' Fitness

Stay in shape with Spa Carnival's state-of-the-art exercise equipment, jogging track and aerobics classes. Each ship's spa features a staff of knowledgeable fitness experts ready to assist you.

Stress Sails Away

Feel the stress sail away as you pamper your body and mind. Relax and revive with a trip to our steamroom and sauna. For the ultimate in relaxation, soothe your tired and aching muscles with a full-body massage.

Look Your Best

Look and feel your best as you stroll around the ship and ports. Spa Carnival features a variety of beauty treatments for both men and women including: facials, loofah treatments, manicures, pedicures and hairstyling.

Source: Carnival Cruise Lines.

---

superliners. This has been developed to appeal to young people and families which are target markets that might not have previously considered a cruise. Each superliner features a Nautica Spa complex that includes a fully equipped gym, an aerobics room, saunas, steam rooms and a full range of beauty treatments. The superliners also offer a special healthy Nautica Spa menu which incorporates healthy menus. Spa Carnival has been introduced to enable the company to develop this business and details are shown in Exhibit 7.10.

The reasons for customers choosing a Carnival Cruise Line product

The reasons for customers choosing a Carnival Cruise Line product vary according to the origin of the customers, and are explained in Exhibit 7.11. The US customer is more likely to go on a Carnival Cruise as an impulse, rather than those customers who are travelling from overseas before boarding the ship.

Customers often go on a Carnival Cruise to celebrate a special event such as a birthday, honeymoon, or wedding anniversary. Customers are often motivated by the desire to have a 'fun time' in a beautiful and changing setting. It is particularly important in the marketing activity for Carnival overseas to communicate the informal theme and good value associated with their holidays. The use of well-recognized package holiday operators and high street retailers are key to this activity.

Exhibit 7.11   Reasons for customers choosing a Carnival Cruise Line product

Motivators	*	Seeking fun and entertainment
	*	The desire to see new places
	*	Special occasions – weddings, honeymoons, wedding anniversaries, birthdays
	*	Entertainment seeking and gambling
	*	The desire to 'chill out' and get away from it all
Determinants	*	Available by direct sale (particularly applicable in the USA)
	*	Available as part of a package (particularly important in overseas markets)
	*	Good value for money – everything included in the price
	*	New exciting, informal cruise concept

Source: Carnival Cruise Lines.

Research with customers

The company carries out marketing research with all customers, when their holiday is just about to finish. The Bon Voyage comment card is filled in and returned to the company for analysis. Comments cards which have been completed by customers from outside the USA, are sent on to the local office after preliminary analysis.

Comments which are received via these cards are usually very favourable. Some examples of comments received from UK customers are shown in Exhibit 7.12.

Exhibit 7.12   Comments made by passengers from the UK who travelled on Carnival Cruise Lines

'Thanks very much. I have had a really fantastic time. Roel and Mr Paul made it special by singing to me and I also had a cake. Once again, thank you'

'Devin Fleming was absolutely brilliant – and all the staff. We have travelled all over Europe four or five times a year, but this was our best holiday ever. Thank you'

'All your employees have been marvellous and I have enjoyed my holiday with you. The entertainment has been first class, as have all other departments'

Source: Carnival Cruise Lines.

The customers often mention particular members of staff in their comments, which shows the importance of well-developed customer care programmes. Further scrutiny of the Bon Voyage comment cards also reveals the large number of customers that celebrate a special event, while they are on the cruise.

Conclusions

Carnival Cruise Lines has developed a new type of mass-market 'fun' cruise and is attempting to attract different market segments into taking a cruise holiday with the company. This has been very effective in the US market, but the company has work to do to try to change consumer perceptions of the cruise product in other markets.

Discussion points

1 The main problem a company has when it repositions a product is the changing of consumer perceptions. Discuss this statement in relation to Carnival Cruise Line.
2 Carnival Cruise Lines has had to change the product considerably to attract new market segments. Give an outline of this product development process, and highlight the most important features of this programme.

Wensleydale Creamery, Hawes, North Yorkshire

Introduction

Wensleydale Creamery in North Yorkshire, England, is a good example of a company that has combined a tourism venture with traditional food production. The Wensleydale Cheese Experience offers the visitor the possibility of visiting a museum on cheese production, seeing cheese being produced from a viewing gallery and tasting and buying cheese, in a well-designed shop. The site also has a restaurant and gift shop. Hawes in West Yorkshire is in one of the most beautiful parts of Britain – the North Yorkshire Dales, which is a picturesque and mountainous area, and has a long tradition as a holiday region.

History

Wensleydale has been inhabited since Iron Age times. The first recorded origins of Wensleydale cheese date back to the period when the Norman conquerors, having settled in the area, brought religious orders from France to found the great abbeys in the Yorkshire Dales. In 1150, a monastery was built at Fors which is 4 miles from Hawes, and this was later moved to Jervaulx in Lower Wensleydale. The French Cistercian monks continued to make cheese until the dissolution of the monasteries in the sixteenth century. The art was then passed on to local farmers' wives who then produced cheese in their own farmhouses.

In 1897, Mr Edward Chapman started the first industrial-scale production of Wensleydale cheese, from milk which he purchased from surrounding farms. The industrial depression of the 1930s made trading hard, and the Milk Marketing

Board tried to offer contracts to take the milk to a national dairy which was miles away. The dalesmen, led by Kit Calvert, fought against this and established their own Wensleydale Creamery in Hawes with capital of £1085, £200 of which came from Kit Calvert, the Managing Director.

In 1953, Kit built a new creamery for £15 000 and sales of Wensleydale cheese boomed. In 1966, the Milk Marketing Board purchased Wensleydale Creamery and Kit continued to run the creamery until his retirement in 1967. In May 1992, Dairy Crest, a subsidiary of the Milk Marketing Board, closed the Hawes creamery and transferred the production of Wensleydale cheese to the neighbouring county of Lancashire! The news that Yorkshire's famous cheese was to be lost, because of a decision made by a large conglomerate incensed the public and offers of help to rescue the creamery flooded in.

The ex-managers of Hawes Creamery persuaded the owners to sell the creamery to them in a management buy-out which was finally agreed in November 1992. Cheese-making in Wensleydale recommenced on the 16 December 1992. The refurbishment of the creamery was completed in January 1993 ensuring a significant increase in the production of handmade cheeses and the provision of many local jobs.

A visitor centre and a viewing gallery were opened in June 1994 and The Cheese Experience was born. This allows visitors to see for themselves the history, tradition, and skill involved in the production of Real Wensleydale cheese. The attraction was awarded a White Rose Award for Tourism by the Yorkshire and Humberside Tourist Board in 1994.

In recent years, The Wensleydale Creamery has negotiated with the BBC, to use their two animated characters, Wallace and Gromit. Wallace and Gromit, who were created by animator Nick Parks, are well known in their films *The Wrong Trousers* and *A Great Day Out*, for enjoying Wensleydale cheese. The association with 'Wallace and Gromit' has allowed the Wensleydale creamery to use the characters on their cheese products and in their advertising literature.

Wensleydale Creamery products

The Wensleydale Creamery produces Real Wensleydale Cheese which is creamy-white in colour and has a flaky appearance. The cheese is free from additives and is produced by hand in the traditional way. The texture of the cheese is firm, but not dry, and hard. The cheese is uneven and open in appearance when it is sliced. The cheese goes well with crisp apple, and is traditionally eaten with fruit cake and apple pie. The cheese is extremely nutritious, rich in vitamins and will keep well at chilled temperatures.

The creamery makes a full range of Wensleydale cheeses in different shapes and sizes. The company also produces a range which incorporates fruits and a range which relies on the traditional art of smoking. The full range of cheese produced by the creamery is shown is Exhibit 8.1.

The majority of the cheese sales are achieved through the major food retailers and cheese shops. The company also has a limited direct mail

Exhibit 8.1 Range of products made at Wensleydale Creamery, Hawes

THE WENSLEYDALE SELECTION

White Wensleydale cheese has a mild, slightly sweet flavour with a honey aftertaste, whereas blue Wensleydale is robust in flavour.

Originally Wensleydale was sold either 'fresh' – white, or 'ripe' – blue. White Wensleydale cheese is only ripened for 3 weeks and is made from a lightly pressed, finely cut curd leaving a high moisture content giving a slightly crumbly, flaky texture. The celebrated Blue Veined Wensleydale requires six months to mature. It has a smooth creamy texture similar to Stilton but with a mellower flavour.

* NEW 'Real' Blue Wensleydale

Miniatures

* Traditional Wensleydale Cheese
* Wallace and Gromit's Wensleydale
* Cows and ewe's Milk Wensleydale
* Oak Smoked Wensleydale
* Wensleydale with Onions and Chives
* Garsdale
* Coverdale
* Fountains Gold

Matured

* 21 kg Traditional Bandaged Truckle
* 4.5 kg Traditional Bandaged Tall
* 2.2 kg Half Tall in green wax
* Special Reserve Wensleydale

Fruit and Herb

* Wensleydale with Cranberries
* Wensleydale with Apricots
* Wensleydale with Onions and Chives
* Wensleydale with Blueberries
* Wensleydale with Carrot and Orange

NEW Wensleydale with Papaya and Mango

Smoked

* Smoked Traditional Wensleydale
* Smoked Blue Wensleydale
* Smoked Lancashire
* Smoked Mature Cheddar

Others

* Sage Derby
* Red Leicester
* Emmerdale
* Double Gloucester
* Ewe's Milk Wensleydale
* Leicester with Leeks
* Cheddar with Cherrybell pepper and Sundried tomatoes

Source: Wensleydale Creamery, Hawes.

order business, which it is hoping to develop in the future. Limited sales are also made via the cheese shop on the factory site.

The visitor attraction – the Cheese Experience – opened in June 1994, and has experienced great success since then. Details of the Cheese Experience are shown in Exhibit 8.2. The attraction is part of the factory complex in Hawes village and visitors can reach the site in their own car or by coach. The Cheese Experience features a museum, cheese shop and licensed restaurant. One of the main attractions is the viewing gallery where visitors can see the hand production of real Wensleydale cheese. The attraction is open all the year round, except Christmas Day, from 9.00 a.m. to 5.00 p.m. Tours of the creamery are organized daily from 10.00 a.m.

Customers of the Cheese Experience

Customers of the Cheese Experience have grown steadily since its opening in 1994. The customers fall into certain categories which are

---

Exhibit 8.2   Facilities at the Wensleydale Cheese Experience

* *Viewing gallery*

The centre opened in July 1994 and includes a viewing gallery where visitors can see real Wensleydale Cheese being made.
There is a traditional cheeseroom where everything is done by hand. Cheeses are made individually, moulded and wrapped in muslin.

* *The museum*

The museum portrays the history of 'Real Wensleydale Cheese'. There is a video describing the processes involved in the production of Wensleydale cheese.

* *The cheese shop*

The shop offers the visitor the opportunity to purchase a wide range of premium quality cheeses. Free tasting of the 'Real Wensleydale Cheese' is included in the admission price to the museum.

* *Licensed restaurant*

'The Buttery' is formerly the butter-making room which has been converted to a licensed restaurant where visitors can buy meals, snacks and local ice cream. The 'Creamery Coffee Shop' serves drinks, Yorkshire tea and a range of home-made cakes, scones and pastries.

Source: Wensleydale Creamery, Hawes.

---

explored in Exhibit 8.3. The Cheese Experience is visited by a growing number of individuals or groups from a wide cross-section of socioeconomic groups. Visitors can arrive on foot, by private car, or on one of the many coach trips organized to visit the attraction. The company is currently trying to increase visits by coach parties and offers guided tours to parties of fifteen or more. The parties are encouraged to pre-book the restaurant for their visit. The company offers all-inclusive packages which incorporate free admission to the museum if the party books to dine in the restaurant.

Restaurant-only bookings and evening visits are also available for party bookings. The facilities are available for functions and special occasions.

The company has carried out some market research to date to find out details of the visitors to the Cheese Experience. It is clear, however, that the presence of the visitor attraction has boosted cheese sales. Customers who visit the attraction tend to be influenced directly to purchase the cheese when they return home, either in their local supermarket or by direct mail. The Cheese Experience has also experienced a great deal of press coverage and has received many awards, such as the 1994 White Rose Award for Tourism. This has meant that The Wensleydale Creamery has benefited from substantial indirect publicity as a result of this press coverage. This raises the awareness of the general public in the range of products which the company offers.

The company also conducts market research with customers following their visit to the Cheese Experience. It has found that this information collected from group organizers has been the most useful in terms of future development of the business.

The Wensleydale Creamery has the advantage of offering a product which is closely linked with regional tradition. The creamery is almost unique in the UK, where many traditional cheese producers have been taken over by larger industrial cheese producers. This link to history, and the fact that the cheese is still handmade along traditional lines, has meant that the product is very attractive to customers who are

---

Exhibit 8.3 Main customer of groups visiting the Cheese Experience

1. Individuals or couples arriving by private car.
2. Family groups arriving by private car.
3. Individuals or couples arriving in groups by coach. These customers are given a guided tour.
4. Holiday-makers staying in Hawes arriving on foot as individuals, couples or family groups.
5. Local customers visiting the restaurant only as individuals, in pairs, or in family groups.

Source: Wensleydale Creamery, Hawes.

seeking nostalgic views of past ways of life. The position of the creamery in the Yorkshire Dales means that a visit can be easily slotted into a holiday itinerary.

The creamery also has the added attraction for customers of a view of the cheese actually being made and packed. The viewing gallery means that the visitor feels that they have actually observed the ancient tradition of cheese making. This leads to strong feelings of association with the product, which are very memorable.

Conclusions

The Wensleydale Creamery has been successful at combining a traditional food production company with a visitor attraction. The visitor attraction has been very influential in the development of the total cheese business of the company. The company plans to research customer profiles, and views, in more depth in the future, so that it can use this information to target customers more effectively and give them the appropriate products and services. The visitor attraction has also provided the company with extensive coverage in the media which has generated substantial interest in the company.

Discussion points

1 Explore the possible reasons for people seeking nostalgic images of the past. Discuss the ways in which a visitor attraction, based on a traditional food process, can exploit these behaviour patterns.
2 The Wensleydale Creamery allows the visitor to see the actual cheese-making process. Evaluate the importance of this feature to the success of the visitor attraction and company cheese sales in general.

Société Roquefort, Roquefort, France

Introduction

Roquefort-sur-Soulzon is situated in the south of France between the regions of Languedoc and Auvergne. The village is perched at about 2000 feet above the town of Millau, near to the beautiful Gorges du Tarn River.

Roquefort is world renowned for the 'king of cheeses', which is made from ewe's milk and matured in the caves at Roquefort. The production of Roquefort cheese is approximately 20 000 tones per year, and approximately 15 per cent of the production is sold abroad, particularly to the USA, Belgium, Germany and Switzerland. There are several dozen brands of Roquefort cheese on the market, and the Société group controls approximately 82 per cent of the production.

Société has developed a visitor attraction in the village of Roquefort which allows visitors to gain an insight into this very special cheese production. This attraction is called Visite de Caves – Les plus belles caves de Roquefort.

The production of Roquefort cheese

Roquefort cheese is made by a number of producers in the Roquefort area from ewe's milk, which is the richest milk in cheese making. Ewe's milk is approximately three times more expensive than cow's milk and therefore makes the cheese expensive to produce.

The cheese is made in the traditional way at the producers. The *Penicillium Roqueforti* is introduced into the milk in the early stages of production. The cheeses are transported to Roquefort after one day of manufacture, two to three days of draining and five days of salting. The cheeses in this form are white with no internal blue veining. The cheeses are now ready for ripening.

The cheeses are referred to as 'loaves' and are slid into a tray containing thirty-eight large needles which pierce the cheese. This piercing allows carbonic gas produced by the fermentation of the curds to escape and allows penetration of air into the cheese.

The cheeses are placed vertically on trays and are placed in the Roquefort caves. The *Penicillium Roqueforti* develops and forms the characteristic blue-green veins inside the cheese which becomes soft and full of flavour. This process lasts three to four weeks.

The second ripening of the cheese is carried out to develop the *Penicillium Roqueforti*, more slowly, and to exclude micro-organisms from growing on the outside of the cheese. The cheeses are wrapped in pure tin foil and returned to the caves. The master-ripeners will determine when the cheeses are ready, by withdrawing samples of the cheese with a sampling rod. The tin foil is then removed, and aluminium foil is used to wrap the cheeses ready for sale.

The ripening of the cheeses in the caves at Roquefort is key to the production of the Roquefort cheese. The Roquefort mountain was formed by gigantic rock upheaval which formed a mass extending to 1.25 miles in length and 1000 feet in width. Inside the rocks, there are faults or 'fleurines'. These fleurines have draughts of fresh air flowing through them at a constant temperature of 46 °F and 95 per cent humidity. This underground breathing is unique in the world, and can be explained by a complex set of issues relating to geological form and climate. The ripening of the cheeses in the Roquefort caves is key to the development of the cheeses.

Roquefort cheese is rich in calories, minerals and vitamins. A large part of the protein present in the cheese is pre-digested and is therefore directly assimilable. It is rich in B vitamins, and the enzymes in the cheese help with the digestion of certain foodstuffs. These factors, along with the very special flavour, make the cheese unique in the world and very sought after.

Visite des Caves

The village of Roquefort has become a very special place to visit in the south-west of France. The opening of the highest bridge in the world nearby at Roquefort – Sur-Soulzon, in 2004, has increased the number of visitors to the area. There are a number of Roquefort producers in the village which have developed visitor attractions so that visitors can learn about their very special cheese production methods. Société is the largest producer of Roquefort cheese, and it has developed a sophisticated visitor attraction which appeals to all age groups. Details of the visitor attraction are shown in Exhibit 9.1.

The tour around the attraction lasts from one to two hours, and incorporates the use of special techniques such as a *son et lumierè* spectacle with the serious educational information. Visitors can actually see into the special caves, and can view the cheeses maturing on the wooden slats. The end of the tour incorporates a tasting session of the

---

Exhibit 9.1   The Visite de Caves – visitor attraction

Location	Roquefort Village
Tour details	1 to 2 hours tour through the caves, exhibitions and museum
Highlights of the tour	* A *son et lumière* show which shows the production of Roquefort and the development through the centuries
	* A visit to the ancient caves, dating back to the 17th century
	* A viewing of the fleurines in the rocks which go to the plateau of the Grands Causses
	* The museum and demonstrations of the Penicillium Roquefort
	* Tasting session of different cheeses and shop
Cost of the tour 2005	Adults 3 euros
	Special tariff 2 euros
	Children under 16 – free
Opening hours	Various opening times according to the season

Source: Société Roquefort

---

full range of cheeses and a shop, where cheese and other merchandising items can be bought.

The visitor attraction has developed more sophisticated techniques since it opened in 1957. An excellent film of the cheese production process now forms part of the tour because this does not happen in the Roquefort village, but in many small to medium-sized production factories.

Visitor numbers have been growing since the attraction opened in 1957, and over 6 million people have visited the attraction since then. The great majority of visitors come from France, but the number of visitors from outside France is growing as the cheese has been marketed throughout Europe on a wider basis in recent years. Most of the visitors to the visitor attraction arrive by car, in independent groups. A small percentage of the visitors arrive as part of an organized tour, and a large proportion of these are either American or Japanese. The attraction is also visited by schoolchildren and students. The visitor attraction is also used by Société as a marketing tool by showing corporate clients, such as food retailers, around.

It is very important that young people visit the attraction because they will be enthused with the mystique of Roquefort, and be more inclined to buy the cheese regularly as they grow older. The company is keen to encourage visitors from outside France because this acts as a powerful marketing tool for the export market, which is an area the company is working hard to develop.

The visitor attraction is an important part of the tourism strategy for the south-west of France. Promotional leaflets for the attractions are distributed widely around the tourism offices, which are very well developed in France. Roquefort is situated in an area of outstanding beauty and there are a number of other attractions in close proximity to the site. This encourages tourism development in this area of France.

The real spectacle of Roquefort, however, is the mystique and legends surrounding the production of such a unique product. The visitor attraction at Société provides the visitor with an excellent insight into an ancient and special tradition.

Discussion points

1 Discuss the importance of the visitor attraction at Société for the development of an export business for the cheese.
2 The development of the visitor attraction at Roquefort has relied on the appeal of an ancient production process. Evaluate the importance of this for the development of a successful industrial tourism venture.

Industrial tourism in France

In recent years, the industrial tourism market has grown dramatically in France. This is evident from the fact that a publisher now produces guides to industrial tourism for all the regions of France, featuring over 1000 workplaces which open their doors to the public, as well as industry-based museums.

The guides, which are published by Editions Solar, differentiate between three distinct audiences:

- professionals involved in the appropriate field
- school pupils and higher education students
- the general public.

The authors divide the establishments featured in the guides into five groups:

- heritage attractions and museums
- research centres
- manufacturing industries
- artisan or craft workshops
- services.

The guide to the Bretagne and Pays de la Loire regions of north-west France, listed a wide range of establishments in some nine *départements* or counties. Perhaps it is not surprising that a quarter of these establishments were mainstream food and drink manufacturers. Another ten establishments were in fish farming or seafood production and processing.

Industrial tourism permeates most areas of the French economy as can be seen from the following examples of workplaces, included in the guide:

- the local newspaper in Morlaix
- a hydroelectricity power station in Northern Brittany
- potters and wood turners

- working flour mills
- printers
- a cement works in the Mayenne Département
- an abbey where the nuns make cheese
- a local radio station in Laval
- farms producing and selling foie gras
- wine producers
- oyster 'farms'
- the airport at Nantes
- a bus company
- salt pans on the coast
- a food industry research establishment
- biscuit factories
- a naval dockyard at Lorient
- an Yves Rocher cosmetics plant in Southern Brittany
- an audio-visual production company in St Malo
- textile factories.

The guide also features a number of industry-based museums including industries as diverse as cars and printing, mushrooms and cider, wine and salt. Some of these are what would be termed in France, *ecomusées*, in other words, museums that present heritage themes in their correct geographical setting and which tell the story of the way in which people have made a living in the area over time.

The vast majority of establishments in the guide offer guided tours, either for the safety of visitors or to enable them to fully understand the processes involved. It can also be essential for security reasons. Many companies do not charge visitors, but a number insist on people making prior appointments. A significant minority offer guided tours in English, German, Spanish and Italian, reflecting the nationality of the majority of foreign visitors.

The experience of industrial tourism in France illustrates a number of consumer preferences when it comes to visiting workplaces. It shows that people, particularly like to visit:

- places where famous branded products are produced, for example, Remy Martin cognac, Cointreau liqueur and the Ricard brand of pastis
- unusual producers such as oyster farmers
- organizations that provide a public service that is used by everyone, and which is paid for through taxes, such as electricity generating plants
- production processes which are traditional and/or picturesque, including cutlery in Thiers, cheese on farms across France and pottery manufacturers around the country
- high-technology industries such as computer-aided design
- products and services that are part of everyday life, such as newspapers, salt, biscuits, and banks

- factories where products can be bought at discount prices, such as those textile producers who have on-site factory shops
- establishments where visitors hope to receive free samples, if it is a desirable product such as wine or chocolate
- controversial organizations including nuclear power stations.

The development of industrial tourism in France began to be exploited in the early 1990s. Two reports dating from 1993, in *Tourism Eco* and *La Gazette Officielle du Tourisme*, give an interesting picture of the industrial tourism market in the early 1990s, in France.

It was estimated that over 5000 enterprises opened their doors to visitors and that, between them, they attracted some 10 million visitors. Four 'attractions' attracted over 100 000 tourists per annum with the top attraction being a tidal power station in Brittany which attracted some 350 000 visitors in 1992. The other three most popular workplaces were all connected with the food and drink industry (Swarbrooke, 1995).

The same source reported that, at the time in question, some 67 per cent of French people had already visited an industrial tourism attraction while only 57 per cent had visited a major national museum. When questioned, some 75 per cent of French people said they would definitely or probably visit an industrial attraction while they were on holiday. This early interest in industrial tourism has continued to grow in popularity.

Many commentators would argue that this popular interest in industrial tourism, reflects the growth of postmodernism and the rapidly changing nature of industrial and economic change, in France and beyond.

We can see evidence of this growing interest in industrial tourism in the UK, including Scottish whisky distilleries, Cadbury's World and breweries. In recent years, destinations have developed industrial tourism products including programme of workplace visits such as 'Quality North' in the North-East, and 'Sheffield Works'. However, interestingly, in both cases the vast majority of workplace visitors have been local people.

Discussion points and essay questions

1 Discuss the main reasons why an enterprise might choose to open its doors to visitors.
2 Compare and contrast the likely motivators for visiting industrial tourism attractions, for the three market segments identified at the beginning of the case study, namely, professional people, educational visitors and the general public.

British Airways — environmental policy

Background

British Airways is the world's leading international airline and one of the most profitable. The financial results of the company continue to set standards for the whole industry. The conversion of British Airways from the public sector to a profit-motivated business and the accompanying long-term operational and marketing campaign which accompanied this turn around have been documented by Horner and Swarbrooke (1996).

More recently, the company has established its 'Environmental Campaign' which is a long-term strategy to try and improve the company's performance and reporting measures in this area. This case study aims to evaluate the development of this environmental campaign, and the response of consumers to these initiatives.

Introduction

British Airways has an enviable financial performance for an international company in this sector. The Chairman, Rod Eddington, commented on the company's financial performance in the Annual Accounts for the period 2004/05, in the light of difficult trading conditions, as follows:

> In recent years, we have become accustomed to dealing with major threats to the viability and success of our business. This year has been no exception. We have had to cope with a high fuel price, against a market background of fierce competition and excess global airline capacity.

The fact that we have continued to improve our profit margins – and have moved a step closer to our 10 per cent margin target – is a reflection of the hard work put in across the airline. I am pleased that this year we have been able to provide a financial recognition of this effort to all our employees, through the employee reward incentive programme.

A summary of the financial position is shown in Exhibit 11.1.

British Airways is an international airline which has developed as a result of global strategic alliances with other airlines. Details of these are shown in Exhibit 11.2.

The airline has had an impressive long-term development concentrating on improvements in operational efficiency and improving marketing operations and customer services. In 2005, 36 million people flew on British Airways and the company treated each of them as an individual, offering excellent customer service. Customer loyalty figure suggest that the airline is matching up to their expectations for service levels and value for money. The airline is not complacent however, and is constantly looking for ways to improve the experience of customers who choose to fly with the airline.

In 1995/96, the company launched a three-year plan which cost £500 million, to improve the travel experience for all passengers. This involved radical enhancements to every aspect of customer service. The first stage of this programme involved the increase in leg room by 25 per cent in the Club World long-haul business. To help with the programme, specially designed 'cradle seats' were introduced which give substantially better support and comfort for the back.

In the same year, the First Class service was improved and customers were provided with their own individual compartment within the

Exhibit 11.1   British Airways key group statistics

£ million	2004/05	2003/04
Turnover	7 813	7 560
Operating profit (£m)	540	405
Operating margin (%)	6.9	5.4
Manpower (MPE)	47 472	49 072
Passengers (m)	35.7	36.1
Cargo (000 tonnes)	877	796
Available tonne km (m)	22 565	21 859
Revenue tonne km (m)	15 731	14 771
Revenue passenger km (m)	107 892	103 092
Passenger load factor	74.8	73.0

Source: www.britishairways.com

Exhibit 11.2   The franchisees and alliance carriers of British Airways

Alliances

British Airways co-operates with other airlines forming different types of alliances, which enable us to extend the number of destinations and benefits we can offer you. When you fly with these airlines, you will enjoy similar levels of service and the high standards that you expect from British Airways, either on the ground or in the air.

When you book online, or via any other booking method, you will be advised if you will be travelling with another airline.

Use these links to find out more about each type of alliance:

> **one**world alliance
> BA Connect
> Codeshare carriers
> Franchise carriers
> Airline alliances at-a-glance

oneworld alliance

By operating as part of this alliance, we are able to offer you an extensive worldwide route network and a wide range of customer benefits. Other members of the **one**world alliance are:

> Aer Lingus
> American Airlines
> Cathay Pacific
> Finnair
> Iberia
> Lan
> Qantas

You can find out more from the dedicated website which explains the benefits you can expect from the **one**world alliance.

Codeshare carriers

We operate a number of 'codeshare' routes with other airlines, which means that you travel with another independent airline with whom we work closely. Wherever possible we codeshare with airlines who are able to provide a level of service that closely matches our own.

The flight has two codes – the British Airways flight number, as appears on your ticket, and the flight number of the other airline operating the service.

British Airways Executive Club members receive a number of benefits when travelling with alliance or partner airlines, including the opportunity to collect and spend mileage.

(Continued)

Exhibit 11.2 *(Continued)*

Airline alliances at-a-glance
The table below shows the types of relationship that British Airways operates with other airlines.

Carrier	oneworld	Codeshare	Franchise	BA Executive Club benefits
Aer Lingus	X	X		X
Alaska Airlines				X
America West				X
American Airlines	X	X		X
BMED	X*		X	X
Cathay PacificB	X	X		X
Comair Pty Ltd	X*		X	X
Finnair	X	X		X
GB Airways	X*		X	X
Iberia	X	X		X
Japan Airlines		X		X
Jet Airways#				X
LAN	X	X		X
Loganair	X*		X	X
Qantas	X	X		X
SN Brussels Airlines		X		X
Sun-Air of Scandinavia	X*		X	

Notes: * **one**world affiliate members
available to Indian residents only

Source: www.britishairways.com

cabin, which they could use for themselves, or as a mini-meeting room, or as a bedroom with a fully flat 6ft 6ins (198 cm) bed.

A new approach to in-flight customer service was also introduced and staff offered a more personalized style and à la carte menus. Check-in times were also improved for First Class and Club passengers with the introduction of 'queue-jumping' channels.

The airline also stated publicly in the late 1990s, that it was committed to the environment. One of the company's corporate goals is 'To be a good neighbour, concerned for the community and the environment'.

To monitor progress in this regard, the company publishes annually an Environment Report. The Chairman, Rod Eddington, stated his commitment to the environmental policy in a statement which appeared in his Company Environment Report for the period 2004/05. This statement is shown in Exhibit 11.3.

> ## Exhibit 11.3 Rod Eddington's commitment to the environment policy of British Airways
>
> We recognize that we will not win the respect of the wider community if we do not seriously address the environmental impacts of aviation. We have a longstanding programme of measures designed to reduce our noise and emissions footprint at the airports where we operate, focussing particularly on our main Heathrow base. We are also actively involved with international initiatives aimed to help the industry manage its key environmental issues.
>
> On the issue of climate change, we have played a leading role in encouraging the industry and policy-makers to embrace an approach which includes emissions trading. British Airways is currently the only airline trading emissions in the voluntary United Kingdom government scheme and we support the inclusion of aviation into emissions trading within the European Union. At the Aviation and Environment summit in Geneva in March 2005, I urged the global aviation industry to think about new ways of working together to reduce our impact on climate change, or risk facing additional taxation.
>
> Taking a responsible approach to social and environmental issues remains crucial to our business performance and its future success. This report reviews our performance and progress over the last year, but it also highlights major challenges ahead.
>
> We are committed to work to meet these challenges, to ensure that our business is both profitable and sustainable over the long term.
> ROD EDDINGTON
>
> *Source*: www.britishairways.com.

Aviation and the environment

The potential for damage to the environment as the demand for air travel increases, has been recognized and documented by many commentators. A summary of the types of damage which aviation travel can cause to the environment is listed in Exhibit 11.4.

Exhibit 11.4 shows that, although air travel is an integral part of the modern world, with tourism and business travel being recognized as making a major contribution to economic development, it has tremendous potential for damaging the environment. It has been recognized by British Airways that managing the impact on the environment in a responsible and acceptable way is central to the long-term survival of the airline. To help with this process, the Aviation Environment Federation has been established, which is concerned with all the environmental and amenity effects of aviation.

The European Community's programme of policy and action on the environment, 'Towards Sustainability', specifically targets five sectors,

---

Exhibit 11.4   Environmental damage caused by air travel

Noise

* Noise – aircraft noise affects the local community
* Noise from the ground power units
* Noise from the engine running

Waste

* Waste from the aircraft and catering
* Hazardous waste from engineering
* Effluent
* Office waste

Emissions to atmosphere

* Atmospheric impact of aviation
* Local air quality affected by ground transport
* Emissions from ground vehicle fleet
* Emission from maintenance processes

Congestion

* Congestion in the air
* Traffic pressures on the ground

Tourism and conservation

* Impacts at destinations including waste, congestion, emissions and noise
* Conservation issues

Source: Aviation Environment Federation and British Airways.

---

including both transport and tourism, as critical to development of a strategy for sustainable development. British Airways define sustainable development as 'the means, in practice, that the global society must seek to use natural resources more efficiently to protect natural "capital" for future generations'.

There has been *regulation* on aspects of airline operations such as noise, emissions, and waste. *Fiscal measures* have also been applied and may be expanded further. Local noise charges at airports, are examples of a fiscal measure. Self-interest of the airline companies involved can lead to environmental measures being taken. Fuel economy in aircraft, for example, can save the airline money in the long term, and give environmental advantages.

The British Airways environmental policy

British Airways has addressed environmental issues, historically, through individual departments. It was considered so important, however, in 1989, that a central Environment Branch was established to focus on this important area. The company now has a clear environmental policy, consistent with best industry practice, which is shown in Exhibit 11.5. The full statement of the company's environmental policy is published each year in the Annual Environmental Report.

The British Airways social and environmental policy is shown in Exhibit 11.6.

The transparency of the environmental policy and the method of reporting its activities in the Annual Environmental Reports has brought considerable recognition to the airline.

BA tour operations and environmental policy

British Airways operates a tourism business in their British Airways Holidays division. The potential damage to the environment by tourism has been recognized and steps need to be taken to help organizations work towards sustainable tourism practices. British Airways has worked with several organizations which have been set up to raise awareness of the issues related to bad tourism practice. These organizations are summarized in Exhibit 11.7.

British Airways is trying to take positive steps to encourage environmentally responsible tourism. The company has developed a scheme, the British Airways Tourism for Tomorrow Awards, which encourages tour operators to protect the environment at resorts. Organizations apply for these awards and the overall winner is chosen from each of five world-wide regional winners and receives the Global Award. There are two special awards aimed at encouraging organizations in the mass tourism sector to behave in a more environmentally friendly manner. The awards are publicized through the British Airways global network.

British Airways Holidays is also encouraging a more environmentally friendly approach. An environmental co-ordinator was appointed after a review in 1993. A series of programmes and initiatives were started up in the 1990s, following this appointment. Details of these are shown in Exhibit 11.8. These initiatives are in their early stages of development but are already providing a lead in the tourism industry. An example of an Earthwise guide for one British Airways Holiday destination is shown in Exhibit 11.9.

An example of environmental literature which is given out before travel is shown in Exhibit 11.10. These guides encourage holiday-makers to treat the environment with respect and cause minimum damage while they are on holiday. The guides also provide special features related to the individual destinations. Early research by British Airways in the 1990s indicated that consumers who booked a holiday with them had little real interest in the environmental impact of their holiday.

Exhibit 11.5 Responsibilities for implementing the environment policy

Staff

All staff are responsible for safeguarding, as far as they are able, both their working environment and the greater environment surrounding our operations. This includes:

* complying with environmental standards and procedures
* notifying management and supervisors of potential hazards
* avoiding needless wastage of energy and materials

Line management

All line managers, in relation to activities under their individual control, are responsible for identifying and ensuring compliance with environmental regulations affecting our environment. Each Director shall address environmental matters regularly, identify items requiring action and make sure they are followed up. Line managers must:

* establish individual responsibilities, objectives and accountabilities for subordinate staff in environmental matters

* develop and maintain procedures to protect the working and external environment

* monitor implementation of procedures and working practices and take swift and appropriate steps to put deficiencies right

* ensure that a statement of environmental impact, tailored to specific requirements, is prepared as part of the planning of facilities and operations, and for modifying or abandoning them

* provide channels for employees and contractors to be consulted on environmental matters

* investigate and report all environmental incidents and near misses and take necessary follow up actions

* set quality standards covering relevant discharges and disposals including any that are not covered by statutory requirements

* review regularly the use of materials and energy in order to reduce waste, optimize recycling and select materials compatible with environmental objectives

* maintain accurate and comprehensive records of discharges and other waste disposals to the environment, including breaches of compliance limits

* report any breaches to the relevant regulatory bodies or internally as appropriate and take action to bring operations within compliance

Exhibit 11.5 (*Continued*)

Director of Safety, Security and Risk Management and Head of Environment

Authority for environmental matters is devolved through the Director of Safety, Security and Risk Management to the Head of Environment who is responsible for:

* periodic assessments, audits and review of facilities and operations to ensure compliance with this policy

* provision of support and advice on environmental matters throughout British Airways operations

* promoting workable procedures, codes of practice and working co-operatively in emergencies

* encouraging initiatives to implement this policy, and research to reduce environmental problems

* active co-operation by British Airways with government, local authorities and other external bodies to provide an informed and constructive background to regulatory processes

* keeping staff, relevant authorities and, as appropriate, the public informed of our efforts to protect and improve the environment

* interpreting and ensuring implementation of this policy, and updating it as required

Source: British Airways, 2005.

Exhibit 11.6   British Airways social and environmental policy

British Airways will strive to improve its environmental and social performance and to contribute to a better quality of life for everyone, now and for generations to come.

This will be achieved by:

* aiming to improve our economic, environmental and social performance, integrating environmental and social factors in our management systems and programmes and in our commercial decisions

* identifying significant aspects and impacts of our activites, including changes, on society and the environment and developing programmes to minimize these impacts

(*Continued*)

Exhibit 11.6   (*Continued*)

* setting clearly defined objectives and targets addressing our environmental and social issues

* meeting or exceeding requirements of relevant rules and regulations

* using natural resources efficiently, minimizing waste and harmful releases to the environment

* working constructively with organizations concerned for communities, society and the environment

* raising awareness of environmental and social issues with staff, partners and suppliers, who we will seek to influence to adopt similar policies

* undertaking open dialogue on our environmental and social programmes with our staff, customers and other stakeholders

* engagement on relevant major public policy issues such as climate change

* providing support, advice and training to staff on matters relating to our environmental and social performance

* monitoring, auditing and reviewing our performances

* regularly reviewing policies and management systems in these areas in order to drive for continual improvement

Specific aspects of social and environmental performance are covered in other policy documents, including the Code of Conduct, the Health, Safety and Environment Manual, and the Employment Guide.

Authority for monitoring compliance with this policy is devolved to the Head of Environment, who will review and update it as required.

Source: British Airways, 2005.

Conclusions

British Airways will continue their long-term environmental policy and will be trying to communicate their successes via different communication mediums, including their Annual Environmental Report. Work will continue on trying to encourage people to take a more responsible attitude to tourism in co-operation with such bodies as the World Wildlife Fund (WWW).

Customers at present, however, seem to have a limited interest in environmental measures, and seem to be more interested in other features such as destinations, facilities, entertainments and price.

Exhibit 11.7   Organizations established to raise awareness of issues relating to bad tourism practice

Tourism Concern – pushing forward the debate about what is good or bad tourism and questioning the direction in which the industry should be moving.

Campaign for Environmentally Responsible Tourism (CERT) – encourages awareness and feedback on experiences as a tourist. Activities include publishing a set of guidelines and distributing them to tour operators to pass on to their clients.

The International Hotels Environment Initiative (IHEI) – targets the hotel sector and encourages positive action.

Green Globe – set up under the auspices of the **World Travel and Tourism Council (WTTC)** – offers a package of practical environmental advice to various sectors of the industry who join as members.

ASTA (American Society of Travel Agents Inc.) and **PATA (Pacific Asia Travel Association)** have published codes of practice.

Source: Aviation Environment Federation and British Airways.

Exhibit 11.8   British Airways Holidays environmental programmes and initiatives 1990s

1. **Life-cycle analysis of a holiday destination**
   The company commissioned a detailed study of the impacts of their product at a specific destination – the Seychelles.
   A number of issues were highlighted including water pollution and exploitation of endangered species for souvenirs.

2. **Earthwise guide**
   The British Airways brochure for travel from the UK contains a panel of environmental guidelines for holiday-makers.

3. **Traveller donation schemes**
   Some brochures contain details of donation schemes in support of conservation projects in places such as Kenya, India, Thailand, Venice, Florida and California.

Source: British Airways.

Exhibit 11.9 Earthwise guide

Fragile Earth – Wherever you go be a friend to the environment

British Airways Holidays is committed to improving environmental practice and performance in all aspects of its business. The company held an environmental audit of its operations in 1993 and is working actively as a member of the tourism industry to safeguard holiday destinations for future generations. Through its Traveller Donation Scheme, we actively support important conservation work in countries around the world.

Travel wisely

* Find out as much as you can about the wildlife, culture and history of your destination. Try to understand the local community and its customs.

* Support the local economy by using locally-owed services and buying regional produce – from souvenirs to the local brew.

* Don't buy products like ivory, coral or tortoiseshell, which are made from endangered species.

* Corals are living creatures, easily damaged just by touch. Avoid standing on them and resist the temptation to collect any corals, shells or other reef species.

* Protect the local environment – dispose of litter carefully and avoid disturbing or damaging wildlife or plants.

* Conserve energy, turn off lights and air conditioning, and save water.

* Ask permission before taking photographs of local people, show respect for religious symbols and rituals. Avoid giving presents or money to local children – if you wish to help youngsters, it is better to give to a local school.

* Dress modestly particularly outside the main tourist areas.

* You can help conservation efforts by visiting parks and reserves. Your support will encourage local authorities to protect their heritage.

* If you witness or encounter environmental abuses, please write to the country's tourist board or an environmental organization. If you have any comments or suggestions we would be glad to hear from you. Please write to: Environmental Coordinator, Marketing Department, British Airways Holidays, Astral Towers, Betts Way, Crawley, RH10 2XA.

Source: British Airways Holiday brochure.

Exhibit 11.10 British Airways fact sheet given to holiday-makers before travel to Thailand

ENVIRONMENTAL INFORMATION

You may find it hard to imagine as you visit some of the more beautiful sites, but the natural environment in Thailand is under massive pressure.

British Airways Holidays want to give customers some background information to help customers to view Thailand through a green lens. It should help you to ensure that your visit to Thailand does not contribute to the growing pressure on the country's environment.

As the population grows and industry booms, so does the demand for land building. Each year, Bangkok – which accounts for about three-quarters of national economic output – concretes over another 8 000 acres of farmland.

Bangkok has virtually no sewage facilities, which puts huge pressures on the city's canals (or klongs) and on the great Chao Phraya River which flows through the city's heart. Happily, there is now an Environmental Protection Act which gives top priority to sewage treatment in Phuket and Pattaya. Business people face fines and even jail sentences for pollution related offences.

If you find yourself wondering why the streets are so congested, just remember this extraordinary fact: vehicle sales have been growing at about 35 per cent a year. An estimated 800 new cars arrive every day – that's an extra two miles of cars bumper to bumper. Thais not surprisingly, are waking up to their environmental problems. Look out for posters featuring a pair of angry 'Magic Eyes', part of a major Bangkok campaign to discourage litter.

Population growth has been phenomenal in recent decades. The population of Bangkok today is larger than the entire population of Thailand in 1910. There is even a Bangkok restaurant dedicated to the theme of contraception. It is called 'Cabbages and Condoms'.

With a surprisingly high number of young Thais involved in some form of prostitution, AIDS is now a growing concern. Now AIDS is putting sex tourism firmly in the spotlight, with Thailand ranking alongside or possibly ahead of the USA.

For a lesson in eco-history visit the beautiful Vrinannek Teak Mansion in Bangkok. Once the home of King Rama V, the building dates from a time when teak trees were still Thailand's most valuable resource. With 81 rooms, this is said to be the largest building ever made out of golden teak. Teak contains a special oil which helps it resist heavy rain, hot sun and insects. A solid piece of the wood, it is said, can easily last 1 000 years.

But the world's appetite for tropical timber has chewed great holes in Thailand's forests. Coupled with tree-felling by farmers and

(Continued)

Exhibit 11.10   (*Continued*)

opium poppy growers, the result was that the country's forest cover was cut in half between 1960 and 1985.

Despite logging bans and attempts to replant logged areas, Thailand continues to lose its forests. Today the country's rainforests and other natural treasures need urgent protection. Remember, this is a country in transition, from an agricultural economy to one based on industry. But ask yourself: can any country afford to lose its natural resources at this rate? The answer, surely is, no. Visit one more of Thailand's wonderful National Parks and see for yourself what is at stake.

Source: British Airways.

Targeting the subgroup which have a particular interest in environmental policies will be crucial in increasing overall awareness and interest.

Discussion points

1 Evaluate the reasons for an apparent lack of interest amongst consumers in the UK in environmental issues of tour operation and airlines when purchasing holiday products.

2 British Airways is trying to communicate their environmental policies to customers with the aim of increasing interest and encouraging concern. Discuss the most appropriate way of communicating this information to customers, in your opinion.

TUI, Germany– environmental policy

Introduction

TUI (Touristik Union International) is the largest tour operator in Europe. The company is based in Germany and has developed a wide range of mass-market tourism products which are distributed in major countries throughout Europe. TUI has developed its tourism business by ownership and part investment in a range of tour operators, hotel companies, incoming agencies and distribution companies. The TUI Group is shown in Exhibit 12.1.

It can be seen from the exhibit that TUI participates in the ownership of tour operators in a number of European countries, including Germany, Austria, the Netherlands, Switzerland and Belgium. It also has substantial interests in hotel companies and incoming agencies in destinations which are of major importance for the TUI Group. Through its participations in hotel companies, TUI safeguards its influence on hotel quality and the group's financial performance. The TUI hotel-portfolio consists of the thirteen brands, including RIU, Grecotel, Iberotel, Dorfhotel and Club Robinson.

The company was quick to capitalize on an increase in European travel and tourism which occurred in the 1990s, despite the difficult economic conditions which occurred throughout Europe during this period.

TUI AG reported a profit in 2004 of €137.6 million. The TUI Group performed very well in the period 2003/04, and was able to expand its market position nationally and throughout Europe. The four business segments of the TUI

Exhibit 12.1   TUI Group, 2004

Retail – companies and brand

TUI Germany	Walters Reisen GmbH Germany
TUI Austria	TUI Reise Center Austria
TUI Poland	Scan Holiday Poland
TUI Switzerland	MOSTRAVEL Russia
TEMA Finland	Thomson UK
Austravel UK	Callers-Pegasus UK
Team Lincoln UK	TUI UK
Budget Travel Ltd Ireland	TUI Ireland
Sportreiser Norway	Star Tour Norway
TEMA Norway	Fritidsreson Sweden
Sportresor Sweden	TEMA Sweden
Jetair Belgium	TUI Belgium
Nouvelles Frontiers France	JV France
TUI France	arke Netherlands
De Boers Wendel Netherlan	Discovery Netherlands
Groups Incentive Travel Netherlands	Holland International Netherlands
TUI Reisbureau Netherlands	

Tour operators – companies and brands

1-2 Fly GmbH Germany	Airtours Germany
Discount Travel Germany	Fox-Tours Germany
Gebeco Germany	Litur Tourismus AG Germany
OFT REISEN Germany	Europa Germany
Gulet Touropa Touristik GmbH Germany	TU Travel Shop Germany
Sportsrejser Denmark	Star Tour Denmark
TEMA Denmark	Finn Matkat Denmark

Airlines

TUI AG Germany	Hapag-Lloyd Express GmbH
Hapag-Lloye Germany	Germany
Thomsonfly.com UK	Britannia Uk
TUI Belgium	Corsair France

Hotels

TUI Hotels & Resorts Germany	Atlantica Hotels Cyprus
Dorfhotel Austria	Gran Resort Hotels Spain
Grecotel Greece	Grupotel Dos SA Spain
Iberotel Germany	Magic Life Austria
Nordotel Spain	Paladien Hotel Paris
RIU Spain	Robinson Germany
Sol y Mar Egypt	

Exhibit 12.1   (*Continued*)

Incoming agencies

TUI Germany	Travco Egypt
TUI Bulgaria	TUI China
TUI Dominican Republic	Travco Dubai
Tui Greece	Serenade Tours Italy
Pollmanic Kenya	Gulliver Travel Croatia
Aeolos Lebanon	Tui Malta
Holiday Services Morocco	Summertimes Mauritius
Mex Atlantica Tours Mexico	ATC Namibia
TUI Portugal	Dunubius Romania
TUI Spain	Aitken Spence Travels Ltd,
ATC African Travel Concept, South Africa	Sri Lanka
Tunisia Voyages Tunisia	Ranger Safaris Ltd Tanzania
Aeolos Travel Cyprus	Tantur Turkey

The group also own tour guide organization, business travel organization, information technology businesses and logistic companies.

Source: TUI, 2004.

Exhibit 12.2   Financial performance of the TUI Group 2003/2004

		2003	2004
Turnover	€	19 215	18 046
Net earnings/share	€	1.54	2.74
Cashflow	€	902	964
Total	€	12 989	12 319
Balance sheet total	€	1 722	1 470
Equity ratio	*percent*	21.3	24.3
Employees	*number*	64 257	57 716

Source: TUI Annual Accounts 2004.

Group – business tour operating, hotel companies, incoming agencies and share holdings in distribution – all performed positively in the 1995/96 financial year. The good financial performance, which is shown in Exhibit 12.2, allowed the Group to further enlarge its position as European market leaders in the tourism business.

The TUI environmental policy

The TUI environmental policy has been developed as a central strategy of the Group (Horner and Swarbrooke, 1996). TUI's environmental strategy is an integral part of the TUI quality strategy. The TUI corporate policy states: 'the protection of an intact nature and environment are of outstanding importance to us'.

It is the aim of the Group to try and preserve the national basic substance of the product that the Group is offering in the form of the sea, the beach, peace and quiet, landscape, the animal world and nature.

The Group appointed Dr Wolf Michael Iwand in 1990 as their environment manager to manage the Group's environmental policy. He still reports directly to the board of directors. The Group has recognized that it is key for any major tourism business that it makes major efforts to minimize the environmental effect on the natural environment which holiday-makers are visiting. It is only by taking a positive approach to environmental planning that tourism companies will continue to be able to be successful in the future.

Exhibit 12.3   TUI's planning objectives

Time period	Ecological objectives	Measures	Economic objectives
Short term	Reduction of environmental pollution and impairment	Education/ consulting Programme organization Hotel management	Quality control Product optimization Ensuring returns
Medium term (up to 2005)	Environmental relief Prevention of environmental pollution and impairment	Environmental standards/ eco-labelling Environment information systems Environmental quality goals	Management of risk and opportunities/ innovation
Long term (up to 2030)	Environmental relief Prevention of environmental pollution and nuisance Environmental improvements	Eco-controlling Ecological product control Environmental impact assessment	Securing the future Securing and improving revenues

Source: Department of Environment, TUI 1997.

The Group established short-, medium- and long-term objectives in relation to the environment in the late 1990s. These planning objectives are shown in Exhibit 12.3.

It can be seen that this programme outlined a series of measures which the Group hoped to achieve up to the year 2030. This includes moves towards 'eco-labelling' and 'eco-auditing' which originate from Brussels. The Group had four main aspects to the drive for sustainable tourist development. The first of these involved reducing pollution by all means and by low-cost activity. The second aspect was the establishment of financial and technical feasibility at the destinations. The third aspect was to stimulate environmental awareness among vacationers and clients, and to achieve satisfaction by environmental quality. The final aspect was to ensure that a measurable return on investment was secured.

In the first stages of their environmental initiatives, TUI worked with experts and environmentalists, local authorities and hotel partners to

---

Exhibit 12.4   Holiday-making and environment friendliness – the late 1990s

TUI destination criteria

* Bathing water and beach quality
* Water supply and water-saving measures
* Wastewater disposal and utilization
* Solid waste disposal, recycling and prevention
* Energy supply and energy-saving measures
* Traffic, air, noise and climate
* Landscape and built environment
* Nature conservation, species preservation and animal welfare
* Environmental information and offers
* Environmental policy and activities

TUI hotel criteria

* Wastewater treatment
* Solid waste disposal, recycling and prevention
* Water supply and water-saving measures
* Energy supply and energy-saving measures
* Environmentally oriented hotel management (focus on food, cleaning and hygiene)
* Quality of bathing waters and beaches in the vicinity of the hotel
* Noise protection in and around the hotel
* Hotel gardens
* Building materials and architecture
* Environmental information and offers of the hotel
* Location and immediate surroundings of the hotel

(*Continued*)

Exhibit 12.4 (*Continued*)

TUI carrier criteria

*   Energy consumption
*   Pollutant and noise emissions
*   Land use and paving over
*   Vehicle/craft, equipment and line maintenance techniques
*   Catering and waste recycling and disposal
*   Environmental information for passengers
*   Environmental guidelines and reporting
*   Environmental research and development
*   Environmental co-operation, integrated transport concepts
*   Specific data: vehicle/craft type, motor/power unit, age

Source: General information brochure, TUI Travel, 1997 Catalogues.

---

ensure that the holidays on offer were as environmentally friendly as possible. The Group established environmental criteria for their destinations, hotels, and carriers. Details of these are shown in Exhibit 12.4.

Information on the TUI environmental programme

The early environmental initiative involved the group in collecting information concerning the environment collected by the Group which was stored in the TUI Environmental Database.

This information was used in planning and in the holiday brochure. The hotels which are contracted by TUI were examined using a comprehensive environmental acceptability checklist. The Group worked in local environmental action which tried to allay problems such as malfunctioning sewage plants or improper tipping of rubbish and brought together tourist officials, local authority representatives, local politicians and hoteliers in 'round table' meetings, in order to find joint solutions. TUI has also worked with its airline partners and other carriers over the past decade, to improve their environmental friendliness on the criteria outlined in Exhibit 12.4.

Customers and the TUI Environmental Policy

TUI recognized that an unspoiled environment is key for customers when they are choosing holidays. They reflected on the main characteristics for 'Quality Tourism' that were researched by Opaschowski (1993) and are shown in Exhibit 12.5. It can be seen that a large number of the characteristics which were chosen by respondents were related to the environment.

TUI researched customer views on the environment with a customer questionnaire. The results of TUI's market research and customers' letters they receive were reflected in its environmental measures,

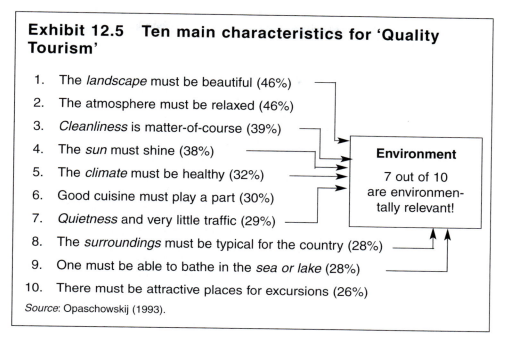

Exhibit 12.5   Ten main characteristics for 'Quality Tourism'

1.   The *landscape* must be beautiful (46%)
2.   The atmosphere must be relaxed (46%)
3.   *Cleanliness* is matter-of-course (39%)
4.   The *sun* must shine (38%)
5.   The *climate* must be healthy (32%)
6.   Good cuisine must play a part (30%)
7.   *Quietness* and very little traffic (29%)
8.   The *surroundings* must be typical for the country (28%)
9.   One must be able to bathe in the *sea or lake* (28%)
10. There must be attractive places for excursions (26%)

Environment

7 out of 10 are environmentally relevant!

Source: Opaschowskij (1993).

which helped to ensure that the Group ensured the best customer orientation from the environmental standpoint.

Tour operators, holiday regions and hoteliers tried to improve their environmental measures in response to customer demand. The customer has, however, been spoiled with reduced package prices across Europe over the past decade, owing to intense competition in the market. Customers have also been going to more exotic locations and are seeking more thrilling diversions.

TUI recognized that the task of persuading these hedonistic citizens of the leisure era to save water and energy, and to avoid discarding litter, even during the most relaxed weeks of their year, was difficult but not impossible. The Group recognized that reasoned briefing on the ecology of the destination and the environment in resorts rather than preaching was required. The publication of seawater analysis and beach qualities were practical examples of this. Publicity for new national parks, cycle tracks and footpaths were other practical examples.

TUI still has an active role in the development of sustainable tourism. This is seen as being a critical role of the Group as tourism business worldwide continues to grow. The current activities of TUI in the development of sustainable tourism are shown in Exhibit 12.6.

It can be seen from this exhibit that the activities of TUI in the development of sustainable tourism are far reaching. The Group has also developed sustainable criteria for whale watching and nature excursions to help to protect creatures and the environment. It has also developed relationships with Co-operation Partners to help in the fostering of the development of sustainable tourism.

Exhibit 12.6 World of TUI activities to support tourism development

Reducing negative environmental impacts through continuously improving eco-efficiency (energy consumption, water consumption, waste generation, land and nature consumption ...) in thousands of holiday hotels. The pioneering role is played by TUI's own hotels.

Integrating environmental quality standards and social standards in a TQM concept and its active implementation.

Intensive lobbying for strictly controlled master plans within a co-ordinated regional development for tourism development (integration of local, communal and regional needs).

Supporting all measures for prudent visitor management i.e. the control and management of visitor flows in time and space measures for the renovation and renaturization of 'overexploited' tourism areas.

Supporting phased protected area policies in holiday regions (nature protection, landscape protection, species protection, eco-system protection) with fixed clearly defined protection and utilization regulations. TUI's 'environmental quality performance indicators' for destination quality include the percentage of protected area per holiday region and 'biological diversity'.

Support and funding of holiday regions for application and classifiction as UNESCO MaB (Man and Biosphere) – biosphere reserves (positive examples: Lanzarote, Minorca, Donana).

Supporting measures for the 'invalorization' of natural areas with high biodiversity through the strategy 'protecting through controlled use' = combining nature protection and economic value generation through compatible forms of utlization, particularly for

major protected areas (national parks, nature parks, and biosphere reserves).

Supporting local councils and regions in the implementation of the development processes of local Agenda 21 (examples: Calvia/Majorca, Alps, Caribbean). Cooperation and participation of all parties involved in tourism (tour operators, service providers, agencies, environmental associations/NGOs, local inhabitants)in joint local Agenda 21 processes, sustainability projects and round-tables / forums ...

Joint consideration of financing concepts and supporting measures through links with institutions (World Bank/GEF, IWF, European Commission, European Investment Bank, DES/GTZ) and the integration of public and private sectors (e.g. public private partnership) in project co-operation.

Source: TUI, 2004.

Communicating with consumers

TUI recognized early on that long-term briefing of consumers on their environmental measures was the way to improve recognition of the environment in relation to tourism. Market research in Germany showed that German tourists are environmentally conscious and consider this when choosing holidays. It is important that the environmental measures taken by TUI are communicated to the customer in an effective way. TUI produces millions of TUI brochures every year

Exhibit 12.7   Early environmental information in TUI travel brochures

'Nature and Environment'

Extracts from TUI catalogues, explaining the 'Nature and Environment' situation for the exemplary cases of Fuerteventura, La Palma and Namibia.

Fuerteventura: Fuerteventura's beaches are acclaimed by our guests as the best in Europe. They are regularly cleaned, and the coastal waters are monitored within the international Coastwatch Network. Five bathing beaches on Fuerteventura were awarded the European Blue Flag in 1995. Due to the low amount of precipitation, the island is one of the driest in the archipelago. The extensive grazing of the many goats has intensified the island's desert character, and erosion, which is perhaps its greatest problem, is increased. Water supply is difficult. Because of the geological conditions, groundwater is scarce. The population is supplied by four seawater desalination plants, while the larger hotels often have their own facilities. For a renewable supply of energy, the 'Parque Eolico' with 45 wind turbines came into operation in 1994. A second wind park is planned. A Nature Conservation Act designates 13 protected zones, amongst which are the unique and particularly endangered dune landscapes of Corralejo and Jandia. Together with the ASCAN environmental organization, TUI supports the ECO ISLA Fuerteventura project.

La Palma: La Palma boasts one of the ten Biosphere Reserves on Spanish territory, a piece of nature that is unique worldwide. 40% of the island is already protected under nature conservation law. Last year, however, forest fires took toll of some 5 000 hectares. Although the 'Green movement' is strongly represented on La Palma, environmentally sound measures such as the construction of new sewage plants or the introduction of controlled waste management systems are currently only at the planning stage. The new Development Plan makes a positive step forwards: this stipulates that 80% of the island must be held free from development.

Namibia: The government of Namibia has limited the number of tourists per annum to a maximum of 650,000 to preserve the country's unique landscape. Tourist accommodation in nature reserves will continue to be owned by the government in future; ecological sensitive areas like the skeleton coast are protected by strict environmental legislation. More and more lodges are using solar energy for producing hot water. On account of natural conditions (e.g. climate) Namibia suffers from water shortage. Therefore our request: please use water economically!

'Ecologically Sound Hotel Management'

Extracts from TUI catalogues, explaining 'Ecologically Sound Hotel Management' for the exemplary case of Cyprus

Columbia Pissouri, Pissouri: Own biological sewage plant with re-use of purified water for garden irrigation. Use of solar energy for hot-water supply. Waste separation and composting. Avoidance of disposable products.

(Continued)

Exhibit 12.7   *(Continued)*

The Annabelle, Paphos: Own biological sewage plant; re-use of purified water for garden irrigation. Use of solar energy for hot-water supply, waste separation and use of returnable bottles. Automatic tailor-made air-conditioning equipment.

Source: TUI.

---

which all incorporate information about the environment. This includes both good and bad points about the destination and tries to state realistic facts about the environmental conditions in different parts of the world. The company recognize that communication of environmental initiative brochures was an important part of the communication strategy. An early example of this type of communication is shown in Exhibit 12.7.

The customer can compare the information which he reads in the brochure with the conditions that he finds at the destination. If the environmental situation concerns the customer he will express his dislike at the resort, to the representative, or in writing to the company, when he returns home. He can also fill in questionnaires provided by TUI to express his feelings.

TUI also thinks that the travel agent has a key role to play in the education of consumers on environmental matters. TUI provides seminars for travel agents so that they understand the necessity for good environmental quality. This education of the travel agent is a large task, however, given that TUI goes to about 150 destinations every year. TUI has set up an on-line programme for travel agents containing the latest environmental information to help with the process. The number of travel agents which use this service, at the moment in Germany, is very limited, but TUI hopes that this will increase in the future.

The future of the TUI environmental policy

TUI has recognized that its environmental policy will help the company to be successful in ten to twenty years' time. The policy is therefore part of the long-term strategy of the company. TUI has predicted that tourism will have to be organized in a sound, safe and environmentally friendly way in the future. The company does not see itself offering 'eco-tourism' products, but minimizing the environmental impact caused by 5 million TUI customers who travel abroad every year.

The company is predicting that there will be a day in the future when consumers base their travel decisions on environmental information provided by the tour operator and travel agent. The key factor in this is the point when the consumer is prepared to pay more for a better environment. Consumer behaviour which favours companies which have well-implemented environmental campaigns is supported by environmental campaigning organizations such as Greenpeace. TUI believes that it is logical for the company to prepare itself for the day when consumers ask for environment-related information before they book their holidays. At this stage, the company which is not in a position to provide this information will lose business.

Conclusions

TUI is the largest tour operator in Europe and has been active in pursuing an environmental policy for all their tour operations business. The company considers that this is an important part of their future strategy, despite the fact that the consumer has limited interest in the environment in relation to tourism, at the present time.

Discussion points and essay questions

1 'Mass tourism and ecological soundness do not go together – but there is much one can do to lessen the impact of one on the other' (Dr Iwand, TUI). Discuss this comment, in relation to TUI consumers.

2 The desire for consumers to travel to exotic destinations has been accompanied with an almost total lack of interest in the environment. Discuss the reasons for this and explore the actions which a mass tour operator, such as TUI, can do about this situation.

Ragdale Hall – health hydro

Introduction

Ragdale Hall was established in the 1970s as a business which offered customers the opportunity to experience health, beauty and fitness treatments. There have been considerable alterations made to the hall during the past twenty years. There have been additions made to the original buildings, and facilities have been regularly updated so that the latest treatments and products can always be offered to guests. Ragdale Hall is situated within easy reach of the M1 and A1, between Loughborough and Melton Mowbray in the heart of the Leicestershire countryside. Guests can arrive at the hall by car or taxi from local railway stations.

Ragdale Hall is set in its own extensive landscaped gardens and combines the charm of traditional Victorian architecture with the most modern facilities, to create one of the most luxurious and relaxing health resorts in the UK.

Ragdale Hall – the company

Ragdale Hall has had many owners during its history. It has been operated as a restaurant and a nightclub with gambling facilities. It became a health hydro in 1972 when Slimming World purchased it. Ragdale Hall changed ownership in June 1990, when it was bought by Gerry Nesbitt and Michael Isaacs – the founders of Our Price Records. These new owners have taken a personal interest in the business and have provided the finance for an extensive refurbishment and extension of the facilities.

The products and services on offer at Ragdale Hall

Ragdale Hall has written a definitive guide to what a health hydro is, so that customers can understand the difference

---

Exhibit 13.1   A health hydro – the criteria

*   Countryside location with resort like feel

*   Provision of healthy, calorie controlled food on a full board basis

*   Absence of alcohol (wine excepted)

*   A no smoking policy in public areas and bedrooms but provision of a small smoking room

*   Provision of high quality beauty treatments, some of which are included in overnight packages

*   Large variety of exercise classes for all fitness levels provided in the inclusive rate

*   Ban on pets and anyone under the age of 16

*   A very high guests/staff ratio allowing the very highest standards of personal care e.g. 5-star hotel 1:1, Ragdale 2.5:1

*   Comprehensive health and beauty consultations to ensure compatibility with treatments and activities offered

*   Provision of some medical/dietary advice when necessary but to ensure safety rather than to give any treatment

*   Casual dress and leisure wear in all areas at all times

*   No conferences, functions, or indeed suits!

*   An organization geared completely towards caring and total relaxation from the choice of staff, type of decor, ambience of the whole complex to the treatments and activities on offer

Source: Ragdale Hall.

---

between luxury hotels with a health and leisure spa and up-market private hospitals and retreats. The criteria which have been developed are shown in Exhibit 13.1.

It can be seen from this list of criteria that the health hydro concept offers customers a very different experience from those at other types of establishments. Customer service in a relaxed and pleasant surroundings is a key part of the product on offer.

Ragdale Hall has been designed to allow customers to put together their own mix of activities and treatments. Customers may choose to have an active or more leisure time. They may want to unwind or tone up, to shed weight or to relieve their worries.

Ragdale Hall offers a full range of services, which are shown in Exhibit 13.2. Guests may choose to purchase a package or may come to

Exhibit 13.2   The range of services on offer at Ragdale Hall

1. **Overnight Accommodation**
   Incorporating a luxury hotel with single and double rooms and suites.

2. **Restaurant and other catering facilities**
   A luxury restaurant which offers meals at different calorie levels. There is also a small self-service bar and snack service facility.

3. **Retail outlets**
   Two shops which offer a full range of beauty products, clothing and other merchandise.

4. **Health treatments**
   A range of treatment rooms surrounding an impressive conservatory seating area. These include revitalizing facials, relaxing massages, aromatherapy, reflexology thermal wraps, stress relief and detoxifying treatments.

5. **Beauty treatments**
   A full range of beauty treatments available including manicure, pedicure and expert make-up. There is also a full hair service and a Sun Centre which offers the safest and most modern tanning technology.

6. **Exercise areas**
   A fully equipped gymnasium which includes the latest resistance fitness equipment, bicycles, jogging and rowing machines. There are fitness co-ordinators who look after customers. The Hall also has an exercise studio with full sprung wooden floor.

7. **Water treatments**
   A luxurious range of water treatments, centred around two indoor pools. Steam room, and a luxurious new spa complex with traditional Scandinavian saunas, plunge pools, hurricane showers, whirlpool spas, floatation tanks and hydrotherapy baths complete this area.

8. **Outdoor activities**
   Including an outdoor swimming pool, tennis courts, etc.

Source: Ragdale Hall.

stay at the hall and put together their own programme of activities. These packages allow the guests to purchase a range of products at one time, and still purchase a range of extra services during their stay. The extra services include body and facial treatment (incorporating Clarins, Declor, Guinot and Kanebo products), fitness activities, and hair and beauty treatments.

All residential stays include:

- comfortable accommodation in a bedroom with en suite facilities
- breakfast served in the room, three course buffet lunch and four course table d'hôte dinner
- a full introductory tour of the hall
- an in-depth consultation with one of the senior therapists, including advice on treatments and an individually recommended exercise programme
- a welcome reception with refreshments, allowing the opportunity to meet the Guest Liaison Officer and Duty Manager who will ensure the break gets off to a great start
- an extensive daily programme of exercise classes to suit all fitness levels
- use of the gymnasium including induction session to cover training principles and safety
- use of the indoor and outdoor swimming pools and water exercise sessions.
- the unrestricted use of the Whirlpool Spa bath as well as separate male and female spa areas with sauna, steam and plunge pool facilities
- unlimited use of bicycles, championship-standard tennis courts, pitch and putt course, croquet and boules areas
- the opportunity to relax and unwind, whether it be in one of the relaxing lounges or outside in the beautiful gardens
- evening talks and demonstrations covering a wide range of interesting topics
- specially tailored packages to suit all needs
- weekend breaks, short or longer holidays, Healthy Option breaks geared around a specific objective, i.e. Focus on Fitness, Stress Buster, Slim and Shape, New You, Total Pampering.

New treatments are always being added to the list of treatments on offer. The staff at Ragdale Hall have just developed a new massage treatment called Ragdale Multi Method Massage, which is now on offer to customers. Two highly skilled therapists work in unison to give the customer a feeling of deep relaxation. Music and the use of aromatherapy oils are used during this type of massage. Ragdale Hall is also considering using further holistic treatments such as kineseology.

The food is considered a very important part of the product at Ragdale Hall. Guests can choose a menu to help them lose weight or they may choose to eat a healthy balanced diet, but with more calorific content. This is particularly important when the guest is taking part in strenuous physical exercise programmes during their stay.

Ragdale Hall has a wealth of experts who can offer advice on special subjects such as:

- bodycare during pregnancy:
  - suitable treatments
  - products which help alleviate the symptoms of pregnancy
  - exercise programmes
- advice for safety in the sun:
  - the best products
  - skin care routines
- care of those forgotten extremities – the hands and feet
- alternative therapies:
  - the concept
  - the difference between each one and who they can help
- stress management:
  - including giving up smoking
  - lifestyle
  - diet
- menopause:
  - treatments and activities to counteract its effects.

Other health resorts in the UK

There are other health resorts available to customers in the UK offering a similar range of products to Ragdale Hall, such as Champneys, Henlow Grange and Stobeo Castle, and hotels which offer in-house spas, such as Chewton Glen in Hampshire. Customers at Ragdale Hall come from all over the UK, although a proportion of these come from areas within a short drive time. It is clear that customers choose the health resort they want to visit according to the range of facilities and treatments on offer and their geographic location. Once a customer has chosen their preferred health resort, they are likely to be very loyal to this and return over and over again.

The guests at Ragdale Hall

A summary of the types of guests which stay at Ragdale Hall is shown in Exhibit 13.3.

It can be seen that the guest of Ragdale Hall is usually female, aged thirty-five and over, working and from a higher socioeconomic group. The interest in health and nutrition has been growing rapidly over the past ten years. There has been intense interest in the mainstream media in the UK, and people are generally much more knowledgeable about health and nutrition than they were ten years ago. Treatments such as

---

Exhibit 13.3   The guests of Ragdale Hall

* 92% of guests are female, 8% are male

* Guests are generally in the age range 35–70

* Guests are usually professional or working women, usually from socioeconomic groups ABC1

* Guests have a personal interest in health and nutrition and are generally trying to lead healthier lifestyles

* 64–65% of guests have visited Ragdale Hall before. The average number of visits per year is 2/3. Lengths of stay vary but the 3-night packages and day packages are very popular

* Guests live in all areas of the UK

* Guests come on their own, but it is more common for them to be in pairs or in small groups

Source: Ragdale Hall.

---

aromatherapy and floatation are widely recognized by people in general in the UK, whereas ten years ago these treatments were considered rather 'freaky' and unusual. This growing knowledge and education about healthy lifestyles, which has been fuelled by the government report 'The Health of the Nation' has meant that people, particularly women, are much more conscious about their general levels of health and fitness.

This growing interest has encouraged the development of the health hydro business, which offers the guest the opportunity to experience health and beauty treatments and 'chill out' from the everyday stresses and strain of modern living. The health hydro now appeals to people, especially women, from different backgrounds. It is not just the reserve of the 'health freak' or the celebrity model.

The benefits guests receive at Ragdale Hall

There are a wide range of benefits which guests say that they receive when they visit Ragdale Hall. These are shown in order of importance in Exhibit 13.4.

Guests leaving Ragdale Hall always express feelings of total relaxation and the desire to go back as soon as possible. It seems that the experience is often almost addictive for a large number of guests. The accompanying example testimonial, shown in Exhibit 13.5, from one guest illustrates this point very effectively.

> ## Exhibit 13.4   The benefits that guests receive from their visit to Ragdale Hall (in order of importance)
>
> *   Relief of stress
> *   Improvements in looks
> *   Becoming more healthy
> *   Escapism
> *   Losing weight
> *   A holiday experience
> *   Recovering from illness
> *   Getting ready for the 'big day', e.g. marriage or birth of a child
>
> *Source*: Ragdale Hall.

> ## Exhibit 13.5   Testimonials of guests – Ragdale Hall
>
> To celebrate our 40th birthdays, my friend and I spent a week at Ragdale Hall Health Hydro last July. There we, too, learned not to feel guilty about spending time on ourselves – and about leaving behind our families, pets, jobs and so on, for the first time ever.
>
> A little bit of pampering not only made me look better, but, more importantly, made me feel good and has helped re-establish a sense of my own worth after years of putting myself last in the pecking order. This is having a knock-on effect of making me more pleasant to live with – as my family will testify.
>
> It strikes me that the hectic lifestyles many women lead, well into middle-age and beyond, goes against the natural rhythm of things. Making time for ourselves to relax and feel good must go some way towards redressing the balance and can only benefit our health overall. Long live health hydros and beauty treatments.
>
> *Source*: Ragdale Hall.

Conclusions

The health hydro concept has developed recently as a response to the growing interest with healthy lifestyles. Ragdale Hall has responded to this trend and offers guests the opportunity to relax and be pampered in luxurious surroundings.

Discussion points

1   Evaluate the reasons for the growth of interest in the health hydro concept. How will this develop in the future?
2   Discuss in detail the *motivators* and *determinants* for customers of Ragdale Hall.

The international spa market

We saw, in Chapter 3, that spas have played a significant role in the historical development of tourism. While their popularity has declined in countries like the UK, it is still a very large market worldwide, and some spas are enjoying a renaissance.

The history of the development of the spa market

The history of the spa market goes back a long way, but the growth of the popular spa began in the 1990s. A report published in 1996 by Deloitte-Touche estimated that every year there were some 160 million visits paid to spa resorts in Europe, the USA, and Japan alone. The same document suggested that there were over 2000 spas resorts in Japan, nearly 450 in Italy, and between 250 and 300 each in the USA and Germany.

Deloitte-Touche's research indicated that the proportion of spa visits to overall population was probably highest in Germany and Japan. However, length of stay for Japanese visitors was one of the lowest in the world at around one to two nights while French visitors were the highest at over twenty nights.

In the same year, the Economist Intelligence Unit published a report, written by Nancy Cockerell, on European spas. This contained a number of interesting statistics, including the following:

- In Germany, spa towns received between 40 per cent and 45 per cent of domestic and international tourist trips, and accounted for around one half of all visits to European spas. Spa visiting, in Germany, was popular with both sexes, and all age and income groups. It was also linked to social tourism and the health service in Germany.

- While German people often also travelled abroad in search of spa treatment, most Italians and French tended to stay at home and use domestic spa resorts.
- The market in France was split between traditional thermal spa resorts and the more modern thalassotherapy complexes. Provision for the former was usually subsidized while that for the latter was almost wholly commercial.
- The motivation for thermal spas was largely medical whereas that for thalassotherapy is not.
- The thalassotherapy market was also younger than the market for the thermal spas.
- In 1994, it was estimated that the European international health holiday market involved around 1.7 million tourists, around 1 per cent of all tourism demand in Europe.

The growing popularity of thalassotherapy is illustrated by the creation of new centres, in recent years, in countries like Cyprus, Morocco, St Lucia, Venezuela, Indonesia, and Japan.

Likewise the increased concern with health and beauty is linked to a growth of new types of resort, including:

- pelotherapy (mud treatment) and heliotherapy (sun treatment) in Israel
- seaweed alyotherapy in Ireland.

To ensure their future, spas are seeking to diversify their offer to attract wider market segments. Some thermal establishments have opened themselves up to day visitors, while others have established other health facilities such as outdoor jogging tracks. Many resorts have sought to become leading venues for major sporting or cultural activities and events. They are also developing better leisure shopping attractions. They are aiming to make themselves attractive to more market segments by offering 'something for everyone'.

The consumer

There are differences between consumers who choose to go on a spa holiday and those who choose to go for a day spa experience. Market research in the UK (Mintel, 2005) showed that it is women from the eighteen to twenty-four year old age group who are most likely to express an interest in going on a spa holiday. Evidence suggests that older consumers (over forty-fives) have little or no interest in going to a spa complex. The rise in day spas has also attracted a new audience with women from higher socioeconomic groups, showing a particular interest in this type of experience (Mintel, 2005).

The spa market today

The spa market has now become international in nature with consumers travelling to spas as a total holiday, but a larger percentage of the business is part of a total holiday package. This desire to have a spa as part of a hotel complex is a relatively new trend that has fuelled international hotel development across the world. The focus on in-house spas in hotels has brought dividends to a number of hotel groups across the world. The Mandarin Oriental Hotels for example, in London, Miami and New York have been voted the best in town according to a survey of 17 000 *Conde Nast Traveller* readers in the USA and the UK (Caterer-online.com, accessed 5 April 2005).

The development of spas has also led to the growth of certain resorts on an international basis. Examples of some of these resorts are shown in Exhibit 14.1.

There has been a growth in spa operators who specialize in spa experiences. Some examples of these in the UK are shown in exhibit 14.2.

It can be seen from Exhibit 14.2 that competition is quite tough in the UK market, with specialist tour operators competing head on with mainstream operations.

Exhibit 14.1   Examples of worldwide spas

Name of spa	Location
Shambhala Spa	Parrot Cay, Turks and Caicos Islands
Mandara Spa	JW Marriott Phuket Resort and Spa, Thailand
Les Sources de Caudalie	France
Banyan Tree Spa	Seychelles
Spa Village	Pangkor Laut Resort, Malaysia
Willow Stream Spa	The Fairmont Banff Springs, Canada
Six Senses Spa	Soneva Fushi Resort and Spa, Maldives
Chiva-Som International Health Resort	Thailand
Mandara Spa	The Datai, Malaysia
Mandara Spa	One and Only Ocean Club, Bahamas

Source: CNTraveller.com, 2002.

Exhibit 14.2   Spa operators, UK, 2005

Spa operator	Type of business	Countries offered
A Spa to Life	Wellness and holistic healing trips	Europe and Barbados
Caribtours	Tailor-made holidays including spa escapes	Caribbean
Champneys Health Resort	One of the world's largest destination spa groups	UK, India, Switzerland
Erna Low	Promotes spas worldwide (in addition to skiing holidays)	Hungary, Malta, Spain, Switzerland, Cyprus, Portugal, Germany, Austria, Italy, UK, S Africa, India
Thermalia	Health and wellbeing holidays	Europe, Sri Lanka, S. Africa, Jordan, Cyprus, Slovakia, etc.
Luxury operators e.g. International Travel Connections Ltd,	Visits to spas as part of a package	Worldwide
La Joie de Vivre Travel,		Tropical Locations
Mainstream operators e.g. First Choice Holidays, TUI, UK	Visits to spas as part of a package	Worldwide

Source: Mintel (2005).

Countries that have developed spa/well-being tourism

France was traditionally a country that developed the spa business across the country with different spa and well-being destinations. There has been a more recent development of alternative spa destinations which has helped the countries to boost their tourist revenues. Exhibit 14.3 outlines some examples of these destinations.

It can be seen from this exhibit that it is important for the national government of a potential spa and well-being country to actively promote the destination and get involved in developments and standards.

Exhibit 14.3 Countries that have developed spa/well-being tourism

Country	Type of spa business	Comment
Hungary	Historical bathhouses, hot springs and spas. Cultural establishments, thermal waters	Government sponsored development (launched in 2001, the Sze Cheni Plan)
Thailand	Spa centres date back 2500 years using local herbs. Thai healing famous	Many spa brand operators Thai government formed the Federation of Thai Spas in 2004
Japan	Wellness tourism based on hot springs. Long history of spa tourism going back to AD552 Wellness hotels	Development of wellness hotels, thalassotherapy centres
Austria	Wellness tourism. Range of treatments including innovative ideas such as beer baths. Bathing treatments Alpine treatments	Sponsored by the Austrian National Secretary for Tourism

The future of the spa industry

Mintel (2005) identified six main trends that are likely to occur in this market. These can be summarized as:

- the emergence of global spa brands – Banjan Tree for example
- expanding target markets – for example families, males, and older consumers
- spa combination holiday – for example golf for the man, spa treatments for the woman
- growth in medical spas – for example in Central Europe
- increase in quality standards – for example standards set by the European Spas Association (AESPA)
- standardization of training – for example the development of Diplomas in Spa Therapies.

It is predicted that the increase in obesity levels will fuel the growth of spa and well-being tourism across the world. Consumers will become particularly interested in the benefits offered by traditional water spas, and budget airlines will enable the consumers to get to different destinations on a more regular basis.

Discussion points and essay questions

1 What are the main opportunities and threats that will affect the future growth of the European spa market?
2 Apart from the desire to improve his or her health, what other factors might motivate a tourist to visit a spa?

Adventure tourism in New Zealand

Introduction – what is adventure tourism?

There has been a growth in the interest of consumers in adventurous pursuits as part of a holiday. But what is adventure tourism? Swarbrooke et al. (2003) identified that there is no single characteristic that sums up the nature of adventure. They did however, identify certain characteristics or qualities that are associated with adventure tourism, and these are shown in Exhibit 15.1.

They also identified the themes that have been influential in the historical development of adventure tourism, and these are shown in Exhibit 15.2.

It is well recognized that adventure travellers are not one uniform group. Adventure travellers are sometimes older people who want to experience new things, the backpackers who want holidays that are different and a new group of

---

Exhibit 15.1 The core characteristics of adventure tourism

- Uncertain outcomes
- Danger and risk
- Challenge
- Anticipated rewards
- Novelty
- Stimulation and excitement
- Escapism and separation
- Exploration and discovery
- Absorption and focus
- Contrasting emotions

Source: Swarbrooke et al. (2003).

Exhibit 15.2 Themes in the historical development of adventure tourism

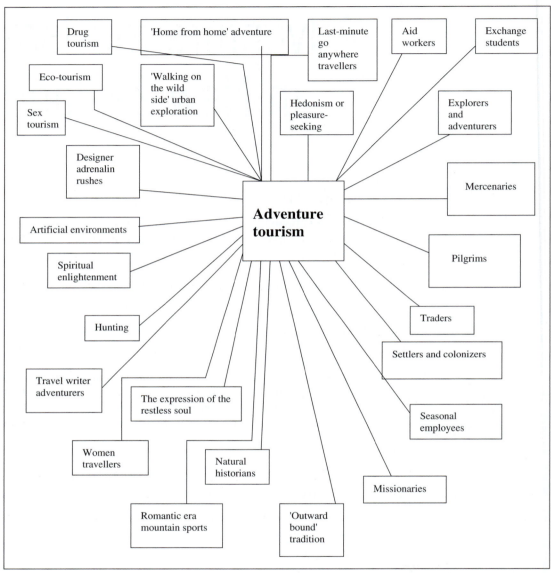

consumers who see adventure as an exciting alternative to the more traditional holiday (Mintel, 2001b).

The different types of adventure travel have also been identified by Mintel (2001b) and these are shown in Exhibit 15.3.

It can be seen from this exhibit that adventure travel incorporates a wide range of different experiences and activities. It also appeals to a wide cross-section of market segments.

> ## Exhibit 15.3   Difference types of adventure travel
>
> **Destination driven adventure travel** – the consumer picks a particular country or region to explore
>
> **Vehicle travel** – the travel is based around a vehicle, e.g. boat or Landrover
>
> **Non-vehicle travel** – the travel is based around walking or running
>
> **Activity-driven adventure travel** –- e.g. camping, hiking, cycling, scuba diving, snorkelling, etc.
>
> **Family adventure travel** – the family go as a unit for an adventurous experience
>
> **Multi-activity travel** – the travel package incorporates a number of activities
>
> **Extreme activity travel** – extreme sports are the basis of the travel
>
> **Ethical adventure travel** – the travel involves some element of sustainability
>
> **Prestige adventure travel** – the travel is prestigious and involves status building
>
> *Source*: Mintel (2001b).

Adventure tourism in New Zealand

New Zealand has become recognized as a destination that encourages adventure travel in many different forms. The wide open spaces and temperate climate have provided the country with an opportunity to exploit this type of tourism. Exhibit 15.4 shows that the country is wanting to actively develop this type of tourism experience.

There are a wide range of operators that have developed in New Zealand to underpin the development of adventure travel. These are shown in Exhibit 15.5.

The country has also developed adventure experiences which are possible because of the wide open spaces that are available in the country. One example of this is the Great New Zealand Trek which it is possible to complete on foot, bike or horseback. Details of this trek are shown in Exhibit 15.6.

Certain areas of New Zealand have promoted themselves as being particularly suitable for adventure travel.

Queenstown, for example, has promoted itself as being particularly suitable as a town where tourists can undertake a wide range of adventurous activities. The marketing literature which promotes this on their web page is shown in Exhibit 15.7. It is interesting that this web

Exhibit 15.4   Adventure tourism in New Zealand

New Zealand's landscape and temperate climate lends itself to outdoor activity. The country is renowned for its range of adventure pastimes – the best known being bungy jumping, jetboat riding, rafting and skiing. But adventure means different things to different people and the best aspect of the New Zealand adventure scene is that it provides activities rated from 'soft' to extreme' – from hiking and waterskiing to mountain climbing and caving. The adventure tourism industry makes the most of having a country surrounded by sea, criss-crossed by rivers and lakes, covered in native bush and with a central spine of spectacular snow-capped mountains. There's something for everyone who enjoys the outdoor lifestyle and the special sense of freedom the relatively sparsely populated land provides.

Source: www.newzealand.com.

Exhibit 15.5   New Zealand adventure

More adventures than time

Being a creative bunch, New Zealand adventure operators are always adding new dimensions to activities available, as well as new activities themselves. The best source of information on these is from the homepage of www.newzealand.com where thousands of operators are listed. Where available, the websites of the official professional bodies associated with or related to these pastimes are listed.

4WD (four wheel drive) – www.nzfwda.org.nz
Abseiling
Bungy
Canoeing/kayaking – www.rivers.org.nz
Caving – www.massey.ac.nz
Diving – www.nzunderwater.org.nz
Fly by wire
Gliding – www.gliding.co.nz/
Hang gliding – www.nzhgpa.org.nz
Heli-hiking
Heli-skiing
Horse riding
Hot air ballooning
Hunting
Jet boating
Motorcycle tours

Exhibit 15.5 (*Continued*)

Mountain climbing – www.mountainsafety.org.nz;
www.alpineclub.org.nz; www.climb.co.nz; www.nzmga.co.nz;
Orienteering – www.nzorienteering.com
Parapenting
Parasailing
Rafting – www.intraftfed.com/Members.htm; www.slalomnz.org.nz
Rock climbing – www.climb.co.nz; www.powerband.org.nz
Sailing/boating – www.msa.govt.nz; www.cbes.org.nz;
www.nzmarine.com; www.yachtingnz.org.nz
Skiing – www.snow.co.nz/skicouncil/
Sky diving
Snowboarding – www.snow.co.jz/skicouncil/
Surfing – www.slsnz.org.nz
Water-skiing
Windsurfing
Zorbing – www.zorb.com/zorbnz.htm

Source: www.newzealand.com.

Exhibit 15.6   The Great New Zealand Trek

Travel the length of New Zealand on horse, mountain bike or foot in The Great New Zealand Trek. This is a unique way for people to travel the country in 12-week-long stages of around 250 kilometres.

The first stage is from Cape Reinga o Kohukohu in Northland from 11–19 March 2006. Stage 2 will continue from the Hokianga in 2007 and so on until participants reach Bluff in Southland in 2018.

Participants choose their mode of transport and travel between 30–45 kilometres per day for six days with a rest day halfway.

The Great New Zealand Trek is supported by a crew of 80 people and will offer luxuries from professional caterers, massage, luggage, transport, hot showers, movies, bar, café, to entertainment such as a talent quest, mechanical bull, karaoke and slave auctions.

The week lets participants experience the outdoors while meeting like minded people from around the world.

The 'open route' system will ensure the enjoyment and safety of participants. Instead of controlling the pace with a lead and end rider, the track, which is off road wherever possible, will be marked with red ribbons and position marshals along the way allowing people to travel as fast or slow as they wish.

(*Continued*)

Exhibit 15.6 *(Continued)*

'After all it is a holiday', says event organizer Stephen Old.

Stephen Old organized the inaugural Great New Zealand Horse Ride in 1996 attracting 483 riders, including 56 from Australia, making it the largest horse ride of its kind in the world.

Since organizing his last Great New Zealand Horse Ride in 2000, Old has worked in the film industry as Horse Coordinator for *The Lord of the Rings* trilogy and *The Last Samurai* followed by stunt work on *King Arthur* in Ireland.

'The Great New Zealand Trek is a very unique experience that I believe will grow into a Kiwi icon capturing the interest of people from all walks of life', says Old.

The Great New Zealand Trek will raise funds for the Multiple Sclerosis Society of New Zealand.

Source: www.newzealand.com.

Exhibit 15.7 Queenstown – the active capital

All of our South Island trips have at least one free day in Queenstown because there is so much to do here! This glamorous town is nestled on the shores of Lake Wakatipu beneath the majestic Remarkables mountain range. Today this premier visitor destination is known as the 'adrenaline capital of the world' but Queenstown originally got its name because 'it was fit for Queen Victoria'.

Queenstown has more than its share of breathtaking scenery and a diverse range of attractions, but it's the 'cruisy' locals whom international visitors find most enchanting. We located our main office in Queenstown because our staff enjoy the outdoor lifestyle so much – but we're not the only ones who like it here. In 1998 Queenstown was again voted 'Friendliest Foreign City' in a poll of 37 000 readers of Conde Nast Traveler, a top US publication. In the same publication, we were positioned as the 14th best city in the world (the only New Zealand destination to rank in the top 20) alongside others such as Vienna, London, Paris, and Hong Kong. In the winter, Queenstown transforms into a popular ski resort to rival its glamorous sister city, Aspen, Colorado.

For adrenaline junkies who live for the next rush, Queenstown is the perfect place to spend a few days bungy jumping, white water rafting, jet boating, or trying whatever the newest craze happens to be. Others who prefer a more relaxed pace can take one of the many scenic walks, join a wine tasting tour, ride up the gondola, or relax by a warm fire at one of the local pubs. There are also plenty of bars and clubs to choose from if you'd like to go out for a night on the town.

Exhibit 15.7 (*Continued*)

Your guides can help you plan your free day in Queenstown when you arrive and even make bookings for you, but we'll try to cover some of the many activities, walks, tours, and trips available here. Don't worry, most tours can be booked when you get to town and there are lots of 'combo' packages available if you can't choose just one! There's enough to keep even the most active person busy, and it's the perfect place to just sip a latte at an outdoor cafe and do some world-class people watching.

Hiking

Although there's plenty of opportunity to, you don't have to spend money to have a good time in Queenstown. There are about a dozen well-marked *hikes* in town that you can explore on your own, and many more just a short taxi ride away (and hitchhike back like we locals do). Ask your guide for a map or pick one up at the Department of Conservation (DOC) office when you get into town. Our favourite is up to Ben Lomond for amazing views of the lake, town and surrounding mountains. Start at the Fernhill round-about just past the youth hostel, and take One Mile Creek Track up to Lomond Crescent via Skyline Road, then Bobs Peak at Skyline Chalet. The last hour up to the summit is pretty steep, but worth the climb (Moderate, 3 hours to Saddle one way; a quick ride back down, and you can take the gondola one or both ways. For an easier hike, take the Sunshine Bay walking track that starts/finishes about 1 km past the Fernhill roundabout on Glenorchy Road (Easy, 1 hour return). Or stroll along the lakefront in Queenstown Gardens and learn to play frisbee golf (Easy, 15 to 45 minutes).

Mountain biking

You can often borrow one of our bikes or rent a *mountain bike* in town to explore some of the famous single tracks in the area. Charge down Skipper's Canyon if you dare, or ride up to Moke Lake with a picnic on a nice day. For a gentler ride, try the Frankton track or the Sunshine Bay track.

Bungy jumping

Queenstown is the home of *bungy jumping*. A.J. Hackett created the very first commercially available jump, the Kawarau bridge, which is still in use today. Since that first site in 1988, bungy jumping has become a worldwide phenomenon and there are now numerous sites to choose from in town.

Jet boating

Jet boating is also very popular for a real-life rollercoaster ride. Just imagine what you can do in a very powerful, highly manoeuvrable

(*Continued*)

Exhibit 15.7 (*Continued*)

craft that only requires 2 inches of water! The most famous ride is through the dramatic Shotover Canyon where you'll skim across the river inches away from the cliff face. There's a multitude of jet boating trips available in and around Queenstown.

Whitewater rafting

Many people choose to go *rafting* while in Queenstown, and once again there are lots of rivers (Class II–V) and operators to choose from, ranging from novice-friendly to experienced paddlers only. Depending on the time of year and river, you could enjoy a scenic helicopter ride to the put-in.

Skydiving

Want something even more extreme? How about flying to high altitude over stunning scenery. As the anticipation builds, the countdown begins, your tandem instructor gives the signal – and together you make 'the Ultimate Jump'. Free fall at awesome speeds of up to 200 kph. The speed, the sensation of flying and the sheer excitement make *skydiving* an adrenaline rush that cannot be equalized.

Golf

Arguably New Zealand's most scenic *golf* course, Kelvin Heights was opened in 1975 and is located on a peninsula overlooking Lake Wakatipu, close to picturesque Queenstown. The magnificent setting ensures that this is a course much sought out by local and overseas golfers. The sheer beauty of the surroundings makes it a delightful course to play in any season. The snowcapped peaks of the nearby mountains, together with the ever-changing colours of the lake will ensure a round you'll long remember and cherish. Millbrook, away from town is very prestigious 'Country Club' resort and world-class golf course.

Fishing

If you want fresh fish for dinner, it's not far from your plate. New Zealand has some of the best trout and salmon fishing in the world, and Queenstown is a renowned fishery and popular base for anglers in the South Island. From a few hours *fishing* from a boat charter on Lake Wakatipu with an experienced guide to helicopter-accessed fly fishing in a remote area for the more experienced fishermen, there are options for every level of angler. Or bring your own rod and try your luck in some of the numerous lakes and rivers around Queenstown.

Wine tasting

The Queenstown and Central Otago wine region is the fastest growing wine region in New Zealand. This area is renowned for its Pinot Noir and has won more gold medals for this variety than any

Exhibit 15.7 (*Continued*)

other New Zealand Region. This region is also achieving recognition for quality Chardonnay, Riesling, Pinot Gris and Sauvignon Blanc varieties. Wine tours of the vineyards in the area are available and there's a new tasting room overlooking Lake Hayes featuring the best of the bunch.

Other things to do

High-country Horses – spend an hour, two hours or a whole day in the saddle, soaking up the stunning scenery in nearby Glenorchy.

Accommodation

Blue Peaks Apartments & Lodge – quality visitor accommodation and true Southern hospitality – we stay here on our trips.

A Line Hotel and Aurum Apartments – very nice, centrally located – another place we sometimes stay.

Heritage Hotel – very nice, located on Lake Wakatipu.

Thomas's Hotel – on the Waterfront – Queenstown's closest lakeside accommodation, right in the heart of town. Four floors of accommodation – with rooms ranging from standard or budget (twins, doubles, triples) to multishare rooms, all with en suites.

Colonial Village Motel and Apartment Accommodation – Queenstown motel accommodation offering character, charm and stunning views.

A few great examples of some of the 'boutique' accommodations to be found around Queenstown

The Stone House – located in the heart of Queenstown, New Zealand's spectacular adventure playground, The Stone House offers exclusive and intimate boutique accommodation combining personalized old-world charm and modern comforts.

The Dairy Guesthouse – provides luxury bed and breakfast accommodation in Queenstown, New Zealand. Experience fine lodging in the heart of Queenstown.

Brown's Boutique Hotel – designed along traditional European lines, this small intimate hotel is only three minutes walk to the centre of town and features stunning views of the Remarkables mountain range from every room.

Source: www.activenewzealand.com/queenstown.

page also gives hints for booking a range of accommodation and links to other companies' web pages which operate some type of adventurous activity in the area. This allows the traveller to put together their own holiday package.

Conclusions

New Zealand has become an important destination for a wide range of adventure based holidays due to the geography and climate of the country, both of which are eminently suitable for this type of development.

Discussion points and essay questions

1 Discuss the reasons for a growth of interest in adventure based holidays.
2 Find an example of one travel company that operates in New Zealand. Discuss the ways in which this company has advertised to potential customers and discuss any improvement that you would make to their campaign.
3 Critically analyse the natural and human-made factors that are necessary for the development of adventure travel in a region or country.
4 Evaluate the types of people who are likely to favour an adventure based holiday. Explore the ways in which you would promote a destination to these types of people.

Gay and lesbian tourism in Australia

A definition of gay and lesbian tourism

The growth of marketing to gay and lesbian tourists can be attributed to the wider acceptance in society, of diversity and acceptance of gay and lesbian consumers in general (Adams, 1993). Stuber (2002) argues that gays and lesbians now fit into a market segment because they can be measured, are accessible by a variety of communication methods, have fairly homogenous consumer behaviour and are stable as a group. He also states that it is well recognized in the industry that the strategic marketing of tourism products and services to gays and lesbians will be a profitable undertaking that can bring about success for a wide variety of organizations involved in the tourism process. These tourism organizations include destination marketers (for example, New York, Key West, and San Francisco in the USA, Brighton and Blackpool in the UK), events organizers (for example, the Mardi Gras in Sydney, the Sydney Olympics 2000, where gay and lesbian tourists were encouraged, by tour operators (such as Olivia, the US-based package holiday company).

Gay and lesbian tourism in Australia

Australia now markets itself as a destination for groups of travellers who have special needs. This includes backpackers and singles, the over fifties, families, and gay and lesbian travellers. The country promotes its perfect climate, dazzling beaches, great restaurants, vibrant communities, friendly atmosphere and festivals and dance parties, as being particularly attractive to gay and lesbian travellers (www.australia.com).

The fact that Australia has a population which is drawn from many ethnic religious and cultural groups means that the country has a level of understanding that means that the population accept that being 'different' is acceptable. All areas of Australia promote themselves as being suitable for gay and lesbian travellers to visit. Sydney is considered to be the gay and lesbian capital of Australia, with a wide range of hotels, clubs, restaurants and shopping outlets that are targeted at the gay and lesbian traveller. The details of Sydney as a gay and lesbian venue are explored in the official website of the Australian Tourism Board (www.australia.com) and we can see an extract from these web pages in Exhibit 16.1.

Exhibit 16.1 Sydney, New South Wales – a gay and lesbian view

Sydney – According to Gore Vidal (and he should know) 'San Francisco thinks it's the city that Sydney is'. There are few doubts now that Sydney is one of the great gay and lesbian destinations in the world. Perhaps it's the long warm summer, perhaps it's the history as a penal colony, perhaps it's because Sydney just loves to party so much, but whatever the reason, the lesbian and gay communities have made their mark on Sydney and stamped it as a world centre for tolerance, diversity, flamboyance and a damn good time.

Sydney has the biggest gay and lesbian population in Australia and it shows. From building sites to restaurants, bars to beaches, shops to hospitals, there does not seem an area or industry without a significant gay or lesbian presence.

February is the time when all this comes to the fore with the Sydney Gay and Lesbian Mardi Gras, the biggest celebration of gay and lesbian pride, culture and arts in the world, where the spectators for the Parade each year is bigger than for any other event. The national prime time television coverage never fails to win its time slot. The Festival is the biggest gay and lesbian arts festival anywhere and the party is the largest of its kind in the world.

Throughout the rest of the year the gay and lesbian population does not hibernate. The bars, clubs and venues thrive. There are more dance parties throughout the year, more celebrations, art activities, community events and fireworks.

Gay and lesbian activities are centred in Oxford Street in Darlinghurst and King Street in Newtown. Cafes, bars, cinemas, shops catering to the market abound in these areas. However increasingly lesbians and gay men are not confining themselves in these 'ghettos'. Leichhardt has long been a recognized 'dyke' centre. Marrickville, Bondi, Elizabeth Bay, Bronte, Surry Hills, Redfern are suburbs with a strong gay presence.

Exhibit 16.1 (Continued)

In central Sydney it would be harder to find accommodation that is *not* lesbian or gay friendly, than accommodation that is. Virtually all the major central hotels are used to and welcome the influx of gay and lesbian tourists around Mardi Gras and are happy to receive them all year round. Smaller hotels in the areas of Darlinghurst and Surry Hills depend on the lesbian and gay market and are well versed in the ways of catering for the community.

Keeping up to date with the stream of venues and events in Sydney is easy. Pick up any of the free community publications for the latest information.

Sydney Star Observer, Capital Q, Sydney Morning Herald
Entertainment venues – A full list is given. An example is:

The Albury Hotel, Oxford Street, Paddington NSW 2021: Crowd – mainly young gay men and friends and quite a few straight people who come to see the shows. Expect – fabulous drag seven nights a week, gorgeous barmen, plus singers and entertainment in the cocktail bar. Speciality – Drag, drag and more drag.

Eating out – Eating out is one of the things Sydneysiders do best. Considering the range and quality of restaurants and cafes, it is little surprise Sydney home kitchens are some of the most underused in the world. For gay and lesbian travellers there is no need to seek out queer specific eating places. Anyone is hard pushed to go to a restaurant without finding a 'family member'.

Shopping – Gay and lesbian specific shopping is mainly focussed on Oxford Street and in Newtown again.

Aussie Boys is a two-storey store for lesbians and gay men with a strong emphasis on party clothes, from stylish shirts to shorts. However, everything from underwear to sunglasses is available along with a few souvenirs and gorgeous little items for friends and family back home.

Sax Leather offers off-the-peg leatherwear and accoutrements, everything from your polished chrome codpiece to leather briefcases. Harnesses, masques, crops, paddles, jackets, shorts, bras . . . teddy bears. Sax produce most of their own goods themselves but also have other suppliers.

Mephisto Leather sells made to measure leatherware, from leather jeans to something you've scribbled down on the back of a beer mat. They also have an extensive range of PVC and rubber wear. All goods are made on the premises so you can check their workmanship while you're there.

Another made to measure leather outlet, Karnal Leather is focussing on the lesbian market but more than happy to put something outrageous together for the boys. Let your fantasy become reality.

(Continued)

Exhibit 16.1 *(Continued)*

The Bookshop Darlinghurst offers the best selection of gay and lesbian titles in Australia and possibly beyond. If they don't have it, they'll order it specifically for you. Great place to discover more about the growing staple of Australian gay and lesbian writers. Staff are friendly, and informed. They give good lit. Open till 11 pm, great for late evening browsing.

In operation since 1974, The Feminist Bookshop offer 'books for a changing world'. Great selection of works that often cannot be found elsewhere along with cards, posters, T-shirts and gifts.

The Toolshed offers a large selection of adult toys and magazines, clothing and swimwear. Many dance parties sell tickets through these shops.

Grace Bros City's recently refurbished store has had Sydney's gay and lesbian population pouring in. The 3rd floor is so full of 'beautiful things' that it might have been created specifically for gay men. There are also four gorgeous eating places which completely redefine the concept of in-store dining.

Health and well being – When shopping and partying get too much, it is time to relax, unwind, or work out. An example of a gym is:
City Gym, Crown Street, East Sydney, NSW 2010.

Gay games – Every four years, the Gay Games are held somewhere in the world. It is a vast gathering of people participating in sport and cultural activities with more competitors than the Olympic Games. The Gay Games are about inclusion and participation. Anyone can enter regardless of sexuality or ability. The Games are a marvellous time of friendship, support, celebration and sporting achievement.

Community support – Sydney has a full and active network of support and community groups. These are a few of the key ones:
Sydney Gay and Lesbian Mardi Gras
2010 Lesbian and Gay Youth Services
Gay and Lesbian Counselling Services
Clover Women's Club
Transgender Support – Gender Centre

Source: Australian Tourism Board, www.australia.com.

A full listing for all the major destinations is also given for the following cities on this webpage:

- Victoria – Melbourne
- Canberra
- Western Australia – Perth
- Tasmania – Hobart
- Northern Territory – Darwin
- Queensland
- Brisbane and Gold Coast.

Exhibit 16.2   GALTA

About GALTA – Gay and Lesbian Tourism Australia

What is GALTA?

A national network of tourism professionals dedicated to the welfare and satisfaction of all gay and lesbian travellers within and to Australia. GALTA – Gay and Lesbian Tourism Australia Ltd is a non-profit organization operated by a team of elected individuals who work with federal, state and regional tourism bodies, corporations, businesses and individuals to develop and grow the gay and lesbian market and increases the awareness of gay and lesbian travellers and their needs.

Why does GALTA exist?

GALTA recognizes the needs of two distinct groups. One is the gay and lesbian traveller seeking quality tourism related services that provide a genuine interest in and welcome them. The other is businesses who wish to make their product or services available to these travellers.

What does GALTA do?

GALTA represents members by forming close alliances with local, State and National tourism bodies, assisting members in attracting a qualified niche market. Through newsletters, symposiums/workshops, trade shows, fair days, regional networking functions/dinners, the website and publications such as the TSD – Tourism Services Directory, GALTA provides members with a wide distribution and exposure to gay and lesbian travellers around Australia.
GALTA also enjoys a successful close working relationship with IGLTA – International Gay and Lesbian Travel Association.

Where is GALTA?

GALTA members are located across Australia from major capital cities to rural and coastal destinatons. Members represent major hotels and resorts, airlines, tourism organizations, accommodation places, restaurants/cafes, travel services, individuals and media, all of whom are dedicated to the professional development and growth of gay and lesbian tourism niche market to, from and within Australia.

When does GALTA work?

GALTA operate 365 days a year. It recognizes the importance of gay and lesbian cultural festivals and pride events around the country and maintains a regular presence at these events. It also recognizes the needs of lesbians and gays who travel all year round to capital cities and other destinations for both work or pleasure.

Source: www.galta.com.

The Mardi Gras in Sydney

Sydney Gay and Lesbian Mardi Gras is probably the world's greatest celebration of gay and lesbian culture, art, fun and community. It started off as a small protest march and has become a large festival that happens every year in February, which draws visitors from across the world. The festivities begin at the festival once it goes dark, and there is a week of dance, parties, films, sports, art and debates. The festival is also accompanied by a shopping spree with stores donating to Australia's largest HIV/AIDS charity – the Bobby Goldsmith Foundation. There is a wide spectrum of music and entertainment, and drag queens jostle for attention in the crowd.

The parade features floats, marketing groups and events. The Mardi Gras Party at Fox Studio, which has shows, costumes and dancing all night, is a major event. This festival encourages gay and lesbian travellers to visit Sydney in February, but also acts as a magnet for all tourists to visit the city to take part in the spectacular event.

GALTA – Gay and Lesbian Tourism Australia

GALTA has been established to deliver a service to all gay and lesbian visitors to Australia. Details of GALTA are shown in Exhibit 16.2.

Conclusions

Australia has been very focused in establishing a well-recognized gay and lesbian tourism business. They have taken a strategic view of this development using well-balanced management principles and practices, so that gay and lesbian travellers can be accommodated alongside the other visitors to Australia. The Mardi Gras festival in Sydney has proved to be a particular magnet for gay and lesbian visitors.

Discussion points and essay questions

1 Evaluate the reasons for Australia being particularly committed to the growth of gay and lesbian tourism.
2 Discuss the importance of festivals such as the Mardi Gras festival Sydney for the development of gay and lesbian tourism.
3 Discuss the ways that a country or city can balance the development of gay and lesbian tourism with other forms of tourism development.
4 Assess the nature and importance of having a well-developed tourism infrastructure to underpin the development of gay and lesbian tourism.

easyJet

Background

The European air-travel market has opened up because of the deregulation of the industry and this has brought about the establishment of a whole variety of cut-price airlines which will offer airline seats at increasingly competitive prices. There is already evidence in Europe that air ticket prices are beginning to decrease with the increased competitive nature of the market, although there is still a long way to go before the fiercely discounted market as exists in the USA is achieved.

Stelios Haji-Ioannou – the man and his business idea

Stelios Haji-Ioannou is the son of a Greek shipping tycoon. He graduated from the London School of Economics and gained a Master's degree in shipping trade and finance at the City University Business School.

It was predicted that he would join his father's shipping empire after graduation, but he was keen to escape from his father's shadow and develop as an autonomous personality. He became increasingly interested in the airline business and proceeded to study the American discount airlines.

He took the American airline company Valujet as a model for the type of business which he thought he could develop for the European market. The Valujet company experienced the tragic crash of one of its planes into the Florida Everglades in May 1996, and it is this, it is said, which showed that his plans for a budget airline would have to incorporate safety features.

This was particularly the case for him, because he and his father were already facing charges of manslaughter because one of the company tankers, the 232 000-tonne *Haven* had blown up in Genoa in 1991, killing five crew and polluting the Ligurian coastline.

Despite the problems which the American company Valuejet had, he became increasingly convinced that the idea of a discount 'no frills' type of airline would work in the European market. The incident which finally convinced him of this was when he tried to fly to Corfu from London, only to find that the fare was more than the cost of a 14-day package holiday to the same place. This seemed to be a ridiculous situation which should be addressed. Stelios Haji-Ioannou took Freddie Laker and particularly Richard Branson of Virgin airlines as role models for his own idea. He knew that he could not survive in the airline business with just a clever idea, but needed clear business planning and management control. He had the advantage of having the opportunity to get substantial financial backing from his father, but has never played down the fact that without this backing he would never have been able to establish the business. The establishment of an airline business, after all, requires considerable investment over a substantial period of time.

He finally approached his father in March 1995, armed with a comprehensive business plan, in order to obtain financial backing for the company. His father backed him with a £5 million advance which meant that he was now in the position of being ready to set up the business that he had dreamed about and planned.

The business idea that Stelios Haji-Ioannou envisaged was summarized by a statement which he made in 1995: 'Our research has shown that people in both Britain and Europe are crying out for an American style operation which will give them instant access to really cheap, reliable and safe air travel' (Stelios Haji-Ioannou, 1995).

Stelios still owns a small shareholding in the easyJet business but has given up the role of company chairman to become a non-executive director.

The development of the easyJet business

The development of the easyJet business has proceeded well since the formation of the company in 1995; details of this are shown in Exhibit 17.1.

This development has depended on a simple but clever idea. The airline would offer a 'no frills' service between a limited set of destinations at the lowest possible price. There would be no in-flight meals and only soft drinks and peanuts would be served. The company would sell direct and cut out the travel agents' 15–20 per cent commission, and there would be no tickets or fancy staff uniforms.

The business concept was summarized by its founder in 1995, when he was talking to the press: 'If we were a restaurant, we would be McDonald's. If we were a watch-maker, we would be Swatch' (Stelios Haji-Ioannou, *Travel and Trade Gazette*, 25 October 1995).

Stelios Haji-Ioannou decided to locate his prefabricated head office next to Luton airport which is an hour's drive from London. The home base for the flights would be Luton airport where he could get flight slots. He then leased two Boeing 737s complete with pilots, in November. The first flights to Glasgow and Edinburgh commenced in 1995, and were quickly expanded to serve six cities, including Amsterdam, Barcelona and Nice. The company increased the number

Exhibit 17.1   The development of the easyJet company

1994	Stelios Haji-Ioannou has business idea for easyJet.
March 1995	£5m investment by Loucas Haji-Oiannous. Company established and prefabricated building set up at Luton airport as company headquarters. 2 aircraft leased.
18 Oct. 1995	easyJet commences selling of seats. Lorraine Chase launched easyJet at Planet Hollywood, London.
10 Nov. 1995	First easyJet flight.
24 Nov. 1995	Glasgow and Edinburgh services commenced.
26 Jan. 1996	Aberdeen service commenced.
1996	Commencement of flights to Amsterdam, Barcelona and Nice. Purchase of first aircraft.
1997	Increased frequency of existing routes. Plans to expand to Nordic countries, Geneva, Madrid, Berlin and Jersey. Purchase of 3 aircraft and 2 aircraft leased.
2002	Expansion to offer 89 routes from 86 European airports operating 64 aircraft.
2002	Merger with Go-fly to become Europe's number one low-cost airline.

Source: easyJet.

of flights per day to each location, and expanded the network to other European destinations during the period 2000–06. The purchase of Go-fly in August 2002 also expanded the network further.

The easyJet concept

The concept of a 'no frills' airline which offered cut-price fares has been developed by easyJet and incorporates many features, which are shown in Exhibit 17.2.

In the early days, the product concept came under criticism from commentators in the travel and tourism industry. One particularly controversial area of the business was the decision by the founder to develop a direct booking service, which cut out the travel agency commission other airlines have to add on their final ticket price. Comments concerning this came from all areas of the travel industry, including

---

Exhibit 17.2   The easyJet concept

Head office	Prefabricated building. Paperless offices. Located at Luton airport.
Staff	Senior staff headhunted from major airlines. Minimum staffing levels. Large numbers of part-time telesales operatives paid on commission-only basis.
Uniforms	Cabin crew dressed in orange polo shirts, sweatshirts and black slacks.
Product	Direct sales single journeys to range of destinations. Very low prices. Tickets sold direct with no use of travel agents. Ticketless system. No food – only soft drinks and peanuts served. Open seating.
Company livery	Orange and white livery. Telephone booking numbers emblazoned on side of aircraft in orange for easy recognition.
Positioning	Emphasis on budget accommodation with minimum service levels.

Source: easyJet.

---

easyJet's potential competitors. One of the comments at this time was: 'While there is room for two low cost carriers and together we will bring down fares, easyJet is making a huge mistake by ignoring the opportunity of distribution through the travel trade' (Tim Jenns, Chief Executive, Ryanair UK, *Trade and Travel Gazette*, 1 November 1995).

There was no doubt in the trade, however, that the easyJet type of operation would be replicated in the market over time. Many analysts have predicted the growth of these type of airlines in Europe. One analyst made predictions as follows: 'You will see deep, deep discounts being offered by a plethora of "peanut carriers" creating massive potential savings for ordinary customers' (Ian Lowden of Simat, Helliesen and Eichner, 1995).

easyJet's mission statement is shown in Exhibit 17.3.

The financial performance of easyJet for the period 2001 to 2005 is shown in Exhibit 17.4.

Competitors

Competitors have entered the market in recent years to challenge the easyJet hold on the market. These competitors include Ryanair, currently seen as easyJet's main competitor.

> ## Exhibit 17.3 easyJet's mission statement
>
> To provide its customers with safe, good value, point-to-point air services. To effect and to offer a consistent and reliable product and fares appealing to leisure and business markets on a range of European routes. To achieve this they will develop their people and establish lasting relationships with their suppliers.
>
> *Source*: easyJet.

Some of these new airlines will be close competitors of easyJet, depending on the routes that they develop and the customers that they target. The major airlines will also discount fares and try to stress their particular advantages, including more regular flights from mainstream airports, better levels of service and higher safety perceptions among customers.

easyJet customers

Stelios Haji-Ioannou originally envisaged that the customer for easyJet would be the leisure traveller. It is becoming apparent, however, that business travellers are becoming a large part of the easyJet market, particularly on the short-haul day-return routes. It is clear that the company is trying to change customer buying behaviour patterns which existed previously. The company is trying to encourage the impulse purchase of airline travel, rather like the behaviour patterns more commonly associated with the purchase of fast-moving consumer goods or clothing. 'We are encouraging people to take impulse purchase decisions to fly' (Stelios Haji-Ioannou, 1996). The company is encouraging this type of impulse purchasing decision by using a public relations campaign which shows the price of its airline seats as being comparable or cheaper than that of a pair of jeans.

The growth in passenger statistics for the airline is shown in Exhibit 17.5. Research carried out by easyJet has shown that many different market segments are making the decision to fly with easyJet.

The main customers for easyJet originate in the UK, although this differs according to the route. The customers originate mainly from the catchment area of the airports from which the company operates. The socioeconomic profile of the customers is mixed, but tends towards the B and C1 socioeconomic groups. The customer is usually working in a professional job and lives in an urban area.

The town of Milton Keynes is seen by the company as being particularly representative of the type of area in which the customers of the airline live. Customers of the airline tend to be regular travellers abroad, although this picture may change in the future. Leisure travellers are a particular target group, and the cheap fares mean that they are much more likely to go abroad for a weekend, perhaps, on an

Exhibit 17.4 Summary of selected financial information for five years – 2005

	2005 million	2004 million	2003 million	2002 million	2001 million
Revenue	1 341.4	1 091.0	931.8	551.8	356.9
Total operating profit before exceptional costs	48.9	50.7	48.4	69.6	41.9
Profit on ordinary activities before taxation	67.9	62.2	51.5	71.6	40.1
Retained profit for the financial year	42.6	41.1	32.4	49.0	37.9
Fixed assets	718.2	640.2	650.6	541.4	216.6
Current assets	892.7	684.7	477.0	523.9	291.5
Creditors: amounts falling due within one year	(397.6)	(314.7)	(260.9)	(260.6)	(113.4)
Creditors: amounts falling due after more than one year	(276.1)	(157.7)	(65.3)	(48.6)	(76.3)
Provision for liabilities and charges	(97.5)	(63.1)	(42.9)	(28.4)	(1.9)
Net assets	839.7	789.4	758.5	727.7	316.5
Cash flow from operating activities	169.8	160.5	77.2	84.2	83.4
Committed contribution to associate	—	—	(1.9)	(0.8)	—
Dividend received from joint venture	0.2	—	—	—	—
Return on investment and servicing of finance	23.1	12.6	11.8	10.7	1.7
Taxation	2.9	(6.2)	(16.5)	0.5	—
Capital expenditure	(108.9)	(61.9)	(175.3)	(3.4)	(29.0)
Acquisitions and disposals	—	3.4	1.1	(267.2)	—
Managemet of liquid resources and financing	83.9	71.3	79.7	286.7	159.2
Increase/(decrease) in cash in the year	171.0	179.7	(23.9)	110.7	215.3

Source: easyJet Annual Report, 2005.

Exhibit 17.5 Passenger statistics for easyJet

As the growing passenger figures detailed below indicate, since its advent in 1995 easyJet has made air travel an affordable option for many more people by offering a reliable, quality service at great value fares.

Full year	Annual total ('000)
1995	30
1996	420
1997	1 140
1998	1 880
1999	3 670
2000	5 996
2001	7 664
2002	11 400
2003	20 300
2004	24 300
2005	29 558

Source: easyJet.

impulse. The one-way fares are particularly attractive to customers who do not plan their return travel date. This means that the easyJet seats are particularly attractive to students, and people studying and working throughout Europe on short- or long-term contracts.

Business travellers who work for small to medium-sized enterprises (SMEs) in particular are very interested in the easyJet product, because they themselves will often be responsible for the cost of the airline ticket and will therefore be keen to keep the cost of the tickets down. easyJet has also tried to target purchases of airline tickets by larger businesses, in a controversial advertising campaign which stressed the extra costs of buying their staff seats on conventional carriers.

Business travellers can now travel around the cities of Europe on a much more impulsive basis, pulling off deals and visiting suppliers and customers. The cheaper airfares will encourage them to travel more readily and with less thought.

Students who have previously been put off extensive regular travel around Europe as a result of high-priced airline tickets are now being encouraged, by companies such as easyJet who are offering a cheaper alternative, to travel more readily. Students are also being poached from the rail companies because prices are now comparable. This type of behaviour is illustrated in this statement: 'I would not have been able to do this in the past because of the cost. Now it is the equivalent of a rail fare' (Barnaby Jenkins, student, aged 23, purchased a long weekend in Barcelona).

easyJet has also been attractive to professional people who had previously travelled by train for business meetings and events. This is particularly noticeable on the Scotland–England route where rail travel has been relatively expensive and slow. This type of switching behaviour pattern is shown in this statement: 'I could have gone by train but when I discovered how much it was with easyJet, I decided this was the way to go' (Open University tutor).

easyJet predicts that the type of consumer profile will continue to develop and change over time as consumer behaviour patterns and competition change. The company has had to increase advertising costs more recently (from £30.5 million in 2004 to £32.8 million in 2005) owing to the maturity of the market and to support the brand in Germany.

The future

It is clear that the deregulation of the airline industry in Europe will continue to encourage small specialist airlines to enter the market. This will result in changing consumer buying patterns as prices drop and competition and choice increases.

Conclusions

easyjet has been one of the first airlines to have been set up to respond to the changing air travel scene in Europe. The business idea was simple in approach, but required the entrepreneurial spirit and financial backing which Stelios Haji-Ioannou could bring to the company. Longer-term development will now be the key for the business to flourish.

Discussion points

1 Evaluate the reasons for consumers being increasingly more willing to purchase airline seats as an impulse decision.
2 Analyse the relationship of price and consumer purchasing behaviour in the short-haul airline market.

Las Vegas, Nevada, USA

Introduction

Las Vegas is situated in Nevada on the western side of the USA. It is 2591 miles from New York City, 288 miles from Los Angeles and 576 miles from San Francisco. The city is visited by approximately 37 million visitors each year, and has over 135 000 hotels and motel rooms spread throughout the metropolitan area.

The city's average room occupancy rate is approximately 95 per cent and major projects are planned for Las Vegas in the future. These include developments by Trump International in early 2007 and the MGM Mirage 'Project City Center', a resort hotel to be built by 2010.

Las Vegas is unsurpassed as a resort because of its impressive range of entertainment, casinos, dining, nightlife and host of other attractions. It has become known as the city that never sleeps, offering the visitor a unique one-stop multidimensional vacation.

The history and development of Las Vegas

Las Vegas, which means 'The Meadows' in Spanish was well known as being an oasis-like valley which attracted Spanish travellers on their way to Los Angeles during the gold rush. John C. Fremont led an overland expedition west and camped in Las Vegas Springs on 13 May 1944.

Nevada was the first US state to legalize gambling. This led to the position today where more than 43 per cent of the state general fund is provided by gambling tax revenue. Legalized gambling suffered a brief lull in 1910 when a strict anti-gambling law became effective in Nevada. Legalized gambling returned to Nevada during the Great Depression. The first major resort growth of Las Vegas was completed by Tommy Hull when he built the El Rancho Vegas Hotel-Casino in 1941.

The success of this hotel-casino fuelled the massive expansion boom which occurred in the late 1940s when construction of several hotel-casinos and a two-way highway from Las Vegas to Los Angeles took place. One of the earliest resorts was the Flamingo Hotel, which was built by mobster Benjamin 'Bugsy' Siegel who was murdered by an unknown gunman.

The resort was developed extensively during the 1950s. The Desert Inn opened in 1950, and the Sands Hotel in 1952. Other resorts which opened in the 1950s were the Hacienda, the Tropicana and the Stardust hotels. The Moulin Rouge Hotel-Casino opened in 1953 to accommodate the growing black population.

The city realized as far back as 1950, that a way to fill hotel rooms during the slack periods in the year was to encourage the convention business. A 90 000 square foot exhibit hall, the Las Vegas Convention Center, was opened in April 1959. The Las Vegas Convention and Visitors Authority, which is supported mainly by room tax revenue, now attracts more than 2 million convention delegates every year.

Las Vegas has always been at the forefront of gambling and entertainment technology. The resort was one of the first to have multiple slot machines in the 1960s. Video machines were introduced in the 1970s and computerized slot machines were soon to follow.

Las Vegas developed the concept of the mega-resort when it lost exclusive rights to gambling casinos because gaming was legalized in Atlantic City, New Jersey, in 1976. The first of these mega-resorts was the Circus Circus Hotel-Casino, which incorporated an entertainment park, hotel and casino.

Other mega-resorts which have been developed include The Mirage Hotel-Casino (1989), The Excalibur (1990), The Treasure Island (1993), and the MGM Grand Hotel and Theme Park (1993). These mega-resorts involve huge investment plans. The MGM Grand Hotel and Theme

---

Exhibit 18.1   The history of Las Vegas

*	1892	Discovered by Spanish explorers
*	1911	The city of Las Vegas is incorporated
*	1931	Hoover Dam construction begins
*	1941	El Rancho Vegas opens
*	1946	Bugsy Siegel opens Flamingo Hotel
*	1959	Las Vegas Convention Center opens
*	1975	Nevada gaming revenues reach $1 billion
*	1989	Mirage opens – 3039 rooms
*	1990	Excalibur opens – 4032 rooms
*	1991	Construction of MGM Grand Hotel and Theme Park begins

Exhibit 18.1 (*Continued*)

*	1993	Grand Slam Canyon Adventure Dome opens
*	1993	Treasure Island opens – 2900 rooms
*	1993	Luxor Hotel opens – 2526 rooms
*	1993	MGM Grand Hotel and Theme Park opens – 5005 rooms
*	1994	Work begins on the Fremont Street Experience
*	1994	Boomtown opens a 300 room hotel-casino
*	1994	The first non-stop charter service from Europe begins from Cologne, Germany
*	1994	The Fiesta, the first hotel-casino in North Las Vegas opens
*	1995	Clark County population is estimated at more than 1 million residents
*	1995	Visitor Center Hoover Dam opens
*	1995	Announcement of construction of $420 million Paris Casino Resort
*	1996	The Orleans Hotel and Casino opens
*	1997	The New York-New York Hotel & Casino opens on 3 January. More than 100 000 people a day visit the new resort during its first days of operation
*	1997	Sheldon Adelson breaks ground in April to build the 3000 suite, $1.8 billion Venetian Resort Hotel Casino on the grounds of the original Sands Hotel
*	1997	The Aladdin Hotel closes on November 25, making way for a $1.5 billion resort hotel and shopping complex
*	1997	Harrah's Entertainment Inc. buys Showboat Inc. in a $1.154 billion deal
*	1997	The Frontier Hotel, owned by the Elardi family, is sold to Phil Ruffin, a Kansas industrialist, for $165 million
*	1998	Starwood Hotels & Resorts buys the ITT Corporation for $14.5 billion. The purchase includes the acquisition of Caesars Palace and the Desert Inn
*	1998	Northwest Airlines inaugurates non-stop service on 1 June from Tokyo to Las Vegas, while Japan

(*Continued*)

Exhibit 18.1 (*Continued*)

		Airlines inaugurates non-stop service on 2 October. Korean Airlines starts three non-stop charter flights from Seoul to Las Vegas in August
*	1998	The Bellagio, billed as the most expensive hotel in the world ($1.7 billion) opens on 15 October.
*	1998	A 66-year-old Las Vegas resident hits a $27.58 million progressive Megabucks jackpot on 15 November at the Palace Station Hotel Casino
*	1998	Annual gross gaming revenue in Nevada hits the £8.1 billion mark, while the number of visitors to Las Vegas totals 30.6 million people
*	1999	Harrah's Entertainment Inc. purchases the Rio All-Suite Hotel and Casino for $888 million on 1 January
*	1999	MGM Grand Inc. buys Primadonna Resorts, taking 100 per cent ownership of the New York-New York Hotel & Casino and Whiskey Pete's, Buffalo Bill's and Primm Valley Resort & Casino in Primm
*	1999	Mandalay Bay opens on March 2 with 3300 rooms, as does the Four Seasons Hotel with 424 rooms
*	1999	Phase one of the Venetian Resort Hotel Casino opens on 3 May with 3036 suites
*	1999	Circus Circus Enterprises changes its name to Mandalay Resort Group
*	1999	Paris Las Vegas opens on 1 September
*	2000	A $3 billion deal closes selling Caesars World Inc. including Caesars Palace, to Park Place Entertainment
*	2000	The Resort at Summerlin changes its name to The Regent Las Vegas
*	2000	MGM Grand Inc. announces the purchase of Mirage Resorts Inc. in the largest corporate buyout in gaming history
*	2000	The new Aladdin Resort & Casino opens in August on the Strip
*	2000	The Desert Inn is bought by casino/hotel entrepreneur Steve Wynn who implodes it to make way for construction of Wynn Las Vegas, a 2700-room, $2.7 billion property

Exhibit 18.1 (*Continued*)

*	2000	The MGM Grand Hotel & Casino satellite registration/hotel check-in facility at McCarran Airport opens, the first facility of its kind in North America
*	2001	Clark County's population reaches 1 498 274, while Las Vegas gets to 506 111
*	2001	Station Casinos opens the Green Valley Ranch Resort & Spa, a $300 million dollar property in Henderson
*	2001	The 3 millionth marriage certificate is recorded in Clark County on 9 February
*	2003	Clark County's population reaches 1 641 529; Las Vegas' grows to 535,395
*	2003	In April, Caesar's Palace opens the Colosseum, a $95 million contemporary replica of its namesake in Rome and home to Caesars Palace's newest resident performer, Celine Dion
*	2003	The Stratosphere releases plans for its latest thrill ride, a teeter-totter like device situated nearly 900 feet above Las Vegas Boulevard, aptly called X Scream
*	2003	Las Vegas Premium Outlets open in downtown Las Vegas
*	2003	The Fashion Show mall completes a $1 billion expansion, including a towering outdoor multimedia platform called, 'The Cloud'
*	2003	Mandalay Bay opens new 1120-suite tower, THEhotel
*	2004	Harrah's Entertainment purchases Binion's Horseshoe
*	2004	The Strip dims its lights for President Ronald Reagan's passing. Other dignitaries to receive such a remembrance upon their passing have included President John F. Kennedy, Rat Pack members Sammy Davis Jr, Frank Sinatra and Dean Martin, and George Burns
*	2004	The Las Vegas Monorail, a $654 million mass transit system, opens to the public
*	2004	Las Vegas Sands releases new details about its planned $1.6 billion Palazzo casino resort on the Strip Palazzo casino resort on the Strip

(*Continued*)

Exhibit 18.1 (*Continued*)

*   2005   Las Vegas celebrates its Centennial year throughout 2005, beginning with the New Year's fireworks display, Las Vegas will celebrate its 100th birthday on May 15, with the world's largest birthday cake and a re-creation of the 1905 land auction that started the Las Vegas community as we know it today

*   2005   Wynn, Las Vegas, the destination's newest mega-resort, is scheduled to open April 28, 2005

Source: Las Vegas on-line visitor guide.

Park, for example, cost $1 billion to build its elaborate hotel, casino, theatres arena and theme park.

The city has also been keen to encourage leisure shopping. The multi-million dollar project 'The Fremont Street Experience' was opened in 1995. This shopping centre was designed by the Jerde Partnership to create a lively urban centre which incorporates light, sound and entertainment. A brief summary of the history of Las Vegas is shown in Exhibit 18.1.

Las Vegas today

Las Vegas has become America's top resort destination, offering the visitor an unparalleled range of hotels, casinos and entertainments. The climate is very warm, particularly in the months of April to September. Las Vegas averages 294 days of sunshine per year, and the average daily rainfall is very low. The dazzling strip offers a wide range of entertainment, and The Fremont Street Experience offers the visitor an exciting shopping experience. Las Vegas has its own international airport – McCarran International Airport, where an average of more than 750 scheduled and charter flights arrive every day. Las Vegas has abundant nightlife and offers superstars, five major production shows, and Broadway musicals all year round. The city also has the extravagant strip casinos where visitors marvel at the glittering array of buildings and lights.

Hotels and Motels in Las Vegas

The city has approximately 131 000 hotel/motel rooms (in 2004) which appeal to a wide cross-section of visitors, whether they be holiday-makers, convention visitors or business travellers. The city has accommodation which ranges from multi-suite accommodation, which is bigger than an average home, to low budget one room hotel accommodation. Many Las Vegas hotels offer a wide range of added-value services, including multilingual staff, gaming lessons for the novice gambler, entertainments, golf courses, travel and entertainment reservation desks, and tour attraction desks. Las Vegas has thirteen of the fifteen largest hotels in the world and has specialized in the development of mega-resorts, which incorporate hotels, leisure facilities, casinos and attractions. Large hotels include MGM Grand, Luxor, The Mirage, Circus Circus, Bally's and Caesars Palace.

A full range of restaurants offering a wide range of cuisines is also available in Las Vegas.

Casinos in Las Vegas

Gambling is one of the major attractions of Las Vegas. The city offers non-stop gaming in a variety of casinos. The gambler can take part in poker, craps, baccarat, blackjack, roulette and slot machines on a twenty-four hour basis. The resorts also offer classes in gambling for those visitors who are unfamiliar with the games.

The range of casinos in Las Vegas is shown in Exhibit 18.2.

The city also hosts year-round gaming tournaments which have their own rules, entry fees and promotional packages that may include a

---

Exhibit 18.2   Casinos in Las Vegas

* Aladdin Hotel and Casino
* Bally's Las Vegas
* Boulder Station Hotel and Casino
* Caesars Palace
* Circus Circus Hotel/Casino/Theme Park
* Day's Inn Town Hall Casino
* Fitzgerald's Casino-Holiday Inn
* Golden Nugget Hotel and Casino
* Hard Rock Hotel and Casino
* Harrah's Las Vegas Casino Hotel
* Hotel San Remo Casino and Resort
* Imperial Palace Hotel and Casino
* Lady Luck Casino and Hotel
* Las Vegas Hilton Superbook
* Luxor Las Vegas
* MGM Grand Hotel/Casino
* The Mirage
* New York-New York Hotel and Casino
* The Orleans Hotel and Casino

Source: The Las Vegas Official Visitors Guide.

two- or three-day stay, dining specials, parties and banquets. Most tournaments are open to the public and take place at casinos or resorts.

Las Vegas Shows

Las Vegas offers the visitor a range of spectacular shows in many of the resorts and hotels in the city. The shows on offer in the 2004 season are shown in Exhibit 18.3.

There are also adult shows, comedy shows and magic shows.

Recreation in Las Vegas

A full range of recreation facilities are available for the visitor to Las Vegas. The weather encourages sport on a year-round basis. Most of

---

Exhibit 18.3   The shows in Las Vegas, 2004

Air Play – Tropicana Las Vegas

American Superstars – Stratosphere Las Vegas

Bite Stratosphere, Las Vegas

Celine Dion – Ceasars Palace

Chippendales – Rio in Las Vegas

Clint Homes – Harrah's Hotel & Casino, Las Vegas

Crazy Girls – Riviera Las Vegas

Elvis-A-rama – Elvis-A-rama in Las Vegas

Fashionistas – Krave – Las Vegas

Folies Bergere – Tropicana Las Vegas

Jubiliee – Bally's Las Vegas

KA-Cirque Du Soleil – MGM Grand, Las Vegas

La Cage – Riviera, Las Vegas

Lance Burton Master Magician – Monte Carlo Las Vegas

Le Femme – MGM Grand Las Vegas

Blue Man Group – Venetian Las Vegas

Barry Manilow 'Manilow, Music & Passion' – Las Vegas Hilton

Midnight Fantasy – Luxor Las Vegas

Mystère-Cirque Du Soleil – Treasure Island, Las Vegas

'O'-Cirque Du Soleil – Bellagio Las Vegas

Penn & Teller – Rio Las Vegas

The Magic of Rick Thomas – Stardust Las Vegas

Rita Rudner – New York/New York Hotel and Casino

Exhibit 18.3 (*Continued*)

Tony n' Tina's Wedding – Rio Las Vegas

Tournament of Kings – Excalibur Las Vegas

We Will Rock You – Paris Las Vegas

ZUMANITY – Cirque Du Soleil – New York/New York Hotel and Casino

Source: The Las Vegas Official Visitors Guide.

---

the Las Vegas resorts have swimming pools and many also have health clubs. Championship golf courses and a host of tennis facilities are available to golfers and tennis players.

Attractions and sightseeing in Las Vegas

The hotels and casinos of Las Vegas offer a varied range of attractions. The latest range of these attractions is shown in Exhibit 18.4.

It is possible for visitors to Las Vegas to visit areas of outstanding beauty in the surrounding area. There are scenic destinations such as the Great Basin National Park in Northern Nevada, the Grand Canyon in Arizona, Death Valley in California, and Bryce Canyon and Zion National Park in Utah. Visitors can travel to these areas by car, bus or plane.

Exhibit 18.4   The range of family attractions available in Las Vegas hotels and casinos, 2004

1. **The Stratosphere Tower**, the tallest free standing observation tower in the USA. High Roller roller-coaster and Big Shot Ride.

2. **The Fremont Street Experience**, 2.1 million lights in a canopy transform five blocks of Downtown into a light and music show.

3. **Adventuredome** at Circus-Circus Hotel-Casino, and the MGM Grand Hotel-Casino.

4. **The Dolphin Pool** at The Mirage Hotel, 1.5 million gallon pool with dolphins.

5. **The Pirate Baths** at The Treasure Island. Lifesize British frigate with cannon blasts, explosions, and a sinking ship.

6. **Gondola ride** at the Venetian.

Source: The Las Vegas Official Visitors Guide.

Getting married in Las Vegas

Las Vegas has become known as the wedding capital of the world. There are more than 50 wedding chapels in the city and more than 100 000 couples obtain wedding licences every year in Las Vegas. There is no waiting period and blood tests are not required for weddings in Las Vegas, which explains the reason for its popularity. There are many organizations that can organize any style wedding for visitors. This ranges from a black tie affair, to exchanging vows on a motorcycle at a chapel's drive-up window. The more exotic type of wedding ceremonies include getting married in a hot air balloon or being married by an Elvis Presley impersonator. The Excalibur hotel can provide medieval costumes for a ceremony which is reminiscent of Merry Old England. The Tropicana has a thatched roof bungalow in a Polynesian setting, which is also offered for wedding ceremonies.

The Las Vegas Convention and Visitors Authority

The Las Vegas Convention and Visitors Authority (LVCVA) was created in 1995 by the Nevada Legislature to manage the operations of the Las Vegas Convention Center and to promote Southern Nevada throughout the world as a convention location.

The LVCVA has been very successful and there has been remarkable growth of visitors coming to Las Vegas because it is an excellent resort location. The Las Vegas Convention Center opened in 1959 with 90 000 square feet of space. The Center is now one of the largest meeting facilities in the USA, with more than 1.6 million square feet of usable space available.

The LVCVA also operates The Cashman Field Center with 100 000 square feet of meeting and exhibit space, a 10 000-seat baseball stadium, and a 2000-seat theatre.

The twelve members of the LVCVA board of directors have overseen the growth of Las Vegas as a business, conference and resort destination. They have a set policy to increase the number of visitors to Las Vegas and Clark County each year. The LVCVA board of directors has representatives from Clark County, the City of Las Vegas, North Las Vegas, Henderson, Boulder City and Mesquite, as well as representatives from the hotel/motel industry, and business and financial communities. The LVCVA board can use their combined knowledge and experience to help Las Vegas maintain its leadership in the tourism and convention business.

Visitors to Las Vegas

Growth has shown a steady rise over the past decade (Exhibit 18.5), with tourist numbers of over 37 million in 2002.

The volume of visitors to Las Vegas is fairly evenly spread throughout the year.

The spend by visitors to Las Vegas is also growing steadily, with visitors spending $33.7 billion in the Las Vegas area during 2004. The average visitor spend depends on the reason for the visit. Trade show delegates and convention visitors spend more than the average leisure visitor. This shows the importance of trade conventions and delegates for the Las Vegas economy.

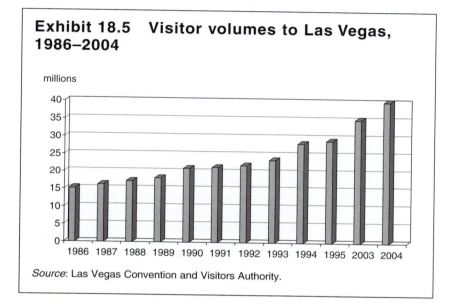

Exhibit 18.5 Visitor volumes to Las Vegas, 1986–2004

Source: Las Vegas Convention and Visitors Authority.

Exhibit 18.6 The growth in convention attendance in Las Vegas, 1986–2004

Year	Number of conventions	Attendance
1986	564	1 519 421
1987	556	1 677 716
1988	681	1 702 158
1989	711	1 508 842
1990	1 011	1 742 194
1991	1 655	1 794 444
1992	2 199	1 969 435
1993	2 443	2 439 734
1994	2 662	2 684 171
1995	2 826	2 924 879
2003	24 463	5 657 796
2004	22 286	5 724 864

Source: Las Vegas Convention and Visitors Authority.

Exhibit 18.7   Las Vegas Visitor Demographics

	1993	1994	1995	2003	2004
Male	49%	50%	52%	50%	52%
Female	51%	50%	48%	50%	48%
Mean age	47.4	47.1	48.9	50.2	49
Retired	27%	26%	27%	30%	26%
Married	68%	66%	68%	73%	73%
US resident	85%	86%	87%	88%	87%
International	15%	14%	13%	12%	18%

Source: Las Vegas Convention and Visitors Authority, *Las Vegas Visitor Profile Study* (2004).

The Las Vegas Convention and Visitor Authority have been trying to encourage the growth of the convention and trade show market in Las Vegas. The success of this activity can be seen when the growth figures for this type of business are considered. The figures for the 1986–2004 period are shown in Exhibit 18.6, and show an explosion of convention visitors in the early part of this century.

The demographic profile of visitors to Las Vegas is shown in Exhibit 18.7. It can be seen that there is an approximate equal split of male and female visitors, and a large proportion of the visitors to Las Vegas are from the USA itself. International visitors only represented 13 per cent of all visitors in 2004, which is a fairly constant figure.

The Las Vegas Convention and Visitor Authority undertakes an annual visitor profile study which reveals some interesting information about the behaviour of visitors when they are in Las Vegas. The highlight of this survey for 2004 is shown in Exhibit 18.8.

It can be seen from Exhibit 18.8, that there is high repeat purchase behaviour among visitors to Las Vegas with over 80 per cent of visitors during the 2004 period being in this category. The tourist represents a high percentage of visitors to Las Vegas, but business and convention visitors are an important part of the market, particularly as they have a higher per capita spend on average. Arrival by air represents an important part of the market, although arrival by other methods of transport such as car or bus is also important. This will be explored in more detail later. Room occupancy is predominantly in pairs, although the single and triple occupancy is also important. Single occupancy is particularly important in the business and convention market.

Visitors to Las Vegas often come on multiple visits during any one year and short stays are more common than longer vacations. Visitors with children represent a small part of the market which is probably explained by the high incidence of gambling in the resort, which is not always appealing to this group. Large numbers of the visitors to Las Vegas do participate in some gambling during their visit, and often spend a large proportion of the day in this activity. A smaller proportion of visitors also gamble outside Las Vegas. A large proportion of

Exhibit 18.8   Las Vegas visitor profile highlights

	1994	1995	2003	2004
First vs repeat				
First time visitor	22%	28%	17%	19%
Repeat visitor	78%	72%	83%	81%
Purpose of current visit				
Vacation/pleasure/gamble	74%	71%	67%	67%
Business/Convention	14%	15%	17%	16%
Other	12%	14%	16%	17%
Transportation				
Air	44%	44%	45%	47%
Automobile	39%	41%	43%	43%
Bus	11%	8%	9%	8%
Recreational vehicle	6%	6%	3%	2%
Room occupants				
One	14%	13%	13%	11%
Two	70%	67%	72%	74%
Three	11%	13%	8%	8%
Four or more	6%	7%	7%	7%
Other trip characteristics				
Number of visits in past year	2.5	2.4	1.7	1.8
Adults in party	2.7	2.6	2.6	2.6
Nights stayed	3.1	3.5	2.6	3.6
Visitors with children	8%	11%	10%	10%
Expenditures per visitor ($)				
Food and drink (per day)	22.99	22.53	208.81	238.8
Transportation (per day)	14.05	9.16	48.93	64.64
Shopping (per trip)	74.52	66.18	97.25	124.39
Shows (per trip)	20.34	26.01	42.26	47.21
Sightseeing (per trip)	3.77	4.70	5.05	8.01
Hotel/Motel room (per night)	52.16	54.47	81.43	86.22
Gambling behaviour				
% who gamble while in LV	92%	89%	88%	87%
Daily hours gambled	5.0	4.1	3.6	3.3
Gambling budget ($)	479.77	513.73	490.87	544.93
% gambled outside LV	38%	35%	N/A	N/A
Origin				
Eastern States	9%	10%	8%	10%
Southern States	12%	12%	12%	13%
Midwestern States	14%	13%	16%	7%
Western States	50%	51%	52%	48%
CA	33%	35%	34%	31%

(Continued)

Exhibit 18.8   (*Continued*)

	1994	1995	2003	2004
AZ	5%	3%	5%	6%
Foreign	14%	13%	12%	13%
Ethnicity				
White	80%	79%	83%	80%
African American	7%	7%	6%	6%
Asian/Asian American	7%	7%	4%	7%
Hispanic/Latino	6%	6%	7%	7%
Other	1%	1%	1%	0%

Source: Las Vegas Convention and Visitors Authority, *Las Vegas Visitor Profile Study* (1994, 1995, 2003, 2004).

visitors to Las Vegas come from the Western States of America and California (79 per cent in 2004). A smaller percentage of visitors come from abroad (13 per cent in 2004). The large majority of visitors have a white ethnic origin.

A breakdown of the way that visitors travelled to Las Vegas is shown in Exhibit 18.9.

There has been a steady growth in visitor arrivals by air over a ten-year period, especially by passengers travelling on scheduled airlines, as opposed to charter airlines where there has been a small decline. The growth of arrivals by scheduled airline can be explained by the fact that the business and convention visitors are growing in numbers.

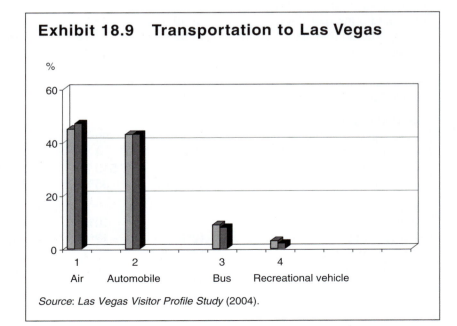

Exhibit 18.9   Transportation to Las Vegas

Source: *Las Vegas Visitor Profile Study* (2004).

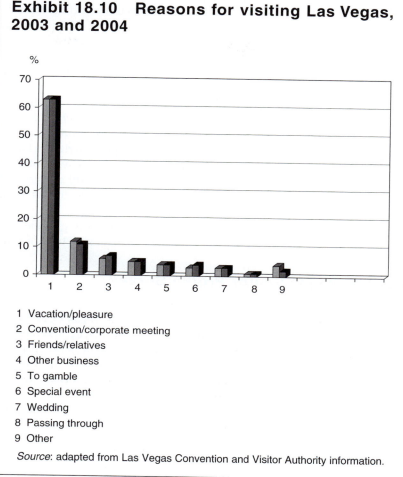

Exhibit 18.10   Reasons for visiting Las Vegas, 2003 and 2004

1 Vacation/pleasure
2 Convention/corporate meeting
3 Friends/relatives
4 Other business
5 To gamble
6 Special event
7 Wedding
8 Passing through
9 Other

Source: adapted from Las Vegas Convention and Visitor Authority information.

Convention attendees are much more likely to use scheduled airlines, than charter airlines.

The reasons for visiting Las Vegas have also been researched by the Las Vegas Convention and Visitor Authority. The results of this are shown in Exhibit 18.10.

Tourists come to Las Vegas for a variety of reasons. One of the primary motivations is vacation and pleasure, which is available in the resort at casinos and hotels. Las Vegas also offers the tourist unparalleled entertainment opportunities, including shows, eating experiences and attractions.

One of the issues for the hospitality operators in Las Vegas has been the balance between gambling and other activities, particularly when they have been trying to encourage children to visit their operations. The tourist has also been encouraged to visit Las Vegas by the impressive range of golf courses which have been developed around the fringes of the city.

It has become very fashionable to get married in Las Vegas, and the city has become known as the wedding capital of the world. More than 100 000 couples obtain wedding licences in Las Vegas every year, and then can choose where to get married from a range of more than fifty chapels throughout the city. Many of the large resort hotels have their own chapels and offer the prospective bride and groom tailored wedding packages. The Excalibur resort for example, offers couples the opportunity of getting married in medieval costumes, while the Tropicana resort offers couples the chance to get married in a thatched roof building and a Polynesian setting.

It has become popular to get married in Las Vegas because of the lack of formalities required compared with other American states, where waiting periods and blood tests are required before the marriage ceremony. This makes getting married in Las Vegas attractive both to domestic and international visitors.

It is also becoming popular among foreign visitors to combine a visit to Las Vegas with a more extensive tour of other parts of the USA.

The Las Vegas Visitor Profile Survey

The Las Vegas Visitor Profile Survey is conducted on an ongoing basis so that an assessment of the Las Vegas visitor and trends in visitor behaviour is shown over time. The survey involves personal interviews with a sample of visitors near to hotel-casino and motels (3300 during 2004). Statistically significant differences in the behaviour attitudes and opinions of visitors from year to year are highlighted in the annual report.

A summary of the results from the 2004 survey is shown in Exhibit 18.11.

Exhibit 18.11   Summary of the 1995 Las Vegas Visitor Profile Survey

Demographic profile

Married	73%
Employed	67%
Retired	26%
White	80%
40 years old or older	72%
From Western USA	48%
Household income of $40 000 or more	85%

Reasons for visiting

For vacation or pleasure	63%
Attendance at convention or trade show	10%
Participation in a gaming tournament	1%

Exhibit 18.11   (*Continued*)

As part of an incentive travel programme	0%
For business	5%

Trip characteristics and expenditures

64% of visitors travelled in parties of two
Average party size – 2.6 persons
10% of visitors were in parties including someone aged under 21
Average length of stay in Las Vegas was 4.6 nights and 4.6 days
92% of visitors stayed in hotels

Gaming behaviour and budgets

87% of visitors said they gambled while in Las Vegas
The average gambling budget was $544.93 in 2004

Entertainment

82% of visitors attended shows during their stay
Visitors who did not visit a show gave reasons such as they did not have enough time or that they only came to Las Vegas to gamble

Note: Sample size: 3300 personal interviews.

Source: Las Vegas Visitor Profile (2005).

This survey shows that a high percentage of visitors to Las Vegas were white, married and over forty years old. A high percentage of visitors came for vacation or pleasure, although attendance at conferences was also important. A large proportion of visitors stayed in hotels, and gambled regularly while they were in Las Vegas.

Profile of international travellers to Las Vegas

Las Vegas has managed to attract international visitors to the city and it is now the seventh most popular city to visit within the USA for overseas visitors, surpassed by New York (Number 1), Los Angeles (Number 2), Miami (Number 3), Orlando (Number 4), San Francisco (Number 5) and Honolulu (Number 6).

The principal source of international travel statistics for the USA and Las Vegas is the International Trade Administration (ITA), which conducts an ongoing survey of international travellers to the USA. The Office of Tourism Industries (OTI) within the US Department of Commerce's International Trade Administration is now responsible for reporting international visitor statistics in the USA. The origin of visitors arriving by airplane is shown in Exhibit 18.12.

There are differences between travellers from different countries, in terms of the types of activities they take part in during their stay in Las Vegas and their average daily expenditure. Gambling and shopping

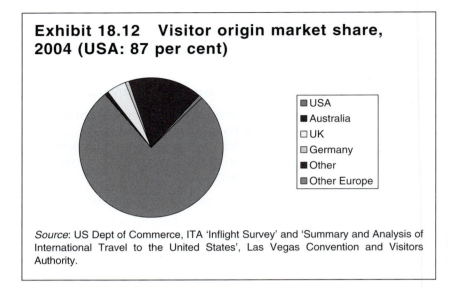

Exhibit 18.12   Visitor origin market share, 2004 (USA: 87 per cent)

Legend:
- USA
- Australia
- UK
- Germany
- Other
- Other Europe

Source: US Dept of Commerce, ITA 'Inflight Survey' and 'Summary and Analysis of International Travel to the United States', Las Vegas Convention and Visitors Authority.

are the top leisure activities for all overseas visitors to Las Vegas. Visitors from countries such as Australia, Republic of China, Taiwan, Switzerland and Germany are particularly interested in casinos and gambling. The Japanese, an important part of all overseas visitors, are particularly heavy spenders in Las Vegas.

One of the challenges which the Las Vegas Convention and Visitor Authority will have for the future is how to attract an increasing number of overseas visitors, particularly in the quieter periods of the year. The hotels, resorts and casinos will have to decide on their particular target market and design their products and services accordingly.

Conclusion

Las Vegas has developed as the entertainment capital of the USA. The early development as a gambling centre has evolved into a wider leisure and entertainment base as gambling restrictions were lifted in other areas of the USA. Las Vegas attracts visitors from the USA, and a growing number of overseas visitors who book either independently or as part of package holidays. An important part of the development of Las Vegas as a destination has been the growth of the city as an ideal location for trade fairs, conferences and conventions. The city has ambitious plans for the growth of this business into the next century.

Discussion points

1 Las Vegas has been developed as a place to visit for gambling activity. Discuss the opportunities and threats which this could bring to the city in their quest to attract new market segments to Las Vegas.
2 Las Vegas has become the 'wedding capital' of the world. Discuss the reasons for this market development. Outline the opportunities that this development brings to Las Vegas and the wider business community.

Taiwan: the emergence of a new major outbound tourism market

Taiwan has a population of around 23 million and its economy has grown in recent years at an average rate of nearly 9 per cent per annum.

In the early 1990s, the Taiwanese government sought actively to encourage its population to take holidays abroad, because it would promote the country's image abroad and helps with international relations for the country which has an unusual existence, owing to its lack of recognition by the People's Republic of China.

Travel restrictions have been relaxed and increased disposable income has stimulated the growth of outbound tourism from Taiwan. The number of Taiwanese tourists travelling abroad has grown dramatically from 1.6 million in 1988 to a little under 7.5 million in 2002.

Of the tourists who took international trips in 2003, nearly 80 per cent visited other Asian destinations. The only other major destination was the USA, with around half a million Taiwanese visitors. Indeed, in 1995, around 117 000 tourists from Taiwan and the People's Republic of China visited Las Vegas alone (Las Vegas Visitor and Convention Authority, 1996). In the same year, by contrast, only 14 000 Taiwanese tourists visited Africa.

Of Asian destinations, a few account for the overriding majority of Taiwanese tourists. Hong Kong topped the list in 2003 with a massive 1.9 million visitors, followed by Japan with 500 000, Thailand with 392 000, and Singapore with 125 000. Taiwanese arrivals in Hong Kong however, did fall by 23.7 per cent in 2003 after growing strongly in the early part of this century. As a recently developed country, Taiwanese tourists are relatively inexperienced and still tend to travel on highly organized group tours.

Unlike most Asian destinations, Taiwanese inbound tourism is not growing rapidly. Between 1979 and 1995, foreign tourist arrivals grew from 1.34 million to just 2.33 million. However, the growth in outbound tourism looks set to continue and as the Taiwanese become more experienced tourists they will probably take more independent holidays and explore new destinations.

Acknowledgement

The authors would like to express their thanks to Professor C. Michael Hall for providing the data which has been used in this case study.

The inbound market to the Republic of Cyprus

The Republic of Cyprus, which joined the European Union in 2004, has become one of Europe's leading tourist destinations over the past twenty years or so. After the Turkish invasion of 1974, which left some of this leading resort under Turkish occupation, the Republic of Cyprus had to restructure its tourism industry and develop new resort areas and attractions. Its success in this rebuilding after 1974 is clearly demonstrated by the fact that in 2005 it attracted 2.5 million visitors.

In this case study we discuss the inbound tourism market industry, trends and key issues. Let us start by looking at the volume of inbound tourism. All data used comes from the Cyprus Tourism Organization, unless otherwise stated.

In 2005, Cyprus received 2 470 057 international tourist arrivals. The top ten national markets from which these tourists came were as follows:

1	UK	1 391 842
2	Germany	182 682
3	Greece	130 151
4	Russia	97 595
5	Sweden	88 119
6	France	52 777
7	Ireland	52 705
8	Norway	48 276
9	Israel	40 934
10	Switzerland	40 280

Exhibit 20.1 Comparison of arrivals from selected countries in 2004 and 2005

Country	Tourist arrivals 2005	Tourist arrivals 2004	Approximate percentage change 2004–05
Ireland	52 705	44 286	+18
France	52 777	46 792	+12
Austria	36 984	28 636	+29
Russia	97 595	83 816	+16
Finland	29 285	31 670	−7
Lebanon	13 755	14 569	−6
Spain	4 908	5 397	−9
Iceland	223	481	−55

Source: CTO, 2006.

However, Cyprus also attracts tourists from outside Europe and the Eastern Mediterranean. In 2005, the Republic of Cyprus welcomed 22 046 visitors from the USA, and 10 755 from Australia. However, a substantial number of these are likely to be people with friends and relatives in Cyprus.

Tourist arrivals in Cyprus tend, like most countries, to fluctuate year on year, and the total 2005 arrival figure was around 5 per cent up on that for 2004. However, there were larger fluctuations, both up and down, in the market from specific countries between 2004 and 2005, as can be seen from Exhibit 20.1.

These decreases and increases in visitors from particular countries between 2004 and 2005 could be a result of a number of factors as diverse as:

- economic recession in the generating country
- the opening of new airline routes
- marketing efforts of the Cyprus Tourism Organization and tour operators in these particular countries.

In recent years, Cyprus has tried to market itself, with some success, as a winter tourism destination. However, its visitor arrivals are still highly seasonal and focused on the summer months. For example, in July and August 2005 Cyprus recorded 338 972 and 336 587 tourists respectively, compared with 58 894 in January 2005 and 72 600 in February. In other words, tourist arrivals are some six times higher in the peak month than in the least popular month. However, some markets are more seasonal than others, as we can see from Exhibit 20.2.

Again, these visitor numbers could be the result of a wide variety of factors including everything from climate in the home country and motivation for visiting Cyprus, to school holiday periods in the different countries.

Exhibit 20.2 Approximate percentage of tourists from selected countries who visit during particular months

Country	January	March	May	August	October
UK	2	5	12	4	12
Germany	3	11	12	8	11
Greece	6	8	8	12	7
Sweden	1	4	15	15	14
France	2	3	13	11	12
Russia	1	2	11	15	11

Source: CTO, 2006.

Let us now turn our attention to the spending of international tourists in Cyprus. The Cyprus Tourism Organization estimates that in 2004, tourists spent Cyprus £982 million (about £1.2 billion sterling). However, there are significant differences between different countries in terms of spend per head per day, as we can see from Exhibit 20.3.

These significant differences could reflect, for example:

- the types of segments being attracted and their tastes in accommodation
- the numbers of people who may not be paying for accommodation because they are planning to stay in property belonging to friends or relatives during their visit. This phenomena has grown dramatically in recent years.

However, spending per day by various nationalities also changes dramatically year by year. For example, Norwegians spent Cyprus £28 a day in March 2004 but Cyprus £34.62 in March 2005. On the other hand, between August 2003 and August 2004 the per day spend of US tourists fell from Cyprus £29 to Cyprus £17.

At the same time there is another aspect to tourist expenditure, and that is the amount spent per whole stay. This is a function of per day spending and the length of stay, and, as Exhibit 20.4 illustrates, there are also significant differences between national visitors in terms of length of stay and per trip expenditure.

Again there are factors that will influence this situation, for example, in terms of preferences for different types of vacation and accommodation, and access to privately owned, non-commercial accommodation.

There are also variances between one year and another for international countries. For example, in August 2004, Russians stayed an average of eleven nights in Cyprus compared with fifteen in August 2005. Spend per trip in August 2004 by Danish tourists had fallen from Cyprus £396 to Cyprus £277 by August 2005.

Exhibit 20.3 Per head per day spending of selected national markets in March 2005 and August 2004 (Cyprus £s)

	Spending per person per day in Cyprus £s	
Country	March 2005	August 2004
UK	32.70	40.60
Germany	36.67	36.19
France	33.50	46.11
Russia	36.79	43.95
Israel	59.63	47.53
Finland	31.66	33.94
Greece	43.84	17.07
Italy	62.52	48.14
AVERAGE	36.02	40.67

Source: CTO, 2005, 2006.

Exhibit 20.4 Length of stay and per trip expenditure of selected countries in April 2004 and March 2005

Spending per person per day	Average length of stay March 2005	Average per trip per person March 2005	Average length of stay August 2004	Average per trip spend per person August 2004
Country				
UK	10.7	350.49	13.0	526.74
Russia	9.6	354.07	11.1	490.84
Israel	2.8	166.98	5.3	251.55
Sweden	17.0	583.31	8.9	279.57
France	9.0	300.37	10.5	465.42
Greece	4.7	204.45	16.3	278.65
AVERAGE	9.64	347.26	11.90	484.07

Source: CTO, 2005, 2006.

If we continue the theme of national differences we could look at two other examples, namely, the difference in preferences for areas of Cyprus and types of accommodation. Exhibit 20.5 illustrates some of these differences.

Approximately 55 per cent of all tourists to Cyprus are from the UK, so let us now focus a little more on this market, which is so crucial to the Republic of Cyprus. We also look at how successfully Cyprus is attracting UK tourists compared with other destinations. The data in this section is largely from the work of the statistics office of the UK government.

Exhibit 20.5 Differences in use of place of stay and accommodation in Cyprus by selected months in 2004

Percentage of tourists staying in this resort

Country	UK	Russia	Germany
Ayia Napa	11	18	20
Larnaca	6	12	9
Lemesos	15	33	10
Lefkosia	1	3	2
Paphos	40	30	43
Paralimni	22	2	8
Polis	2	1	4

Type of accommodation as percentage of tourists from the country

Country	UK	Russia	Germany
5-star hotel	9	24	11
A-class apartment	12	3	4
Visiting friends or relatives	5	9	8

Source : CTO 2005

In 1971, Cyprus (before the Turkish invasion) was the destination for about 1 per cent of outbound tourist trips from the UK; by 2000 this figure had grown to 3 per cent. This compared, in 2000, with 2 per cent to Turkey, 4 per cent to Portugal and Italy, 7 per cent to Greece, 18 per cent to France and 28 per cent to Spain.

However, UK tourist numbers to Cyprus have fluctuated dramatically, even between 1999 and 2005:

```
1999 =   958 000
2000 = 1 310 000
2001 = 1 476 000
2002 = 1 302 000
2003 = 1 281 000
2004 = 1 333 000
2005 = 1 392 000
```

Therefore between 1999 and 2004, the number of British tourists rose by an impressive 36 per cent approximately. However, over the same period the number of British tourists to Turkey rose by a little over 40 percent, to Spain by 32 percent and to Egypt and North Africa by 32 per cent. Furthermore, while UK tourist trips to Cyprus peaked in 2001, those to Turkey, Spain and Malta were higher in 2004 than ever before. So it is clear that Cyprus is facing major challenges in the Eastern Mediterranean.

It also faces competition from newly emerging destinations in the Balkans and the Middle East. For example, tourism to the United Arab Emirates and Bulgaria grew between 2002 and 2004 by 44 per cent and 105 per cent respectively!

Cyprus Tourism Organization data on the UK market also throws some light on the characteristics of the UK market, including the fact that in 2004:

- 43 per cent of UK tourists chose to stay in Paphos and 20 per cent in Paralimni, while only 9 per cent selected Ayia Napa and 8 per cent Larnaca as their holiday destination
- most Britons who wish to stay in four- and five-star hotels took their vacations in Paphos, while those who prefer apartments are most likely to be found in Paralimni
- a quarter of all tourists who stay with friends and relatives stayed in Larnaca
- 35 per cent of all people staying in houses and apartments they own took their vacations in Paphos
- two-thirds of all stays in one-star hotels were in Lemesos
- very few British tourists stay in Lefkosia, Polis or the hill resorts.

Conclusions

The Republic of Cyprus has been highly successful at attracting international tourists in recent years. However, it remains heavily dependant on the UK market and is facing increasing competition from emerging destinations in the Eastern Mediterranean and the Middle East in particular.

Events such as the Gulf War showed how vulnerable Cyprus can be to events many hundreds of kilometres away, and it is also beginning to face competition, controversially, from the so-called Turkish Republic of Northern Cyprus, even though this is still not recognized as a country by the United Nations.

The Cyprus Tourism Organization has clear strategies for developing tourism in the Republic, but it remains to be seen how successful it will be in the future.

Discussion points and essay questions

1 To what extent is the fact that over 50 per cent of tourists to Cyprus come from the UK a strength or a weakness for Cyprus.
2 Explain the likely reasons which lie behind the spending patterns illustrated in Exhibits 20.3 and 20.4.
3 Discuss the reasons why British, Russian and German people appear to favour different areas of Cyprus for their vacations.

4 Discuss how seasonal the market is in Cyprus compared with other destinations, and suggest ways in which seasonality might be reduced.

Exercise

Visit the Cyprus Tourism Organization website and look at the latest data on inbound tourist arrivals, spending and revenue, length of stay, place of stay, type of accommodation, and so on. Also try to find the same data for earlier years to help you identify trends in the market.

Then, on the basis of this data, devise a five-year marketing strategy for Cyprus, with an emphasis on which national markets and market segments Cyprus should target and how it should target them.

Susi Madron's Cycling for Softies

Introduction

Susi Madron's Cycling for Softies is a limited company which was established in the early 1980s. The company developed the market for arranged tours to allow customers to explore France on a bicycle away from the usual tourist haunts. The company added the possibility of cycling in the Italian regions of Tuscany and Umbria for the 1997 season. The company is unique in only offering cycling holidays. Other companies such as Belle France and French Cycling Holidays have entered the market, but have never gained the reputation of the original.

History of the company

The company was established by Susi Madron and Roy Madron in 1980. The partners had regularly visited France and experienced the joys of cycling around the unspoilt areas which were rarely visited by tourists. They had stayed at small family hotels during these tours and had realized that the joys of cycling, coupled with a stay at a reasonable hotel with excellent food, was a powerful and attractive combination. They had also noticed that there were no companies in the UK offering help to arrange similar tours.

Susi and Roy Madron decided to return to the UK and set up a company which would offer customers the opportunity to visit these beautiful areas of France on a bicycle, staying at pre-arranged hotels offering comfortable accommodation. They decided to call the company 'Cycling for Softies' because the cycling tours would incorporate a touch of luxury, customers would be able to stay at comfortable hotels rather than the more traditional accommodation and camping experience usually associated with cycling holidays.

The company was initially run from the back bedroom of Susi Madron's house but, as business developed, it became necessary for the company to obtain premises. Premises in the centre of Manchester were obtained in 1995. Over the next seventeen years the company grew rapidly. Agents were recruited in France to handle the customers as they arrived in France. Nine bases were established in France and all had a good stock of bicycles of various sizes.

In 1995 the company moved its headquarters to peaceful office accommodation on the outskirts of Manchester. The company had recruited agents in Australia, New Zealand and South Africa by this time, to handle their overseas business. These agents were all ex-customers of the company. In 1997, the company expanded their product to Italy, although they still see their main objective as selling their current French products to a wider and more sophisticated market. Since the late 1990s the company has continued to expand their product offerings.

Susi Madron and her staff

Susi Madron has provided the inspiration and leadership for the development of the company. It was her initial idea of providing cycling and accommodation itineraries that established the company. She has a personal interest in providing customers with an exciting and enjoyable experience in a country that she loves.

She has received many prestigious awards for her ideas and business skills, and has written widely on the subject. In 1985, she received a BBC Radio 4's Award for Small Business Enterprise. In 1988, she published a book entitled *Susi Madron's Cycling in France*, published by George Philip, London. Susi Madron has also recruited a loyal and experienced staff from the UK, France and other countries to help her with the development of the business.

Products

The 'Cycling for Softies' concept is very well defined by the company. This concept is shown in Exhibit 21.1.

The first products offered by the company provided a bicycle for the duration of the holiday and a hotel booking at the start and the finish of the holiday. Maps and ideas of hotels to stay at en route were also provided. It became clear during the early years that customers would also like the company to book all the accommodation for the whole duration of the holiday. The company therefore started to offer these services if the customer wanted them. The company has developed close relationships with the proprietors of hotels to allow them to offer this service.

The current product range is shown in Exhibit 21.2 and the regions which the company offers are shown in Exhibit 21.3.

Exhibit 21.1 What 'Cycling for Softies' actually means

Lots of warmly welcoming small family-owned hotels

Food! What the French do best. Always good and authentic, often wonderful

Cycling along quiet country roads and the little unexpected surprises you might find around any corner. Perhaps the smell of ripe peaches, dropping from the trees, or the fields of sunflowers stretching to the horizon

The freedom of choosing your own pace and your own route, and cycling as little or as much as you wish

The friendliness of the people you meet and the sense of well-being you feel as you enjoy each day at a time

Not having to worry because we do all the planning and organizing for you, so all you have to do is relax and enjoy your own personal adventure in typical French countryside.

Source: Cycling for Softies.

Exhibit 21.2 Current product range offered in each destination

THE GENTLE TOURER. Cycling Holiday in France
Your favourite option is a wonderful combination of exercise and luxury. You stay two nights at each hotel, or even three or four nights if you wish; generally doing a circular route, giving you time to explore the region everyday, or have a day off every other day, just to relax.

A TWIN BASE. Cycling Holiday in France
Divide your time between two hotels. It allows you to rest and relax or cycle and explore and you don't have the inconvenience of packing up and moving on too often.

THE SUPER SOFTIE. Cycling Holiday in France
Idea for a short break. The whole of your stay is in one hotel. Choose a base which is completely off the beaten track, or perhaps one in the centre of a medieval town buzzing with cafe life and chateau visits.

REGION TO REGION. Cycling Holiday in France
A long distance ride taking you from one region to another for both toughies and softies to suit your fitness.

Exhibit 21.2 *(Continued)*

A LA CARTE. Cycling Holiday in France
We can design your holiday to fit around other plans.

SHORT BREAK/ADVENTURER. Cycling Holiday in France
Three nights booked with us, either three booked together (cycling short break) or two at the start and one at the finish of the holiday, and the rest of the time you can arrange your own itinerary and book your own hotels [adventurer]

GROUP CYCLING HOLIDAY in France
Each year we run a limited number of group cycling holidays. For 2006 we are running a 7 nights tour in the Loire on July 9th and September 10th. The holidays include 4 nights in Chinon and 3 nights in Azay le Rideau.

Source: Cycling for Softies.

Exhibit 21.3   Regions of Europe currently offered by Cycling for Softies

1.   Mayenne and Sarthe
2.   Chateaux of the Loire
3.   La Venise Verte
4.   Cognac and Charente
5.   Dordogne and Garonne
6.   Rivers of the Tarn
7.   Gascony
8.   Provence and Luberon
9.   Burgundy and Beaujolais
10.   Alsace and Wine Trail

Source: Cycling for Softies.

It can be seen from Exhibit 21.2 that customers can choose how much of their holiday is pre-booked by the company and how much is tailor-made or fits in with the arranged holiday route through one of the regions. The company is very flexible and will even arrange special requests for customers. For example, the company can arrange accommodation only for customers who have their own bicycles or they can book special accommodation equipment and routes for customers with young children or special needs. This means that there is flexibility offered to customers when they are choosing their particular package.

The length of holiday in the regions shown in Exhibit 21.3 can vary from seven, nine, ten or fourteen days, according to the customer's requirements.

Prices of the holidays

Prices for the holidays are based on the holiday package excluding travel. Travel can be arranged if required, and prices for this are quoted in the brochure. An example of prices for one of the regions – Rivers of the Tarn, for 2006 – are shown in Exhibit 21.4.

Promotion

Promotion of the holidays is carried out in two main ways. The company produces a colour brochure each year which is sent to customers on request. The company also organizes 'Cycling for Softies' presentations, in the North and South of England and in Scotland, where prospective customers can meet and talk to staff and chefs from the hotels. These presentations are organized in areas of the country where the bookings record is good and are held in February and March each year.

The company advertises in national newspapers, mainly on Saturdays and Sundays at the beginning of the year. This includes advertisements in *The Times*, *Guardian*, *Sunday Times*, *Observer* and *Independent*. Word-of-mouth promotion is considered to be a key part of the promotion, which generates sales, by friends and family of past customers.

The company also sends mail shots out to the customers who have booked with the company before. A 'welcome home' card is also sent to all customers to be at their home when they arrive back from their

---

Exhibit 21.4   Holiday prices for 2006

No. nights	Price
3 nights	£377
5 nights	£628
7 nights	£879
9 nights	£1025
10 nights	£1098
12 nights	£1244
14 nights	£1390
14 nights to region	£1423

Source: Cycling for Softies.

holiday. This has proved to be an excellent method of promotion for the company.

Distribution

The holidays are distributed mainly by direct mail. The company relies on newspaper advertisements and word-of-mouth to generate interest. The company sends out a brochure to people who ring in after seeing an advertisement, or hearing about the company from their friends and relatives. A very small number of sales are handled via travel agents.

The company employs agents in Australia, New Zealand and South Africa, who handle the bookings from these countries on behalf of the company. The company database of past and present customers is very important in the distribution of the brochure. Past customers are often contacted and a copy of the new brochure is always sent out after publication. The Internet site – www.cycling-for-softies.co.uk – has become an important method of distribution in recent years.

The customers

A profile of the customers of Cycling for Softies is shown in Exhibit 21.5. It can be seen that the holidays attract customers from all over the world. Most people book as couples or families or as two or three friends together. Stressed-out professionals, worried academics, relaxing retirees and overworked home-workers all find the holidays stimulating and refreshing. The customers are mostly twenty-five to

---

Exhibit 21.5   The customers

Demographic
* 50% male/50% female
* Age range – mainly 25–65, but all age ranges can be accommodated

Socioeconomic
* Mainly A/B socioeconomic groups
   Some C1s

Lifestyle
* Professional people – 50% of customers are employed in the medical profession; 21% in education
   Lawyers, doctors, writers and celebrities, and self-employed business people are also regular customers
* Interested in the healthy outdoors, good diet, and often taking multiple holidays a year

(*Continued*)

Exhibit 21.5 (*Continued*)

Country of origin

* Mainly UK based
* Limited business n America, South Africa, Australia and New Zealand

Note: All figures are approximate.

Source: Cycling for Softies.

Exhibit 21.6   Comments made by Cycling for Softies customers

'There is the sheer bliss of cycling for an hour or two without seeing a car, and the awful torment of trying to decide which flavour of ice cream to try next'

'France seen from a bike is just blissful'

'We got exactly what we expected, and more. As we hadn't cycled for over 30 years we were a little concerned as to how we would manage, but everything was so well organized; we had no problems'

'On the last day poodling along the river bank back to Chinon was heaven'

'We loved the small hotels and freedom to potter, buy trout, picnic . . .'

'I spent one day cycling then the next day walking in the hills and sketching the wild flowers which are glorious in May. The peace and tranquillity took my breath away'

'An elderly gentleman on a very elderly bike stopped and offered to help us. He had a large plastic bag hanging from the handlebars and as we struggled to understand each other, we noticed that several snails were crawling out'

'We particularly liked the more "regional" hotels and food'

'The food was fabulous. You could call it 'Cycling for Gourmets''

Source: Cycling for Softies.

---

sixty-five years old, but the company can arrange holidays for people from other age groups. The customers are interested in 'getting away from it all' or 'chilling out'. They are often busy professionals who spend little time with their children during the year. This type of holiday allows them to spend a lot of time with their families in a peaceful and stress-free environment.

The repeat purchase business of the company is very high. Approximately 70 per cent of the holiday-makers who book each year have booked with the company before. In the American market, repeat purchase is even higher at 90 per cent. Some of the statements made by the customers in letters written to the company, on their return, reflect some of the experiences which they gain from a Cycling for Softies holiday. Examples of these are shown in Exhibit 21.6. The company is now keen to offer the French holidays to customers from a wider geographic area, and is particularly interested in developing the overseas market. Customers are encouraged to fill in questionnaires about every aspect of their holiday on their return. These are scrutinized carefully and if any problems emerge, these are acted on swiftly by the company's management.

Conclusions

Susi Madron's Cycling for Softies' is an example of a business which has been developed on the basis of one person's unique and original idea. The cycling holidays in the most beautiful areas of France attract a loyal group of customers who use the company to provide one of their holidays in a year.

Discussion points

1 Critically evaluate the way in which the Cycling for Softies business has been developed because of an individual's understanding of the behaviour of a particular group of people.
2 Evaluate the reasons for the growth of interest in cycling holidays for professional people in the UK. In your opinion, will this interest be mirrored in other countries of Europe, and the world.

Glossary of terms

The following glossary of terms is offered as a service to those readers who may be unfamiliar with some of the terms used in this book. It is not meant to be a definitive set of definitions but rather a simple, easy-to-use interpretation of some key words and phrases.

ACORN – a method classifying residential neighbourhoods on the basis of who lives there, for use in marketing research or direct mail.

Advertising – any paid form of non-personal presentation of ideas, goods or services by an identified sponsor.

All-inclusive – a type of package holiday where one price covers everything that guests will require in the destination, namely accommodation, food, drink, activities and entertainment.

Allocentric – a term, coined in 1977 by Plog, which refers to those tourists who are adventurous, outward-looking and like to take risks.

Backpackers – term used to describe tourists who tend to be younger people who take relatively long trips seeking out places which are 'off the beaten track', making relatively little use of the mass tourism infrastructure, and trying to minimize their expenses.

Brand – the name, symbol or design, or combination of these, that is used to identify the products or services of a producer to differentiate them from competitors' products or services.

Brand loyalty – the propensity or otherwise of consumers to continue to purchase a particular brand.

Business tourism – tourist trips that take place as part of people's employment, largely in work time, rather than for pleasure in people's leisure time.

Catchment area – the geographical area from which the overwhelming majority of an organization's or product's customers are drawn.

Commission – money paid by a producer to an external agent who helps the organization to sell its products, usually expressed as a percentage of the selling price.

Competition – the process by which two or more organizations endeavour to gain customers at the expense of the other organization or organizations.

Concentrated marketing – the focusing of the marketing effort on just one or two of the available market segments.

Consumer – the person who actually uses or consumes a product or service.

Consumer behaviour – the study of which products people buy, why they buy these products, and how they make their purchasing decisions.

Critical incident – this concept suggests that the tourist's satisfaction or otherwise depends on what happens at times when something out of the ordinary occurs.

Culture – the sum total of knowledge, attitudes, beliefs and customs to which people are exposed in their social conditioning.

Customer – the person who actively purchases the product or service, and pays the bill. The term is often used interchangeably with 'consumer' but they are different. For example, in business tourism, a company is the *customer* as it pays for the travel services, but it is the employee or business traveller who actively travels, and is therefore the *consumer*.

Demand – the quantity of a product or service that customers are willing and able to purchase at a particular time at a given price. Where there is a desire to purchase a type of product or experience which is not currently available, for whatever reason, we talk about *latent demand*.

De-marketing – action designed to discourage the purchase of particular products or services.

Demographics – the study of population structure and its characteristics such as age, sex, race and family status.

Desk research – the collection of secondary data in marketing research.

Destination – the country, region or local area in which the tourist spends his or her holiday.

Determinants – the factors which determine whether or not someone will be able to take a holiday and, if so, then what type of holiday he or she will be able to take.

Differentiated marketing – the development of a different marketing mix for each market segment.

Direct marketing – selling directly from the producer to the customer without the use of intermediaries such as travel agents.

Discounting – a reduction in the list price of a product or service to encourage sales.

Disposable income – the money which remains once all expenditure has been subtracted from the income of an individual or family.

Distribution – the process by which products and services are made available to customers by producers.

Domestic tourism – tourism where the residents of a country take holidays as business trips wholly within their own country.

Eco-tourist – someone who is motivated by a desire to take a vacation that allows him or her to see the natural history of a destination and meet the indigenous population.

Ethics – the moral values and standards that guide the behaviour of individuals and organizations.

Excursionists – people who take leisure trips which last one day or less and do not require an overnight stay away from home.

Family life cycle – the stages through which people pass between birth and death, that are thought to influence their consumer behaviour.

FIT – fully-inclusive tour.

Geodemographics – an approach to segmentation which classifies people according to where they live.

Green issues – a commonly used term that is used as an umbrella for a variety of issues relating to the physical environment, from recycling to pollution, wildlife conservation to 'global warming'.

Growth market – a market where demand is growing significantly.

Hedonism – the constant quest for pleasure and sensual experiences.

Heterogeneous – a market that consists of segments or sub-groups which differ from each other significantly in terms of their characteristics and/or purchasing behaviour.

Homogeneous – a market made up of people whose characteristics and/or purchasing behaviour are wholly or largely identical.

Inbound tourism – tourist trips from a foreign country to one's own country.

Intangibility – the characteristic of a service by which it has no physical form and cannot be seen or touched.

International tourism – those tourist trips where residents of one country take holidays or business trips to other countries.

JICNARS – the Joint Industry Committee for National Readership Surveys.

Leisure – leisure is considered to be 'free time', in other words, the time which is not devoted to work or other duties. However, some people also use the term to describe an industry which provides products and services for people to use in their spare time.

Leisure shopping – shopping that in contrast to ordinary shopping involves shopping as a leisure activity not as a necessary task of everyday life. It also implies that products are purchased for the pleasure involved in buying and consuming them rather than because of their utilitarian value.

Lifestyle – the way of life adopted by an individual or group of people.

Market – those consumers who currently are, or potentially may become, purchasers and/or users of a particular individual or group of products services.

Market leader – the product which has the largest share of a single market, in other words, it is purchased by more people than any of its competitor products.

Market share – the proportion of sales of a particular type of product achieved by an individual product.

Marketing mix – the four controllable marketing variables – product, price, place and promotion – which marketers manipulate in order to achieve their marketing objectives.

Marketing positioning – the position in the market which a product is perceived to have, in the minds of consumers, in relation to variables such as quality, value for money, and level of service.

Marketing research – the process of collecting, recording and analysing market-related information. It includes published or secondary data of specific data or primary research. It is designed specifically to provide data which helps an organization improve the effectiveness of its marketing activities.

Media – this can refer to either the news media or the advertising media, in other words, the media in which advertisements may be placed.

Model – a representation that seeks to illustrate and/or explain a phenomenon.

Motivation – those factors which make tourists want to purchase a particular product or service.

Niche marketing – the targeting of a product and service at a particular market segment which is numerically much smaller than the total market.

Off-peak – a period when demand for a product or service is habitually lower than at other times which are termed peak periods.

Outbound tourism – tourist trips from one's own country to a foreign country.

Perceptions – the subjective interpretation by individuals of the data available to them, which results in them having particular opinions of, and attitudes towards, products, places or organizations.

Perishability – a characteristic of tourism products whereby they have very limited lives, after which they no longer exist and have no value. For example, an airline seat is no longer an existing saleable product once the aircraft has departed.

Point of sale – refers to techniques which are used at the point when tourists actually buy products or services to encourage higher sales. This could involve window displays in travel agencies, for example.

Postmodernism – a sociological theory that has major implications, if it is a valid theory, for the study of consumer behaviour in tourism. It is based on the idea that in industrialized, developed nations, the basis on which people act as consumers has been transformed in recent years. The theory suggests the traditional boundaries, such as those between high-brow and low-brow culture and up-market and down-market leisure activities are becoming blurred and are breaking down. Authors, notably John Urry, have looked at the implications of post-modernism for the tourism industry.

Post-tourist – a tourist who recognizes that there is no such thing as an authentic tourism product or experience. To the post-tourist, tourism is a game and they feel free to move between different types of apparently totally contrasting holidays, from an eco-tourism trip to Belize one year to a sun, sand, sea and sex trip to Benidorm the next year.

Product-service mix – the combination of tangible elements and service that is aimed at satisfying the needs of the target market.

Promotion – the techniques by which organizations communicate with their customers and seek to persuade them to purchase particular products and services.

Psychocentrics – a term coined in 1977 by Plog referring to inward-looking, low risk-taking, less adventurous tourists.

Psychographic – the analysis of people's lifestyles, perceptions and attitudes as a way of segmenting tourism markets.

Purchase decision – the process by which an individual decides whether or not to buy a particular type of product and then which specific brand to purchase.

Qualitative research – research which is concerned with customers' attitudes and opinions which cannot be qualified.

Quantitative research – research which is concerned with the statistical data which can be measured and expressed numerically.

Repositioning – the process by which organizations attempt to change the consumer's perceptions of a product or service.

Seasonality – the distribution over time of total demand for a product or destination, usually expressed in terms of peak and off-peak seasons to distinguish between those times when demand is higher than average and vice versa.

Segmentation – the technique of dividing total markets into subgroups whose members share similar characteristics as consumers.

Service gap – a concept coined by Parsuraman et al. which is based on the idea that tourist dissatisfaction is caused by perceived gaps between expectation and actual outcomes.

SERVQUAL – a technique developed by Parsuraman et al. which is designed to measure service quality.

Snowbird – people who live in areas which are cold in the winter, who take long trips to warmer destinations to escape the cold weather.

Social tourism – a broad area which is primarily concerned with providing opportunities to participate in tourism for those who would not normally be able to go on the trips for primarily financial or health reasons.

Target marketing – marketing activity aimed at a particular group of consumers within the overall total population.

Tour operator – an organization which assembles 'package holidays' from components provided by other sectors such as accommodation and transport. These packages are then sold to tourists, usually through travel agents.

Tourism – the activity in which people spend a short period, of at least one night, away from home for leisure or business.

Tourist – a consumer of tourism products.

Typology – a classification that subdivides a group into subgroups which share similar characteristics.

Undifferentiated marketing – a broad-brush approach to marketing in which the market is not subdivided into segments.

Up-market – Products aimed at the more expensive, higher status end of the market.

Virtual reality – a set of technologies which replicate real-world experiences and can be developed as a leisure product.

Visting friends and relatives (VFR) – tourist trips where the main motivation is the desire or need to visit friends and relatives.

Visitor – a widely used term for someone who makes a visit to an attraction. Visitors are not all tourists in the technical sense in that they will not all spend at least one night away from home.

Visitor attractions – a single site, unit or entity which motivates people to travel to it to see, experience and participate in what it has to offer.

They may be human-made or natural and can be physical entities or special events.

Word of mouth – the process whereby consumers who have experienced a product or service pass on their views, both positive and negative, about the product or service to other people.

Bibliography and further reading

Adams, M. (1993). The gay nineties. *Inventive*, September, 58–62.

Ahmed, Z. and Krohn, F. (1992). Understanding the unique consumer behaviour of Japanese tourists. *Journal of Tourism Marketing*, **3**, 73–86.

Ahmed, Z. U., Johnson, J. P., Ling, C. P., Tan, T. W. and Hui, A. K. (2002). Country of Origin and brand effects on consumers' evaluations of cruise lines, *International Marketing Review*, **19.3**, 279–302.

Andreason, A. R. (1965). *Attitudes and Consumer Behaviour: A Decision Model in New Research in Marketing*, ed. L. Preston. Institute of Business and Economic Research, University of California.

Beard, J. and Raghob, M. G. (1983). Measuring leisure motivation. *Journal of Leisure Research*, **15**(3), 219–228.

Bejou, D., Edvardssen, B. and Rakourski, J. P. (1996). A critical incident approach to examining the effects of service failures in customer relationships. The case of Swedish and US airlines. *Tourism and Travel Research*, Summer, 35–40.

Boorstin, D. (1992). The Image: A Guide to Pseudo-Events in America. Vintage Books.

Buzzell, R. D. (1968), 'Can you standardise multinational marketing?' *Harvard Business Review*, November–December, 102–13.

Calantone, R. J. and Johar, J. S. (1984). Seasonal segmentation of the tourism market using a benefit segmentation framework. *Journal of Travel Research*, **25**(2), 14–24.

Calantone, R. J. and Mazanec, J. A. (1991). Marketing management and tourism. *Annals of Tourism Research*, **18**, 101–119.

Calantone, R. J. and Sawyer, A. (1978). The stability of benefit segments. *Journal of Marketing Research*, 15 August, 395–404.

Calantone, R. J., Benedetto, C. A. and Bojanic, D. C. (1987). A comprehensive review of the tourism forecasting literature. *Journal of Travel Research*, **28**(2), 28–39.

Calantone, R. J., Benedetto, C. A. and Bojanic, D. C. (1988). Multi-method forecasts for tourism analysis. *Annals of Tourism Research*, **28**(2), 28–39.

Calantone, R. J., Schewe, C. and Allen, C. T. (1980). Targeting specific advertising messages at tourist segments. In *Tourism Marketing and Management Issues* (D. E. Hawkins, E. L. Shafer and J. M. Rovelstand, eds) pp. 149–160, George Washington University.

Clark, H. F. Jnr (1987). Consumer and corporate values: yet another view on global marketing. *International Journal of Advertising*, **6**, 29–42.

Clift, S., Luongo, M. and Callister, C. (2002). *Gay Tourism–Culture, Identity and Sex*. Continuum.

Cohen, E. (1972). Towards a sociology of international tourism. *Social Research*, **39**, 64–82.

Cohen, E. (1979). A phenomenology of tourist experience. *Sociology*, **13**, 179–201.

Collin, P. H. (1994). Dictionary of Hotels, Tourism and Catering Management. P. H. Collin.

Cooper, C. P., Wanhill, S., Fletcher, J., Gilbert, D. and Fyall, A. (2005). *Tourism: Principles and Practice*. Pearson.

Crofts, J. C. and Erdmann, R. (2000). Does national culture influence consumers' evaluation of travel services? A test of Hofstede's model of cross-cultural differences. *Managing Service Quality*, **10.6**, 410–419.

Culler, J. (1981). Semiotics of tourism. *American Journal of Semiotics*, 1(1–2), 127–140.

Dace, R. (1995). Japanese tourism: how a knowledge of Japanese buyer behaviour and culture can be of assistance to British hoteliers in seeking to develop this valuable market. *Journal of Vacation Marketing*, **1**(3), 281–288.

Dalen, E. (1989). Research into values and consumer trends in Norway. *Tourism Management*, **10**(3), 183–186.

De Mooij, M. (1997). Global Marketing and Advertising: Understanding Cultural Paradoxes. Sage Publications.

Deloitte-Touche (1996). *Highlights of the International Market*. Deloitte-Touche.

Dibb, S., Simkin, L., Pride, W. M. and Ferrell, O. C. (2001). *Marketing Concepts and Strategies*. 4th European edition. Houghton-Mifflin.

Economist Intelligence Unit (1996). Market segments: spas and health resorts in Europe (by N. Cockrell). *Travel and Tourism Analyst*, **1**, 53–57.

Elkington, J. and Hailes, J. (1992). *Holidays that Don't Cost the Earth*. Victor Gollancz.

Engel, J. F., Blackwell, R. D. and Miniard, P. W. (2001). *Consumer Behaviour. International Edition*. 9th edition. Dryden Press.

Engel, J. F., Kollat, D. J. and Blackwell, R. D. (1968). *Consumer Behaviour*. Holt, Rinehart and Winston.

Euromonitor (1994). International Marketing. Data and Statistics 1994. 18th edition. Euromonitor.

Euromonitor (1996). Market Direction Report 19:1. Travel and Tourism. Euromonitor.

Euromonitor (1997). *European Marketing. Data and Statistics 1997*. 32nd edition. Euromonitor.

Euromonitor (2004). *World Income Distribution*. London: Euromonitor International.

Feifer, M. (1985). *Going Places*. Macmillan.

Foxall, G. R. and Goldsmith, R. E. (1994). *Consumer Psychology for Marketing*. Routledge.

Frochet, I. (1996). Histoqual: the evaluation of service quality in historic properties. In *Tourism and Culture Conference Proceedings: Managing Culture Resources for the Tourist Volume* (M. Robinson, N. Evans and P. Callaghan, eds), Business Education.

Frommer, A. (1996). *Arthur Frommer's New World of Travel*. 5th edition. Macmillan.

Gallup and American Express (1989). Unique four national travel study reveals traveller types. News release. American Express.

Ghoshal, S. (1987). Global strategy: an organizing framework. *Strategic Management Journal*, **8**, 425–440.

Gilbert, D. C. (1991). An examination of the consumer decision process related to tourism. In *Progress in Tourism, Recreation and Hospitality Management* (C. Cooper, ed.), vol. 3, Belhaven Press.

Gray, H. (1970). International Travel – International Trade. D. C. Heath.

Guido, G. (1991). Implementing a pan-European marketing strategy. *Long Range Planning*, **24**(5), 23–33.

Gummesson, E. (1988). Service quality and product quality combined. *Review of Business*, 9(3).

Hall, C. M. and Johnston, M. E. (1995). Polar Tourism – Tourism in the Arctic and Antarctic Regions. John Wiley and Sons.

Halliburton, C. and Hünerberg, R. (1993). *European Marketing – Readings and Cases*. Addison-Wesley.

Hampton, G. M. and Buske, E. (1987). The global marketing perspective. In *Advances in International Marketing* (S. T. Cavugsil, ed.) vol. 2, pp. 259–77, JAI Press.

Harcourt, B., Carroll, P., Donahue, K., McGovern, M. and McMillen, J. (1991). *Jovonovich Group*. Monichville, NSW.

Harrison, D. (1992). Tourism and the Less Development Countries. Belhaven.

Hitchcock, M., King, V. T. and Parnwell, J. G. (1993). *Tourism in South East Asia*. Routledge.

Homma, N. (1991). The continued relevance of cultural diversity. *Marketing Research Today*, November, 251–258.

Horner, S. and Swarbrooke, J. (1996). *Marketing Tourism, Hospitality, and Leisure in Europe*. International Thomson Business Press.

Horner, S. and Swarbrooke, J. (2005). *Leisure Marketing: A Global Perspective*. Elsevier Butterworth-Heinemann.

Horton, R. L. (1984). Buyer Behaviour. A Decision Making Approach. Charles E. Merrill.

Howard, J. A. and Sheth, J. N. (1969). *The Theory of Buyer Behaviour*. John Wiley and Sons.

Inove, R. (1991). An army of Japanese tourists in Ampo in Japan. *Asia Quarterly Review: Special Issue on Resort Development*, **22**(4), 2–10.

Jenner, P. and Smith, C. (1996). Attendance trends at Europe's leisure attractions. *Travel and Tourism Analyst*, (4), 72–93.

Kashani, K. (1989). Beward of the pitfalls of global marketing. *Harvard Business Review*, September–October, 89–98.

Kaynak, E., Kucukemiroglu, O., Kara, A. and Tevfik, D. (1996). Holiday destinations: modelling vacationers' preferences. *Journal of Vacation Marketing*, **2**(4), 299–314.

Kotler, P. (1984). In A. B. Fisher, The ad biz gloms on to global. *Fortune*, 12 November, pp. 77–80.

Kotler, P. (1994). Marketing Management: Analysis, Planning, Implementation and Control. 8th edition. Prentice-Hall.

Kotler, P. and Armstrong, G. (2004). *Marketing Management: Analysis Planning, Implementation and Control*. 10th edition. Pearson Education.

Las Vegas Convention and Visitors Authority (published annual). *Las Vegas Leisure Guide*. LVCVA.

Las Vegas Convention and Visitors Authority (various) *Las Vegas Marketing Bulletin*. LVCVA.

Las Vegas Convention and Visitors Authority (1997). *Las Vegas Official Visitor Guide*. Winter/Spring. LVCVA.

Las Vegas Convention and Visitors Authority (published annually). *Las Vegas Visitor Profile Study*. LVCVA.

Laws, E. (1991). Tourism Marketing: Service and Quality Management Perspectives. Stanley Thornes.

Leeflang, P. S. H. and van Raaij, W. F. (1995). The changing consumer in the European Union: a meta-analysis. *International Journal of Research in Marketing*, **12**(5), 373–387.

Lett, J. (1989). Epilogue to Touristic Studies in Anthropological Perspective, in Hosts and Guests. The Anthropology of Tourism, ed. V. Smith. 2nd edition. University of Pennsylvania Press.

Levitt, T. (1983). The globalisation of marketing. *Harvard Business Review*, May–June, 92–102.

Levitt, T. (1986). *The Marketing Imagination*. Free Press.

Lowyck, E., Van Langenhave, L. and Bollaert, L. (1992). Typologies of tourist roles. In *Choice and Demand in Tourism* (P. Johnson and B. Thomas, eds), Mansell.

Lundberg, D. E. (1990). *The Tourist Business*. 6th edition. Van Nostrand Reinhold.

Lunn, J. A. (1974). *Consumer Decision Process Models in Models of Buyer Behaviour*, ed. N. S. Jagdish, pp. 34–69, Harper and Row.

Mathieson, A. and Wall, G. (1982). Tourism: Economic, Physical and Social Impacts. Longman.

McDonald, M. H. B. and Morris, P. (2000). *The Marketing Plan*. Butterworth-Heinemann.

Middleton, V. T. C. and Clarke, J. (2001). *Marketing for Travel and Tourism*. 3rd edition. Butterworth-Heinemann.

Mintel (2001). *Adventure Travel. Global*. November. Mintel.

Mintel (2001). *All Inclusive Holidays*. June. Mintel.

Mintel (2002). *Outbound Travel. Japan*. February. Mintel.

Mintel (2005). *Spa Holidays – UK*. January. Mintel.

Moscardo, E., Morrison, A. M., Pearce, P. L., Long, C. T. and O'Leary, J. T. (1996). Understanding vacation destination choice through travel motivation and activities. *Journal of Vacation Marketing*, **2**(2), 109–122.

Moutinho, L. (1987). Consumer behaviour in tourism. *European Journal of Marketing*, **21**(10), 3–44.

Munt, I. (1994). The 'other' post-modern tourism: culture, travel and the new middle classes. *Theory, Culture, and Society*, **11**(3), 101–123.

Nicosia, F. M. (1966). *Consumer Decision Processes*. Prentice-Hall.

O'Guinn, T. C. and Belk, W. (1989). Heaven on earth: consumption at Heritage Village, USA. *Journal of Consumer Research*, **16**(2), 227–238.

Ohmae, K. (1982). *The Mind of the Strategist: Business Planning for Competitive Advantage*. Penguin Books.

Opaschowski, H. (1993). *European Tourism Analysis*. BAT-Leisure Research Institute.

Packard, V. (1957). *The Hidden Persuaders*. Longmans, Green and Co.

Parasuraman, A., Zeithaml, V. A. and Berry, U. (1985). A conceptual model of service quality and its implications for future research. *Journal of Marketing*, **49**, 41–50.

Perreault, W. D., Dorden, D. K. and Dorden, W. R. (1979). A psychological classification of vacation life–styles. *Journal of Leisure Research*, 9, 208–224.

Piercy, N. (2002). Market-led strategic change – a guide to transforming the process of going to market. Butterworth-Heinemann.

Plog, S. (1977). Why destination areas rise and fall in popularity. In *Domestic and International Tourism* (E. Kelly, ed.), Institute of Certified Travel Agents.

Plog, S. (1987). Understanding psychographics in tourism research. In *Travel, Tourism, and Hospitality Research: A Handbook for Managers and Researchers* (J. R. B. Ritchie and C. R. Goeldner, eds), John Wiley and Sons.

Reisinger, Y. and Turner, L. (1999). A critical analysis of Japanese tourists: challenges for tourism markets. *European Journal of Marketing*, **33**(11–12), 1203–1227.

Ritzer, G. (2000). *The McDonaldisaton of Society*. 3rd edition. Pine Forge Press.

Ryan, C. (1991). *Tourism, Terrorism, and Violence: The Risks of Wider World Travel*. Conflict Study 244. Research Institute for the Study of Conflicts and Terrorism, London.

Ryan, C. (1995). Learning about tourists from conversations: the over 55s in Majorca? *Tourism Management*, **16**(3), 207–215.

Ryan, C. (ed.) (1997). The Tourist Experience: A New Introduction. Cassell.

Savani, G. (1986). Selling travel to the over-50 crowd. *Direct Marketing*, **49**, October, 42–45.

Seaton, A. V. (1994). Tourism and the media. In *Tourism Marketing and Management Handbook* (S. J. Witt and L. Moutinho, eds), Prentice-Hall.

Seaton, A. V. (1996). Tourism and relative deprivation: the counter revolutionary pressures of tourism in Cuba. In *Proceedings of the 'Tourism and Culture: Towards the 21st Century' Conference* (M. Robinson, N. Evans and P Callaghan, eds), Centre for Travel and Tourism/ Business Education.

Seaton, A. V., Jenkins, C. L., Wood, R. C., Dieke, P. V. C., Bennett, M. M, MacLellan, L. R. and Smith, R. (eds) (1994*). Tourism: The State of the Art*. John Wiley and Sons.

Sharpley, R. (1994). *Tourism, Tourists and Societies*. 2nd edition. Elm.

Sharpley, R. (1996). Tourism and consumer culture in postmodern society. In *Proceedings of the 'Tourism and Culture: Towards the 21st Century' Conference* (M. Robinson, N. Evans and P Callaghan, eds) pp. 203–215, Centre for Travel and Tourism/Business Education.

Shaw, S. (1999). *Airline Marketing and Management*. 4th edition. Ashgate.

Sinus GmbH – N. Homma and J. Ueltzhoffer (1990). The Internationalisation of everyday research markets and milieus. ESOMAR Conferences on America, Japan and EC '92. The Prospects for Marketing, Advertising and Research. Venice, 18–20 June.

Smith, V. (ed.) (1989). *Hosts and Guests: The Anthropology of Tourism*. 2nd edition. University Press.

Solomon, M. R. (1996). *Consumer Behaviour*. 3rd edition. Prentice-Hall.

Steward, J. (1996). Tourism place: images of late imperial Austria. In *Proceedings of the 'Tourism and Culture: Towards the 21st Century' Conference* (M. Robinson, N. Evans and P. Callaghan, eds) pp. 203–215, Centre for Travel and Tourism/Business Education.

Stuber, M. (2002). Tourism Marketing Aimed at Gay Men and Lesbians: A Business Perspective. In *Gay Tourism Identity and Sex* (S. Clift, M. Luongo and C. Callister), Continuum.

Swarbrooke, J. S. (1995). Sustainable tourism and the development and regeneration of rural regions in Europe: A marketing approach. In *Proceedings of the 'Expert Meeting on Sustainability in Tourism and Leisure'* (G. Richards, ed.), Tilburg University Press.

Swarbrooke, J. S. (1999). The Development and Management of Visitor Attractions. Butterworth-Heinemann.

Swarbrooke, J., Beard, C., Leckie, S. and Pomfret, G. (2003). *Adventure Tourism – The New Frontier*. Butterworth-Heinemann.

Tordjman, A. (1995). European retailing: convergences, differences and perspectives. In *International Retailing Trends and Statistics* (P. J. McGoldrick and G. Davies, eds), Pitman.

Urry, J. (2002). The Tourist Gaze: Leisure and Travel in Contemporary Society. 2nd edition. Sage.

Usinier, J. C. (1993). *International Marketing: A Cultural Approach*. Prentice-Hall International.

Vellas, F. and Bécherel, L. (1995). *International Tourism: An Economic Perspective*. Basingstoke: Macmillan.

Voase, R. (1995*). Tourism: The Human Perspective*. Hodder and Stoughton.

Wahab, S., Crompton, L. J. and Rothfield, L. M. (1976). *Tourism Marketing*. Tourism International Press.

Walsh, K. (1992). The Representation of the Past: Museums and Heritage in the Postmodern World. Routledge.

Weirmair, K. (2000). Tourists' perceptions towards and satisfaction with service quality in the cross-cultural service encounter – implications for hospitality and tourism management. *Managing Service Quality*, **10.6**, 397–409.

Westvlaams Ekonomisch Studiebureau, Afdeling Toerislisch Underzoeu (1986). Toerishische gedragingen en attitudes van de Belgen in 1985: Reeks vakontieanderzaeken.

Wood, K. and House, S. (1991). The Good Tourist: A Worldwide Guide for the Green Traveller. Mandarin.

Wootton, G. and Stevens, T. (1996). Business tourism: a study of the market for hotel-based meetings and its contribution to Wales' tourism. *Tourism Management*, **16**(4), 305–313.

World Advertising Research Centre (2003). *The Asia Pacific Marketing Pocket Book*. Biddles.

World Advertising Research Centre (2005). *The European Marketing Pocket Book*. Biddles.

World Tourism Organization (WTO) (1992). *Tourism Trends to the Year 2000 and Beyond*. WTO.

World Tourism Organization (WTO) (1995). *Global Tourism Forecasts to the Year 2000 and Beyond*. Vol. 1. WTO.

World Tourism Organization (WTO) (1996). *Yearbook of Tourism Statistics*. WTO.

World Tourism Organization (WTO) (2004). *Tourism Market Trends*. WTO.

World Tourism Organization (WTO) (2005a). *Compendium of Tourism Statistics*. WTO.

World Tourism Organization (WTO) (2005b). *Tourism 2020 Vision*. Vols 1–4. WTO.

Zaltman, G., Pinson, C. A. and Angelman, R. (1973). *Methodology and Consumer Research*. Holt, Rinehart and Winston.

Index

Academic typologies, 83
Accommodation sector, 148, 270–5
Accor, 33, 93
Activity tourism, 37
Adams, 301
Advertising Standards Authority (ASA), 258
Africa, 22
Ahmed and Krohn, 265
Ahmed et al., 196
Airtours, 205
All inclusive market, 201
Albert Docks, Liverpool, 143
America, 19–22
Andraeson, 40, 41
Antartica, 27
Archers, 204
Asia, 25
Australia, 26
Australian Tourist Board, 362

Backpackers, 131
BAL Leisure Research Institute, 183
Beard and Ragheb, 54
Bejou, Edvarsson and Radowski, 211
Boorstin, 84
Branding, 164, 165
British Airways, 186, 198, 213–326
British Tourist for Conservation Volunteers, 186
Brittany Ferries, 205
Budget cruising, 205

BUNAC, 129
Business:
    environment, 190
    tourism, 29, 146
Buzzell, 193

Cadbury's World, 312
Calatone and Johan, 8
Calatone, Mazanec, di Benedetto and Bojanic, 8
Calatone and Sawjer, 8
Calatone, Schewe and Allen, 8
Carnival Cruise Line, 197, 285–299
Caribbean, 21
Center Parcs, 5, 7, 17
Characteristics of tourism services, 48, 70
Chartered Institute of Marketing, 5
Chaucer, 12
Children's holidays, 203
Clark, 193
Cliff and Ryan, 217
Club 18–30, 30, 93, 131, 206, 252–260
Club Medíteranée, 5, 202
Coca Cola, 191
Cohen, 84, 86
Collin, 4
Cooper et al., 75
Consumer:
    behaviour research, 156, 158, 236
    satisfaction and national differences, 221
Computer Reservation Systems (CRS), 169
CN traveller, 347

Couples only market, 206
Crotts and Erdmann, 196
Cruise market, 205, 285–299
Culler, 84
Cultural Tourism, 35
Cyprus tourism, 395–401
Cyprus Tourism Organization (CTO), 397, 398

Dace, 261
Dalen, 87, 91, 99
Da Vinci Code, 204
Definitions of:
    marketing, 7
    tourism, 4
Deloitte-Touche, 345
Determinants:
    external, 64
    group travel, 65
    personal, 63
Dibb et al., 91
Different types of tourism, 12, 28
Direct booking, 206
Disabled tourists, 136
Disney, 193
Disneyland, 20, 92, 165
Distribution – see place

easyjet, 205, 367–374
Eco-tourism, 208
Educational tourism, 35, 134
Edvardsson and Radowski, 216
Elkington and Hales, 178
Engel, Blackwell and Miniard, 6
Engel, Kollat and Blackwell, 76
Ethnic minority tourists, 136
Euromonitor, 105, 109, 115, 117, 118, 119, 120, 121
Euroconsumer, 197
Europe, 40
Expedia, 200
Excursionists and day trippers, 133

Fairmont Hotels and Resorts, 275
Family:
    life-cycle, 129
    tourists, 93
First Choice, 277–284
Foxall and Goldsmith, 42

Frochet, 214
Frommer, 185

GALTA, 365
Gallup and American Express, 87
Gay and lesbian tourism in Australia, 361–366
Germany, 124
Ghoshal, 193
Gilbert, 45, 47
Gítes d'Enfant, 129
Global Distribution Systems (GDS), 169
Globalization, 189
Goldsmith, 44
Graceland, 204
Grecotel, 186
Green tourists, 177
Guido, 191
Gummesson, 211

Hall and Johnston, 27
Halliburton and Hünerberg, 191
Hampton and Buske, 193
Harcourt et al., 26
Harry Potter, 204
Hedonistic tourism, 36, 130
Health tourism, 32, 207
Heartbeat, 204
History of tourism, 13–26
Hitchcock, King and Edwards, 26
Hollywood, 204
Homma, 191
Horner and Swarbrooke, 4, 5, 45, 75, 84, 98, 127, 162, 163, 164, 183, 190, 194, 200, 313
Horton, 44
Howard-Sheth, 42, 43, 70
Human resource management, 216

ICD marketing Services, 245, 249
Inbound and outbound tourism receipts, 113
Industrial tourism in France, 310–312
Inove, 25
Intermediaries, 169
Internet, 169

Japanese markets, 261–265
Japanese Tourist Board, 262
JICNARS, 92

Kashani, 191
Kotler, 191
Kotler and Armstrong, 7, 45, 162, 163

Las Vegas, 220, 375–394
Last of the summer wine, 204
Laws, 215
Leading Hotels of the World, 270
Leeflang and van Raaij, 192
Leisure:
    motivation scale, 54
    shopping, 262–266
Lett, 193
Levitt, 7, 191
Lowyck, Van Langenhave and Bollaert, 90
Lundberg, 19
Lunn, 42

Mackie, 25
Market segmentation 91, 147, 230
Marketing:
    communications, 170, 171, 172
    intermediaries, 217
    mix, 161
    planning, 9, 10
    research, 153–163
Mattieson and Wall, 4, 5, 76, 179
McDonald's, 191, 193
McDonald and Morris, 9
Middleton and Clarke, 45, 46, 70, 71, 96, 98
Middle East, 24–25
Mintel, 255, 263, 281, 282, 283, 345, 346, 348, 349, 352
Motivators:
    expressed and real, 56
    multiple, 55
    shared, 56
Motivators and:
    determinants, 51
    different market segments, 58
    different types of tourism product, 59
    gender, 59
    the individual, 55
    timing of purchase decision, 60
Moutinho, 76
MTV, 194, 198
Munt, 197
Mystic Seaport, 20

National Trust, 186
New generating countries, 229
New tourism products, 231
Nicosia model, 42
No frills airlines, 205

Organisation for Economic Co-operation
    and Development (OECD), 126
Ohmae, 191
Old Deerfield Village Museum, 19
Old Sturbridge Village, 20
Old Trafford, 205

Packard, 8
Parasuraman, Zeithamle and Berry, 214, 215
Perreault, Dorden and Dorden, 86, 91
PGL, 8, 93, 129, 203, 241–251
Piercy, 7
Place (distribution), 167
Plimouth Plantation, 20
Plog, 8, 93, 129
Point of sale (POS), 168
Popular culture, 204
Price, 165
Pricing strategies, 166
Product positioning, 162
Product life-cycle, 163
Promotion, 170
Purchase decision making, 142
Purchasing methods, 235

Quality, 211–213

Ragdale Hall, 338–344
Reisinger and Turner, 195
Religious tourism, 31, 134, 208
Retail travel agent, 168
Ritzer, 196
Russian tourists, 207
Ryan, 52, 67, 216, 217, 219
Ryanair, 205

Saatchi and Saatchi, 255, 257
Saga, 8, 93
Sandals, 202
SARS, 97
Savini, 8
Savoy, 270–276
Seaton, 22, 45, 88, 99

SERVQUAL, 214
Sex in the City tour, 204
Sharpley, 14, 83, 84, 85, 196, 197
Shaw, 97
Short breaks, 137
Sinus GmbH, 191
Smith, 87
Snowbirds, 135
Social tourism, 34, 137
Société Roquefort, 306–309
Solomon, 6, 44
Spain, 125–126
Spas, 345–350
Stress and tourism, 218
Stuber, 361
Susi Madron's Cycling for Softies, 402–409
Swarbrooke, 94, 96
Swarbrooke et al., 351
Swarbrooke and Horner *see* Horner and
    Swarbrooke

Taiwan, 393–394
Thomas Cook, 13, 17, 23, 253, 252–260
Thomson, 205
Tordjman, 192
Tour operation sector, 144, 149, 241–251,
    252–262, 327–337, 402–409
Tourism:
    arrivals and receipts, 103
    concern, 178, 180
    demand, 103–111, 113–127
    in regions of the world, 13
    sectors, 141
    trends, 202

Tourist behaviour, the future, 230
Tourist satisfaction, 211–213
Travelocity, 200
TUI, 183, 184, 198, 327–337
Typology of motivators, 54
Typologies of tourist behaviour, 51, 53

United Kingdom, 119
United States of America, 119
Urry, 88
Usunier, 193
USP, 10

Vellas and Becharel, 193
Virtual reality and fantasy tourism, 232
Visiting friends and relatives, 28, 32
Visitor attractions, 60, 94
Voase, 197

Wahab, Crampton and Rothfield, 45, 46, 76
Walsh, 197
Warner Brothers, 204
Wedding market, 203
Weirmair, 195, 196
Wensleydale Creamery, 300–305
Westvlaams Ekonomisch Studiebureau, 86
Wickens, 88, 99
Wood and House, 178
World Advertising Research Centre, 106, 107
World Tourism Organization (WTO), 21,
    103, 104, 109, 110, 111, 114, 115, 116, 117,
    195, 198

Zaltham, Pinson and Angelman, 42